ABOUT THE AUTHOR:

Pamela studies and teaches spirituality from various perspectives, believing the spirit calls to the creativity and artist in all of us. She has a 2006 Doctor of Ministry degree from the University of Creation Spirituality, now Wisdom University, and a 1982 Master of Divinity degree from Iliff School of Theology in Denver and a 1972 B. A. in history from University of California, Los Angeles.

Since 1982 she has been an ordained minister in the United Methodist Church in Northern California.

Ultimately her home is in Oro Fino, in the far north of California, with her husband Earl. She is surrounded by, and often taught by a dog, cats and wild creatures of all sorts.

MAP OF TERRITORY COVERED IN STORY.

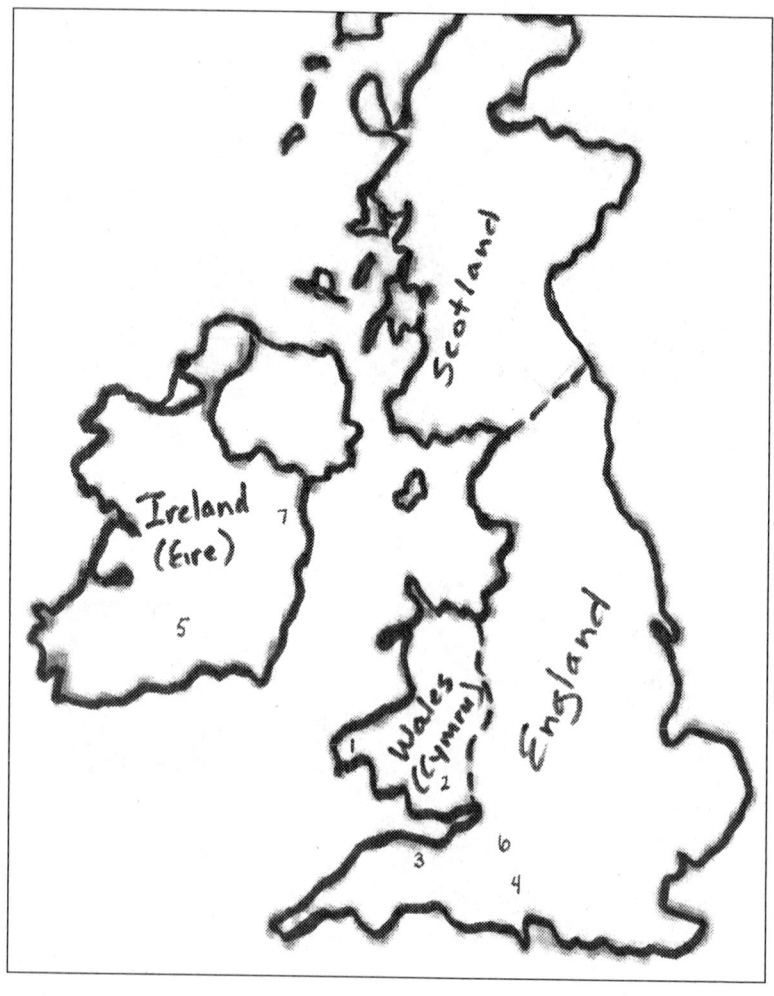

1. Eogan exile home. Pembrokeshire Coast. St. Bride's Bay
2. Caves of Ana
3. Refuge. Exmoor. Lynmouth/Lynton
4. Stonehenge.
5. Shreedrum - Eogan clan territory - Munster - today's Cashel.
6. Glastonbury
7. EiNeill clan territory.

TRADE ROUTES IN 5TH CENTURY. TORRIDA'S, PAPALLAS' AND PELAGIUS' POSSIBLE JOURNEY

8. Rome 9. Carthage. 10. Ephesus 11. Palestine 12. Egypt

The hills of Exmoor, looking down on cove.

The rapids at Watersmeet in Exmoor

Marloes Sands on the Pembrokeshire Coast in Wales

The Town of Cashel in County Tipperary today.
It was once known as Shreedrum

Shreedrum, in today's Cashel, close-up

The top of Shreedrum, today's Cashel.
The replica of the sacrificial stone with St Patrick's Cross.

ACKNOWLEDGMENTS

The crowd is huge. I have many friends, colleagues and members of churches over the years who have encouraged me in this adventure.

I especially appreciate those of you who, after asking 'when can we read you novel', for 25 years, still ask the question.

I thank the dissertation committee at the University of Creation Spirituality for a serious encounter with the story and my analysis of writing it. I thank Dr. Mel Bricker, Dr. Linda Allen, and Dr. Jeremy Taylor for their critique and encouragement.

I thank Molly Young Brown who took on the task of coaching me through the transition from private spiritual journey to publication.

For all the writers on Celtic mythology and thought in the last two decades, especially Mara Freeman who has inspired me with her grace and wisdom.

I appreciate my husband Earl who has listened to oral readings of this story in its various stages with patience and insight, and even traveled to Ireland with me.

I am deeply indebted to my sister Lucia for her encouragement. My mother, Luella, who has a joy of life that has always been infectious; who has opened my eyes to wonder and beauty so many times. To my sister Valerie and brother Douglas and their families who listened to and absorbed my thoughts over the years.

I thank those who have entered the realm of ancestor: My father, Glenn Coy, the scientist, naturalist, amateur historian who gave me the desire to learn everything I could about every subject. My grandfather, Dr. Owen Coy, a professor of history whose legacy in our family made me want to be an historian. My great grandfather, Rev. Charles Fremont Coy, a circuit riding minister of the Methodist Episcopal Church whose legacy suggests being a minister might just be in my blood.

I thank Dr. Clyde Reid who continually asked me when my story was going to be written. I kept telling him 'soon', but he died before he could see the finished product. But, Clyde, I know you had a powerful belief in time as an illusion. So maybe I can share this with you after all.

I thank the non-humans who have helped with this story. A lot of research was done with my dog, Bonkers, now gone, by my side. Many long, thoughtful walks were taken with him, encouraging my imagination. There were the cats, Simon, Malachi, foster cat Shadow. There was the rabbit Buster.

Today the dog teacher is Popcorn; the cat teachers are Hidey, Pepper. And, of course, there were wild creatures I've encountered; too many to mention.

I also thank all the people I met in Ireland, Wales and England who knowingly and unknowingly led me to clues for this story. For the hosts in the various b&b's whose names have been changed, though their graciousness was wonderful. I thank them for making me feel like part of the family.

PRELUDE – THE JOURNEY OF WRITING

I am a lover of the study of history. The events of the past, I have always felt, are clues to the reasons for the events of the present and future. People who say they hate studying history always surprise me. 'It's old and dead,' they say. Yet for me, it is still alive. We need to listen and remember. I want to bring history alive through story, through intuitive history.

What is 'intuitive history'? Many things that did actually happen in the past cannot be 'proven'. There can be clues to what might have happened and why, but it is very hard to prove an event. The attempt to prove is often tainted by the prejudice of the historian.

For instance, the existence and experience of the average individual cannot be proven. The very existence of particular active, powerful, talkative, productive women can rarely be proven in history. Historical documents have tended to be written by those in power. Women have rarely been in power in the last 5,000 years. Yet my intuitive mind tells me that women have always been active, talkative, and productive. Proof can rarely be found of the thoughts and activities of the 'victims' of violence, only the results of violence. Wars are fought and the historian can note that a certain tyrant was overthrown; but rarely is a word said about the peasant whose fields were burned or who lost a leg in the battle and grieves the loss of family members.

The un-provable parts of history may be the most important. It may be the sorrow, grief and triumph of the average person that is shaping our present time. We need to discover and remember. In order to understand the present and future it may be that we need to go back and touch the lives of these average people. We can only do that by taking the facts as far as they will go and then letting our imagination or 'intuition' do the rest of the work.

I believe strongly that some fabric of creation is healed when we take that time.

I trust that there is a mystical interconnection. I feel a pull or a flow to a place or time. Discoveries and new clues along the way are my reward for listening and following. It is kind of like a time and space treasure hunt.

As an intuitive historian, I get to travel to a place and soak in the clues. The journey is always exhilarating and unexpected. An invisible force seems to guide me. Voices I hear are not with the ear, but with the heart. I learn something new about myself as well as about the place I visit. I hope you will join me and imagine. Let history come alive.

The historian gets to play in the realm of this dimension called time. There are scientists and philosophers today who call us to re-examine our assumptions about time. How far are we from our ancestors of 1500 year ago? How far are we from those who will live 1500 years from now? What can we learn from them? What can they learn from us?

Ordinary people are sacred to my work as an ordained minister of the United Methodist Church. It may be that no one will write about individuals in my congregations in history books, but they are profoundly important people. I suspect that is true of every living creature. All life is profoundly important. Your life is profoundly important.

There is an essence, a spark, which allows for life. It keeps humans going in the worst of times. It allows them to discover the best that life has to offer. The search for that spark is an element of most major religions, often overshadowed by the doctrines of those religions. In my religion, Christianity, it is present in the teachings of Jesus as he tells us about the power of love. It is present in Hebrew Scripture in the wisdom literature. You can hear it in the first story of creation, in some of the psalms and some of the proverbs and the words of the prophets. You find it present in your faith tradition whatever that may be. As an intuitive historian, I search for that spark in the lives of our ancestors.

For many years, the writing of this story was a personal, spiritual journey. As with many spiritual journeys, it is often hard to find the right words. The late Dr. Clyde Reid, a Jungian counselor in Denver, Colorado, was a friend and mentor. He gave me the courage to listen to and follow the story in its deepest dimensions. While as a student at the Iliff School of Theology I was affected deeply by the teachings of Dr. Vincent Harding who was and is able to weave the study of history with a deep spirituality. His compassionate study of the horrors of slavery and of the courage of the civil rights movement is empowering. When I approached him 25 years ago with the story of my encounter with the past, he simply said, 'that shows just how interconnected we all truly are.'

I was finally able to fully write this story, and my thoughts about it, as a dissertation for the Doctor of Ministry degree at the University of Creation Spirituality, now called Wisdom University. I appreciate the gift that the school gives its students as we explore aspects of the spirit, the world and the universe. Dr. Matthew Fox, has opened us all to a sense of the mystical, which is grounded in living and acting in the world. He has mined the historical landscape and discovered the mystics that were often either written out of history, or changed by previous historians to be more suitable for their particular interpretation of history. He reminds us that it is all about celebration.

I'm more recently indebted to Dr. Joanna Macy for her work in deep time. As she works to give people courage to face a much needed transformation, away from ecological destruction and escalating global violence, she suggests we listen to our ancestors as well as our descendants.

Before I take you on my journey, I want share these words from Carl Jung,

> "I had the feeling that I had pushed to the brink of the world; what was of burning interest to me was null and void for others, and even a cause for dread. Dread of what? I could find no explanation for this. After all, there was nothing preposterous or world-shaking in the idea that there might be events which overstepped the limited categories of space, time and causality."[1]

May we all be pushed to the brink of the world!!

I have woven together the story of Anaias, the people around her, and my own journey, historical research and my thoughts. Please travel with me as I weave her story and my story together. May your story be a part of it also.

PRONUNCIATION AND MEANINGS GUIDE

Here are a few of the names – obviously not the full set:

Anaias – "of Ana" – First and last 'a' like the a in 'pat', second 'a; like the 'i' in the French 'vin'.- stress on the middle syllable

Seabhac – 'little hawk' – s like a sh sound – bh -live a 'v'. -stress on the last syllable – "Shevak"

Papallas – follower of Pallas – a's like the a in 'pat' – stress on the middle syllable.

Owain – "o" like exclamation 'oh',- 'ain' like the word 'one' – stress on the last syllable.

Giosai – 'a good and generous man' – "g' like in george. stress on last syllable.

Ciallach – 'wise one' – 'c' in beginning and 'ch' at end like k in king. – stress on last syllable

Pa'abhallia – "like a fruit bearing tree' – 'a' like above. 'bh' like 'v' – stress on middle syllable – "Povalla

Geanta – 'modest' – g like 'george' – stress on middle syllable.

M'alda – 'gentle' – stress on the first syllable

Here are some general pronunciation tips –

a – pronounced like a in "pat"

a (with an m or n) pronounced like the "i" in the French 'vin'

o – as in 'pot' – *u* as in 'fool' – *e* as in 'her'

bh when it is initial like a 'v' in veil.- *bh* in the middle like a 'v' or 'w' in towel *bh* at the end is silent

c like k in king when together with a-o-u like the c in cock

dh – with e or i like 'y' in yea *dh* with a,o,u like a g *dh* at the end is silent

gh similar to the dh

mh as a nasal v as in "vain" or as 'au' in German 'haus'

mh at the end is silent – *ng* as in angle *s* when together with a,o,u as in sun

s when with e or i as in sure – *sh* – like 'h' in hav

t when together with e or i is like ch in chin – *th* – like h or silent.

APPROXIMATE TIMELINE

*dates in legends can be guessed only, not known
BCE – before common era (was called BC)
CE – common era (was called AD)
ca. – approximate date

A SHORTENED VERSION OF THE TIMELINE IS:
Anaias lived as the Roman Empire was failing, about a century before the King Arthur legends and about 400 years before the Vikings invaded Ireland and 600 years before the Normans invaded Ireland.
Anaias' time was close enough to the time of Saint Patrick and theologian Pelagius to allow them, potentially, to meet.

ca 3500 BCE – Newgrange constructed
ca. 3-2000 BCE – Stonehenge constructed
ca 2100 BCE – Firbolg culture
ca 1500 BCE – Tuatha De Danaan
ca 800-900 BCE – Milesians
ca 700-500 BCE – Arrival of Celts in Ireland – Wales 3 C – B.C.
ca 200-300's BCE – Finn Mac Cumhaill
54 – Caesar invades Britain
60 – Boudicca Queen of Iceni revolts against Roman Army
312 – Constantine legalizes Christianity
325 – Council of Nicea
347 – Saint Jerome's birth
354 – Saint Augustine's birth
354 – Pelagius birth according to historians
382 – Saint Jerome begins translations in Bethlehem
ca. early 400's Saint Patrick's birth (432 is a ritual date)
ca. early 400's – Story – time of Seabhac/Anaias' birth
405 – Jerome completes his translations.
410 – Roman Emperor orders end of British occupation
418 – Pelagius condemned
420 – Jerome's death
430 – Death of Augustine
500's – Saint Kevin of Glendalough
500-700's timing of King Arthur stories
500-800 – Irish spread gospel around Europe
800-900's – Viking raids
1000's – Brian Boru lost battle and Vikings became part of Ireland
1100's – Norman Invasion

Wisdom's Calling

Part 1

CHAPTER 1 – MEETING ANAIAS IN DENVER COLORADO

January 1, 1982 – The new year had come and I was facing my last year in seminary. What the year would bring was a mystery. I love the first day of the new year and the limitless possibilities. I got a little wild as I danced around my small apartment to a traditional Irish tune. The rhythms took me from somber to joyful to 'hard on the furniture'.

Suddenly I was on my knees. I met Anaias. She was screaming hysterically and indiscriminately into the darkness of an ancient night and I intercepted her pain. Her sorrow was being felt in my psyche; the feelings grabbed my gut and yet they felt distant, ancient, and strange.

There had been a massacre. The blood of Luann was spilling out onto her lap and the ground as she held her. Luann was dead. All around her was death. She screamed in horror, her emotion ricocheting off of time and space.

I found myself entering into her sobs not knowing why. "Who are you?" I cried out.

"I am Anaias, the daughter of the Goddess Ana. Do you know who has killed my people?" The voice came through me as a thought into my brain.

"I don't know anything about you, but I am willing to listen to you," I whispered.

"I must find Papallas and with him we will find these murderers." The feeling turned to bewilderment. "Who are you?" The voice inside me said.

As I told her my name she asked, "Are you a daughter of Ana?"

I responded, "I am a follower of Jesus, studying to be a minister."

"As a woman, are you allowed to lift the cup?"

"In my church, I am."

"I celebrate with you then. Women are being honored again, I'm glad. But I warn you, beware of those who call themselves Christian. It can be a dangerous religion," she responded.

I sorted out my thoughts until I concluded that this voice was from another place and time. "Where are you?" I asked.

She was silent for a moment. I could feel her thinking about the same situation. "You must have heard my pain. The loss was great but it is in the past. I must have broken through into your time. I wish Papallas were here. I would love to share this moment of new life with him."

She stopped, "But, I'm rude, you ask me where I am. I don't

know what you call it in your time, but I have lived on an island aflame with the green fire. I have learned many lessons that I might share with you if you are willing to listen," she answered.

"I'll try to listen."

"Will you tell my story to your people, so we won't be forgotten?" she asked

"I'll try."

I got out notebook paper and began to write about the massacre. It was nighttime. Anaias was up the hill in a forested area meditating, as was her practice before a ritual. She heard screaming and shouting. She ran down the hill to see shadowy figures struggling. She saw glistening swords in the firelight. She reached one of the figures and with her dagger lashed out, and struck the person, drawing blood. Then they fled into the forests. She didn't see any faces. She saw her dearest friend Luann on the ground.

I was shivering from the power of the encounter and the cold of the day that suddenly descended upon me. I drew a hot bath and as the water flowed, deep wrenching sobs came out of me for a loss that happened in another place and time.

'Why!?' she asked. She had touched a person in her future, as I touched one in the past. We both asked 'why the killing?' Why?!

As I wrote the story my first guess about the location was that she had lived somewhere in Ireland. I also guessed the time was the 5th century.

CHAPTER 2 – TIME AND SPACE

Can we intuit past events? How could a woman from the 5th century communicate with me? My rational mind said it was impossible.

I never again had as clear a communication as I had on January 1, 1982. After that, it was just a sense of her presence, a nudge. My rational mind fought against anything more. Yet, I had had that first vision and I wanted rational answers.

I continue to ponder the possibility of communication through time and space.

Archaeologists and historians have artifacts, ruins and manuscripts to work with. Does the past also leave behind strong feelings, anger, joy, longing?

Rubert Sheldrake's theory of morphic resonance suggests that there are different qualities of places and times that induce emotions, feelings, habitual attitudes and states of mind. "Mechanistic science has little to tell us about those qualities of time and place."[2]

Many of us have experienced going into an office and feeling, "There is some really negative stuff going on here!" Or, the opposite may occur. We may go to a house of strangers and feel peace and comfort. In intuitive history, we allow ourselves to go to an historic battlefield and feel the terror and suffering. We allow ourselves to find places where peace broke out and hope grew.

Sheldrake examines feeling locked into a place. Sheldrake suggests, "in addition to individual memory, through morphic resonance there will also be a component of collective memory through which a person can tune in to the past experiences of other people in the same place."[3] He adds, "The quality or atmosphere of the place does not depend just on what is happening there now, but on what has happened there before and on the way it has been experienced."[4] It is this atmosphere that the intuitive historian uses as a tool, along with the other historical tools to tell the story of the time and the people.

According to Einstein's ideas, time and space are not absolutes. They are inter-related dimensions and relative. Time is just one dimension of our universe. Maybe it does not mean as much as our rational mind tells us it does. Could an event that has happened fifteen hundred years ago, in some dimension, be happening now?

Kurt Goedel, a good friend of Einstein, made shocking assertions on the relativity of time. Goedel used mathematics and equations of relativity to show that time travel was not just fantasy, but scientific possibility. Goedel pointed out that time never really passes. We are not revisiting anything. To answer his horrified critics, he suggested that time is, "that mysterious and seemingly self-contradictory being."[5]

His ideas and proofs fell on silence in the scientific community. Even today, scientists recoil at his mathematical proofs, but have to ignore the science that is clearly there. As Goedel's biographer, Yourgraf says, "attempts to neutralize the Goedel universe shows how dangerous it is to break the conspiracy of silence that has shrouded the Goedel-Einstein connection."[6] Yourgrau suggests that this silence keeps the world from moving forward with the theory of the relativity of time and all its implications.

Physicist Brian Greene helps us out. He compares the perspective of classical physics and quantum physics. In classical physics events leading up to something are described with certainty, as if the event was happening now. For instance, I say that Anaias screamed to me about a massacre. I search for a time in history when a massacre happened, locked into a certain time and place. In quantum physics there is a probability, but not a certainty, that events unfolded in a certain way.[7] In this view, that Anaias screamed to me about an event, is, in itself, an event. There is a time-lessness about the vision. I can study the vision side by side with the historical facts. We move outside of 'time' to collect the intuitive elements.

Greene suggests that we see time as a block of ice or loaf of bread as opposed to a flowing river. If we do that, we can then visualize cutting off blocks of 'space-time'. These would be timeless moments. He says, "Moments don't change. Moments are. Being illuminated is simply one of the many unchanging features that constitute a moment."[8] What happened, happened in any moment. Even time travel would not allow you to change what happened.

Then Greene opens the door to the 'many worlds' framework. In it, he proposes that every potential outcome is realized in its own separate parallel universe.[9] Could events of the past be happening now, in a separate parallel universe? Could Seabhac, Owain and Beechna be thriving right now in a parallel universe? Could beings like the Tywa, and the Tuatha de Danaan and other 'mythical creatures' come in and out of our space from a separate parallel universe?[10]

The 'many worlds' and 'parallel universe' theories offer enticing possibilities for the expansion of what we call rational experience.

There are possibilities with superstrings and wormholes. According to the theories, a wormhole is a tunnel through space, the superstring keeps us connected to our own conscious in the 'now'. Superstrings and wormholes suggest to us that their may be dimensions that we cannot even perceive because of our limited brain capacity. This is the realm of the quantum scientist and it is also the realm of the mystic.

Ira Progoff points out that there is a one-sidedness to

rationalism.[11] It is less an expression of the scientific attitude than a outworn faith in a narrow version of science. This faith in the scientific attitude is comparable in many ways to the development of the rigid attitudes of the Middle Ages. He suggests that now science is no longer being conceived in terms of a restrictive rationalism, but is understood in the full generic meaning of the word science. Science is knowing. It is man's total quest for knowledge; where-ever that takes us.

I call my task "intuitive history". Ira Progoff agrees that the work of theoretical physics and the hunch-like intuition correspond. Carl Jung, in depth psychology work, began to formulate the principle of 'acausal relationship' that he named synchronicity. We sometimes call it 'coincidence'.

Carl Jung was friends with Wolfgang Pauli, Nils Bohr and Albert Einstein. He was aware that there was a connection with the atom as the basic unit of the physical world and the psyche of the human being. Now, as scientists are finding infinitely smaller units of the 'atom', we are finding even deeper connections within consciousness.

Jung saw that as great sums of energy can be released by breaking the atom, equivalent sums of energy can be released by delving into the psyche.

Carl Jung's theory of synchronicity allows us to bring together nonphysical as well as physical phenomena. The rational scientific and the non-rational consciousness are two sides of a single reality. Jung felt that the experience of synchronicity affirms that the individual is an interactive part of a larger whole.

Ira Progoff suggests, "The unfoldment of a human life is thus taking place on two distinct planes, simultaneously on two separate dimensions of reality. The one is the individual's perceptions of his life, his motivations and his actions. The second dimension is more than individual. Within this field, synchronicity operates. It encompasses the patterning of the universe across time, at each specific moment of time. Synchronicity is 'meaningful coincidence.'"[12]

Therefore, we are called to take these coincidences both seriously and playfully. Progoff says, "One cannot do anything about it, neither to cause more synchronistic events to happen nor to avoid them. By definition one cannot cause synchronistic events, but...can increase sensitivity to synchronistic events, especially to harmonize one's life with them."[13]

Yet at their deepest the artist, poet and mystic, and maybe the intuitive historian, are able to open themselves to the dimensions that interconnect us all no matter what the time or space or height or depth.

I have written and researched this story and pondered its meaning for me, and for whoever reads it. I have decided that the meaning is greater than anything I can understand. I have also decided that the moment of my communication with Anaias was a moment of extreme importance.

In June of 1982 I became an ordained minister of the United Methodist Church. I was appointed as an associate in Santa Clara, California. I had the joy of counseling people on their spiritual journey; baptizing babies and adults, serving the cup and loaf in communion, and best of all, I sometimes got to preach the word. After a couple of years I was appointed as the solo pastor to a small church in Biggs. There I got to minister to a whole community, and preach every Sunday. Because of my encounter with Anaias, I have never taken my position as a woman pastor lightly. It was and is an astonishing breakthrough, when one looks at the history of women's spiritual struggle in the western world.

At the time the number of women being ordained was small. We could all fit around a table at our Annual Conference in California and inquire about each other's well being. At the same time I was trying to understand the message of Anaias in 400 CE, I was witnessing an magnificent opening to and influx of women into the ordained ministry of the church. Although many Christian denominations have trouble with women in leadership even today, a major shift has started. Are the ancestors somehow breaking through time to cheer us on?

CHAPTER 3 – IN SEARCH OF ANAIAS – TRAVELS TO IRELAND.

May 12, 1985 – It was my first trip out of the country. I decided to head out 'intuitively". With just a backpack full of necessities and one reservation at the YWCA, I figured I would go where Anaias led me. As the plane touched down in Shannon, I experienced the shock of green against the blue ocean and the blue sky. The day was an amazingly cloudless one. My seatmate was visiting her boyfriend near Cork and was worried because his family believed in the little people and apparently the little people didn't like her. I wished her well as we both went into the town of Limerick to catch a train in opposite directions.

On the train to Dublin, a woman sat next to me and narrated the plight of her country. Yes, it was green, but how could it help but be green with all the rain? The problem was there wasn't enough sun to make the crops grow. I was used to the rainless droughts of California, and was curious about these sunless, soggy droughts in Ireland. Looking out at the endless green fields, I remembered that Anaias spoke of the massacre taking place in the forest, so I asked the woman on the train where the forests were. "Oh, forests, the British took all the trees years ago." It was just the beginning of tales I would hear of the hardships of the Irish-British relationship.

The people of the Republic of Ireland are very friendly. As I arrived in Dublin a man grabbed my hand and told me to follow him quickly to a bus. I followed him in spite of my doubts, and luckily I found it went to downtown Dublin. He was just the person I needed to meet, a professor at Trinity University. I told him of my interest in Irish history and my quest to find out about a woman who lived in the 5th century. He thought for a moment and then began to tell me of ruins and artifacts from that time period. He suggested that I visit the Book of Kells, Glendalough and Kildare.

I got to my room at the YWCA by dinner time. It had been a convent with gardens and well-kept lawns. I went to my room and started to freshen up for dinner, but jet lag overcame me. I slept through the meal. I woke up at midnight, wide awake, and hungry. I found a few crackers and cheese left over from the airplane flight. I opened the window to the lush grounds and heard, for the first time, the song of the nightingale. I was ready for the story to unfold.

I listened for the inner voice of Anaias. Instead a growling voice came, "Why are you here?! Go home!"

I ignored the voice and planned the next day. At 5 a.m. a noisy cricket match began in the field outside the window. Several school girls were calling to each other outside my door, in a deep Irish brogue. I was in Ireland! I would find Anaias!

At breakfast I ate with a woman who found out I was a protestant. She assured me that the Irish Catholics in the Republic were tolerant and settled. She even told me where she thought I could find a Methodist Church. She had worked for many years in Manchester because people in the Republic were poor and had to go to England to earn any money, even though they disliked the English.

I took a walk into Dublin Bay. I found that I could follow the tide, walking on the sand, formerly ocean bottom, for a long distance. Signs warned me not to walk too far or I'd be drowned by the incoming tide. By evening, the water would be crashing onto the sea wall.

I still had plenty of time to make the early train to town. The Dart was the fast rail line and it zipped me into Dublin with time to spare. I was at Trinity College before the doors to the Book of Kells opened to the public. No one else was there but the librarian. I was able to stand for a long time examining the intensity of the artwork, the elegance of the printed word. I remembered that, as a teenager, I was fascinated by this book and the illuminators. The Irish had provided a place of pilgrimage from the 5th century, through the middle ages. In a time of darkness in the rest of Europe, a light still shone around Ireland. The brightness of the shining was on these pages of the Book of Kells.

Next, I bought a tour to Glendalough, one of the primary places of pilgrimage in the 5th century. The location was on two shimmering lakes in the Wicklow Hills. The tour guide told us about Saint Kevin who had gone there to be alone with God. A huge village grew around him because the world was hungry for his wisdom. Kevin was serious about wanting to be alone and wandered up to the more secluded second lake. There he lived in a cave and on occasion would wander into the middle of the lake and pray with his hands reaching to God. Birds would come and build nests in his hands; his prayers were so long and constant.

The community continued for years after Saint Kevin's death. It was ravaged by invasions of local warlords, the Vikings and the Normans. This particular tour was so short I wasn't able to get to the upper lake. A small voice told me, though, this was not the time of Anaias. Saint Kevin was born decades after Anaias had died.

May 15, 1985 – Dublin – I took the regular commuter bus to the town of Kildare to visit Bridget's abbey. Bridget, or Bridey or Bride (pronounced Bridey) had been converted by St. Patrick. She nursed her ailing father who was still a pagan. As she sat at his bedside, she took reeds and wove crosses, and talked to him of the Christ. Before her father died, he accepted Christ. Bridget went on to become one of the most important women of Irish history and folklore.

Her spiritual power was recognized throughout Ireland. She was often present with women giving birth, and is even said to have gone back in time to be at Holy Mary's birth and then at Christ Jesus' birth.

After her father died, she decided to dedicate her life to the church. When the bishop came to accept her as a nun, she was accidentally ordained as a bishop when the he read the wrong ritual. Ritual was ritual, though, and the title stuck.

Bishop Bridget was the Abbess, in the 5th Century, of the church in Kildare. The name "Cill dara" literally means 'church by the oak'. Bridget had chosen this spot for her church because it had an ancient oak and yew tree, both sacred trees to the pagan Irish.

The literature at the church told the story of an ancient, sacred flame that had burned since the time of Bridget in the 5th century. Legend said that when she was alive, she and each of the 19 nuns would take a day and stoke the fire. When Bridget was dying, and the women were grieving, she told them that as a sign of eternal life, she would forever keep the fire burning on her day. When she died, the 19 women continued to stoke the fire. On the 20th day, miraculously, the fire was burning hotter than it had the night before. Bridget kept the flame burning for over fourteen hundred years.

The rule, for those fourteen hundred years, was that men were not allowed near the sacred flame. Even Cromwell, who ravaged Ireland in the 17th century, had tried to put it out. He was frightened away by the women who protected it. Over time, though, the church fell into disrepair, and Bridget maybe got busy with other things. In the 1900's an unnamed bishop doused the flame.

I came to the sign indicating where the vault for the flame had been. It was a brick cave-like structure, with ash visible. I sat silently. I felt Anaias with me, and the words came to me, "We will light this flame again. The world needs the power, and the fire, of women more than it ever has."

As many know already, Bridget, Bridey or Bride was also the name of an ancient goddess of Ireland. She was the goddess of new life and was often depicted milking a cow. She is the young maid symbolizing the new life that comes after the cold and frost leave. She was the goddess of spring, or Imbolg, and the flame. In mythology she had the same eternal flame that the saint had, and it kept burning with the help of 19 priestesses, as she watched over the 20th day. Her divine presence, whether saint or goddess, is strong in Ireland.

From the church I walked down the hill following a sign that said 'Bride's Well'. I had purchased a book in Dublin on the importance of wells in Ireland, each with a ritual and a sacred healing power. The 'little people' blessed those who visited a well on pilgrimage. Or, maybe it was the Christian God. Maybe it was Mary the Mother of the Christian God. Anyway, I turned down a path with high stone walls covered with moss. A horse looked over the wall and seemed to welcome me. Birds seemed to lite purposefully on my path. A butterfly landed on my shoulder. I came to an open field and a flock of sheep came running to me, baaing. They really seemed to be greeting me. More than that, I felt friendly, excited, eyes watching me walk down the path. When I finally came to the simple well, I felt an overflowing of joy. Here was the essence of ancient Ireland.

This was a well as it might have been centuries ago. It was a simple low circle of stones, with the Celtic words 'Tobar Bride' (well of Bridget). Then the English words, 'say the rosary', suggested that worshiping the goddess Bride was not an option. As an added inducement to proper prayer, a statue of the Virgin Mary, encased in glass, stood nearby.

I reached into the well with my hands and brought the water to my head as in baptism. I prayed, "Open me to the story. Trust me with it." I felt a gentle blessing fall over me. I heard a voice say. "Thank you for coming." I guess that was enough, I filled my water bottle with a little of the water for future blessings, and caught the bus back to Dublin.

Energized by the discovery in, and blessing of Kildare, I was interested in what other local towns might contain a treasure of blessing. But the words came, "The ancestors of the north and the Kingdom of Tara were not my people, they were descendants of the EiNeill and rivals. Go south to find my kinfolk."

May 18, 1985 – I took the express bus to Cork. That was as far south as one could go in Ireland. On the bus, we traveled quickly though the flat and green countryside. It was raining. The rain turned to ice crystals and pelted the bus window. I fell asleep.

I was jarred awake by a bump in the road. There, before me, framed in a rainbow, was a magnificent cathedral on top of a high rock. My heart began to beat wildly. "This is my home!" a voice said. The bus rush on past the town.

In Cork, I found a bed and breakfast in a private home up a steep hill. It was the home of a single mother trying to make ends meet by renting a room. Asking advice of my host, I found out the town was Cashel. She graciously offered to drive me down the steep hill to the bus station the next morning so I could spend the day exploring the town and return to Cork by evening. The next morning I crowded into her car along with her children going to school.

The rock had been known as 'St. Patrick's rock'; also known as Shreedrum. In the 5th century, it had been the home of the Kings of Munster. I met an American woman on the bus. She had just left her boyfriend after an argument. Together we walked up to the rock as she told me her troubles. As I approached, I stopped hearing her words. I heard a voice within me, "Walk slowly, this is a place of royalty. Our return is a sacred moment."

My new friend bought a ticket and got into the tour-line. The ticket taker spoke to me and startled me, "There's a tour in 10 minutes."

I looked around and asked him what structures might have been on the hill in the 5th century. "Oh I don't know. Only St. Patrick's cross. Even Cormac's castle is newer than that." He pointed to steps that took me into a small dark chapel and to an ancient cross. It was actually a cross placed on the ancient coronation stone of the kings of Munster. The original was preserved underground. A replica was on the lawn outside. I went into the darkened room.

"I have returned as promised," a voice inside me said. It was Anaias. The words seem to be an ancient challenge as well as a statement of victory.

I wandered outside. A tour guide was telling the familiar story, "It was here that St. Patrick baptized Aengus, King of Munster. When the King stood on this stone, St. Patrick sprinkled his head with holy water. Patrick declared Aengus' salvation in the name of the Father and the Son and the Holy Spirit, bringing down his staff with each name of the Trinity. When the ceremony was done, he saw the king's bleeding foot. "Why didn't you cry out?" Patrick asked. "I thought it was part of the ritual!" Aengus replied.

All of the tourists laughed at poor Aengus. Anaias seemed to call me away from the laughter. It was an insult to laugh at this king.

The tourists walked into a church that had been built centuries later by the Normans. Anaias asked me to walk to the front of the sanctuary and imagine myself holding the cup and performing mass. Maybe it was more than just Anaias talking to me. Maybe it was all the women who had been denied this privilege of offering the cup of Jesus through the centuries. Anaias seemed to be telling me that she had once served the cup, but someone around Patrick's time had stopped her. As I stood in that spot, I realized how fortunate I was to be a woman pastor, even with all the challenges before me.

The tour guide continued, "The buildings on this rock withstood the Vikings and the Normans. During the invasion of the English under Cromwell, all Catholics were to be killed. When Cromwell's armies came to Cashel, all the people of the town fled to the rock and hid in this sanctuary knowing they would be safe in God's house. Cromwell ignored the sanctity of the place and ordered that the canons aim at the Cathedral on the high hill. Everyone in the church was killed." We all looked at large pieces of the tower that had been destroyed by the canon-fire. I imagined the screams.

I remembered Anaias' scream asking why. I thought of the atrocity of Cromwell in the name of Christ. I held my breath.

"Did the massacre of your people happen here?" I asked as I

walked around the grassy sunlit rock, with yellow dandelions and crocus pushing though the springtime grass.

"No. . .this was a sacred space, but look over there." I looked out toward the distant mountains. "See that dark cloud? It was there long ago, but was not a sign of the weather. Then it was a heavy evil energy that sought to kill whatever was good and right." She brightened, "But then there are the caves of the wise ones in those hills. They saved me."

I turned back to the tourists and asked the tour guide what was out there. The guide responded, "Oh that's the valley of Aherlow, very nice for picnics. The Galtee Mountains are in the distance."

"Are there caves there?" I asked, curious about finding these 'wise ones'.

She answered brightly, "Well, legend says there were robbers who hid in the hills. There must be caves."

I returned to my house in Cork. I knew something now. Anaias was from the 5th century and had been present when St. Patrick baptized Aengus. I also felt she didn't like Patrick very much. I could almost pinpoint the dates. I needed to learn about the meeting of the pagan world and the Christian world.

The next day I moved to a bed and breakfast near the University of Cork. I made my way to the history department. A young heavyset woman greeted me.

I politely said, "I'd like to talk to someone who is a specialist on the coming of Christianity to Ireland, the time of St. Patrick."

"St. Patrick did not bring Christianity to Ireland!" she said indignantly. "We didn't need him for that. We were Christian long before he came." She calmed down and made an appointment for me to see the professor of ancient Irish history.

The next day, through his pipe smoke, the professor said historians knew little about the people St. Patrick met in southern Ireland. They built their homes out of wood, and were very poor. There apparently had been a famine in the land at that time causing many to flee to Wales to find food. Apparently, the tribes of the northern part of Ireland, known as Tara, did not suffer the same fate and so were able to conquer the regions of the south.

In my bedroom in the bed and breakfast, there was an Irish storybook on the bookshelf. In one of the stories, I learned that the ancient Tuatha de Danaan had arrived by boat at the southern shores of Ireland. They set up their realm on its shores. Their goddess Danaa had told them to follow the sacred bees that swarmed from the hives they brought with them on the boats. They had followed a swarm of sacred bees up the Suir River, first stopping in what is now Clonmel 'honey meadow.' The bees were sacred to Danaa and to the followers of Diana in Greece. Honey was the most sacred of foods. It was formed in a place of dark mystery and sweetened the world. The Tuatha de Danaan may have come from ancient Greece or Turkey and brought their Goddess with them.

Danaa was probably another name for Diana. Both names can be traced to An in the Middle East. In Wales there was the goddess Ana, another name for Danaa. Anaias was a daughter of Ana. The hostess of the bed and breakfast knocked on the door and offered a hot water bottle for the bed. I fell into a deep comfortable sleep. I felt very close to Anaias. I had found her.

The next morning I knew I needed to leave Cork and go to the mouth of the Suir River and follow the river inland as the Tuatha de Danaan had done. They had followed honeybees. I would follow the story of Anaias. I hauled my bags onto a bus to Waterford, the mouth of the Suir River. I walked along the waterfront, realizing that I was exhausted from carrying all of my luggage on and off the bus. I had started with a backpack but had added souvenirs that required more bags. Intuitive history cannot take place from a bus. You need to be able to get out, stand on the ground, and ask the soil questions.

May 20, 1985 – I wandered into a local pub offering lunch and bought a ham and cheese sandwich. I shared my problem with a couple of locals. The two men were brothers with cousins in the States. They insisted that I needed a Guinness to really solve the problem. We talked about my need to go to Tipperary. They agreed that I would enjoy it there. They also agreed that I should hire a car from a cousin who could get me a good deal. No more buses.

I left the pub and walked to the car rental kiosk with the cousin's name, and a deal was made. With my credit card number as collateral and extra insurance, I got my tiny bit of Irish freedom. So what that I had never driven manual transmission, and the Irish drive on the 'other side'? I took off in my tiny rental car during the Waterford rush hour. I saw a sign pointing toward Clonmel and took the turn.

There before me was a steep, narrow, medieval road with cars on both sides. My driving skills gave out and I hit the side of a parked car. The other car, a sturdy Mercedes, was not injured but my rental car was missing a headlight glass. A couple of young men came to examine the damage. They lifted my tiny car, disengaging it from the parked car. They drove me down the hill and wished me well. Mortified, I continued my journey.

Soon I forgot my troubles as I found myself traveling on country lanes along the Suir River. I travelled through Clonmel, 'honey meadow', up by the Galtees. It was May and the day was long.

As I approached Tipperary, I pulled over and looked at the map. I decided that I could easily approach my bed and breakfast on a perimeter road. I carefully approached, took the wrong turn anyway, and ended up in the middle of town. A roundabout in front of me totally unnerved me. My car stalled and flooded. Cars were honking.

A woman in an apron came up to me with groceries in her arms. "Do you need help, dear?" I nodded wordlessly. She threw her bags in the back seat. I moved over. She quickly drove the car to my b&b, took her bags out and continued her walk home. My hostess was upset that I was so late. I found my way to my room and fell asleep.

The next day I discovered Irish brown bread and cheese and took a picnic to the valley of Aherlow. I felt the giddiness of returning home to a place I had never been. I also felt the apprehension of discovering the place of Anaias' sorrow.

As I drove in the hills that separated Tipperary and the Aherlow valley, I was surprised to hear the growling voice again. "Why are you here? Go home. We don't need you!"

Suddenly I was in a forest. It was the first forest I had seen in Ireland. I pulled off the road. A sign declared that the international community had helped plant this forest. It was now lush and moss filled.

As I drove into the valley, I saw a beautiful small ruin of a church. I approached a sign on the ruin, 'Here 15 monks were slaughtered, by Cromwell's army, as they prayed.' I felt the fear and horror and heard the ancient screams, but they weren't Anaias' screams.

Here was the valley of Aherlow. It was green and meandering with the Galtee Mountains in the distance. It was a beautiful place, but not beyond atrocities.

My time was limited. If only I could come back to this place for a year and just live. "Yes, come," I heard a voice say.

There was a sense of another presence there. It was as though I was being watched by a gentle, joyful spirit, or two or three. Was I encountering the world of the fairies? Anaias had mentioned them, and Irish folklore was full of stories of 'the wise ones.' Maybe I didn't need to find any caves, but only needed to be receptive and open.

Hunting down legends, the next day, I wandered over to a town called Hospital and a hill called Knockany. The hill was named after a women named Annie who was raped and killed by a King of Munster. Her ghost inhabited the hill and screamed for vengeance. The legend reported that her screams could still be heard during a storm.

I approached the hill in my car thinking I might find a way to hike to the top. A sudden wind started blowing with icy rain pellets that crashed down threatening to break my windshield. Still determined, I pulled on my raincoat and got out of the car, but the wind and ice chased me back. Then I heard what sounded exactly like a woman screaming. Was that Anaias? Had a king of Munster committed the massacre and then raped her? I heard the growling voice, "Go away, we don't need you." Anxiety clutched my stomach as I sat in the car. I convinced myself there was nothing present that I needed to fear. I also convinced myself that I didn't need to climb this hill; this wasn't part of the story of Anaias.

My two weeks in Ireland had ended. I drove to a b&b in Limerick. At breakfast Mr. Barney, our host, told of the story of Irish soldiers in the Punjab in India who had learned of Ireland's near independence and had refused the orders of their British commander. "The commander shot them and their brains splattered on the wall behind them." Mr. Barney had tears in his eyes. The way he told the story it might have happened just last week. It had happened in 1929. Rage in the land was strong and ancient.

I got on the plane with a new sense of Ireland and my story. I had even more questions. More than anything I wanted to write the story of Anaias. Something happened 1500 years ago and she was screaming to me that we not forget today.

After all this traveling around Ireland when I sat down to write the story, my storyteller was called Seabhac, not Anaias and did not seem to be in Ireland. Where was she?

On July 1, 1985 I became pastor in the community of Riverbank, just outside of Modesto. We sang and laughed, shared the cup and loaf in remembrance of God's love for us, baptized babies as a symbol of their membership in the family of God in Christ Jesus, buried the old ones in the awareness of the Resurrection and eternal life. We had feasts and rummage sales.

I would go to the basement of the church and try to write the story that was unfolding of the life of this woman of Ireland. The story came slowly. My work as pastor took not just my time but my heart and complete consciousness. I would put the manuscript into the drawer for months at a time. In my dreams, Anaias would yell at me to take it out and write.

CHAPTER 4 – A FAMILY IN EXILE

She sat on the hillside overlooking the sea. It was the nesting time for the cloud of birds that soared overhead. They called to each other like laughing children. For thousands of years, birds of all sorts, gannets, gulls, curlews, cormorant, and puffins had migrated to this spot in time to herald the coming of long sun-filled days and make their nests. They nested in large colonies on rocky shores and promontories of the nearby islands. The gannets were spectacular divers. They plunged from the high cliffs in pursuit of fish.

Seabhac, a little girl, was a tiny speck to them on the cliff side. Not really noticing her, many made their nest on the peninsula cliffs rather than on the distant islands. These unlucky nesters were fair game for the child who was collecting eggs for her family.

The trick was to climb down the cliff, with one hand holding on to the tangled bushes above, and the basket, and with the other hand reach into the nest. By feel alone, she might find one speckled egg, which she would transfer to the basket. The next time the hand appeared, it would be braver, and grab two or even three eggs. Her basket was filled with enough eggs this day to call her task done.

On this day, as on so many others, her eyes were tracing the shapes on the horizon, looking for sea craft from her beloved home. It was her home though she had never lived there. She could sit for hours watching, waiting. She had heard the story over and over again of the throne of the righteous Eogan family that had been usurped by the evil family of the EiNeill. She was an Eogan and her family would once again rise up and overtake the throne on the high hill of Shreedrum. Her uncle, an optimistic man, after all these years, told her that the gods sent the family into exile so that they might strengthen themselves. They would return, as the ancient heroes had, with wisdom and knowledge to bestow upon their people.

She had never been to that place, but her feet longed to be there. That there were lands far beyond the edge of the sapphire blue sea amazed her. She often dreamed of being on a great ship crossing over to that mysterious and wonderful land. She dreamed of being dressed in jewels and finely woven capes and being applauded by the people for her wisdom. But it would be enough for now to see a ship appear. She'd meet some kinfolk and have the late night stories of the bard and her mother and father come alive. Her imagination was all she had to fill in the empty spaces left by her family's stories.

She gasped and stood and leaned forward as if that would help her see better. A speck had suddenly appeared on the horizon as if it came from some magical place. She was sure she had never seen this perturbance before. This must be the craft they had been waiting for. She was filled with excitement.

Seabhac ran quickly down across the red clay field until she reached the path that took her through the beech trees. She tried not to spill the eggs from her basket. A crowd of birds seemed to follow her as she entered a grove, calling to her as she ran. Two tiny lights flew along behind her, not quite birds, not quite people, entranced by her excitement. She then came to the final descent to the village, which was a limestone staircase and she slid most of the way. As she reached the village, she was nearly breathless but ran faster to the round stone building that was her home.

She carefully set the eggs down as she cried out.
"They're coming! Mama, I see them!"

M'alda was busily scrubbing the workday grime from the pile of woolen pants belonging to the men in the family.

This daughter had sharper eyes, and a more vivid imagination, than any of her other children. It was hard to know which was active now. Seabhac was only eight but she seemed to have an uncanny understanding of the activities of the adults. She seemed to know what it meant to be a people in exile, longing for home. It was a home she had never known.

M'alda remembered Eire and their home there. Her brother would be king if they ever returned. She had almost given up hoping. She had begun to forget life as a royal family. She had been married to the handsomest and strongest man of the clan in a state ceremony on the royal hill of Shreedrum, the home of the king of Munster and his family. She had given birth to a son and a daughter in the royal rooms. Her father, the king, had celebrated the births with banquets and dancing.

Then came the vicious war. While holding her oldest daughter in her arms she had seen her father decapitated in the field below the Shreedrum. His blood splashed around him as his defenders also fought to their death. Their red blood covered the green grass. The surviving family, her mother, brother, husband and two children went into hiding, eventually fleeing to Cymru. It had been a hard life, in a cold, rocky and windswept land. She wondered if the goddess Danaa was punishing her and the rest of the Eogan dynasty. The druid, Boandas had fled with them and continually admonished them that the family had angered Danaa in some way.

M'alda had given birth to six children while in exile, but only Giosai, Seabhac and little Geanta had survived. The two children born in Eire, Ciallach and Pa'abhallia had no memory of life there.

One day, they hoped, the allies would come on ships. One day they'd bring word that the hill of Shreedrum was free of the EiNeill clan.

Would this be the word, or only more refugees?

Seabhac was tall for her age, with red hair, the characteristics of a person with the blood of an ancient race, the Tuatha de Danaan. The Tuatha de Danaan was a mystical race. They had once ruled Eire, but were defeated in battle by the Milesian invaders. As their influence and political power waned, they disappeared from sight. They were still around, though, invisibly living in caves and underground shelters. They could be present, at any time, as pure and powerful spirit. The Eogan clan was descendent from them, but had intermingled with the Firbolgs and Milesians and diluted the mystical blood. Occasionally a person would be born with the almost pure Tuatha de Danaan blood flowing through their veins. They would have wisdom and vision and would bring great and needed changes to the people.

M'alda endured. There was work to do. Slowly and gracefully she looked up, never missing a beat with the scrubbing. "Slow down Seabhac and watch your feet. Whom do you see?"

"The ship, the red hulled one that comes from the Muscraige," Seabhac hissed out in her breathless condition. "I can see it!"

"You've claimed that several times during this last season. Let's wait and see. No doubt, your father and uncle have seen it if it is a ship."

"Oh mama, where are they? Can I tell them, please?"

"They're working now in the fish hut. It's not a business for a girl. Your sister needs a playmate," she said, trying to steer Seabhac to a less serious pursuit. She knew, even as she said it, that it would be useless.

Seabhac stooped for a moment as though she were trying to awaken the normal child in her. Little Geanta was splashing about in the creek right outside the hut, trying to catch a water bug and was having trouble with the task. Seabhac's heart fell. She wanted to please her mother, but she wanted to be part of unfolding events that seemed so much more exciting than a game that Geanta could create.

She wanted to be with her father and uncle and hear their plans. She wanted to be part of the family's destiny.

Her mother just thought of her as a girl of eight. Part of her wanted to be. . .really did want to be!

Tousling her shiny long red hair, she ran off in the direction of the fish hut.

As she ran down the hill, she encountered the old druid Boandas whose eyes widened as she appeared. Their eyes met for an instant as she ran past him. She always felt chills when she looked into his eyes. She shook off the feeling.

As she saw her father she yelled again, "I see them! They're coming!"

Her father, Finn, was a stocky man with red hair like hers and with shining blue eyes. He looked up from the salmon he was cleaning and gutting. The catch had been a good one. Seabhac smiled as she saw the pile of fish. They would eat well today and trading would be good.

The salmon brought wisdom to her people as it had to the ancient one, named Finn Mac Cumhaill.

To bring wisdom to the Firbolg kings a druid of the Tuatha de Danaan had transformed a special salmon into the source of all wisdom. It was to be cooked and eaten by an ancient king of the Firbolgs.

When the servant Finn tried to serve it, he accidentally touched the fish, burned his hand, quickly licking the burn. By this action Finn obtained the wisdom meant for the Firbolg king. Through his wisdom, Finn became a leader of his people.

That was the end of the ancient kings. The new kings saw themselves as servants of the people, like Finn Mac Cumhaill, if they were to be wise. They also ate a lot of salmon. There was always hope that another salmon would contain that same absolute wisdom. That was why the druid, Boandas, had been there. That was why the men were given the task of cleaning and dressing fish.

Her father smiled at his brother-in-law, Nad Fraich. Finn was used to his daughter's excitement. "Again?" he said softly.

Many times she thought she saw a ship but it was only an illusion.

They never ignored her, though. She might be right. This was the time. It had been four seasons since some word had been heard from their allies.

Wiping the fish guts and blood from their hands, the two men walked together to the edge of the cliff. The ocean was glassy against the intense blue sky.

It was most likely the Muscraige clan. They had been loyal to the dynasty of Eogan and had helped them go into hiding. The last time they came, it was to bring more refugees as the power of the EiNeill clan grew. They had a talent for judging the good weather that was rare on the Irish seas.

The High Druid stood back a distance to watch this girl. He was concerned.

There was just a tiny dot on the horizon.

"How did she see it? The ship is barely visible even now?" her uncle said to Finn.

Excitement rose in her father's chest, and a tightening. What would the report be? Could they go home finally? With that one thought, he received the flash of memories of Eire with its rolling green hills and icy wind and light glinting through clouds. That light made one sure the goddess and gods were laughing at the rain, the weather. Their laughter gave rainbows. There was the comfort of knowing that the Tuatha de Danaan continued to watch over them from the nearby caves with their protective powers. The mystery and magic of the land were what he missed the most. He had missed his home, longed to step on its soil, to feel it beneath his feet, to hear it speak to him in soft whispers.

The EiNeill clan was treacherous and bloodthirsty. The Irish of the north used violence and terror to make their living. They often took slaves from the villages they pillaged along the coastal lands. The battle with the EiNeill clan had come from the pressure of too many sons looking for space to rule.

It had been the Muscraige, the Ciarraige, the people Ui Fidgenti and the Fir Maige who protected the Eogans. The Eogan clan would reward their allies when time came to return home.

If it was time to return, his brother-in-law would have to act like a king. Here he was cleaning and preparing the fish. The family would have to transformed itself. The years had been difficult.

Nad Fraich's wife would have been queen if she had not died in childbirth. He had only Aengus, his son, left. This son was in line to be king if he died. He was not certain Aengus had the strength to rule, but he loved him.

The children would have to be trained. Finn had married into the royal family. His wife, M'alda, a princess, was a laboring wife. His five surviving children had done their childhood playing and learning here. The native peoples had welcomed them, because the Eogan clan had come in peace.

Many in the clan had intermarried with the Cymran tribes. It was natural that they might have mixed their blood. All were free to do so, but they would then move out of the line to the throne. Those in direct line to the throne included his nephew Aengus and then his sons, Ciallach and Giosai.

Nad Fraich took over. The family needed to get ready for this messenger. The village would be cleaned and swept, the sacred fire built up into a huge fire that could be seen for miles around. There would be a blessing by the druids, who would come with the honey-wine ceremony. Extra herbs needed to be collected. The salmon would be readied for a royal feast. The finest of the lambs would be sacrificed.

The visitors would recognize that they were royalty by the care they took with preparations. Whoever this messenger was, they would return to Eire with reports of the glory of the waiting king of Shreedrum. His mother would know what to do.

He shouted to his waiting niece, "Seabhac, run and tell your mother that the messenger is coming. Have her tell your grandmother. We have until sundown to get ready for our guests."

Seabhac stood gaping, overwhelmed.

Her father saw that she seemed stunned at the idea. He stamped his foot toward her, making her jump, "Run now!"

She scampered again up the hill. She had been right. She had seen it. They were coming. The excitement overtook her.

She made her way through the woods of hazel and oak and along the edge of the stream. She stopped there to shout the news to birch and alder trees and the finches and sparrows and crows. "They're coming," she shouted. The little people needed to know.

Sheep grazed on the hills above them. They were mostly used for the fleece and wool, only occasionally was one sacrificed for a royal feast. This would be the day. They were her friends.

"They're coming!" she shouted to the sheep knowing they deserved to know the reason one of them must die.

She called to Giosai, "They're coming!"

He looked up and ran to the edge of the hill to see for himself. As she ran up the hill to his side, he looked back at his flock, "Do I have to kill one of them?"

"I think so," she said softly. "I suppose it is for a good cause."

She looked out at the flock. She knew her brother would rather not kill these friends he had protected, but they both liked the taste of lamb.

She hugged her brother and ran off to find Ciallach. He was nowhere. She gave up and ran to the village. A sparrow flew along side her as if listening to the unfolding events.

By the time Seabhac got back to her mother the word had been spread. Everyone had their assignment.

"Your father has told us that your eyes are sharp. Good work Seabhac with your vision, but where have you been!!" Not stopping for an answer, M'alda added, "Help us make the oatcakes."

Her mother had already gotten down the honey pot. A clay bowl was filled with oats. A bit of geranium and anise and currants were readied.

Seabhac momentarily hesitated as she remembered that this was babies' work. Then she watched her little sister Geanta work her fingers through the gooey mess. Seabhac remembered the reward at the end of the mixing. You got to lick your fingers after the cakes were formed. She decided that her sister needed help.

M'alda heated stones for the cooking pot. The cakes would be put into the pot, covered by a large piece of slate, and allowed to steam.

While they were working, her sister Pa'abhallia arrived with a basket of roots, turnips and carrots. A pile of greens lay on the table, ready to be prepared for the stew. It was always good to see Pa'abhallia. As an oldest sister, she had sometimes been like a mother to Seabhac when M'alda had to go out into the fields. After she married Korca, she moved out of the village into his. He was Cymran. It was very obvious that Pa'abhallia, pregnant, was now going to be a mother herself.

"So, you did see it this time?" Pa'abhallia said with a teasing smile.

Seabhac glowed. "It's a really large ship, with a red sail," she added, to stake a claim on knowing the most about the arrival.

"A red sail?" her mother said in a teasing tone. "The ship was so far away. Could you really tell the color?"

"Of course she's sure. She saw a tiny dot on the horizon." Pa'abhallia mocked her. "Seabhac, even with your hawk eyes how could you tell it was red?"

Her mother and older sister laughed, enjoying the joke of questioning this overserious little girl.

Seabhac was silent. It was okay to be teased. The ship was coming. Red, green or yellow – it was coming. The word would travel for miles and the scattered family would gather. Stories would be told. There would be dancing and eating and drinking of honey-wine. There would be the ritual. The bard would sing a new song of this visit. Spirits would soar.

Licking their fingers, Seabhac and Geanta wandered out into the village in time to see Giosai carrying a slaughtered lamb. Blood was dripping from the carcass down his back. The druid, Boandas carried the sacrificial knife that had done the work and walked behind Giosai. No animal was killed without asking the spirits to forgive the people who did the task. It was brought to the women who would prepare it for roasting.

Seabhac joined her sisters and other relatives in the central kitchen. Pa'abhallia was barking orders at Sema and Timna, her cousins. They were crushing the grain with the mortar and mixing in water, herbs, leavening, and the cow's milk. It would be a savory herb bread. Seaweed had been freshly collected by her brothers and was being leached. Timpani who gathered berries, Rewa who collected mushrooms, Croa who made vinegars from the wild crab apples, all brought their supplies to the central kitchen.

A stew was made with the roots and greens. The huge pot was filled with glowing stones and covered.

Her grandmother, Danathie, arrived with the strongbox, carried by Ciallach. It was made of the hard shale with iron straps. Seabhac had seen it opened only twice before. She knew that it contained glorious jewels. There was amber and woven copper. The combs with garnet and sapphire inlay were from the old days in Eire. In those days, when she was queen, her grandmother would have had servants to dress her and comb her long hair now white. Now they had to make due.

M`alda moved about preparing the meal. Seeing the box made her pensive. She needed to appear the part of royalty. Her hands were rough from the work, but her heart and spirit were ready.

Seabhac watched as grandmother brought out the glittering jewels. Morganna came in with robes of finely woven linen. They were embroidered with the emblem of the kings of Munster. Her grandmother had been silent to this point, lost in her own thoughts. "Ah Morganna, you've done beautiful work. The color is right as is the fine stitchery." She fingered the robe that had been worn by her husband. Morganna had repaired the tears that came from the fatal battle. She had redyed the cloth, faded from the years of disuse, a vibrant green.

Most of the village fabric, linen or wool was dyed by Morganna in the house at the edge of the village. Dying the fabric was a messy but fascinating business. With vats of color, the bags of heather, bod weed, oak knots, or sometimes marigolds or dandelions, she could come up with shades of gold, yellow and pink.

The robes Morganna brought today were only for the one of the Eogan clan in line to be king of Munster, of Shreedrum. The source of this green was Morganna's secret, taught to dyers thru the generations.

After leaving a few jeweled combs and broach pins, her grandmother motioned to Ciallach to lift the strong box and follow her. "Let's meet your uncle and father in the meeting house. You are in the line of kings. You will need to dress also."

They left the cookhouse. Danathie looking stately as Ciallach followed, bent over by the weight of the box.

Seabhac watched them leave. She wanted to see into that box that contained the family destiny. She knew she would see more tonight.

M'alda said softly, "Pa'abhallia, finish your work. You'll dress tonight. You are one of the women of the family. I think Seabhac can tend to the cooking now."

Pa'abhallia looked startled. She was used to being outside these events. Seabhac felt a flood of pride for her sister. She felt a little envy that she would get to be part of the pageantry. Pa'abhallia pulled away from the bread she was kneading. Backing toward the door, she seemed almost to dread the night's events. Seabhac couldn't understand the look she saw on her sister's face.

"Seabhac, see to the cooking." Her mother turned to her, "Be sure to leave a dish outside for the spirits, so they'll know to join us."

Seabhac jumped up. She had never been given such a task before. It was as if she were an adult. She looked around the cookhouse as if to grasp the four corners of the world.

"Can you do that?" Her mother smiled at her look of shock.

"Yes, mama, of course I can." She grabbed the partially shaped loaf, getting ready to put it into the pan. Everything needed to boil, bake or simmer. She would have to keep the fire going at a constant temperature.

Giosai had chopped wood. That, with the peat, and the hot red stones, would keep their part of the feast cooking.

The fire never truly went out in the house, nor did the fire in the central meeting hall. It was said that the flame came from Eire. Danaa the grandmother of all, and mother of the goddess, Bridey, had given the fire. Her mother assured her that the same flame had burned in the castle in Shreedrum.

As the evening wore on, aunts and uncles from the hills around the village appeared. They brought food and musical instruments. Many were already dressed in the various Eogan clan colors. People were laughing as they arrived. There was joy in the arrival of old friends.

The sky was glowing red with the setting sun. The ship was so near, they could see the people on board. The beach had been transformed into a banquet hall with tables and flowers.

More ships had been seen on the horizon. They had no idea how many people were coming on the ships.

Boandas ordered Giosai back to the flocks to find two more lambs to ritually kill. They baked a few more loaves. There was plenty of salmon. There would be enough food for all of Eire, even the EiNeills, Seabhac thought. She looked around at the flasks of ale piled in a corner by the rock cliffs. Toblianas, her uncle, had obviously emptied his warehouse of ale for this night's festivities.

She recognized several cousins she hadn't seen in years. Her heart began to pound with excitement. Whatever was said tonight, this all might change. They might all be packing this very night and be transformed into royalty. She knew it was true and she, for one, would be ready.

From the house up the hill, she saw her sister and mother emerge with their hair up in the copper combs, and long green linen robes. She breathed in. She had never seen such beautiful women!

Seabhac looked around to find her father but she didn't see him. There was the king. He stood before her now dressed in the deep green linen with a gold and sapphire belt. Behind him was her cousin and playmate, Aengus, as finely dressed. They often play-acted but reality was different. Could Aengus really be king one day? She laughed to herself.

"Seabhac, they're really coming," Aengus whispered breathlessly. The look in his eyes betrayed both fear and excitement. It obviously had not often occurred to him that he might be asked to be king. Of all the people in the village, he most shared her amazement at their royal destiny. They spent many hours roaming around the hills, talking and pretending.

She giggled, and bowed deeply, "Your highness, you honor me..."

He laughed nervously and hit out at her and then he ran on to join his father.

Her brother Ciallach came next looking older than his thirteen years and obviously intending to impress anyone he could.

Unconstrained joy consumed her as she saw the bard at the edge of the cliff above the village. He was coming down the trail carrying his harp in his pouch, protecting it carefully from the elements. He was needed to tell the story of this night and weave it into the story of the past. She loved him.

The bard, Cormonthuc, was tall with brown curly hair and expressive light blue eyes. Those eyes held in them whatever emotion he sang of, sadness, anger, joy, love. He had often looked at her when he sang of love and she dreamed of being his wife and traveling throughout Cymru with him and one day singing triumphantly with him on Shreedrum.

As he came into sight Seabhac held back, wanting him to come to her, but Geanta ran ahead of her and jumped into his arms. He nearly dropped his harp. "Wow, what a greeting. . . my you've grown . . . you little flower you," he said, laughing to Geanta as she giggled in his embrace.

He put her down gently and his eyes caught Seabhac's as she stood staring at him. "Ah, here is the lass I've been longing to see." He held his arm out to her, his harp at his back.

"Come give me an embrace."

She ran to him and felt herself melt into his strong arms. He laughed and sang a small song into her ear about a man's heart beating in time with his true love's. She felt their hearts beating together.

Just at that moment, the drummers who had been gathering on the beach began their steady rhythm. The greeting was for the coming guests and was also meant to be a chilling warning in case they weren't friends arriving after all. All those who had any rhythm at all were inducted as drummers, including Morganna who had often been heard keeping time in her hillside dyer's hut.

As the lead ship entered the cove, Ciallach, and the other young men headed out to meet it in their small curraghs to help unload and to bring the guests to the shore. They were also armed and prepared for a surprise attack.

At the moment of the curragh launching, the tin pipes started to play a sonorous tune. The words that came to mind were of a people longing to go home, but willing to settle for a greeting from old friends. A mixture of sadness and joy filled the air with the music.

The first people came ashore to shouts and shrieks from the women. Many embraced old friends. They brought honey direct from Danaa's hives in Eire. There were baskets of Irish mussels and strips of dried venison from the red deer. After a few quick words, everyone knew that the exile was not over. These people had fled their lands and would now join them in exile. The EiNeills were stronger and had attacked even the Muscraige communities. All were disappointed. But friends were gathered and there was reason to celebrate.

The tables were set. There was cheering as each roasted lamb was brought out. The fragrance of the savory bread filled the air. The laverbread, seaweed, patties were piled high. The roasted salmon was set out on plates. All gathered around, laughing and eating. Pitchers of ale and flower water were set out.

As the food disappeared, the bard took center stage, on a terraced slope up above the banquet. He began to sing of the ancient journey of the people of Eire, of the early kings of the Fir Bolgs and Milesians. He told of the coming of the Tuatha de Danaan. They came with the goddess Danaa and her honey for making the sacred honey-wine. In the song, he noted that some say the Tuatha de Danaan came from the stars. Other say they came on low flat ships from the land to the south were the weather was fair and figs and olives and exotic fruits flourished.

As the people listened, they remembered their traditional restlessness. Many of the men thought of rushing to the waiting ships to find these lands. Tomorrow maybe.

The bard sang of the wisdom and bravery and the strength of the women and queens. He sang of the present conflicts, but glory of the Eogan dynasty that was and would be. He asked them to ponder what the goddess was thinking now. Events would unfold, as they must. The king and his family must hold to the belief that his return would come soon.

He reminded them of the ancient tribes of Eire, the Artraige, 'bear-people', the Osraige, 'deer people', Sordraige, 'boar people'.

He sang of the future. People from the south would come and beg for a place among them and would help them defeat the Romans. He sang of the evil glory of the Romans and how the gods were plotting their defeat. He sang of the care all must take against ignoring the desires of the gods and goddesses who had brought them this far and protected them even now.

The partygoers began to feel uneasy about the darkness of the singing. The bard, sensing this, came back to a happier tune and finished his story by bringing two beautiful Cymru women, two Eogan cousins, and two young Muscraige refugee women onto the stage with him. Seabhac felt she had been stabbed as he kissed the women. They were all laughing. He didn't seem to even notice her. She felt her heart beating alone.

She thought about his songs and the words about people from the south. Who would they be and why would they come?

Local sailors would collect items for trade and disappear on ships heading south. There had been trade between their villages.

Morganna had become famous among the traders for her fabrics. Seabhac had noticed that new items were appearing. There was beautiful amber and delicately painted metals.

For people from the south to come themselves would be interesting. She thought she would like to meet them and hear about the lands far away from here.

All lights were extinguished except those on a flat rock shelf a little above the bard. Boandas, the High Druid, said words in ancient language. A druid priest and priestess appeared. The priestess had a glowing object in her hand. It seemed to be on fire. Seabhac realized that it was a cup of bronze, covered with embedded jewels.

As the druid priestess, Katika, lifted the cup, she acknowledged the goddess who she called Ana. She called on the Tuatha de Danaan, the Tywa, and all other unseen spirits of the lands and the seas between. She acknowledged all of the unseen ancestors that might have come over on the ships and who dwelt in the village. She acknowledged all the other earthlings; the watching spirits and birds, deer, squirrel, and others that might be wondering about this event and all this noise.

As she lifted the cup, it seemed that a glistening cloud of light and shadow surrounded her and the cup. It was as though those ancestors and spirits were drinking of the sacred honey-wine. Seabhac felt the hair on her skin lift as an energy drifted over and touched the people.

The wind blew from the sea. A flock of gannets flew over, glowing in the moonlight. Seabhac shivered. She had heard that the Tuatha de Danaan, the ancient ones, came to these celebrations unseen by all who were not initiated into the sacred rituals. She knew that the Tywa were often around her in disguise. She felt light and joyful at the thought of their presence.

Katika held the cup high in her hands as the lights swirled about her. Suddenly, behind her, Torrida, a huge, bearded man appeared, holding his cape open over her head as if to clear away the spirits. He took the lifted cup and held it up to the crowd. Everyone was transfixed by the drama.

The priest and priestess then faced each other and drank from the cup. The cup was then offered to Boandas who stepped down from the rocky shelf and offered it to the King who offered it to his mother. Danathie then offered it it to her daughter, M'alda then to Aengus. Before Aengus was able to drink, Ciallach took the cup and drank from it. There were gasps in the crowd watching. Ciallach smiled innocently at them all.

Suddenly from the side of the stage, several young women appeared carrying flasks of honey-wine. Cups were and filled with the sweet, spicy, sacred drink. Seabhac got only a sip of the sweet drink that burned as it went down.

It was in this sacred setting that the dancing began.

As the drummers and pipers joined together, Nad Fraich, the king in exile, his mother, Danathie, the queen, joined in the dance. Finn danced with M`alda and Pa'abhallia danced with her Cymran husband Korca. Everyone joined them, young and old.

Men and women moved together as the gods and goddesses did. They sang and laughed together as their feet moved to the music.

The celebrating went on into the night.

Seabhac fell asleep on the beach next to her girlfriend Elihf, her little sister Geanta and her two girl cousins. They awoke to the incoming tide. The rush of water over their bodies brought them to their feet.

CHAPTER 5 – IN SEARCH FOR THE EXILES: DISCOVERING DEEP ECOLOGY

"Our story tells us of the sacredness of life, of the astonishing complexity of cells and organisms, of the vast lengths of time it took to generate their splendid diversity, of the enormous improbability that any of it happened at all." [14]

I've often told friends that I did not know whether I was writing the story of Anaias or whether Anaias was writing the story of me.

After traveling to Ireland, I felt that I needed to have a better understanding of the mind of Anaias. The closest we have in this world to the mind she might have had is the indigenous mind.

I trekked to Peru and met the descendents of the Inca. I traveled to the Southwest and sat at the feet of Navajo weavers, Tohono O'odam basket makers and Pueblo Potters. I listened to the stories and tried to understand a life that was close to the earth. At the same time, I was trying to listen to the story of Anaias.

The story was unfolding outside of Ireland. I didn't know why. I didn't know where.

I had three theories. The first was that she was on the Cornwall Peninsula. The second was that she was on the Welsh coast. The third was that she was in Scotland. Scotland was growing less likely since I had discovered the family was from southern Ireland.

In 1992, I received a piece of mail from a place called Schumacher College, in the Devon region of England and east of the Cornwall Peninsula. The school offered a class on 'Deep Ecology' featuring Arne Naess. It was a modern day philosophy that was close to the earth. The subject intrigued me. I could explore the Cornwall Peninsula and go to the class at Schumacher College.

I arrived in London on December 31st. The New Years celebration was wild outside my hotel at Piccadilly Circus. I brought in the year 1993 realizing that it had been 11 years since my vision and I didn't seem to have a true picture of the woman who had called to me.

On January 1st, I took a walk north to Regents' Park. It was empty and cold. An elderly, well-dressed man appeared with a paper sack.

"Good afternoon!" he said brightly.

I responded to his greeting. Hearing my American accent, he knew I was a tourist.

"Come, help me feed the robins"

I went with him to the Royal Rose Garden off to the side of the main garden. There he reached into the bag and brought out seed. He seemed to know each section of the garden and how many robins lived there and how much to feed each one.

He poured feed into my hand and showed me how to hold it. He explained that the tits would want to get the food first, but it was for the shyer robins. I was to close my hand to the tits and open it for the robins.

I stood silently as my hand filled with tiny hungry English robins. So tiny, so fragile. I felt honored.

The next day I picked up my rental car. After the fiasco in Ireland, I was ready for the differences in English roads. I spent extra to rent an automatic transmission, so at least I didn't have to worry about shifting when I was figuring out how to make a left turn.

It was 2:30 p.m. by the time I headed west. It grew foggy. In England in January, the sun goes down around 3:30 p.m. The fog and darkness made me tense. Traffic was thick. I was driving too slowly and cars were flashing their lights behind me. My knuckles turned white on the steering wheel.

Suddenly before me, Stonehenge seemed to rise above the fog. I couldn't stop, but I tried to keep my eyes on the road while transfixed by the ancient mysterious stones.

Finally, I pulled into a parking lot to get gas. There was a motel there. I took out my credit card to get a room. I'd be late to class but it would just have to be.

The next morning was much nicer as I drove into the town of Totnes and followed the signs to Dartington. In Dartington, I discovered a few things. I discovered real cider, that people really live in thatch-roof houses and the ecology can be deep.

I met Arne Naess, Norwegian athlete, mountain climber and philosopher. The philosophical idea he had was that we should live as though we are a part of all creation. Along with the teacher Bill Devall from California, I discovered that there was an international movement of people opening again to our spiritual connection to creation. We are connected beyond ourselves. We are connected to other humans, to grizzly bears, whole rain forest ecosystems, mountains and rivers, and to the tiniest microbes in the soil.[15]

Was this the way Anaias saw the world? Since Anaias lived, the western world experienced an enlightenment. Science made us observers rather than participants. We learned to dissect and compartmentalize. It was a good thing. The scientific discoveries of the last centuries have been astounding and have helped improve the lives of humans. The discoveries have also opened us to the incredible intricacy of the creation. However, for many of us, after we learned about the intricacy in nature and the earth we returned once again to mystery.

We are called to become participants again, but with an even deeper amazement. The mystery of our generation comes not from what we don't know, but comes from what we do know. The processes of the earth are magnificent, and intricate. We are just small beings walking across its surface.

Today, though, as small as we are, our technology, use of resources and resulting pollution is making a dangerous difference.

Was this woman from the 5th century also my teacher? What could I learn from her journey? How could her life, so long ago, affect my life? Somehow, I felt she could, and would.

On the third day of classes, I took a break. I was irresistibly drawn back to Stonehenge. I approached the stones and wondered whether Anaias had been here. I had a sense of both danger and celebration.

After that I drove to the end of the Cornwall Peninsula. This land was not a part of my story. I needed to return home and do some more research.

I came home to minister to my congregation. I was in a new church in the Salinas Valley now. The towns of Soledad and Greenfield were in the fertile valleys of America's salad bowl. Serendipity stepped in as I learned, after the appointment was set, that my great-grandfather, Charles Fremont Coy, had been a pastor there in the early 1900's. As I visited my parishioners, I often stopped in at the old mission ruins, from the days of the early Spanish settlements.

The Soledad mission however had difficulty because the land was fertile and vineyards grew luscious wine grapes. The local indigenous tribes introduced the monks to the soothing hot-springs in the hills. The monks became very relaxed. The bishops removed those monks and sent new, more serious replacements. They too, however, found life in the Salinas valley too enjoyable. The mission never achieved prominence in the mission system.

The towns of the Soledad and Greenfield had been home to immigrants from northern Italy from the 1800's. Now they were home to immigrants from Mexico. All were attracted by the lush soil and abundant harvests.

Anaias' presence in my life lead me to call together a Salinas Valley group of the Sierra Club. I worked hard to send out letters, to plan meetings, and to provide interesting programming on the natural history of the region. I eventually became active in the leadership of the local Sierra Club chapter that included protecting the Monterey Bay and Carmel Valley. The whispers from ancient Ireland gave me a reverence for the greenfires of life.

CHAPTER 6 – THE ISLAND

She stood on the cliff again, looking out to sea. It had not been good news. They would not be going home. Seabhac called out to her goddess, "Bridey, Bridey, take us home!!!" She stamped her feet to show her anger. The gannets called back.

The sound of birds had been deafening. Suddenly there was silence. A fog bank swiftly covered both her and the cliff. Through the mist, she saw an island. It had flickering lights over it, similar to the lights over the priestess' cup. Were the ancestors calling to her? It was like a door to the land of Eire.

She slipped down the sandstone slope to the tiny cove below. A curragh was moored there as a further invitation to her. Although she had no skill as a boat woman and was only eight years old, she untied the boat. She jumped into it as she pushed it into the water. She picked up the oars inside and began paddling toward the island. She barely heard her dog barking at the shore.

The tide was going out and pulled the little boat quickly away from the shore. Occasionally she saw glimpses of the island through the fog. The sight encouraged her to paddle vigorously. The fog was heavy and little else could be seen. She lost track of time or space. She was floating on top of the waters of Danaa, the mother of all. It felt safe and exciting.

Suddenly the fog lifted and the sun came out. Like a bursting bubble, the vision was gone. She was alone floating in a little boat far from shore. She froze in panic as the tide continued to move out quickly. She saw the bird-nesting island and started to paddle toward it but the winds began to blow and the waves started to push the tiny boat toward the rocky cliffs instead of the sandy beach.

A large black cloud filled with ice crystals blew furiously across the water and began pelting the tiny boat with ice.

The waves grew, flipping her and the boat over. Suddenly she was in the sea and the boat was nowhere. She felt the coldness of the water like a thousand needles. She was pulled under water for a moment that seemed like forever as she struggled to hold her breath. As she was thrust upward by the wake, she gulped the air and screamed.

She saw the overturned boat and she reached for it, but the rage of the whipping waves sunk her down again. The boat spun around and slammed into her body and she felt a sharp pain in her arm. She grabbed for the rope that had held the boat steady when it was on shore. As she tried to grab for it she realized her arm would not move. She screamed again, the gulls screamed back at her. This time the boat came from behind and struck her head. All was blackness.

The storm was over as quickly as it had come. Suddenly all was quiet. Her body floated on the water next to the overturned boat. Two gulls sat on the boat, but they had a radiance around them that suggested they were more than just gulls.

From the top of the cliff, a young man with curly dark hair heard the scream and his eyes followed the trajectory of the sound. Were his eyes tricking him or was that a person floating on the water? Next to the body, he saw a boat being tossed by the waves.

He ran down the cliff, over rocks that tumbled beneath his feet. At the water's edge, he dove in and he swam toward the body and boat. When he reached the boat, he saw nothing. Taking a big gulp of air, he dove under the water and saw nothing. Surfacing again, he felt panic knowing that whoever had screamed was certainly dead, or would be soon. At that moment, he saw a limp figure on the surface of the next wave. In the lull, he lunged toward it, opening his arms. A handful of hair swirled before him, he grasped it. Then he grabbed an arm and then a leg. He changed his hold so that he had her securely. He began to swim toward the shore. She was so limp he didn't know what he would have when he reached the land.

He carefully pulled her onto the beach. Gasping for breath, he looked at her wounds. She was not breathing. He turned her over to empty the seawater from her lungs and blew into her cold mouth. He moved back. She coughed and opened her eyes. Their eyes locked. He was mesmerized for a moment by her eyes. They were hazel colored and filled with terror. There was something more. He had seen something in those eyes. It was something he had wanted to see so badly. He wanted to know her. She began to shiver and gasp.

Seabhac was startled to be looking into the eyes of this boy with dark skin and black hair. He was a stranger but he looked at her with such concern. She stared, trying to remember what brought her here. She tried to move. Suddenly her whole body was racked with pain. Her arm began to throb and felt a hundred times its size. She reached up to her head and brought her hand back to find it covered with blood. Then there was blackness.

He pulled her up the shore away from the thrashing waves. "Pallas, brother, give me your healing powers." He broke some of the seaweed pods, scraped out the gelatinous fluid, and patted it on her wounds, using the leaves as a bandage.

He had heard about creatures of the sea that came as beautiful young women. They could curse you or bless you depending on how you treated them. She seemed very mortal to him. He just hoped he could heal her. Pallas, his ritual god, was of the sea and claimed many as his own. He was also a god of healing and wisdom if you could persuade him to part with it.

He took his cloak, given to him at his recent manhood ritual, and put it over her to keep her warm. He quickly climbed up the path to the hut for help. The trail was steep and the limestone gave way under his feet.

A herring gull laughed at his plight, coming close in flight to the cliff and pulling away at the last moment. A struggling yew tree stuck out of the side of the rocks lodging its roots amid an outcropping of stronger rocks. He reached out and grabbed the trunk, letting the tree and its spirit pull him the rest of the way.

Owain knew that Torrida, his guardian and teacher, had been away at a blessing festival. He hoped he would be home. At the top of the cliff now, he saw Torrida in the distance sharpening the blade of his hunting knife. He was wearing his yellow linen cape. His black curly hair and beard made him look bigger and rougher than he was. Torrida had deep knowledge of human nature, of the nature of the spirits, and of healing. He had traveled to distant lands, picking up wisdom. He had knowledge that he had memorized over years of study with the druidic order and devotion to Pallas.

Owain was gasping for breath as he came into the camp. Torrida slowly put down the sharpening stone and the knife and slapped the dust from his cape and body. All of his actions were done slowly and deliberately to match the obvious panic of this boy. He was so young. Everything was an emergency to him.

"Slowly, Owain, slowly. Nothing can be so serious"

"Master, a girl...the sea took her...I swam out. She is on the beach," he shivered as he spoke.

Torrida realized that it indeed might be serious, "On the beach...she's still living?"

"Yes master, she was breathing. There is a lot of blood. It is especially coming from her head."

"Ah..." Torrida tried not to act agitated but he knew that it was an awkward situation. To bring a strange girl from a nearby tribe into their hut was dangerous. To have her die here would be calamitous for all concerned.

If she were from a Roman encampment, his druid connections would put him in danger of being killed by the last of the Romans. Although the Irish tribe had allowed him to be a part of their rituals, they made it clear that he was not to touch their royal women. His dark skin, hair and eyes betrayed that though he was of an ancient Cymru tribe his blood was mixed with Roman. The Irish didn't mind the Cymru blood but hated the Roman part of him. Some of the other brothers of the druid order felt contemptuous about his mixed blood, especially Boandas, druid of the Eogan clan. The hatreds were ancient.

"Get cloths from the medicine tent and get the hammock...bring the splints and bandages."

"Yes master," Owain was relieved. Torrida's momentary hesitation had increased his panic. He hadn't thought of the political ramifications of helping this girl. He only wanted to look into her eyes, talk to her, feel her energy, and know her.

Loaded down with herb pouches and vials of ointment and fabric, they went down the steep trail. On the beach, Owain felt a cringing fear, unsure of what he would find. Torrida saw her with the caked blood and sand in her hair.

He had not had good luck healing those kinds of head wounds. He knew more, though, than most of the local healers. There were those of the druid order who suggested herbs that might stimulate healing. Those herbs, though, would be especially difficult to administer if she was asleep.

He could tell by her fair skin and auburn hair that she was of Irish royalty. He had seen her in the village on healing days. She had not seemed so adventurous. What was she doing here after the ritual he and Katika had performed? He assumed that most of her people were still sleeping or were cleaning up or settling in with the new refugees.

"Young girl," Torrida said. He hoped for some reaction from her but there was none.

They called it 'death sleep.' She could go on breathing for many days until finally the lack of food and drink killed her.

He looked at the face of Owain and saw the passion in his eyes. Torrida knew he had to try to help her in order to help Owain who was a prize student. Owain had just passed the tests of manhood and had promised himself to the study of the druid arts.

One day he would have to find a woman companion to enhance his knowledge. It was important that the energies of the male and female work together. Pallas, their ritual god, would find him this woman when the time was right.

This girl was too young, no more than eight or nine years. Torrida fought the sense he had that the god Pallas and goddess Ana had brought her here to his island for an important purpose. Even as she was in the death sleep, he felt the strength of her spirit. He shuttered to think that Pallas would call these two young people together. Why would Pallas bring such a threat of violence upon them?

Torrida knew he needed to work quickly to stop infection. He brought the vial of honey made from the healing flowers of the island. This sacred honey could close up the wound and would stop infection. He needed especially to clean the head wound.

He marveled that Owain had remembered the healing power of the seaweed, but frowned as he saw it placed incorrectly on the wounds, knowing that it had at least stopped the loss of blood. He unwrapped the wounds. He washed them in water from his flask. Then he reapplied the jelly from the pod mixing it with the honey salve. He wrapped it in linen bandages. He bound her arm to her body. He would check it for a break in camp.

The girl moaned, but did not open her eyes, as they gently lifted her onto the hammock and began the long slow trip up the cliff. Torrida knew there was danger in this kindness. He also knew that Owain and this girl must work out their destiny.

"Where is Seabhac?" M`alda asked no one in particular, with a touch of irritation in her voice. She had simply asked her daughter to collect eggs on the red sandstone hills. The girl was a hard worker when she wasn't distracted. She was worried about her daughter's daydreaming.

"She is too close to the vision world," Briolag, her visiting cousin, murmured. "You have to keep her nearby and knock her head more often. She'll cause you grief like your sister caused your mother."

"Ah Briolag, we were all full of dreams when we were young. I'll let Seabhac have hers for as long as she can."

"Well fine!" Briolag retorted, "But what if she's been stolen by the little people or kidnapped by someone. You'll never see her again."

M`alda was tired of Briolag's constant opinions on dangers and worries. There were worries enough in the world without creating more. M`alda knew that the little people were often accused of snatching children, but more often, they assisted them out of danger. She remembered many times as a girl being surrounded by the light spirits and laughing with joy. They were not to be feared but honored.

There was, though, the danger of the northern Irish kidnapping young girls, but they usually raided the whole village. There had been none of that in this region. Boandas was always warning them of an impending attack, but she didn't really expect one.

Briolag reached her large hands into the sack of oats and rubbed them to get off the husk. They would be thrown into the large kettle of water in the hearth, together with whatever was available. There were more people to feed today than yesterday.

It was good to be close to the vision world. Having been in exile so long, they were all forgetting. Seabhac's bloodline would be nothing but good for them. M`alda did worry about how the chief druid had been looking at her daughter. She could never forget the day her sister was sent away. She might ask Katika how to protect Seabhac from him. She put a dish of oats and honey out for the Tywa in case they had taken her daughter.

"Giosai," she called to her younger son who often watched the sheep in the same place as his sister. "Where is your sister? She's been gone since early his morning!"

"She was heading to the cliff last I saw," Giosai called back. Giosai was tall and lanky. He enjoyed the solitude as he stood on the hillside guiding the sheep to fresh green growth. He also enjoyed being helpful to his mother, or whoever else needed assistance. Sometimes his imagination led him to dream of going to sea. His father and uncles had often left for long fishing trips, but he was thinking more of the lands far away to the south.

He had listened carefully to the stories of the bard. He wondered about distant places, but his wondering stopped there. He had work to do. He envied his sister because she had such an imagination. The family called her Seabhac, after the hawk, because of her tendency to rise up above the ordinary. She seemed to see a world he could not see. He would never call her flighty like some of the girls. She always came back down to earth with something, a thought, a little more wisdom. She was only a year older than he was and they shared many tasks. In her imagination, though, she was able to travel far away without leaving the family. Until today. Her dog had come home without her.

The world was a blurry swirl as Seabhac tried to pull herself to consciousness. She was obviously in a hut. She sensed danger. Her first impulse was to run, but as she moved, a sharp pain shot through her body. Where did it come from? She concentrated on her body, checking each part. Her legs? No, they seemed fine. Her feet? She wiggled her toes. They were fine. All of this happened quickly as her body supplied the answer. The searing pain from her head and her arm screamed out at her. She reached with her left arm to her right and found, instead of an arm, a packing of ointment and cloth securely bound. She was surrounded by a feeling of peace. She fell back to sleep.

Later, she opened her eyes again and saw a large man with a dark beard and wild hair. The man was deeply engrossed in tying the knots like her father so often did for fishing. She saw a young man at the far side of the room, silently whittling with a knife and piece of wood, he was also dark haired.

She knew she should be afraid because strangers were dangerous. Many from the north of Eire were taking slaves, especially young girls. The chief druid had warned all the girls of the village of the danger of wandering away.

Try as she would, she could not be afraid of these two men. She drifted off to sleep again. Suddenly she was awakened by an explosion of pain in her arm. She cried out.

Owain looked over with a start. He put down his blade and moved slowly over to the girl, meeting her eyes carefully. He wasn't sure if he would see the same look of familiarity in her then that he had seen on the beach.

Seabhac knew now that she could not know this boy, yet she did know him. "Hello..." she said softly in Cymran.

He knelt by her side, "Don't move, you've been hurt quite

badly." He spoke in Cymran but with a thick accent. He was not from a local tribe. She almost began to giggle. There was something about hearing the sound of his voice that filled her with joy. The laughter hurt as it jarred her head and arm.

"You've hit your head," Owain continued, wondering at the smile and then wince that crossed over her.

"How did I get here?" she asked in slow Cymru.

"You were out alone with the curragh...and the storm tipped it over. I had to swim out to you or you would have drowned for sure. Why were you out alone?" Owain tried to be gentle with his reprimand.

"So you are responsible for my life?" she said softly. Bridey, she thought, saw him save me. She has made us friends for life.

"You almost died. It was only because my master is a great healer that we're talking now."

She looked over at Torrida. "I know him. He came to our village!"

"Yes, he says you are from the royal tribe from Eire."

Immediately she remembered her mother, father, sisters and brothers, her dog and the eggs she was supposed to be collecting. She remembered the vision and being caught up in the fog. She remembered the calm and the feeling that the goddess Danaa was actually calling to her.

"I was going to Eire. Our family is supposed to return soon to the throne."

"You can't row into the high seas in a little curragh. Even the best sailor wouldn't try that! It was stupid, little girl."

She felt her face flush, "I can make it home by myself now. I don't need you." She pulled her hand back from his touch.

She flipped her feet over the side of the cot and tried to pull herself upright with her good arm. She felt the anger building in her. Who was he to call her little girl and to laugh at her? He had no right to call her stupid. He couldn't even speak Cymran. He was obviously part of a primitive tribe.

Owain tried to stop her movement and she pulled away.

"Leave me alone. I don't need your insults!" Suddenly the pain in her arm and head met with intensity. There was darkness.

Torrida had listened to this encounter. It was amazing and a relief that she had actually awakened and was so alert that she could get angry. It certainly must be that the goddess had brought them together.

He remembered how he and Katika had met to practice their art and healing together. He had been Katika's healer also. But the smile quickly left as he remembered that any friendship with this girl was dangerous if not impossible.

Torrida knew that if Pallas and Ana were involved they must allow events to unfold. The god's being present did not mean that all was well or safe, only that it could not be stopped.

As he saw her move he worried that she might break open her wounds, but was relieved when he saw Owain catch her and put her back on the bed. She was asleep again.

CHAPTER 7 – OWAIN AND TORRIDA

It had been two days. Torrida was concerned about the length of time it would take for her to heal. "We must get her home quickly," he said finally.

"Why are you worried?" Owain asked.

"This girl comes from the family of Eogan. They have strict rules," Torrida answered.

Owain looked at him. "Weren't you at the blessing ceremony. Aren't you friends with the priest?"

"Only as long as Boandas agrees to our friendship. He has control over many of their affairs and is very jealous of that power. He also hates any connection with the south, with Rome."

"But we're not from Rome," Owain protested

"You and I have the dark hair of the ancient conquerors that brought strange gods and disaster," Torrida responded.

"But it was my father who came from those places, my mother was from local tribes."

"And that may make it easier." Torrida thoughtfully gazed at this boy who had been given to him by his dying mother with the request that he be given to the gods. She was pure Cymru, but spoke excellent Greek and Latin. She was highly educated but was abandoned by her family because of her marriage to Owain's father. She was alone when disease struck. Owain's father had been a Greek sailor who traveled with Torrida but had died when a storm swept him overboard. He had often talked about his wife and children. Torrida felt compelled to find the young widow and her child. Torrida found her, too late for two of her children. She was ravaged with fever, clutching Owain. As she died, he promised to raise him as his own son.

"The Irish are a strange people." Torrida looked out to the sea. "If they felt that we had dishonored this girl they would require us to pay a high price."

"We haven't hurt her," said Owain defensively. "We've saved her life." He looked toward the hut. "She is obviously worth more than any human could pay," Owain blushed.

His face grew hot as he imagined her brothers getting angry rather than grateful that they had saved her.

"They should have been taking better care of her! I'll tell them that!" Owain shouted.

Torrida looked at him, startled. "Don't start the battle before they do! And don't get attached to her. She's just a girl and may not grow into the woman you expect her to be."

"Teacher, you know I am not just seeing a girl. She is deeply different from any of the young girls who live with Katika or in my home village. She is different from any person I have ever met."

Torrida laughed, "You speak as though you are a man with many years experience"

"Maybe I am." Owain stood up as he tried to hide his own smile. He knew he was sounding ridiculous.

"Well," said Torrida, "we will let her heal tonight and must somehow, before dawn, get her to the grove above her village. She'll appear to have healed herself."

"What about the bandages?" Owain asked.

"We will take them off. The bleeding has stopped. They will, no doubt, have healers that will care for her. I'll send Katika," Torrida said.

Owain threw a log into the fire with such force that sparks flew, "So she must suffer for their possible stupidity and egos," He paused, then said, "We saved her. They should be grateful."

Torrida smiled and took his arm. It was still shaking. Torrida said, "The goddess will be grateful and the girl will be grateful." Looking up to the stars, "Let them sort it out," he said pointing upward indicating the divine ones.

Owain took a bowl of stew over to Seabhac. He gazed at the ruffled red hair around her face. It was still covered by a bandage to stop the now occasional bleeding of her head wound.

Her arm was badly sprained and deeply cut, but not broken. The bruising had gone down. Torrida said her sleeping was from the head wound and was natural. She would sleep as the goddess allowed her body to heal. The herbs they applied would help.

"Girl," he whispered.

He waited as she failed to respond, "Girl," he said a little louder.

He started to leave as he heard her whisper, but he couldn't understand what she said.

Her eyes opened as he turned back around. She grinned at him, "My name is not girl, it's Seabhac. Thank you for being my rescuer!"

He blushed, "Well Seabhac, I'm Owain. I was just doing my duty. You shouldn't have been acting so crazily."

"You're right I was very stupid, but I'm glad you were around or I'd be one of the fish girls now."

"Don't joke about it," he said sternly.

He smiled, changing his mind about joking, and knelt down beside her, "How do we know you're not a sea-fairy trying to enchant us?"

She giggled, "Give me that bowl of stew you're holding there and I'll show you that I can eat rabbit. Sea-fairys only eat seaweed, you know."

"So you smell rabbit do you? Your nose is healthy."

She took the bowl from him and began to sip the broth. "It's quite savory, like my father cooks it." She stopped for a moment remembering that she had been away from home for a few days.

Owain sensed her silence and its reason. "We'll have to get you back to your home."

"My father and brothers often warned me that men like you and your teacher would be dangerous."

"So they can't know about us. My master thinks it would be best if you were let off in the grove above your village," Owain warned.

"So my people will have to think I healed myself." She gazed at him intensely, wishing she could tell her family about this adventure.

"Well yes, I guess they'll think that. So you will be famous, I expect, a girl of legends." Owain smiled.

"Maybe I could tell them it was a big fish, a dolphin sent by the sea god, Pallas, who healed me." Seabhac smiled brightly.

"So maybe that is who we are!" Owain laughed.

"It's the way you smell, I think." She teasingly sniffed around him. "I should think gods would smell like flowers. You smell like my older brothers."

"Why don't your smelly older brothers watch over you?" Owain said half-seriously.

"No one watches after me," she said indignantly. "I do what I want."

His eyes widened, "And you are able to drown quite well!"

"I was aiming for the island and here I am."

Owain laughed and patted her good arm, "Eat your stew and enjoy your stay. It'll be a short one."

"I think you should give me a tour of this island before I go." She smiled at him.

"You are in no shape for a tour now." Then he looked at her with tenderness, saying, "But maybe we can find a time and a place to meet when your brothers aren't watching you and I'll bring you back."

She ate the stew in silence as he sat watching.

Still looking at her bowl she asked, "Do you know a lot about the sea?"

"I know some, but I'm going to learn more, I'm studying to be a son of Pallas, the god of the sea." Owain hesitated, then continued, "My father was a sea-merchant. The sailors from Cymru wouldn't travel unless a druid was on board and that's why Torrida and my father became friends."

His eyes were bright. "Oh Seabhac if you could have heard his stories. He told of lands glistening white, of peoples and jewels and colors. There are many lands beyond Cymru, beyond your Eire, taking two full moons to travel."

Her eyes widened, "It is hard to imagine that there are lands so far away?" She remembered the stories of the bard.

"And farther," he continued, enjoying her interest.

"Are you a druid?" she said changing the subject

"I'm learning," he responded.

"Can you foresee my future?" she asked smiling.

He paused, looked at her with patience. "You'll grow into a beautiful woman with many red headed children." He took her hand, "And I'll be your husband..."

She pulled her hand back and giggled, "My father and uncle will see about that!" She watched him blush then added, "But why not dark headed children like you."

"Because I believe your hair shows you to be related to a goddess of Eire, and she will touch all your children with her fire," he answered.

"And you are not of a god?" she asked.

"My father was of the cult of Pallas, a Greek god; he rules the sea and wisdom. I follow my father and Torrida in service to that god."

"And you will follow him as a sailor?" she added.

"And a trader of many wonderful things to eat and wear," he confirmed.

"You can bring me all sorts of amber and fine cloth," she added.

"Fit for a princess. Like you!"

She smiled shyly but did not respond.

"How long have you been in Cymru?" he asked.

"All my life. I keep seeing ships come. There seems to be no end to the fighting in Eire; so more and more of my distant cousins come into exile with us. It's the filthy scum called the EiNeill's who need to be kicked out of our lands."

"So it may be awhile!" he said firmly.

She brightened. "Or it might be next week that we get to go home!"

He patted her hand. "Sleep now." He stood up, "You have a big night ahead of you and we will have many more times of talking." He gazed at her hoping that was true.

It was still light. The days were long now and there would be several hours before they would need to begin the journey to take her back to her home. Fortunately, the low tide would stay for a while and the island would be connected by the narrow passageway to the mainland. The lowest tide would be at midnight. They would then follow the trail up the ridge and ride the cart for a few miles of high flat plains. It would be difficult traveling in the dark, but a nearly full moon would light the path.

They awakened her when it was still dark, and moved her into the cart with the lone small horse pulling it. They slowly made the journey. As Seabhac lay in the cart, she looked up at the sky and saw the many stars. Especially, she wondered about the story that people of the Tuatha de Danaan came from the stars. It was amazing that people lived on those little lights. They were like sparks from the fire that rose high and disappeared.

The cart bounced, she winced. She resolved not to feel pain or show pain. She wanted to show her gratitude instead to Owain and to the goddess Bridey who she was sure was a part of this adventure.

It would be many years before she was a woman and could be married. This person was certainly not someone her father or uncle, the future king, would choose. She liked the idea that her husband would give her dark-haired children who would look like him.

Owain looked back, "Being night, we can't see the rocks and ruts. Sorry."

She gritted her teeth at the pain of the jostling

The stars disappeared as they entered the grove. They continued on the path down the ravine. Then the cart could go no further.

Just as Seabhac thought she could endure no more bouncing, that part of the journey ended. Now she had to walk. "Bridey, healer, make me strong," she thought. As she moved, she let out an involuntary scream.

Torrida would stay with the cart. Owain would help her walk until she was within safe distance of the village. He would leave her there but continue watching until her family found her.

She had only walked a little with Owain on the island. Though she had no broken bones, her muscles were sore and bruised. Her head throbbed as the bandages were taken away. She could feel the oozing start again.

She put most of her weight on Owain. It felt good. He seemed to carry it well. She knew she was too young to be thinking about a husband but this boy was not like a big brother. She felt she had known him for longer than her brothers. As they got into the thick brambles, a narrow path opened to the firelight of the village beyond. Owain stopped.

"I'll be back at the next full moon. You will be having the feast of the fire by then. I will remind you by coming right here and calling." He let out a long mournful night whistle like that of the whippoorwill. "Come when you can the next day to the shore by the island."

Seabhac touched his hand. "Thank you," she said.

She limped forward alone. Suddenly a dog growled then barked furiously. Then the barking became a joyous squeal.

Owain watched her go.

"Who is it?" a young male voice said.

"Aengus is that you?" Owain heard Seabhac call.

Aengus cried out, "By the goddess Danaa! Seabhac we were grieving your death!" With his voice quaking he said, "Are you a ghost?"

"No cousin." She limped up to him. "Just a sick bird finally home," Seabhac immediately started teasing and giggling with him; then she shrieked with pain, having forgotten her wounds.

Owain stayed to listen. It was obvious they weren't very worried about invaders with such a young man on duty. He was relieved that someone had been there for her so quickly.

Seabhac was relieved that Aengus was village sentry this early morning. Aengus would act as though he believed her story whether he did or not. "I nearly drowned!" she said.

"Where are you hurt? How...? Did someone attack you?" Aengus responded.

"No, I was on the rocks climbing and I fell," she explained

"Seabhac, you shouldn't go out alone," said Aengus.

Owain turned back to Torrida. It would be in less than a moon cycle and he would see her again. This boy Aengus seemed to care for her. He didn't feel jealousy, just gratitude. She was just a girl.

CHAPTER 8 – SEABHAC'S STORY

As she leaned on him for support, Aengus helped her limp from the woods above, down to the upper village. Her mother was just beginning to set the fire for cooking the morning porridge.

M'alda looked toward the woods and saw the two emerge. "The goddess! Spirits of death! Who is this come back from the darkness?!! Seabhac!!! Gods!!!"

Her shrieking woke the rest of the village. She ran to Seabhac and touched her face and arms examined the swelling and bruises. She looked back to her head, saw the wound, and continued down to check her torso and legs then she wept.

"My little girl, you're home!!! We said you were dead! They told me maybe you had been kidnapped!! But I had to hope for death!! Here you are. You are really here!!" M'alda broke down in sobs and embraced her.

As she looked past her mother, Seabhac saw her father's stern eyes. "Seabhac, we've been near death ourselves in our grief!! Where have you been, girl!?"

"Father, I went out to collect eggs. I reached too far and fell down the cliff. It took me days to climb up..." she tried to memorize the story as she created it. She knew the goddess didn't look kindly on liars and would somehow make her pay for this lie.

"You should never go out alone!! You know better! You're always wandering off as though you were a boy, or as if you were a trained warrior. Much worse could happen to you." His tone softened. "We're so happy that you're home."

He touched her gently on the cheek. He looked at her arm and head. Realizing that he was forcing Aengus to hold her during the tirade, he took her arm, "Come, let's tend those wounds" Together they walked into the hut and carefully, wincing, she sat on her mat.

By this time, the word had traveled throughout the village. Shrigan, the healer, arrived to look at her wounds.

"I can't believe that you were able to get back here by your own power – up the cliff and here, you're an amazing child." Shrigan turned to the mother and father. "The head wound is worse than any I have seen. I suggest that the Holy Woman be called or it may cause insanity even now."

Shrigan shook her head, saying, "The evil powers can get into the wound when it's soft like this." She touched the fresh scab and Seabhac winced and pulled away.

A voice boomed behind them. "The Holy Woman has been

called." Boandas, the druid, in his white robes and golden chains, appeared. Her mother and father moved aside to make room for him. "This girl has shown great powers of survival. I would like to talk to her alone." He lifted his hand to the mother, father and Shrigan, and they left wordlessly.

Seabhac had never felt comfortable with the druid ... especially now. He was so close to the gods, he would know she was lying. He would condemn her for her friendship with this dark haired boy.

"What really happened girl! You must tell me." Boandas' eyes were hard and penetrating.

Tears filled her eyes. She was silent as her lips began to tremble.

He pushed her further. "The gods are telling me that they will punish you if you do not tell me."

She knew the familiar story of the punishment of the gods and goddesses. She had heard it many times. In the days of the Tuatha de Danaan, Cliodhna, the beautiful daughter of Gebann fell in love with Ciabhan. He was not one of them.

The goddess Cailleach disapproved of the match and lulled Cliodhna to sleep on the beach. The waves washed her out to sea, onto the island of the everlasting. She was trapped there forever, never again allowed to return to her beloved Eire.

Was this the island she had seen? Why would the goddess invite her to the island and then punish her for trying to get there?

She looked at the glaring eyes of Boandas. "I have told the truth. I was fetching eggs..."

"And..." His eyes narrowed.

"It became very foggy and I saw..." she continued trying to figure out if she should trust him.

"And what did you see..."

"I slipped and fell..." She grew confident with her story.

"Because you saw what?"

Her eyes caught his... He knew! Maybe she could tell him....

"I saw the island," she said softly.

"What island?" he whispered back, his face close to hers. There was urgency in his voice.

"Eire! The goddess was calling me to go there."

"You actually saw the island? How were you going to get there?" He looked interested now as if they were sharing a secret of great importance.

"She provided a small boat," she explained exploring his face for sincerity of interest.

"To row to Eire?" He didn't seem to be laughing. He at least took her seriously.

"But then the goddess left and the island was no more and there was a storm." She went faster.

"Now we hear the story," Boandas responded warmly.

"I was thrown out of the boat and tossed to the shore."

"I see, and then you healed yourself and came back to us."

"Yes..." Seabhac said softly, afraid to look into his eyes now.

A woman's voice, with a thick accent, came from behind him. "How does she seem, Boandas?"

"She seems amazingly strong. She saw the island in the cloud." He sounded impressed by her confession.

Seabhac looked up to the most beautiful women she had ever seen. It was Katika, the Holy Woman.

Katika walked up to her and took her hand. Boandas moved back. Seabhac had never before seen anyone make the somber druid move back.

"Of course she did. She is one of us," Katika said to Boandas. "She will be a woman of wisdom. You know that."

"I'll leave you to talk to her," Boandas said, giving Katika a knowing look.

As Boandas left, Seabhac felt that she could breathe again. Tears came into her eyes. Katika said nothing as she checked the head wound. She reached into her bag and brought out packets of strong smelling herbs and oils. She began to mix them.

Then after a time of silence Katika said, "You might easily have died out there with the deepness of this gash on your head. It's healing nicely."

She began to put ointment on it. "I'm surprised that it healed so well without the assistance of someone well trained in the arts."

Katika stopped and looked at Seabhac's face and searched her eyes. Seabhac just blinked. Hoping she would not betray the truth.

"Ana cares for you. I can feel it. You are very young but She wants you for her own. Do you feel that way child?"

Seabhac just knew that she had always loved this beautiful woman, "Yes, I do feel that way." She added, "Did She call me to that island?"

"It may be that She did," Katika said as if to assure Seabhac that she was believed.

"Why did She make it disappear?" Seabhac asked.

"It may be that your spirit just wasn't strong enough to get there. To know Ana, you have to study her ways. You have to grow in the art of listening to her. My sisters learn from her in the distant mountains."

Seabhac looked earnestly at her. "Have you been to that island?"

Katika smiled and touched Seabhac's good arm. "I have been many interesting places. The great Mother has led me on many adventures and I suspect She will lead you also."

Katika looked at the head wound again. "I know only one person who would try to heal a wound like yours. He lives on an island off the shore." She smiled at Seabhac.

"If he cared for you, I suppose it's best not to tell anyone." Looking away and then back as if to change the subject, the Holy Woman then said, "We must talk more about your visions."

Seabhac nodded.

"How many suns have you seen?"

"Eight new suns."

"You're too young now, but maybe I can take you with me for a short time to ask the sisters to read your powers."

Seabhac watched her. She felt excited about going off with this woman.

Katika stood up. "For now you will heal, and all will know that you are miraculously close to the Goddess. You will be very popular for a while."

Katika left, but the fragrance of the ointment stayed behind. 'What was it?' Seabhac thought. It made her feel very relaxed. She drifted off to a peaceful sleep.

They were astonished that she had survived on her own. The healer felt that the wound on her head was quite serious. It had healed well. Her arm had been sprained, bruised, and lacerated. She had bruises and cuts on her legs. That she could walk so far with such wounds amazed them all.

Seabhac found herself immersed once again in the life of the village, leaving every afternoon to watch for ships, collect eggs or play with Aengus. He was her guard to make certain she didn't fall again or get kidnapped. She was not allowed to go out without protection. She figured that Aengus was enough fun and adventurous enough that he wouldn't stop any of her exploring.

There was talk that she was amazingly strong for a young girl. There was certainly Tuatha de Danaan blood in her veins. Maybe Bride herself had chosen her. Some thought that Bride herself might walk in the girl's body; after all, she should have died from the head wound. Maybe the goddess had taken over this girl's body. They certainly needed to be careful just in case.

She began to think about the island. "Momma, when I am old like Pa'abhallia, can I choose my husband?"

"Certainly you may choose, Seabhac. As a royal child, though, the king will help you with your choice. It should be a royal prince to help our lineage be strong. He will be from Eire, and will be a fine young man. You will marry well, and be quite happy."

M`alda thought of her own marriage. Her father had chosen well. Seabhac's father was still so handsome and strong. M`alda sparkled at Seabhac as she spoke. "Because even now you are very pretty and smart."

Her sister Pa'abhallia was standing by the door. "That is if you live to marriage age," she said. She had been out of the village since the accident. "What did you do, little sister, to injure yourself so seriously?"

Seabhac ignored the teasing. "What if I find a fine young man who is not royal?"

"That would be good for friendship. You will not marry him though. Marriage for a royal princess is another matter."

Her mother returned to her work and was silent for a while. Pa'abhallia was collecting and sorting some of the clothing in a pile.

Seabhac was silent. She wanted so badly to reveal her secret.

Then she looked at her sister, "Pa'abhallia was able to marry whoever she chose."

M'alda continued her work as she responded, "Yes, and she made the choice to step out of the line of royalty. Her children could never rule Eire." M'alda looked up at her young daughter.

"You can still make a good choice by following the king's guidance." Then she smiled, saying, "But you have many years before you have to worry."

"Mother, what if we never return to Eire," Seabhac said mournfully.

Her mother stopped working, "Seabhac, shame on you for such an attitude. We shall return and we shall be royal once again. You had better start acting and talking as though you deserve to live on Shreedrum and be of the clan of Eogan."

She shooed her away, "Now go, ask your sister how you can help her with the wash."

Seabhac ran down the hill toward her sister who had taken a load of woolens with her to the place where the stream met the sea. Somehow, even as her mother had spoken, Seabhac knew that her fate would be different.

It wouldn't be easy to be together with Owain on the island, but somehow she would sail off with him on a grand adventure. There was something about the conversation with the Holy Woman that made her even more sure that her life would be filled with excitement. Danaa, the goddess Grandmother, would call her to many new places.

When Seabhac was strong enough, she might even find her way to the island in the mist. She made the wish on the waning moon knowing that the goddesses around her would help the wish grow with the waxing. She knew many moons would turn their course before it could be true and she would have to be patient.

"Quit daydreaming, little girl. What's all this talk about marriage anyway? Help me with this pile of clothes!" Pa'abhallia said in a teasing but firm tone.

Seabhac pulled a wet golden cloak out of the washing pond and began kneading it against the flat rock.

CHAPTER 9 – IN SEARCH OF THE EXILES TRAVELS TO WALES

The next phase of my search was in libraries. Through books, I found the location of my family in exile.

According to Irish historian Gearoid Mac Niocall, 'An Irish dynasty established itself in south-west Wales,...maintaining contact with its homeland in Munster.'[16] This was the Eogan clan.

We hear about Kings and Queens of northern Ireland and their legends. The stories of Aengus and the kings of Munster have been lost to history and legend.

The problem with the Eogan clan is that it tried to live in peace. After the EiNeill clan attacked, the whole family fled to southwest Wales, also known as Cymru. They kept in touch with events through their allies. The EiNeill clan ruled from the north of Ireland and sent out armies to steal lands and plunder, rape and kidnap. Scotland and England, even northern Europe felt the violence of the EiNeill clan.

The Eogan clan bided their time and befriended the people of southwest Wales. As friendly, open refugees, they were also in a good place to pick up cultural influences of Europe, the invading tribes and the fading Roman Empire.

I pulled out the maps and tacked them to the wall. Where was this exile community? Where could Seabhac have been as she played, sat, and stared off into the Irish Sea? Now I knew to look at Southwest Wales.

In 1994, we had only primitive computer information. I was using the 'Archie' search vehicle, (no extensive world wide web at the time). In my search of Wales, I found Aberystwyth and the University there. The town was on the Irish Sea. I could download a map, a bus schedule and a list of activities for March and April. That seemed like an interesting place to start.

March 29, 1995 – I flew to London. After a grueling non-stop flight from San Francisco, I waited in a long line through immigrations eager to hear Anaias calling to me. The guidebook I was using told me to find the National Express buses, down the ramp, beyond the Underground entrance. After several twists and turns, I found my way to the buses. The last bus to Wales that day was supposed to have left five minutes before I got there. Fortunately, the bus was late, or I would have had to spend the night in London. I bought a 'return' ticket to Cardiff,

Wales. Someone was smiling on me.

The bus sped across the English countryside towards Wales. There were daffodils everywhere. We crossed the Severn Bridge. The tide was out leaving Bristol Channel almost without water. I arrived in Cardiff and had to cross a busy street, with my bags, from the bus station to the train station to find the tourist office. They gave me a map and sent me to a nice bed and breakfast on the Taff River. I carried my bags about five blocks, stopping to rest a few times, and finally found the place. As I settled into the tiny room, I felt queasy and headachy. Suddenly I realized my purse was missing. I remembered resting for a minute on the bridge. I rushed out of the b&b, over the bridge and saw my purse with all its contents strewn along the riverbank. I climbed down to the water. The thief had only taken a pocketknife and some candy-bars. Fortunately, I learned along time ago never to carry money and my passport in my purse. That was safe in my money belt. Back at my room, I fell into a deep, exhausted traveler's sleep.

The next day I wandered to the National Museum. I learned about ancient travel between Wales and Rome. Pytheas of Massalia cruised the Atlantic from 322 to 285 B. C. The main trade route seemed be a boat to the coast of what is now southern France, travel on navigable rivers then travel overland to another boat in the Mediterranean. There had been a slave business between Britain and Rome in the 1st century B. C. I saw the housing and weaving looms of early Wales. There were caves everywhere in the shale of the mountains of Wales. There were signs that ancient communities had lived in and around the caves.

My next stop was Swansea on a peninsula that jutted out toward the Exmoor coast. Dylan Thomas called Swansea, 'an ugly lovely town'. It had been gutted by bombing raids during the war. It had been rebuilt in ugly concrete. My new bed and breakfast was twice the price of the one in Cardiff, but it had a beautiful view of the bay. The traffic was noisy, but the view great. I stayed an extra day so I could explore Rossilli, the Gower Peninsula and its beaches along the Bristol Channel.

As I arrived at the edge of the Gower Peninsula, it was foggy. The tide was out. For a moment, there was sun. I enjoyed walking through the tide pools and walking out to an island otherwise inaccessible when the tide was high. Suddenly the fog returned and I had to feel my way back to the bus stop.

In Swansea, I discovered laver bread, seaweed mixed with oatmeal. It is an ancient food, black and slimy and quite good tasting.

My intuition was beginning to tell me to go to Pembrokeshire. However, I had a computer map of Aberystwyth and I could get there quickly by train. That was where I went next. It was Sunday, so the Tourist Office was closed. I was on my own. From the train station, I walked down a side street and stopped at the first clean looking bed and breakfast. It was a small room with a bathroom down the hall.

As I walked the beaches of Aberystwyth, I knew this was not the view seen by the family in exile. I was too far north. The story that was unfolding, though, included the community of women living in the mountains. Aberystwyth was on the edge of the Welsh mountains. I looked to the East.

I decided to head into Snowdonia. I took a bus as far as Machynlleth, famous for his alternative technology center. I found a bed and breakfast right away, but my hostess spoke very little English, only Welsh, and didn't serve coffee in the morning. There was no coffee shop in the little town. I was in trouble. With a splitting headache, I took a bus to the technology center. There before me was a coffee shop. It saved my day. I toured the center and I was fascinated with ways we could make energy thru simple sustainable methods such as with solar and wind power.

The next day, armed with instant coffee in my room, I headed up into the higher mountains. My first stop was the town of Beddgellert. It was a beautiful little mountain town built around the grave of a dog named Gellert. Gellert's master came home from a hunting trip and found his home in shambles and his infant son covered in blood. The dog Gellert was lying next to the boy. The master assumed Gellert had attacked his son and angrily killed him. After he killed the dog, he found a dead wolf. He realized that Gellert had actually saved his son.

After a large funeral for the dog, he named the town 'bedd' meaning grave, 'Gellert', the dog's name. I had a scone and a large coffee as I walked around Gellert's grave. Sometimes we underestimate our non-human friends.

The next bus I got was a real bouncer (bad shocks – a phrase used by a British passenger). The bus driver and most people who got on the bus spoke Welsh. I had learned to say, "Bore da", which I hope meant "Hello".

The grand old mountain of northern Wales is Mount Snowden. It was early spring and the mountain was still buried in snow, and the roads to it were closed. I could get as far as a Snowden ranger station. There I read, in their displays, about legends of people living within the hollow mountains. People who traveled through them could often hear bells coming from inside.

I wondered whether Seabhac and Katika had climbed these high mountains to find the sisters of Ana. I looked out at the snowy mountain range. Was this the place inhabited by the holy women? I couldn't get there, but it was a possibility.

I headed back to Aberystwyth and found the tourist office open. With their help, I got a room at a beautiful ocean-front bed and breakfast called Brendan's. I heard the incoming tide crashing against the sea wall as I slept.

As beautiful as Aberystwyth was, it wasn't place of Anaias' childhood.

April 7th 1995 – I made my way slowly by bus to my next best guess of the Eogan exile home. It was the coast of Pembrokeshire. I chose the town of Broad Haven, on St. Bride's Bay. I took a bus to Cardigan, transferred to another bus to get to Haverfordwest. The bus took me past a town called Nant-y-Coy, on the Coy River. I wondered if my ancestors had come from this region. I arrived in Haverfordwest by mid afternoon and got a room.

The next day I found a local bus schedule that would get me to Broad Haven. The tourist office booked me a room in Mrs. Perry's house. I was staying in her daughter's old bedroom.

Before the sun set I wandered on the beach. Tears filled my eyes. This was Anaias' home. Nothing was like it had been, but the view was right. It was now a tourist spot for beach goers. I sat, watching the sunset, imagining what it must have been like to live in this place, waiting and watching.

The next morning I went to the local museum and read that a Christian community had been formed, south of the village, in an ancient community called St. Bride's on the Dale Peninsula. Legend was that St. Bridget had even visited the community. To the north, on the other side of the bay, was Saint David's. It became a place of learning and pilgrimage from the later part of the 5th century into the middle ages.

My first walk took me to the community of St. Bride's. It was on the cliff side of the Dale Peninsula, the limestone under my feet was bright red. It was obvious that the limestone cliffs were constantly being eroded. I hiked every inch of the public footpath in spite of the drizzle. By the time I got to the town of Marloes Sands, my boots started to fall apart from the damp. I tied them together with a shoelace. I was so elated by my closeness to Anaias, and the young Seabhac, that I probably hiked over 20 miles that day, and arrived home after nine at night. Mrs. Perry was beside herself with worry. My legs cramped during the night. The next day I decided to take a bus to St David's and then, in spite of my sore muscles, walk back toward Broad Haven.

The trek from St. David's was even more arduous as the trail took me down shale cliffs and up the other side. I again got to the bed and breakfast late. By this time, Mrs. Perry was used to it.

St. David's had little to do with my story, so I spent the next days wandering around Broad Haven and the Dale Peninsula, listening to the story and writing it down.

Up the sandstone cliffs was a broad and wide expanse where sheep could graze. Sheep still grazed. Hay grew in the fields.

I sat on the cliff side and looked down at the tiny boat waiting to go out to Skomer Island, a tidal island or to Grassholm Island further in the distance. These two islands showed signs of habitation during the fifth century. Anaias, of course, told me that Owain and Torrida lived on the tidal island. The two islands were now a nature preserve for thousands of birds that nested there. On the edge of the cliff, I saw birds building their new spring nests. The sound of the birds saturated the air. I doubted that any child was harvesting their eggs now.

I was exhausted from my long hikes. I was sure I had found Anaias' childhood home, and the location of the community she set up on the red limestone cliffs.

I headed back to Cardiff and then to London. Wearing an ace bandage on one of my wobbly ankles, I got on the plane for home. The flight home was glorious. I could see every detail of the earth, often called Gaia. I could see the glaciers and fjords of Greenland and the lands and icecaps across Canada. Then the snow gave way to the green farmlands and then the cities.

What a glorious, amazing, life-giving planet we live on.

As the story continued to unfold, I realized that the sisters of Ana probably lived in the region called the Brecon Beacons. It is a region with mining and caves and is accessible to the journey across the Bristol Channel.

With all the activities of ministry I sat down and struggled with scenes from the story as Anaias told them to me. I knew, though, that I needed to find a way to give my writing my full attention.

CHAPTER 10 – BEECHNA'S STORY
BETWEEN DIMENSIONS

"The Tuatha de Danaan retreated into the subterranean world, into the hollow hills – the magical mounds built by the neolithic peoples; and the dwelling places beneath the standing stones of the fairies who became their subjects." [17]

Beechna awakened from her deep and relaxing sleep. The sunlight filtered though the ash tree to signal the late afternoon. She was of the ancient race of the Tywa and their time on earth was the night. The Torca, as her people called 'the big people', were of the day.

Beechna is a different sort of creature. She lives in a dimension not always visible to humans. She's invisible because we see things as we believe they are rather than as they truly are.

The earth is energy. Energy is the basis of matter and can change shape and form. The Tywa are exceptionally sensitive to the energies of the earth. For instance Beechna can fly, not because she has wings, but because of the lightness of her mood. Joy can lift her.

The Tywa are often what we humans call 'shape-shifters.' They can appear in any shape they choose. They can shape themselves into a bird, a deer, a squirrel. Some Tywa can even move through time and space.

She was up early today to meet her new friend, a Torca girl. She would find her running near the cliffs in the early afternoon.

Beechna looked around her. This tree branch was the only home she knew. This was the time of quickening of new life, and the spirit of the tree was growing. She had to make room for all the activity of growing leaves and branches, that would push their way through as the year unfolded.

All her treasures were here. She had the feather robe used by her grandmother at banquets with the Tuatha de Danaan. The banquets never seemed to happen now, but just in case, she hung the robe from an upper branch of her home tree awaiting the invitation. A carefully woven shawl made from fine soft threads of wool became a pillow when it was filled with soft yew leaves.

She reached under the makeshift pillow and began to search. She jumped up. Where was it? She jumped down the base of the tree and searched frantically. Then she sighed with relief. There under the pile of leaves, at the base of the tree, was her amulet pouch. She grasped it in both her hands, kissing it.

She opened the pouch gratefully and caressed its contents. There was a red ochre carving of the goddess, fat and fertile and a small chip of amber from a wide flat plain to the east. Her hand tingled as she picked out the clear crystal, like a permanent piece of ice. It radiated with the absolute order of the universe, all elements in their place.

What a story surrounded this crystal. It was a gift to her grandmother from a people living on high mountains at the top of the world, across the ocean. They were people who shimmered like gold. They were also skilled in the art of weaving.

Her grandmother had not just had the gift of shape-shifting, as was common in Beechna's family; she was a space-shifter. She could 'think' herself anywhere in the world. One moment she was standing next to you, the next she would be standing in the desert surrounded by sand and camels. By morning, she would be back to you, telling you stories and carrying gifts. The treasures in the amulet bag came from those journeys.

During the night Beechna and her brother, Rodnic, searched for food as creatures usually do. This time of year there was plenty of food in the trees and forest floor.

Food was not so easy to find in the season of cold. It was helpful that the Torca left dishes with food for them outside the doors of their huts. Some huts were better then others. She especially enjoyed visiting the weaver's hut. Morganna left oatcakes and berries on her doorstep.

Beechna would then go into the hut while the big person was sleeping. She would try to help Morganna with her weaving. Beechna often accidentally tied herself up in the yarn. Morganna had a basket of finely spun yarn set aside. Beechna would sometimes try to fashion something of her own with that. Sometimes, Morganna would even leave a small woven garment for her.

Rodnic liked to spend time at the fish hut. He would take a stone with him and try to sharpen the knives for the Big People. The smaller knives were good for carving. He enjoyed trying his hand at the art. He would try to mend their nets, but sometimes made the hole worse.

Depending on their mood, sometimes they played tricks on the Torca. They would hide small objects and the next day watch the people look for them, yelling and stamping their feet. Sometimes, Beechna would speak to them in their dreams, especially someone who seemed to be ignoring a problem with a child or an animal.

In later years, the Tywa would be accused by the Big People, or Torca, of kidnapping children and injuring innocent people. This was never true. They were stories made up by people who are afraid of those who are different. The Tywa were always here to help. They were not to help people only. Sometimes the Tywa needed to protect other creatures.

If you took time to listen, each creature had its own wisdom.

Each kind of flower had a personality. The trees had an energy that could be unnerving. Birds, for the most part, had quite a sense of humor. Squirrels, while able to laugh, were too nervous to get most jokes.

As Beechna went out into the day, the beauty of this season: the blue, yellow, red flowers, the brilliant green fields, filled her with joy. She felt lightheaded as her feet rose from the ground.

As her tiny body floated, she looked down to see the ash tree and the ruffled leaves that had been her pillow. She looked far over the treetops to the sea in the distance. She felt absolute joy at the connection she had with all of this. She could hear the sounds of all the creatures, those getting up and those going to sleep.

This is the Tywa task. Each Tywa is tuned into the pulse of living things. This time of year, when the sun is growing stronger, the Tywa can hear the noise of the juices moving hydraulically up the trunk of the growing trees, the crackling roots pushing into the earth. You can get sparked as the new leaves reach out for the ray of sun and chemically turn it into food.

There was noisy action as the birds became frenetic about finding their mate and building the nest and creating new life. There was a visible energy that hopped around the meadows, sometimes in the form of insects, but often just as energy.

The action under the earth was electric with seeds that were invisible suddenly beginning to vibrate with life. Plants dormant a moment ago sent their roots out and sucked the nutrients from the soil. Some of Tywa's relatives lived deep in the earth also, tending to the life and energy below. Tywa beneath the earth's surface could see the sparkling of colors from the crackling of new life within the soil.

The Tywa were to see that all the creatures were finding what they needed to survive. Sure, An, the creator, did most of that work, but she could always use the Tywa's sensitive eyes, ears and hearts. It was also their task, as much as possible, to protect one from another. While birds ate insects and foxes ate birds, no one was allowed to get greedy.

Sometimes there was danger. It came in the form of a sticky energy fog. The cloud could form after a disaster. Where there had been sorrow or fear the negative energy fed on itself. It would affect whatever or whoever got stuck in it, unless you knew how to pump light into it. Sometimes it hovered over a location for years, sometimes it sunk into the soil. The Tywa could sometimes pump light into the darkness. There were some Torca who could, but very few , and they were the Torca of legends.

There were times when Beechna walked into a dangerous energy cloud and nearly could not breathe. Whatever joy she felt would suddenly disappear. If she was flying she would fall. If she was shapeshifting she would return to her Tywa body. She had to fight her way out with all her powers of spirit. She had to try to protect whoever else was caught in it.

The darkness would sometimes cause darkness. She remembered a forest fire at the end of one summer, that killed many animals that was caused by one. Another year it was a flood that destroyed the lands. Then the disaster would create more sorrow and fear.

Torca who were caught up in it sometimes started fights with one another. There would be a Torca war with dead bodies and arrows and spears flying. The Torca seemed too slow and stupid to know that it wasn't an enemy, it was just dangerous energy making them angry.

The Tuatha de Danaa tried to teach the Torca. Sometimes leaders among the Big People did have a sensitivity to all that was around them. Torca could be greedy and selfish, among other things, even without the sticky energy fog.

Beechna felt bad that they were so seriously handicapped that they could not experience the spirits of living things or hear the noises of life around them. Some were willing to learn, to see and to hear.

Off in the distance was a curl of smoke from fire. Obviously, it was a Torca camp. They had probably thoughtlessly killed one of her innocent ones. She hated the smell of roasting animal. She dampened her feeling of rage, knowing that that would stop her flight. Torca were teachable, her mother had said. Maybe they were.

Some creatures of An have to eat other animals. Beechna knew that the foxes caught birds, mice, and squirrels. Somehow, that seemed different from the Torca carefully preparing the animal, flavoring it herbs, cooking it slowly so it would be tender, and then stuffing themselves at a feast without a thought to the suffering of the animal.

Beechna took the shape of a tiny sparrow and flew with wings. She swooped down to the camp. She landed on a tree branch and watched.

She could see a young boy and an older man. Their spears lay unattended. Carefully she hopped down to the lush green bank of the river where the spears lay. She hopped and hopped around the larger of the spears. Fear overtook her. She felt her disguise quicken and flicker. She controlled the fear. This was the spear. She reached out to touch it. It was still fresh from the kill. The energy of the terrified animal still clung to it. Its aura permeated the quiet setting.

The man and boy were laughing. They had no sense of her presence. How could they? They were Torca. They were blind to the wonders of the world. For whatever reason the goddess An allowed them to stomp about and destroy. If they were not so spiritually blind, they would sense her presence and the negative energy of the creature they had killed.

Freshly brewed tea of the farn root sat on the fire in a pot. The fragrance was pleasant. She flew to the cup and sat on the edge. The warmth of the steam was nice but it would be too strong for her to drink. It had herbs that Torca needed to raise their huge bodies. She flew to a branch of a tree.

The man looked over to her and seemed to sense her presence. How could he? Did he know about the light also? He stood up and walked over to her. He seemed to stare at her for a moment. He spoke in a calm pleasant way, and turned to the boy. She liked his voice. But she wondered how she could like him since he was Torca. She shuttered.

She sighed and flew over to the two freshly skinned rabbits hung on a rope above the camp. She asked An's blessing. It seemed, by the response from An, that these men had already asked for it. She looked back at them and sang an especially happy sparrow song. At least they had done that right.

The greatest danger came to the Tywa who had chosen an animal shape.

So many of the Tywa had been brutally injured by the thoughtless arrows of those Torca who thought they needed their stomachs full of pigeon, rabbit, and squirrel.

Her mother and father had often risked taking the shape of deer running through the forests and across the moors. They had been shot with arrows. Once shot, they returned to their Tywa shape, wounded and bleeding. The hunted game would disappear to the Torca, as would the bodies of the Tywa. Their family would find them though.

Beechna, her brother and her grandmother had tended their injured parents. Her mother had died within days of her wounds. Her father lived on for a year or two but was very bitter.

In spite of her grief for her parents, she felt she must serve An.

Of the wild creatures, Beechna most enjoyed being a bird. Some enjoyed being wild cats, for the fear they brought. Some especially enjoyed being the hawk or even eagle. The hawk could sit on top branches and see forever and could quickly fly away. It was never, never mistaken for food.

Some enjoyed a watery playground and danced in the ocean but that was not for Beechna. It was too cold and unpredictable. Those that became sea creatures encountered Torca on ships, and sometimes rescued Torca who fell overboard.

There was also the dog. As dog, you could spend a lifetime with Torca. You could have some influence on them, and try to make them more aware of the world around them.

Rodnic, her brother, most enjoyed being a deer, in spite of what happened to their parents. One gets to run fast over the terrain, and can climb mountains quickly. It is one thing to fly above the earth as the eagle, and quite another to fly upon the earth as the stag. He spent most of his days munching on clover and mint and laughing with her.

Sparrow was definitely Beechna's choice.

She flew off above the forest to find her favorite meal. She lit on a currant bush a mile away from the Torca camp. This was her favorite afternoon spot. She hoped to see the little Torca girl.

Sure enough, on this afternoon the little girl sat there on the ground eating the currants. A basket of eggs was next to her.

Beechna remembered last summer when she and Seabhac had shared a cherry tree. Seabhac was sitting in the branches. Beechna reached up and grabbed a cherry. One cherry was a whole meal to her. The juice and sweetness filled her and energized her. Seabhac reached up with her huge Torca hands. They were little girl hands, but quite large by Tywa standards. She grabbed four or five of the sweet fruits and stuck the whole handful in her mouth, until her cheeks were bulging. Beechna sat amazed.

She and this little girl seemed to communicate without words. But there were some thoughts that were hard to communicate. The little girl seemed to be so perplexed by events that seemed so simple. Get up, get dressed, praise the creatures, praise the spirits of earth and sky, acknowledge An, the One, bring peace, bring trouble, find a place to sleep. Beechna would try to teach Seabhac how to live.

Seabhac stood and walked toward the path to the village, carrying the basket of eggs. She was heading home. Beechna followed her. The little girl stopped by a stream to rest and investigate the creatures there. Without words, Beechna showed her the tiny flowers and the almost invisible bugs.

Seabhac and Beechna now sat on a moss-covered log. The moisture of the recent rain had saturated everything. Beechna felt the dampness through her felt-like clothing.

Joy filled her and she was lifted up, soaring. Knowing Seabhac was watching she extended her arms out and upward, doing a double flip in the air.

The little Torca girl giggled in delight and began to do cartwheels on the ground, flapping her arms as if she could also fly. With a jump, Beechna propelled herself to the first branch of an oak tree. Oak trees were great to fly into; they were filled with joyful energy. The little Torca girl's laughter made her joy greater. Without landing, she flapped her arms, now covered with feathers, her body sleek; she looked like a seagull. She soared with her thoughts and desires to the topmost branches.

Beechna disappeared from Seabhac's sight.

There were some things about Seabhac that Beechna did not like. She could smell the flesh of animals on her. Like other Torca, she actually cooked and ate animals!

On this day, though, something amazing happened. Seabhac and Beechna looked into each other's eyes.

Seabhac said, "Hello, I'm Seabhac, named after the hawk, but I can't fly like you can."

Beechna was so shocked that the Torca girl was talking to her that she just stared. Then she surprised herself by speaking, "I'm Beechna, I'm a Tywa."

It was going to be so much easier teaching this Torca girl, now that they could talk.

Could she talk to the Tuatha de Danaan about Seabhac? The de Danaan did all the appearing and inviting. They lived in Eire and she lived in Cymru now.

Could she fly to Eire? Joy could take her a long way, but not across the sea. Looking up, she saw a gannet with its long wings. She knew, though, that she would not have the stamina to fly so far with wings. She lay down and looked up at the sky.

Then it happened. A shimmering light picked her up and flew her over the water. She landed gently on a barren hillside. As she walked up the rocky side of the hill, she saw an opening. Inside it was cool against the heat of the sun. She saw light coming from the inside of the cave and kept walking.

"Welcome Beechna!" she heard an enthusiastic voice say. "Ask us what you will. We will try to give you good advice." She couldn't see a face, but a shimmering light nearly blinded her as the words were spoken.

"I've met a little girl. She is one of the Big People, but I think she is also one of you. She was actually able to see me and talk to me."

"Yes, we know her and have been watching her. Her people call her Seabhac, but she is Anaias, she is of Ana, the Creator. She will need the guidance of our world, but will not know how to receive it. She will be initiated into our ways. We will be advising her in many ways, through many creatures. Be with her."

"How can I be with her?" Beechna asked, wanting more conversation with these beautiful people.

"You won't always be able to talk to her. When she is fully in her spirit, she will see you and hear you. When she is distracted, she will not know you are there. Try many ways to get her attention and guide her." A feminine voice laughed. The laughter stopped, the voice was soft, "We will guide you also."

Beechna found herself spinning through a rainbow of light. She appeared back where she had been in the beginning. Even though they had not said much to her, she knew she must watch over Seabhac, who would one day be called Anaias.

CHAPTER 11 – IN SEARCH OF FAIRIES

All of my travels were alone. Strange things can happen when you are a lone traveler. Throughout my journeys, I had a sense of being watched. Once in a while, when I was in a field or forest I would see movement out of the corner of my eye. If I turned to look there was nothing there. Yet somewhere deep within I felt that there was a presence. There was never a sense of dread, there was actually a sense of peacefulness and laughter. When I felt the presence, my footsteps grew lighter.

I had this feeling when I was walking down the road to Bridget's well. I felt it again when I was traveling through the Aherlow valley. I felt it as I climbed around the rock of Cashel or climbed the mountains around Mt Snowdon in Wales.

As I sat amid ruins, I felt that the crows were more than just crows. It all made me wonder. I asked myself the insane question of whether the cows were really cows, the sheep were really sheep and the squirrels were really squirrels. Were they shape-shifting fairies fooling my eyes?

There was also the sense that if they were really cows, sheep, horses, squirrels, and crows, maybe they had more spirit than I knew.

When I first arrived in Dublin and was pushing my way through the crowds, I saw a woman. She was tall with red hair and deep blue eyes. Everything would disappear as her eyes and mine connected. Then she would disappear into the crowd. I would feel as though I had been transported to another dimension for a moment. Disorientation often happens when you are a traveler, so I did not think much of it.

Later, when I was in a museum in Cork, I saw her again. I saw her in the town of Tipperary.

When I started to write the story of Anaias, Beechna, who called herself a Tywa, wanted to be a part of the story.

I started researching the 'fairy faith' that has existed for thousands of years in Celtic and pre-Celtic countries
One fairy scholar, W. Y. Evans Wentz, suggests that we are suffering because we don't experience the fairy in its various forms. We need to be open. We need to understand that many people have believed, and still believe passionately in fairies. Because of our lack of belief, the fairy people suffer. One fairy faithful complained about the effects of a lack of fairy-faith, "There is not a wave of prosperity upon the fairies of

the knoll, no, not a wave. There is no growth nor increase, no death nor withering upon the fairies."[18]

Does a race of creature that we call 'fairy' exist? Could there be races of intelligent creatures beyond our ability to perceive? Maybe we don't believe in races from other dimension, even when they come near, because we don't want people to laugh at us.

Maybe we don't experience races from other dimensions because our busy civilized life is too distracting. Evans-Wentz suggests that: "Where under modern conditions great multitudes of men and women are herded together, there is bound to be an unhealthy psychical atmosphere never found in the country." This atmosphere will, "inhibit any normal attempts of the Subliminal Self...to manifest itself in consciousness." Our civilized society keeps us from certain levels of consciousness.[19] How much are we missing by being too civilized?

Evans-Wentz reminds us that there are many highly educated people who believe in 'fairyland'. Maybe it takes a more sophisticated consciousness to experience the fairy. Maybe the fairy is part of a world that is greater than the world we know. Our known world is only a small part of it. "Within which the visible world is immersed like an island in an unexplored ocean." Maybe it is peopled by more species of living beings than this world, because it is incomparably more vast and varied in its possibilities."[20]

New science asks us to reconsider the dimensions of our world. Travel into fairyland that seems to take a few moments, actually takes many years. That sounds like Einstein's theory on space travel. Fairies are able to appear and disappear like the electron wave and particle theories.

As my story unfolded, I was introduced to more than just fairies. Who were those the friendly eyes that I 'sensed' as I traveled? Legend tells us that even today the Tuatha de Danaan live in Ireland hidden, unless they want to be seen. Did I see them in the crowd as I traveled through Ireland?

The legends say the Tuatha de Danaan came from the Pleiades. Is star travel through other dimensions possible?

Many people today claim to see visions. Often, in our civilized era, a person's reputation is damaged because of their claim. Some see them, but are afraid to admit it for just that reason. We reject communications that go beyond our understanding of space, time and agreed upon reality.

Mystics have always challenged us to expand our understanding of the limits of reality.[21] Matthew Fox and Rupert Sheldrake ponder the experience of angels by suggesting that we all expand our understanding of the unnecessary limits we place on reality.[22]

Michael Talbot, in *Mysticism and the New Physics*, suggests that we are taught the proper interpretation of objective reality. We will not see what our culture tells us does not exist. "From the day we are born, we are taught that there is a strict commonality to our perceptions. What one person perceives as a tree or a mountain another person must perceive as a tree or a mountain."[23]

If matter is actually, at its core, energy, what we 'see' is a construct of our human mind. Heinz Von Foerster reminds us that, "Indeed 'out there' there is no light and no color, there are only electro-magnetic waves; 'out there' there is no sound and no music, there are only periodic variations of the air pressure; 'out there', there is no heat and no cold; there are only moving molecules with more or less mean kinetic energy, and so on."[24] We have decided collectively how to make sense of all of the electro-magnetic waves. Maybe it's time to open ourselves to new possibilities of perception and consciousness.

Our rational mind is limited in what it knows and understands. There are always edges to our understanding.

So, I open myself to the possibility of creatures existing beyond my ability to perceive them. That is the great mystery of creation

Sometimes I look into the eyes of a wild creature and wonder if it might not be a Tywa cousin visiting me.

I am not suggesting we have 'faith' in fairies, that we worship them or perform rituals around a belief in them. I am just suggesting that we might want to be hospitable to them, as we would to any other visitor in our life, no more, no less.

CHAPTER 12 – PELAGIUS THE BRITO
CARTHAGE – NORTH AFRICA

"Creation itself was, for Pelagius, the foundational "grace"
or gift, of God.
God also gave humans complete freedom of will, and therefore the
capacity to choose good or evil." [25]

Chaos and order were competing in the lands around the Mediterranean, the heart of the Roman Empire. In the 5th century, the empire had been invaded repeatedly by tribes from outside its borders. It had been a few decades since Emperor Constantine had declared the Empire Christian. The church was feeling its strength and beginning to organize. In many ways, the church saw itself as the protector of the structure of the waning Roman Empire.

A man called Pelagius had come from Britain to Rome in about 384 to study law and theology. His father in Britain had been against his journey. He regretted angering his father, but he had to leave. He joined in the debates about acceptable church doctrine. He was respected and loved in the intellectual circles of Rome.

It was in 405, while in Rome, that he had a tangle with the great Bishop Augustine, not in person fortunately. Another bishop was quoting from a prayer of Augustine. It seemed to Pelagius to turn the individual into a puppet of God. For Pelagius it was important that humans be called to a moral effort, that was the foundation of his faith. Unfortunately he was so shocked and violently indignant that a yelling match broke out between himself and the reader that became famous around Rome.

Pelagius had made friends with a student named Caelestius. Although Caelestius was born to an aristocratic family and was at first heading toward a legal career, the teachings of Pelagius changed his life. Pelagius admired Caelestius for his public speaking ability. He had a keenly analytical mind. Pelagius sometimes flinched when Caelestius began expounding the views that Pelagius held gently. Caelestius seemed to always want to shout their views on sin and grace from every corner of the city streets. In 409, Alaric, the Visigoth, threatened to sack Rome. The two of them headed for Sicily. After they heard that Rome had actually fallen they headed for Carthage. The views of the people of Carthage were rigid. The bishops of the area discouraged debate of any sort. He hoped Caelestius could be quieter. But he wasn't.

Pelagius sat on a low stone wall at the edge of a garden in the middle of Carthage He was a large man. Not only was he tall, but he was extremely wide. His hair was sandy colored and his eyes were blue and intense. Because of his heaviness, he moved slowly and needed to sit often as he walked in the hot sun. Sweat poured down his face today. He lifted his water flask and drank deeply.

His childhood name in Britain was Morgan, 'one who traveled'. He took the Latin name, 'Pelagius' because it had the same meaning. He had traveled more than most people in his lifetime.

The land of his birth was green and wet, the absolute opposite of this place. When he talked about home, people laughed, imagining a primitive and wild place. People who intended to insult him called him a Brito or Scoti. The people in Rome, and now in Carthage, felt themselves to be superior to everyone else in the Empire. No one could imagine that someone as well educated as he was could have come from Britain. No one could imagine that he longed to return home.

He looked forward to the arrival of the merchants from the northern islands. They normally came by ship to the coast of Gaul and then overland to Rome. They were able to bring the honey that could only come from the flowers in the fields of his birth. They brought woolen garments that were soft and sometimes warmer than he needed in this more temperate climate.

He especially enjoyed hearing the news of his home from the traveling druid, Torrida. Although some would say Torrida was a pagan, he had a deep sense of the sacred and a deep sense of acting humbly on earth. Christ Jesus approved, Pelagius was sure of that much. It was not the words you professed to believe that were important to God, it was the life you lived. Torrida was always available for a theological argument. Pelagius always felt the fresh breeze of home when they talked.

At home, all the people were deeply aware of the sun, moon, stars, the winds that blew, the rains that fell, the seasons of the year. They honored the deep rich forests. He recalled the fields of flowers and the bogs and the creatures that lived there.

There was always the sense of another race of people wiser than humans. They were not angels. They were not demons. He was sure that Christ Jesus was with them also. All creation came from God. All creation was filled with the power of free will. That was the sheer genius of God. In Britain, all seemed full of life and therefore full of God.

Now he was in Carthage, though. He would not be seeing Torrida, who only came as far as Rome. He would not be receiving the goods that reminded him of home. God had called him to this time of sacrifice. It would cleanse his soul.

He saw two women walking toward him. One, he recognized. She was Juliana, a widow from Rome.

"Good morning, teacher." Juliana greeted him with a smile. A young woman, standing next to her, looked at him with questioning eyes. He was startled by the intensity of her look.

"I'm here to talk to you about my daughter, Demetrias," said Juliana. She turned to the young woman next to her. Pelagius nodded to the young woman.

Juliana continued, "It seems that she has heard a call from God to forgo marriage and give up her wealth. I told her that we needed to talk to someone learned in the faith. She said she would feel most comfortable talking to you."

Demetrias blushed and smiled shyly at Pelagius.

Juliana continued, "She made the decision just as plans were finalized for her marriage."

Demetrias broke into the conversation. She said earnestly, "It was nothing to do with the man I was going to marry. He is a fine man, but I am called. I know I am called to a life of prayer and devotion to the God of Christ Jesus. Marriage is a commitment that requires a woman's full attention." He now understood her questioning, intense look. He remembered it when he was young and told his father that he wanted to study the Christian faith. His whole family was in distress.

Pelagius smiled at her, "I can only answer as a man. I think a life of prayer as a woman must be very different."

He turned to Juliana asking, "Are you happy with her choice?"

"I'm happy if it truly is a call from God. I'd love to have children and grandchildren, but to know your child has a sacred calling is a pleasure greater than any other pleasure. The groom's family is threatening to sue us, though. Many of our relatives are upset."

He turned to Demetrias, motioning her to sit on a stone bench nearby. He gently said, "I'm deeply moved by your ability to turn way from your wealth. There are many wealthy people who would rather ride in grand carriages surrounded by servants. People with wealth tend to cling to it."

Demetrias responded, "I have heard that you are very hard on the rich. You teach that we must share with the poor."

"Yes," said Pelagius, "you are given wealth so that you can make the world a better place."

He continued, "The teachings of Christ Jesus are about discovering your human goodness. I would say that we measure the goodness of human nature in relation to our Creator. When He created the world, God declared that everything was good. So if every tree and animal, insect and plant is good, how much better is the human? He has given animals teeth and jaws that are more powerful and sharper than the finest sword. But he has given humans intelligence and freedom. He has given us the gift of generosity."

Juliana looked at him deeply, "You believe we are created with goodness? Father Augustine says we are all born wicked and selfish?"

Pelagius responded, "Deep within each of us, even the most wicked, is the ability to do good."

Demetrias responded, "It seems like people, even those who call themselves Christians can be very evil. I heard of a Christian nobleman who flogged his slave for bringing him cold wash water. There was the stable boy whose hand was cut off because he was clumsy in helping the Christian nobleman mount his horse. How can people who have devoted themselves to Christ Jesus be so evil?"

Pelagius answered, "Ah, that is the mystery of human freedom. Your question means you are on the road to great wisdom. For whatever reason, goodness is especially a problem for those with wealth and privilege."

Juliana interjected, "I've heard that you criticize the wealthy people in the empire, but our wealth is what keeps the empire alive." She added, "The rich are doing good things. Some things are getting better. Slaves are required by law to be given housing and food. Peasants aren't imprisoned for a debt. Prisoners are treated better. When there is a famine, action is taken by the government to relieve it."

Pelagius nodded and said, "Yes, those reforms have been brought about by good people making good decisions. Too often, though, the rich and powerful make bad decisions, that feed their greed and selfishness."

Juliana responded softly, "It's dangerous to insult the rich and powerful people."

Demetrias laughed softly, "Teacher Pelagius doesn't worry about the danger." She added, "That's why I wanted to hear your teachings. I've heard that you teach a hard word, as Christ Jesus himself did."

Pelagius said, "And he was crucified for it." They all shifted uncomfortably. He added, "But none of us should back away even when we make the rich and powerful uncomfortable."

"I suppose, but I worry for you," said Juliana. "We're also traveling to Palestine to meet Brother Jerome. That is where Demetrias would like to spend time in prayer. There is a woman, Melania, who has invited her."

"Good for you. I may go there also," Pelagius responded.

Demetrias changed the subject back to his teachings, "How do we know we are making good decisions?"

Pelagius added, "We each have been given a conscience. Day by day, hour by hour, we have to reach decisions; and in each decision, we can choose good or evil. If we choose evil that freedom becomes a curse. If we choose good it becomes our greatest blessings."

Juliana was thoughtful, "They say you don't believe in God's grace."

He chuckled at this familiar criticism, "God's grace touches and leads us to do good things in the world, not good as the world knows them. As we know Christ Jesus we are strengthened in our decisions."

He continued, "Even if we don't know Christ Jesus by name, we can know the good through our conscience. All human beings have that gift. It's easier to do good, though, when we have God's grace in Christ Jesus in our heart."

Demetrias asked, "Some say I must memorize church doctrine so I don't go astray. Some say you don't hold to church doctrine. Is that true?"

Pelagius smiled, saying, "Doctrine is not nearly as important as a right heart and right action. Many people who know the good in their minds still don't do it. In Britain, the place of my childhood, there are those who the church calls pagans. They don't know the right words or rituals. They are, though, tolerant, temperate, chaste, generous and kind. They reject the pleasures and honors of the world and choose the way of simplicity and humility. I believe strongly that that pagan has the virtues of Christ Jesus."

Juliana bristled, "Wild people from the north can be good without proper teaching? Do you really believe that! It doesn't make sense!"

Pelagius continued, "I'll tell you what doesn't make sense. There are those from the civilized homes of Rome, who call themselves Christian who never seek divine wisdom, heavenly riches, and immortal honors. There are those who say they are Christian and are rich and powerful but never help the weak and powerless. Some are even rewarded by being made bishops of our church. That doesn't make sense!"

Demetrias broke the tension, "And so I want to live that life and teach others to seek divine wisdom, heavenly riches and immortal honors. I want to help the weak and powerless."

Tears came to Pelagius' eyes, "And so you shall. Christ says we are the light of the world if we open ourselves to His light. The world today needs your light badly."

Juliana put out her hand. Pelagius took it in friendship. She said, "I would ask that you write a letter with all this advice. We will share it with our family members, and the groom's family members who are having trouble with her decision."

Pelagius held her hand and looking at Demetrias said, "I will. May God go with you both. Blessings on your journey, Demetrias, as you travel to Palestine. I hope to see you there."

He watched them get into a carriage and disappear down the road.

He went to his room to begin writing the letter to Demetrias.

He would then plan this trip to Palestine. Now, in 413, Alaric was again at the gates of Rome, it would be best for him to give up his hope of returning there.

Caelestius chose to stay in Carthage. Pelagius wished that his friend were quieter in opposing the local theologians. Although bishop Augustine did not seem opposed to his ideas, the other bishops seemed to be very rigid in their beliefs, and therefore dangerous.

CHAPTER 13 – BOANDAS' STORY
CYMRU

The Tuatha de Danaan reigned for many years and provided the later immigrant Kelts, who did not arrive in Ireland until approximately 500 BCE, with a rich vein of magical and heroic legend....It is not so commonly acknowledged that they were also an aggressive and violent race and to call oneself a Kelt is not necessarily something to be proud of, even if it does give one hereditary access to the Otherworld"[26]

The days were growing long and warm. The waxing moon brought the village closer to the days of the ceremony of fire. Boandas had returned early from the gathering at the center stones. He longed to be there at the stones on the day of the full sun. But he had duties here, to his people, in Cymru.

The news had not been good. There had been fires in the south caused by sudden thunderstorms. They were followed by earthquakes that buried small villages. Here in the north, the sun of quickening life had been covered by clouds. The grass did not grow. The sheep could not graze. Disease had been killing many of the trees in the sacred groves. This could only be because the gods and goddesses were not satisfied.

Strangers were coming. At first, it was just a few of them wandering into Gaul and they were friendly and willing to fit in. The problem was that they brought gods with strange names into the territory of the old gods. Then, as if word had been spread to those waiting on the other side of the mountains, they came by the thousands. They were followed by tribes that were willing to kill the present inhabitants. The names of the old goddesses and gods of the territory were almost forgotten in some places.

The Brothers of Fireantachd {integrity} set themselves apart from the druid leaders who talked of appeasement with new gods and goddesses and with the new inhabitants, as they had earlier with the Romans.

The Brothers talked about the need for appeasement of the old gods and goddesses. Sacrifice had been the old way and many of them found joy in sacrificing young sheep. They would cover themselves in the blood of the animal and throw themselves on the mercy of the god realm.

Boandas stood naked before the rock in the field with the sheep bound and stunned. He lifted his knife and brought it down forcefully, severing the head. The blood spurted out and Boandas rubbed it into his hair and onto his skin. He sank to his knees pleading with his god, Dagda, to deliver his people to their home. He felt no response, only deep and simmering anger.

Years ago, long before Boandas was born, young men and women in the beginning of life were chosen for sacrifice. Boandas shuddered at the thought of what might be required by the angry gods and goddesses.

Boandas had been brought into the order of Druids as a child. His father had been dressed in the long white robes. He came to their village in southern Eire, when he could, bringing gifts to Boandas' mother. He would interview his sons and daughters, wanting to find out who was smart enough to follow him in the order.

His father would reward him for memorizing long verses of the exploits of the heroes. Boandas worked hard to please his father, not for the rewards, but for the privilege of traveling with him as a druid of the order. When he completed his ritual of manhood, his father had agreed that he should be initiated. Boandas had been thrilled at the decision.

The next year he was taken to the central stones and then by boat to the islands. There he spent seven new suns memorizing the stories of each of the gods and goddesses and their rituals. Whatever territory was yours, the local divinity needed tending. He learned the exact movements of the stars and the importance of the exactness of his own movements. The actions of those in the order were ordained by the gods.

He had been present when his father slaughtered a sheep and washed himself in the blood. The work was quick after that and all around covered themselves in the blood and prayed. The work of the gods kept the social order together, which kept the natural order. If the ancient rules were not kept all life would fade away. Boandas knew he would die before he let that happen.

Part of the memory of this order was of the many invasions. When the Romans from the south pushed into Gaul, they learned to respect the druid priests. The druids could defend their people fiercely. It was well known that Caesar had been afraid of their fierceness.

Some of them tried a more passive resistance, pretending to take in the gods of the empire. That was acceptable as long as the older territorial divinities were primary. When the Roman Empire denied those gods, many of the order rebelled.

Then the Romans began to respond violently. They threatened the sacred groves and forests. In their terror, the brotherhood brought back the very ancient ritual of human sacrifice. They chose the brightest among the youth. A young woman and young man of each village who seemed to be especially close to the gods, were taken to a sacred hill. After a night of dancing, drinking of ale and honey-wine they were asked to become lovers. Large pitchers of sweet honey-wine laced with a narcotic drug were left for them. At midnight, dizzy from lovemaking and the drugs, they were taken to a sacred spot beneath the stars and offered as a gift to the gods with a swift blow to the back of the head. This ritual was performed in villages throughout Gaul and Britain. Immediately the movement of the Roman Empire had halted. The earth returned to its normal rhythms. That was four hundred years ago.

Boandas wondered nervously whether he would be asked again to make a sacrifice among his people. The Brothers of Fireantachd believed it was time for the greatest of sacrifice.

So he had come back to the village to see if any of the young people were worthy of a journey to the realm of the gods. Most of the people in the family of Eogan were quite ordinary.

He had been watching the little girl, Seabhac, who, though she was still very young, was showing her connection to the divine world. But she was of the Eogan family, and she was expected to ascend to the holy hill of Shreedrum. Would the gods and goddesses want him to sacrifice her? He shuddered at the duty given him. It weighed heavily on him.

He worried about the family of Eogan on this strange soil. They must remember the stories and the rituals of the gods of Shreedrum. To remember these stories was the tiresome work of a people in exile. He was exhausted from trying to keep them from impurity.

There were the gods and goddesses of Shreedrum who needed to be appeased; but there were also the local gods and goddesses of this place of exile. For the local gods and goddesses he turned to the holy woman Katika and her consort Torrida for guidance. They were excellent in the arts of healing and skilled in the local ritual. Katika was able to supply all the honey-wine the community needed for the rituals throughout the year, through her knowledge of sacred beekeeping.

They must not, though, be allowed to take control of the minds of the Eogan family. Only Boandas should have that control. He needed both to use Torrida and Katika, and to keep them contained. The family Eogan must not forget whose they were.

Torrida and Katika were not of the pure order. Although they were technically druids, they were too open to outside influences. They were dedicated to gods and goddesses that were outside the acceptable circle of power.

Katika was one of the daughters of Ana, an ancient order of druidic women. They continued to live and train other women in the distant mountains. The Brothers of Fireantachd were often suspicious of their power. She took the young women of all the surrounding villages, both of the local tribes and Eogan, to teach them the secrets of being wives and mothers. The young women who had been with Katika seemed to return to the village without as much fear of his power. Yet he needed her, and would use her when he could. He needed to watch her carefully.

Legends had been told about the wisdom of the Tuatha de Danaan. They were not divine, but were of an ancient race that had learned to move through the dimensions of time and space. They were sometimes helpful to the people who lived where they once ruled in the river valley of the Suir. The members of the Tuatha de Danaan were also prone to anger and were sometimes vindictive and violent.

A child, like Seabhac, born with the actual blood of the Tuatha de Danaan, might bring great wisdom and luck to her people but she might also bring disaster. He had had trouble before. Even now, he felt that she had made too strong a connection to her invisible ancestors. He felt she was lying to him. Katika would be able to learn the truth of what this child had seen, but it was Boandas' job to control the girl.

As he walked over the ridge, he could look down and see the ocean. The blood had dried on his skin as he pulled his white robes over it. He could hear the sound of pipes in the distance. It was time.

CHAPTER 14 – FIRST LOVE
CYMRU

"Fire was an interface between the human race and the divine, in particular the elemental powers of the Upperworld who would determine the fate of the herds, the flocks, and the growing harvest." [27]

The festivities had begun with fires in every part of the village and on the hillsides around in order to communicate with other villages. The druid Boandas blessed the fires. It was the longest day of the year. The sun was back in full force in this season, but the people still awaited fruits of the harvest. There was, of course, confidence that this season would bring everything the people needed for comfort and happiness.

It was Seabhac's favorite time of year. Everyone greeted each other with laughter and hugs on the first morning of the celebration. There was a smile on every face, no matter how cranky the person really was. Even Boandas was jovial on this day.

The druidess Katika, in anticipation of the shearing, spinning and weaving of clothing, blessed the wool of the sheep. Giosai and Morganna were honored during the rituals for their connection with the sheep. Giosai showed his skill in shearing during the contest. Morganna had no competitors. She was the best spinner.

The newborn lambs and calves were welcomed into the village family, and brought through the town by the children.

On the eve before the celebration Seabhac, Elihf and her friends ran through the hills collecting the flowers that were blooming. They wove them into garlands and laid them at the door of every family hut. Fruit producing flowers were carefully avoided.

At the ritual banquet, Cormonthuc, the bard, sang of Eire, the virgin goddess of the Tuatha de Danaan, a daughter of Danaa. One day she was at the bank of a river when a man, named Lugh, in a silver boat floated down to her on a beaming ray of the sun.

Eire was overcome with love and she fell into the boat with him. They had a child named Bri who became a famous queen of the Tuatha de Danaan. Although, Lugh went away from Eire and his daughter for months at a time, he always returned with his expressions of devotion. Bri is alive, even today, as a queen, living invisibly far underground, with the people of light.

Seabhac was enthralled as she listened. She did not expect any attention from the bard this time. She did not mind that Geanta sat at his feet as he played and on his lap as he rested. She simply listened to the story. At the cue, they all stamped on the ground to awaken Bri and invite her to the celebration.

Laughing and singing went on into the night. Some fell asleep.

The nights that followed were about lovemaking and maybe child making. Lugh and Eire were together again. The Sun was penetrating the earth. Torrida and Katika set up a tent in the middle of the village, and to drums and singing, they invited every set of lovers to return to their own hut for a night of passion. With laughter and shrieks of delight from the crowd around them, Torrida and Katika disappeared into the tent.

The fires continued to burn on the hills around the seaside village from the day of the sun's fullness to the day of the full moon. The fullness of the moon indicated that the love between Lugh and Eire had been fulfilled. Many children were conceived during these feast days.

Seabhac had seen Torrida, but not Owain. She was full from the feast and restless from all the stories and the adult festivities. She wandered back to her family hut. She did not go inside because her mother and father were celebrating passionately.

Sitting outside the door, she heard the clear full call of a bird. She giggled and rushed into the now dark woods behind the hut. She did not see anyone.

Owain popped out from behind the tree, and called out again louder. She turned toward him and reached out. "Seabhac! You chase birds?" Owain laughed.

"Yes, I haven't had enough fish and berry pie to eat!" She giggled and chased after him.

He kept out of her reach. "Come at sunrise tomorrow to the edge of the cove and we'll row out to the island."

"Yes! I'll be there," she whispered back to him.

Full of new energy, she ran back to the party. She wondered how she could get away without Aengus wanting to follow. She would have to move quietly.

Every child slept outside during the celebration to give room for the adult's passion. She could easily sneak away with no one noticing. Her parents would be sleeping late anyway after such a wild night.

As she heard the first morning call of the sparrow, she got up. She moved quickly up the hill in the dark. She wanted to get to the cove by sunrise. She was able to avoid the attention of everyone and head up the trail by the ocean, over the cliff, across the red rocks and down to the cove. Owain was waiting with a small curragh.

Seabhac got into the boat. Owain pushed it out onto the full waters and jumped in. Seabhac felt her stomach turn. She turned white.

"Relax little one. I'm rowing this time. You're safe."

She hated it that he called her little one, but she would allow him that judgment. She felt so weak and had learned the hard way that the sea was powerful.

"It's just the sea seems rough!" she said softly.

"It is a perfect day." He laughed, "Just a moon ago you were paddling in a smaller boat than this on your own."

"Yes and I remember the water in my lungs and the fish swimming past my head!!" she laughed. The memory chilled her.

"It'll be worth it. Wait until you see the flowers on this full-sun day."

"I'm so glad to be here with you. I've got so much to tell you." Her eyes became bright.

"And I to you!" he said smiling at her.

They were silent for a while as they moved across the water. The gulls flew over and called to them.

"I want to be a merchant on a boat with you and Torrida!!"

He was silent for a moment. "You may be forgetting that you are a princess of Eire. I doubt that your family would let you go."

"I've come this far. We could just keep rowing," Seabhac responded.

"And your brothers, father, cousins and uncle would chase us down. I don't think so. Besides you're too young to know what you want to do."

Seabhac pouted, "But I don't want to marry some prince and wash clothes on the rocks and bake bread and weave cloth and take care of babies."

"Why not? It sounds wonderful."

"It sounds like missing so much adventure," she explained.

"I don't think you'll miss adventure, little one, you're too hard to hold back." He smiled at her as they came to shore on the island.

As they pulled the boat to the beach, Seabhac felt instantly better. They climbed the sandstone path up the cliff wordlessly. As they reached the top, she was amazed at the fields of wondrous blue, red, and orange flowers and the birds of all sorts that flew overhead. They walked through the fields as though through a rainbow. Taken in by the beauty they ran side by side, chasing birds, squirrels, and rabbits, whatever showed itself. They reached the other side of the island and sat staring out at the sea.

"I wanted to row to Eire to meet the goddess of my land," Seabhac finally said.

"I hope to travel as far as the oceans will carry me," Owain added.

"My ancestors came from the stars they say." She looked at the sky.

"I don't think I can row there," Owain laughed

"But I also heard they came by boat so I don't know which to believe. Lugh comes by boat from the sun," she added.

"Star stuff is about gods, boats are about people with the help of the gods, so I suspect you can believe both." He laughed at his philosophical solution.

"I thank the gods and goddesses for the beauty of this day." She lay back on the grass and watched the clouds silently.

She spoke again, "You said that your father died at sea. I almost died in my little rowing trip. It must be dangerous on the ocean."

"Storms can happen quickly and when you're far from the shore you can't be rescued. My father's death was surprising. Torrida tells me that one moment he was on the deck shouting orders and then he was gone."

"You must miss him," she said trying to sound comforting.

"I rarely saw him. When he did come home from a voyage, I loved his stories. He was gone for months and would come back with gifts for my mother and us children," he said thoughtfully.

"So where are your mother and your brothers and sisters?" Seabhac asked.

"They died of a fever. Torrida came and rescued me," he explained.

"I'm sorry," she said softly.

"Grief and loss make you strong – as does curiosity," he said. A gannet flew over, dipping low to check on the figures lying among the flowers in the meadow.

Seabhac was silent for a moment, and then said, "Katika says I'm young, but she wants to find out if I'm close to Ana."

Owain sat up and looked at her. He picked up a piece of grass and started chewing on it. "Only some of us can be really close to the gods and goddesses."

Thoughtfully, Owain continued, "I think you have to be an adult to really know your powers. Now that I have finished my manhood rituals, I need to be initiated into the order of Pallas. Torrida says he will know after a year whether I am close enough to Pallas to be a priest."

"Will you have to go away to be initiated?" Seabhac sat up.

"I think most of my training will be here on this island, but Pallas is a god of the sea and of distant lands and strangers coming together. I will go away often. As a priest for Pallas I must be on the sea most of my life. He is the god of wisdom and the sea. But that's good."

"You think it is good that we can't be together!?" She stood up with her hands on her hips.

"When I'm home from my journeys, I'll tell you about them. Don't you think that Danaa might want you to learn about the places I visit?" Then he smiled. "Maybe you could be like Lavercam the poetess and bard and travel the lands singing."

"The story says she was ugly." She grimaced at him.

"But her beautiful music made everyone see beauty as she sang," he reminded her.

She added, "And she could run the length of Eire. Can you run the length of this island?" They laughed and ran together. The birds fled as they ran. They stopped suddenly in exhaustion and fell to the ground laughing.

"Can't I go with you?" Seabhac whined.

Owain grinned at this question that had already been asked and answered. He realized she was just a little girl. He would wait for her to grow up. "I think our divine ones will keep on bringing us together."

By noon, she was back on the cliff side and Aengus was calling her name. "Seabhac, you aren't supposed to slip away without me. I had to talk fast or I could have been in a lot of trouble. Where were you?!"

Aengus was red-in-the face, obviously scared.

"We need to have adventures together, Aengus, especially if you're going to be king someday!"

"Together though, remember?" Aengus said with authority.

"I'll race you to that rock outcropping!!!" Seabhac took off like the wind with her red hair bouncing. She laughed with delight at the world that was opening up to her.

CHAPTER 15 – THE YOUNG PATRICK
NW BRITAIN

As all these other events were unfolding, there was an attack on the town of Bannaven Taberniae in northwestern Britain.

Screams tore thru the night as the northern EiNeill clansmen swept into the village. They killed anyone who resisted them and stole whatever looked valuable. Then they set the village on fire. Patrick was asleep and therefore did not resist. Patrick never saw what happened to his family but was blindfolded, bound and thrown onto the EiNeill ship. He was a slave for the next six years in northern Eire.

Patrick's father was Calpornius, son of the priest Potitus. The family had had an idyllic existence with the protection of the Roman Empire. His father and mother had taught him the stories of Jesus when he was a child. That life was now over.

In his shock, he lay in the ship, remembering the lessons of his childhood. He remembered learning about God's anger and punishments. He assumed that his family and whole village had committed some great sin. God's fury boiled over.

During the next six years as a slave, he tried to gain God's favor.

He was ordered to tend the herds of his owner. There were times when he did not have as much food as the sheep did.

In spite of these punishments, his love of God increased. His faith grew stronger and zeal became so intense that on some days he would say as many as a hundred prayers, and almost as many in the night. He did this when he was in the woods or on the mountains. Even when it was snowing or raining, he would rise before dawn to pray.

His faithfulness was rewarded. One night, in his sleep, he heard a voice saying, "It is well that you fast. Soon you will be free." The next day he was tending the sheep and a voice said, "Look, your ship is ready." He looked toward the sea and saw a ship in the distance. He listened to the voice and ran in the direction of the ship. It was a long journey, but God directed his way.

He was stunned and confused when the captain refused to let him come aboard. Patrick continued praying.

There was a reason he was not ready to be on this ship. He realized in his prayer that these men were heathens and would not hear God's call to them. He prayed that if he were allowed on board, he would not be required to perform any of the sexual rituals that were often required.

Suddenly he heard shouting, "Boy, come. We're short handed."

He came on board and explained to them that he was not a follower of their gods but was a follower of Christ Jesus. He explained how powerful his God was and how angry his God could become. They kept their distance.

After three days, the ship came to a port. Everyone had to get off the ship and haul the trade goods across the land. The captain commented on how strange it was that the country was deserted. He had traveled this route many times. He told them of the Roman estates that had offered them food and lodging. Now there was nothing. Their supplies began to run out. They traveled on meager rations for twenty-eight days. Finally, they ate their last bit of food.

The captain came to Patrick, saying, "Tell me this, Christian; you say your God is great and all-powerful. Why then can you not pray for us? As you see we are suffering from hunger. It is unlikely that we will ever see a human being again."

Patrick responded, "Turn, sincerely with your whole heart, to Christ Jesus, because nothing is impossible for him, that this day he may send you food on your way until you are satisfied; for he has plenty everywhere." Patrick led him in prayer.

Suddenly a herd of pigs appeared on the road. They drew their spears and killed many of them. Even their dogs ate well for the next several days. The captain shouted out to him, "I believe in your God!" Kneeling before Patrick he cried, "What do I need to do?"

Almost everyone of the crew bowed in prayer to Christ Jesus with Patrick and the captain. They wept as they embraced Patrick. He began to tell them about the God of Christ Jesus.

For the rest of the journey there was plenty of food.

One of the men who had not accepted Christ Jesus found wild honey and in front of the crew offered a sacrifice to the goddess of the land.

Patrick turned to the crew, "No one who is a follower of my God can eat this honey."

Remembering their time of famine, and the herd of pigs that appeared miraculously, a majority of the crew stayed near Patrick for the rest of the journey and listened to his counsel on what they should eat, and how they should pray.

They did not eat the honey.

CHAPTER 16 – IN SEARCH OF PATRICK

It is hard to find the true Patrick. The story above comes from his *"Confession"*. In his confession, it seems that Patrick was a simple man with a good heart.

His early experiences, and personality, made him strong in his faith and rigid in his dogma.

Some scholars have suggested that Patrick was sent to Ireland not just convert to the Irish but to make certain that no heresies abounded. Mary Aileen Schmiel says, "In fact, the real reason for Patrick's mission was not to convert heathens but to try to bring the determinedly independent and anti-authoritarian Irish church under Rome's aegis."[28]

It would make sense, given his history, that he would do anything to defend the 'true' God.

As I have fit Saint Patrick into the story I have had to move away from tradition. Although legend says he was born in 432 CE, written history says little about his actually dates. The early 400's, in Britain, are all a part of pre-history, except when an event from the Roman Empire intervenes. The only firm dates we have are from the discussions of Augustine and Pelagius. I hang every other date on those dates.

I ask my former history professors to forgive me for giving more attention to the intuitive part of history, but Anaias told me that she met both Patrick and Pelagius, so I have to believe her.

In my ministry in the Riverbank church we started a delightful tradition of hosting a Saint Patrick's day dinner with corned beef and cabbage and shamrocks and bright green decorations. Although people were familiar with the 'Wild Irish Rose', type of Irish music, I introduced them to the traditional indigenous music.

Later, in my churches, I introduced Saint Bridget's day; which coincides with Candlemas; and Ground Hogs Day. In the celebration of Candlemas, Mary and the newborn Jesus emerge from the seclusion, required by Hebrew law for a woman after giving birth to a boy. I experienced the celebration in Oaxaca Mexico as the Christmas decorations were kept up until February 2nd.

Saint Bridget's day celebrates the quickening of life and the return of light. It is celebrated with candles. I ask people in my congregation to be on the look-out for signs of new growth in the midst of February's chill.

CHAPTER 17 – KATIKA'S STORY – THE BEES

There was a steady buzz around Katika as she worked in the bee shelter that held the many sacred hives. The honeybees had a dance language as they flitted in and out, pointing, touching. There was no more sacred act for the daughters of Ana then the tending of the hives, caring for the honeybee and collecting the honey. The cup of honey-wine was lifted at each celebration as a symbol of Ana's mysterious care of all creation.

The honeybee made the golden sweetness in the darkness. After traveling miles to find their particular flower, they would return to the hive and deposit the nectar. The work of making the honey was hidden and mysterious. That mystery made it the stuff of the Goddess.

This was the season of the full sun. Katika celebrated that the hives she had nurtured not only seemed to have survived the cold season, but now thrived as the hills came alive with flowers.

That these honeybees had chosen her hives was a special complement. She had learned the craft of hive making from her guardians outside of the caves of Ana. As a child, she used to linger at the edge of the bee shelter and watch the work of the teachers. Usually the sisters of Ana would reward her with a waxy sweet comb. When she was old enough, they taught her how to dress to avoid stings and led her through the steps of caring for the tiny beings.

First, she needed to build the hive using hazel twigs and straw. Carved bone made the layers or skeps. An opening was made that was just large enough for the bees to enter, but small enough for them to guard. On the other side was a secret opening for the beekeeper to retrieve the honey. The hive was then insulated with a plastering of mud.

If a wild swarm chose her hive, her work had just begun. She needed to make her guests happy. In the wild, the bee had an infinite number of choices. The slightest unhappiness might cause a swarm to leave and find an old log instead.

In the time of cold, the hive would become silent to the untrained ear. The keeper needed to make sure that the bees and queen had enough honey to survive. Over harvesting would be deadly. Katika kept a supply of her harvest, and listened to the low pitch tone of the hive just in case more food was needed. To make the relationship useful, though, the bee needed to be coaxed to make more honey than it needed. Then all were happy.

It was a wonderful relief when the first whisper of new life came and the earth grew warmer, the first flowers appeared and the bees would suddenly explode from the hive.

Katika had many kinds of honey. There was the honey for medicine, the honey for cooking and the honey for the sacred honey-wine.

Some hives would be taken to the fields of medicinal flowers and set down just before the explosion that came as the earth warmed. When the bees headed out, the medicinal flowers were all they saw. The healing honey might calm a person, provide stomach relief, and make the heart beat more strongly. It also fought infection. As it was created in the dark mystery of the hive, it healed in the dark mystery of the body.

Some hives were taken into the fields of clover providing a pleasant light honey for cooking. Some hives were taken into the hills to the few fields of the flower of Ana, a red trumpet like flower that created a honey that was tinged red and had a strong minty taste that enhanced the honey-wine flavor.

She would need to teach Seabhac about tending the honeybee. Seabhac probably had the knowledge in her ancient memory. The Tuatha de Danaan was led to Eire by the honeybees of their goddess grandmother Danaa.

As the Tuatha de Danaan migrated north, they brought the sacred beehives with them. They were told in a vision that when they approached the land Danaa would give them, the bees would swarm. They were to follow the swarm and the land would be theirs.

As they approached Eire, at the mouth of the river Suir, bees swarmed and hovered over the boats. The people scrambled to shore. The bees waited for them and then began to dance and swirl up the Suir river valley until they found a hive in a log in a meadow. They named the meadow Cloin Mealla or honey meadow.

Each year a swarm would appear again and one group of the people would follow it. This way they populated the south of Ireland. The Tuatha de Danaan had to convince the Fir Bolgs, the primitive people who lived there first, that they could share the land. Since the people of the Tuatha de Danaan were very smart and wise, the Fir Bolg looked on them as gods and goddesses. Even today, where you see the honeybee, the spirit of the Tuatha de Danaa is probably present.

Katika remembered when she had been a little older than Seabhac. She was living happily in her village in northern Cymru. She had just been promised to a young man of a neighboring village and a wedding was being planned.

Then, came the horror. The tribes from the North of Ireland attacked her village. They meant to steal everything the people had to survive. As her father tried to defend his property, they killed him. As the vicious hoard hacked her father to death, they turned to her screaming mother and three men grabbed her and took turns raping her. The last one laughed as he strangled her. Katika hid behind a pile of straw as they grabbed her little brother and tied him with rope, hand and foot like a sheep for slaughter. They took him away screaming. She had heard later that they often took the children to be slaves.

She was left alone with her parent's dead bodies, filled with terror that the fiends would return for her. Time stood still. She did not know how long she had stayed in her hiding spot, trembling.

That was when she met Torrida. He was a very young man who had heard that there had been an attack on her village and wanted to see if anyone could be saved.

When he came into her hut she stood with her knife ready to kill him, but Ana stopped her mysteriously. As she looked into his eyes, she knew she was safe and collapsed sobbing into his arms.

He took her to the daughters of Ana in the caves of the north. They adopted her and tended her until she became a part of their order of sister druids.

Katika filled several jars with the cooking honey harvested last fall and headed down to the sea cove village of the Eogan family. She would trade the honey for whatever oats or fish they might have. She stopped first at M'alda's hut. M'alda was outside grinding the harvest of oats into fine flour.

As M'alda saw Katika coming down the hill, she smiled. "Ah, the honey of Bel. We've been waiting," M'alda said.

She jumped up to greet Katika. Together they went into the hut where M'alda had a pouch of oat flour in payment.

Katika knew she had to talk to M'alda, "Has your daughter had more visions?"

M'alda went to get tea from a kettle on the fire. "She always sees more than most of us can. I know, you druids must know just how much she can see, but she is my little girl and I need to protect her."

Katika took the tea and responded, "I know you're frightened because of what happened to your sister. It is unlikely that the same thing would happen to Seabhac."

M'alda sipped her tea and said calmly, "How do you know it won't? The power of de Danaan blood can be for great good, but people are often afraid of it."

"That's why she has to be watched and trained." She put her hand on M'alda's and responded, "I'll do everything I can to make sure she is safe."

Katika left the hut and went on to exchange honey for fabric from Morganna, and berries and crab apples from Croa.

She approached Boandas for the sacred dried salmon.

Boandas was standing by his hut. "I'm waiting for your report on the girl," he said.

Katika laughed nervously, "She's still very young, brother, give us time."

He went to get her a bag for the salmon and as he handed it to her he quietly sighed, "I wish we had time, sister."

CHAPTER 18 – DISCOVERING ANA CYMRU

"The Tuatha de Danaan was fair of form, gifted in the arts, the mind and music. Their magical harps sang by themselves. They were great healers. In the life of the spirit; the arrival of the Tuatha de Danaan in Britain represented a change in consciousness for the British people."[29]

Often Seabhac's attention would be caught by the sea with its changing colors. Sometimes it was calm and sometimes quite angry, sometimes joyful. At times its mood matched Seabhac's. Today, the sun beat down, the sea and the call of the seabirds filled her with delight.

Seabhac heard footsteps in the limestone behind her, and was thrilled to turn and see Katika approaching. Katika settled in beside her. They stared out at the sea together. Seabhac felt a heightened calm with this woman beside her.

Gently, Katika said at her, "You are to be tested by Ana. Although you are young, you must come with me."

Seabhac felt a wave of excitement flow over her, but suddenly the wave ebbed and she felt fear. "Where?"

Katika stood up and put out her hand. "Just come."

Seabhac had waited for this moment but now that it had come, it felt odd and out of place. "Can I come tomorrow?" She didn't know why the dread seemed to be welling up in her.

Katika laughed. "You have no choice but to come with me. Boandas has asked that you be examined. The sisters are waiting." Katika took her hand and held it tightly.

She was led by Katika's firm grip into the woods. She wanted adventure. She was surprised by how much it frightened her. Going into the woods this way, reminded her of stories by some of the old women of the village, of children snatched by spirits that were said to stalk them in the forest.

She trusted Katika, but people told stories about her. She was not like other people.

Her mother had laughed and said the stories of children being snatched by spirits were not true. Then sometimes she felt like her mother was not so sure. That was why she and Aengus always played on the shore. From the sunlit sandstone, you could always see danger. In the woods, you never knew what might be hiding.

The sounds in the woods frightened her. She was following behind Katika, but suddenly Katika disappeared into the thickets ahead.

Seabhac couldn't find the path. A large bird flew toward her. Her face began to burn and her heart beat quickly. She scrambled through bushes and low brambles. The thicket and thorns grabbed her legs and scratched her. She began to cry hysterically.

Katika turned back when she heard Seabhac crying. In a soft voice Katika spoke, "You must be brave, little one. There will be many frightening things, but you must be the brave one, because you see the visions that give people hope."

Seabhac was embarrassed by her outburst.

Katika helped her extract herself from the thorn bush that held her tightly. They worked quietly. Seabhac sniffed and looked down to see her torn cape and blood from the scratches dripping down her arm.

"None of us know the Goddess. Many of us have been chosen to do her work. When you've been chosen you can't turn back. You're young now, we are only seeing who you might be."

As they continued to walk down into the stream fed valley and across a field, they saw smoke in the distance. There were the sounds of laughter. She heard the shrieking of young girls.

Knowing her curiosity, Katika said, "You can meet the others at dinner. They're much older than you and have come for a different purpose."

They came to a small group of huts around a clearing. Katika brought her into a round wooden house. The shelves were lined with clay jars and herbs hung from the rafters. Several colored cloaks hung against the walls. "You will sleep here tonight. I'll call you when the sisters of Ana have assembled."

Katika left her alone to explore the hut.

Seabhac was startled by the approaching sound of laughter. The door opened. She was surrounded by teenage girls.

"The priestess has gone crazy! She brought a baby," one girl said in a taunting tone.

"Did you have an early coming of age, baby?" a dark haired girl said. "Are you a freak?" she added, "Did your parents throw you out?"

This last remark brought gales of laughter. It was an old tale that parents used to place a particularly ugly or deformed baby into the woods to be devoured or to survive on its own in order to avoid the curse obviously put on the family.

"She isn't a freak, but I don't know why she is here," Seabhac recognized the voice. Amala walked through the door carrying a bowl of herb stew.

Amala continued, "She's not one of us. She's here for Katika's purpose and will go home tomorrow. She needs to eat."

Amala had left the village after her coming of age. She had never come home and no one talked about her. The other girls lost interest and ran out the door. Amala left with them.

She remembered Amala's words, "She's not one of us."
'Well, then who am I?' Seabhac thought.

On the table was only a rough wooden bowl filled with a savory stew, left by Amala. The cold damp air of the evening made it welcome. As she ate, the warmth soothed her. She was on an adventure. The Goddess had granted her an adventure. She would be brave!

She walked outside with the bowl. The sky was a soft amber from the sunset. She sat on a stone outside Katika's hut. It was still warm from the day's sun.

She hoped her mother and father knew she was here, and hoped they were not worried. Her father would be coming home to report on the day's events. Her brothers would come into the hut arguing about something. Geanta might be crying for some special favor. Her mother would build up the fire and listen to them all. She missed her evening at home.

Suddenly she realized a red squirrel was eating the stew she had neglected on the stone next to her. She felt a predatory growl come from deep inside of her, as hunger welled up. She shooed away the squirrel. A bird hovered on a branch above her, as if scheming about how to steal more of the stew. They were all out to survive, even at each other's expense. There was a little left in the bowl. Seabhac thought she might just as well share it. She pushed it away and the bird flew down. The squirrel turned around to reconsider.

She went back into the hut. She touched nothing, but examined it with her eyes. She was bored and restless. She looked at the amulet's hanging on the wall. The symbols seemed strange.

She suddenly became sleepy from the strange events of the day and found a straw mat to lie down.

She fell asleep. As she dreamed, she seemed to be traveling through the treetops. She seemed to be soaring like a hawk. Then she saw the women in their multi-colored capes and swooped down. She was startled by the sound of footsteps. She awakened and was again in the hut with the herbs and Katika's cloaks.

The door opened and it was Katika.

It was dark outside. Katika held a torch for light. Flickering colored lights seemed to surround her hair in the light. She was clothed in white. It was a soft shimmering material. She put her finger to her lips. Seabhac was not to speak.

"Come in silence," she whispered. "It is time for Ana to tell us if you are called by Her."

Seabhac followed her into the night. Katika's white cape continued to glisten. Seabhac noticed that the moon was nearly full. The tops of the trees were iridescent. As they walked away from the camp, they came to another grove and then to a clearing where there was an ancient stone circle. There were three fires burning around a flat center stone. There were women gathered in a circle. Three of the women, near the center stone, were wearing white robes like Katika's. The other five were wearing robes of red, green or blue.

"Welcome to the circle of Ana," said an older woman with white hair piled on her head. "We are surprised that Ana would bother one as young as you. We have heard from Katika that you have had visions."

The second woman with dark hair and a soft lilting voice continued, "You appear to have the blood of the Tuatha de Danaan in your veins which would make you wise even as a child. If that is true, we must use your wisdom in these times of chaos."

Katika added, "You have shown yourself to be very brave. I've told my sisters about your fear and how you overcame it."

They all walked up to her with hands outstretched. They closed their eyes and barely touched her. She watched the face of the white-haired one.

Their eyes met. "Come, sit on the center stone, and be very still. Close your eyes and don't look at any of us."

She took her to the flat stone in the center. Seabhac sat with her legs crossed. She closed her eyes. Even with her eyes closed, she could see these women swirling around her. They seemed to be pure energy, moving around her and through her, examining spiritual parts of her that she did not even know about.

Then with her eyes closed, she was suddenly aware of a brilliant light. She felt herself lifted up and saw not only these women but women in high mountains, women beating drums, women with prayer bells, women lifting tiny babies. They all seemed to be singing a similar song but she could not make out the tune. It all swirled around. Then she heard a woman's voice singing the song, then laughing, then crying, and then comforting. Suddenly she heard a shriek. It was from the circle.

One of the women was on her knees crying. "I see it, they are dead!! There is blood!! Why were they killed!!?" She was sobbing. The others went to comfort her.

The dark-haired, soft-spoken one said, "I see it also, this child will witness many deaths. She will not be the cause or the victim. She will have the responsibility."

The white-haired one said, "I see her bringing a great light. I see other lights around her that will light the way for those who are lost. She is leading them. They are grateful. She is responsible."

Katika joined in, "I see her standing with kings, and leaders of alien gods. She is without fear in spite of the hardship and danger."

The women then came to her, each touching her. They spoke in one voice.

"Ana, Mother, guide this child that she may use her powers

wisely. Anaa, Mother, Anaa, Mother, Give her Wisdom, Give her Wisdom. Dance with us, Dance with her, Dance with us, Dance with her. Anaa, Mother, Anaa, Mother, Give her love, Give her love. . ."

As they danced in a circle, Katika lifted her and set her on the ground. She joined in the dancing trying to follow the movements of their feet. They laughed and sang. The moon was above them and glistened. Seabhac thought she could hear drums, pipes, bells, and women speaking strange unfamiliar languages. It was only these nine and the child.

She woke wrapped in the many colored cloaks, sleeping on the stone in the center of the circle. No one was around.

One of the teasers of the previous day greeted her. She came into the circle looking glum. "Get up. You must come and help get the morning meal. I really don't know what help you can be. Maybe you can play while we work."

Her words stung. Seabhac carefully removed and folded the cloaks of blue, red and green that had covered her. The girl looked wide-eyed at the pile of fabric. "Did you really get to be with them?" She seemed reverent.

"Yes, we danced," Seabhac responded smiling.

The girl looked at her with interest, responding, "We saw them here, but we didn't know why they came. They are daughters of Ana. They are as holy as or more holy than priestess Katika."

She continued to look at the cloaks as if trying to decide. She looked at Seabhac, "So you must be Holy too . . "

She waved her hand at her, "Hardly. . .you're just a baby." She laughed, "well come on. . ." She walked into the woods that separated the stone circle from the camp.

Seabhac decided she would rather try to be friends than be forever lonely. She chased after the girl. "Were you brought here also by the Holy One?"

"If you want to get along, don't ask silly questions." Her tone sounded angry. "I was brought here because I am to become a woman. I have important things to learn about keeping a fire and hearth. I suppose I need to learn how to care for babies."

She looked at her arrogantly. "Maybe that's why I have to put up with you."

She continued. "I've learned many things and am the brightest in the class, Katika has said. . ."

She stopped abruptly and glared at Seabhac. "I really don't have time to talk to a child about these things!"

They walked on in silence. Seabhac couldn't argue with her. She was a child. She was nowhere near being a woman.

They walked to a corner of a clearing where many girls were busy stirring the porridge over a small fire.

"You will take breakfast to Katika, and be with her for the morning blessing." An unfamiliar girl thrust a bowl at her. It was a beautiful oakwood bowl intricately carved. Seabhac did not have time to examine it. She winced at the sharpness of the girl's voice. She was obviously not pleased that Seabhac had been given this task.

Seabhac took the bowl into Katika's hut.

Katika was talking to two men who looked concerned. Someone was ill. Perhaps it was one of them. She handed one of the men a pouch. They thanked her and bowed as they exited the hut. There was a familiar smell of herbs as they walked out.

Katika glanced in Seabhac's direction, saying "Come child, I'm hungry. It is hard when they come before breakfast, but they traveled all night. I pray the cure works."

Katika took the bowl and said, "Let's go out and bless the morning." She took the bowl in one hand and Seabhac's hand in another and together they walked out of the hut. Seabhac was surprised to see all the girls of the camp around her door. Katika raised the bowl. "Thank you Mother for the grains of the field, for the nuts and berries that you give for our life. As we eat, may you replenish. Our lives are dedicated to you and to your kindness."

All said, "Hail Ana, Hail Katika"

Katika took a bowl for Seabhac from one of the girls and gave it to her. They returned to the hut.

Katika and Seabhac ate quietly.

Seabhac looked around, curious about the room. She asked, "Are all these bags and jars full of cures?"

"Oh yes," Katika laughed. "Cures come in many forms." She touched Seabhac's hand and added, "The sisters and I agreed that you are young now. Your time is coming though. You will be a cure for many people."

"I will?" Seabhac said wide-eyed.

Katika smiled, "But now, I'll take you home and you will be like you have always been."

"So, I am not chosen?" Seabhac asked.

"Oh, you are chosen, but in these strange times of change and chaos, the Mother will give you the right to choose Her."

"I choose Her, I do!" Seabhac cried out.

Katika laughed at Seabhac's enthusiasm and innocence.

"The day will come when the Mother will stab you and make you a woman." Katika touched Seabhac's stomach. "Only then will you have the wisdom to decide."

Katika looked serious. "And you have the right to decide not to come and join me and the sisters."

They spent the morning learning the names and smells of herbs. They put on gowns and inspected the beehives. Katika took her on a walk around the camp. She saw where the herbs grew and how to harvest them. There was so much to learn. She would not remember most of it. But she was young and had plenty of time.

CHAPTER 19 – A NEW WOMAN

The years went by. Seabhac found herself living a normal life. She was now taller than most of the other girls. She grew restless with the life they were living in the cove. She even lost her temper during the days she could play with Aengus. His games were often rougher than she wanted to be. Sometimes she would slip away to the island and talk with Owain. At one point Aengus found out about Owain and went to the island with her. It was great fun keeping this secret from Boandas.

Then it all changed, when Seabhac woke up with pain in her stomach and blood on her night cloak. She screamed. Her mother came running. M'alda was happily excited. Her father left the hut.

All the women in the village celebrated with her as they took her to one of the huts set aside for women only. She was bathed in herbs. It was explained to her that her relationships with all men including her father would change. No man was to touch her intimately until she chose the man she would marry.

All this had her head whirring. She was asked to remain in this hut and listen to her dreams. Other women of the village would come to her for her advice. It was believed that during her first menses she was closer to the Goddess than she had ever been, or would be again. For this week, she had great wisdom.

The ritual included singing by the men outside the hut while the women talked to her inside the hut. For the duration of the flow, the singing continued. Daily baths continued. Advice giving and receiving continued.

Katika arrived and hugged her. "Now you are an adult. You can decide. We will have the woman ritual tonight."

Katika had kept track of the phase of the moon at the beginning of her womanflow. She noted the tides, the weather, the season. All was important in defining Seabhac and her role as a woman of the clan.

The ritual began. A crowd of women entered the hut. The clothes Seabhac was wearing were taken from her. She stood naked before all of them. They talked about the shape of the earth at her time of first bleeding, how it spoke of who she was. She was to be silent as they recalled the answers she had given them and the answers they had received in the sky, the stars, the blooms and grasses, the insects, the clouds, the rain, the lack of rain. Her words and the whispers of the earth were blended into one. This mixing of messages created one message: Seabhac. This was the story that would propel her into the world. They began to draw designs on the dirt floor. They argued about shapes and content.

She listened carefully and absorbed all that was said. After they agreed on the designs, they brought the pigments and began to color them in with reds, the most sacred color, greens, from the ore to the north, blue, yellow and white from the chalky cliffs to the south. She watched the most beautiful designs unfold on the floor of the womanhut. There were ferns, periwinkles, the hawk, nuthatches, squirrels, foxes, waves, stars, and the moons in its phase, little people peeking thru the intertwining of branches. The animals became unrecognizable and took on the shape of the dreams she had reported. A bone needle was dipped into the pigment of the design on the ground around her. Carefully and slowly, the design was transferred to her skin. Her arms, her torso, her legs became vibrant with colors and figures. This was her new woman body. All, who saw her naked, would know who she is.

As they completed the work, the women of the village laughed and sang into the night.

She awoke alone. She was alone to remember, or wonder if they had really all been there together. It had been five days since it all started, and the stabbing in her body had stopped, as had the flow of blood. Her body tingled from the needle pricks and from the pigments settling into her skin. She was covered with heavy cloaks now. She felt deliciously new and content. She was filled with a sense of deep peace. She had answers to questions that she had been afraid to ask as a child. She had gone though a door closed to her previously, and she liked what she saw. She was a woman now.

Her mother and grandmother came in and sat down.

Her mother brought out a copper necklace. She said, "This necklace has been saved for you. From what we read in you last night, we know that you need to wear this, as my sister before you wore it"

Danathie, her grandmother, carefully unwrapped a pin with a shimmering golden amber stone. "This has been in our family since the dawn of memory. It may have been brought with the people as they migrated to Eire."

Her grandmother put her hand on her cheek gently. "Whatever you choose to do with your life, you are a woman of the family of Eogan. You will honor this family."

Her grandmother then brought out a red cape with gold-flecked fringe. Her face was stern.

"But mother, don't," M'alda exclaimed.

"She might as well have it!" Danathie said and looked at Seabhac with concern.

"Will you tell her...everything?" M'alda hesitated. "I can't bear to hear the story again."

M`alda stood and quickly embraced Seabhac. She held her for several minutes as if she did not want to let go. As she moved away, she looked at her face, as if looking for something. Maybe she was looking for the baby she had given birth to eleven winters ago. She walked out.

Her grandmother remained. She put the cloak around Seabhac's shoulders. She stepped back. "Yes, you are beautiful. You look so much like a woman that wore this cloak before you."

"The cloak you are wearing belonged to Iolaire. She was my daughter, your mother's sister, and your aunt. You must know that after her woman ritual she continued to play, as you may be tempted to. She had the blood of de Danaa as you do. She was tall with the golden red hair like you." Tears formed in her grandmother's eyes.

"She could run fast and could read thoughts of people before they spoke. She was named for the bird that flies even higher than the hawk. Iolaire, the eagle, often wandered through the hills as you do." Her grandmother continued remembering with a smile, "She perched on mountaintops to see her visions."

The smile left her grandmother's face and her voice grew somber again. "Without ever having claimed a man she became pregnant. She would not tell us who the father was. The child was cursed. His hair was dark, as were his eyes. His legs were twisted and the look in his eyes was not right." She clasped her hands over her heart. "The priest Boandas ordered that the child be destroyed."

"Iolaire became enraged. She shouted curses at the priest. We all knew how dangerous that was. He was a much younger man then, and able to do great violence in the god's names. The child was killed anyway, but in a ceremony to the gods, to appease them and to get rid of the curse, which he said would touch us all. Boandas banished her from any of our villages. She used to try to come and steal food. Actually we would put food out for her, but after a few months of her banishment she was not heard from again."

Her grandmother was silent. She started to speak but stopped, as if trying to find a hard voice again.

Seabhac's eyes were wide. The beautiful red cloak began to feel heavy and itchy.

Her grandmother looked at her with narrow slits of eyes. She whispered, "Be careful how you act, you must not bring shame on our family! Boandas is watching you and will punish you severely for any rule you break."

Seabhac had never seen that look or heard that tone from her grandmother before.

Her grandmother's tone lightened. She tried to smile, as she added, "But we know you will only do good. We have not used the cloak since Iolaire left it. None of the daughters of our clan were strong enough to overcome its misfortune."

They were silent for a moment. Seabhac had never heard the whole story of this aunt. She pondered what might have happened to her.

She wanted to know more but did not dare ask.

"You have a great responsibility," her grandmother said as she leaned over to kiss Seabhac. She then stood and left the hut.

The old woman seemed to leave a vacuum behind her. Seabhac began to gasp for air. She wanted nothing more than to be free of all this and run through the hills with Aengus. Was he off limits now!? Would it now be even more dangerous to be with Owain?

She took off the red cloak and the necklaces and stepped away from them in the candlelight.

Early the next morning there was singing outside the hut. It was Aengus and her uncle, her father and Ciallach and Giosai, her brothers. She called a greeting to them and they called back, "Good morning, Eogan woman." She recognized the voice of her father.

She jumped up and felt the cold of the morning. She dressed quickly. As she put on the red cloak, she shivered and said a word to her aunt, "Iolaire, I will make it right for you."

Just then, Katika came in. She put out her hand and touched Seabhac's shoulder, "I see you have the courage to wear your aunt's cloak."

"Did you know her?" Seabhac asked, overflowing with curiosity.

"I can't say," said Katika, lowering her eyes. She was silent for a moment. Katika broke the silence. "Hurry now! Get your things together. The procession is about to begin."

Her mother looked through the door. She gazed at her, saying, "You look so beautiful my little girl." She hugged her. M`alda stopped for a moment and touched the cloak Seabhac was wearing. She said nothing.

M'alda then said, "Let's join the others. Are you ready?"

Seabhac nodded. They stepped out into the sunlight. The brightness startled her. She had been in the hut for so many days.

Her father and her male relatives applauded her. They stayed at a distance. She remembered her new relationship to them.

All of her relatives were gathered outside, applauding her and singing, "May the goddess bless you and all of us. May you be fertile with your new body. Return to us and make us glad!" They threw flower petals on her head and her path. Many of the women hugged her.

At the end of the path was an open cart pulled by two small Cymran horses. Ehilf and another young woman she barely knew were already in the cart.

Ehilf giggled, "You too? Isn't this exciting? I'm glad we are becoming women together."

She turned to the other girl. Ehilf reached out to her, "This is Fina, she's become a woman this week also. My grandmother says that it is common for many girls to become women in the same month. It's good because then we can take lessons from the priestess together." Ehilf took her hand, and held it throughout the journey.

By the road it took until late in the afternoon to arrive at the encampment. Amala greeted them as they got out of the cart, "Welcome new women! The goddess smiles on you! May your time among us make you fruitful." She embraced the two other girls first. When she got to Seabhac, she embraced her for an especially long time.

"And you are finally here as a woman," she said softly.

"It is time for the evening meal," said Amala loudly to all the arrivals. There were about twelve girls from surrounding villages.

This time as they ate the herb stew, Seabhac was here for the same reasons as the other girls. She talked happily with them about the events of the past week

Suddenly Katika appeared. "The ritual begins!" She was in her green gown. "Come!! Now." All the new women rushed to follow her.

It was late but the full moon showered the glen with a silvery shimmer. As they traveled through the thicket, the trees blocked out the light. Suddenly they came to a clearing. Fires lit the way to the gathering spot.

A deep rich male voice sang in the eerie flickering. Two men, sat behind a fire. As they got closer, the women joined them to make a circle. It was Torrida and Owain. Their song was in an unfamiliar language. "E Kaio Lontayne Apollo" "E Kaio Lontayne Apollo" (*We are your light, Apollo*)

Everyone sat in the circle, the singing stopped.

Katika greeted him, "Hail Torrida! These are new women come to find their appointed task."

He responded, "Hail Katika! We welcome them in the name of our gods."

He stood up. His eyes softened as he spoke to Katika. He held his arms out to her and they embraced. The girls all began to giggle at the show of affection.

Torrida looked around the circle at the giggling women. His gaze stopped with Seabhac and he held out his hand to her. "Come, woman, do not be afraid." Seabhac was embarrassed to be singled out. He pulled her to her feet.

"All young women will be asked to be the partner of a young man." He spoke in the thick accent that Seabhac had become used to with her time on the island. He walked around the circle holding Seabhac's hand. He turned and speaking so that everyone could hear, "So you new women, do you know what man you want?"

He walked her halfway around the circle. They stopped where Owain sat. Torrida pointed to a spot next to Owain in the circle. She sat down. They both looked sidelong at each other. Owain reached down so no one would see and took her hand.

Torrida took each of the young women by the hand and walked them around the circle asking the same question. Seabhac did not know if any other words were spoken. She was absorbed in the presence of Owain next to her. She knew their relationship had changed completely.

All had been asked to name their man and returned to the circle. Some said names of young men back in the village. Several said the name of the same man.

A feminine voice broke into the silence. "E Kaia Loytayne Ana" *(We are your light, Ana)* Katika intoned.

"Women have been very brave," Katika said to the group.

"Yes, new women. We are responsible for saving Cymru from the Romans. Boudicca the Queen of the Iceni Tribe surprised the Romans who were coming to attack the druid encampment. With her sisterhood of screaming women, their hair plastered with blue dye and red mud they ran toward the men screaming with the sounds of Ana. The Romans, in spite of their weapons, were so scared they simply ran away," Katika continued.

The young women laughed at the picture drawn by her words.

"After that," Katika continued, "Cartimandua, the Queen of the Brigantes actually signed a treaty of peace that ended the brutal wars." She was silent. "We women are birthers. We prefer peace to war. Our children grow better in peace."

Torrida nodded.

The young women spent two weeks in the clearing, learning how to care for a home and how to raise children. They learned the needs of a husband. They learned how sacred all their tasks were.

Katika took a moment with Seabhac. "I must share something important with you. As you decide what you will do with your life." She touched Seabhac's stomach. She said, "I do not feel the vibrations of a child-bearer in you. You will not have children from your womb." Katika touched her hand. "You are like me in that way. I wasn't given the gift of my own child from my womb. You will be a woman who finds many ways of giving birth and nurturing others."

Seabhac was startled by this news. She thought about those dark haired children she and Owain hoped to have. Did this mean they would just never be born? There was so much she had to learn about the ways of Ana.

All the new women packed up their belongings for the journey home. Amala approached Seabhac.

She frowned. "Be careful of Boandas. Come to the caves, and become our sister," she said.

Boandas returned from a meeting with his Brothers of Fireantachd knowing what he must do. No sooner had he arrived home than he heard about Seabhac's coming of age. He also heard disturbing news about a relationship between Seabhac and the dark boy on the island. All his work of keeping the family pure was unraveling. He would set down the rules to Torrida and Katika. He hoped they would understand and help him.

CHAPTER 20 – PELAGIUS THE FAITHFUL PALESTINE

"Pelagius is one of the most maligned figures in the history of Christianity. It has been common sport of the theologian and the historian of theology to set him up as a symbolic bad man and to heap upon him accusations which often tell us more about the theological perspective of the accuser than about Pelagius."[30]

Excommunicated!! His student, Caelestius had been excommunicated in Carthage. Pelagius was breathless with shock. They both loved the church and loved the debate about the meaning of Christ Jesus and his teachings. He knew how stunned Caelestius must be. He wished he could go to him, but travel was hard for Pelagius now. He had come to Palestine hoping to work with Master Jerome, but had been rebuffed.

He had, though, become friends with Melania, a widow who had renounced her wealth and had come to Palestine to set up a house of prayer for women. She also worked with Jerome. Her aunt Paula had been Jerome's companion but had died suddenly. Jerome had been in deep despair after Paula died. Recently Melania's niece Paulina, only eight years old, had joined them. She was the delight of Jerome's life.

Pelagius had often asked Melania about having an audience with Jerome. She warned him that it wasn't wise. He didn't understand why Jerome disliked him so much.

Demetrias had left Carthage and moved to Palestine and had been living with Melania. They would sometimes slip away together to discuss the faith with Pelagius. Demetrias told Pelagius that Jerome had warned her that his teachings would lead her astray.

She told Melania, though, that she preferred her time with him to time with Jerome. Pelagius seemed to respect her deep thoughts and questions, even though she was a woman. They tried to keep the meetings secret from Jerome who chided Pelagius for spending so much time with mere women.

Paulus Orosius was excitedly on his way to visit Jerome with the news of the excommunication. He had fought the pagan Vandals in Spain and had nearly been killed. He had been in Spain fighting Priscillianism and the teachings of Origen. His zeal against heresy had made him famous.

The great Bishop Augustine in Africa said that he had a

"vigilant intellect, ready tongue and burning zeal." Bishop Augustine had recommended him to Jerome by saying, that he spoke 'with the eloquence of angels.' Now he would show Jerome his true worth by helping him get rid of this false teacher Pelagius.

He burst into the room. "Brother Jerome, I bring you great news! You will be delighted to know that Pelagius' student, Caelestius, has been excommunicated in Carthage!"

Jerome stood and embraced him, "Blessings on your good work. But what about Pelagius himself? I'm tired of being insulted by that fat, slow, porridge eating Brito."

Orosius laughed at the image. "The student's beliefs can't be far from the teacher. I plan to take the papers to the bishop of Jerusalem. Maybe he will condemn the Brito himself."

"Go! Do it! I give you my blessing!! And I thank you for bringing me such good words," Jerome said gleefully.

"Ah, but first come and have a meal with us." Jerome called Melania and Paulina to prepare a meal for his guest. Melania listened to their conversation with concern, as she brought the food and cleared the table.

The next day, Orosius met privately with the Bishop of Jerusalem. He showed him the letters of condemnation of Caelestius from the Bishops in Africa. He reminded the bishop that this man's teacher lived and worked in Bethlehem.

Gathering a small group of examiners, the bishop sent for Pelagius.

It was a hot midsummer day and Pelagius dreaded the meeting. He approached the small group of men, nodding to Orosius. He knew from Melania that he had been with Jerome the last few days.

The Bishop asked directly, "Is it true that you are teaching doctrines that are against the teaching of Augustine?"

Pelagius was angry to begin with and angrier at the question. Before he could stop himself the words came out, "What is Augustine to me?"

There was a gasp. Pelagius realized they misunderstood him. Bishop Augustine was a revered teacher throughout the Mediterranean, and it was dangerous to appear to insult him.

Pelagius laughed, trying to cut the tension, "I simply meant that I would debate Augustine as we all love a good debate. However, he isn't here. I can only debate those present."

The Bishop of Jerusalem laughed saying, "Let me be your Augustine then."

Everyone present joined in the laughter.

Orosius realized that everyone was relaxing. He shouted, "This man teaches that a man can actually live without sin!"

The bishop turned to Pelagius asking, "Is that what you teach?"

Pelagius nodding responded, "Of course I do. Scripture says so!"

Orosius interrupted, "This teaching is denounced by the Council of Carthage. It is opposed by the authority of Bishop Augustine, and Brother Jerome also condemns it!"

The bishop turned to Pelagius. "Explain your belief."

Pelagius responded, "I don't teach that it is easy for humans to be sinless. A person who is prepared to toil and strive to avoid sin and walk in the commandments of God is granted, by God, the possibility of so doing."

One of the examiners shouted out, "But what about God's grace?"

Pelagius responded, "Paul the Apostle said, 'I labored more abundantly than they all, yet not I but the grace of God which was with me.'" Everyone was quiet.

Pelagius continued with the sound of a pastor, "Again, 'It is not him that wills nor him that runs, but of God who shows him mercy.'" He continued, "Or the Psalmist who says, 'Except the Lord build the house, they labor in vain that build it.'"

The bishop turned to Orosius, "Don't you believe that God's grace can free a man from sin?"

Orosius didn't answer.

The Bishop of Jerusalem declared, "To me this man, Pelagius, is incontrovertibly Christian!"

He approached them both and smiled at Pelagius offering his hand in friendship.

Then he turned to Orosius who bowed.

The Bishop frowned, pointing his finger at Orosius, "But you are a blasphemer! You don't believe it is possible to live without sin, even with God's help." The bishop walked away from him.

Pelagius tried not to laugh at Orosius' shock. He knew, though, that Orosius would take the news to Jerome.

Pelagius could not stop Jerome's plotting.

Jerome was sitting in this study as Orosius returned. "Well, what happened?"

Orosius was silent.

Jerome bellowed, "Don't tell me that dog has the Bishop of Jerusalem on his side?" He tried to control his anger. He didn't want to scare Paulina who was in the other room.

Orosius said thoughtfully, "We need help to get the job done."

"Where can we get that help?" asked Jerome.

Orosius smiled, "There are two bishops who have nothing to do. They would love to say they served you. The first was my Bishop in Spain, his name is Heros. He was recently forced out of that country by the terrible invasion of the barbarians."

Jerome shook his head. "That was terrible and frightening for our church and for the empire."

"Yes, Heros stayed until the last moment, but was finally forced to leave. He has come to Palestine in order to hear God's will for him."

"He sounds like a brave man, just the kind we need in the church."

"With me, he is willing to fight heresy to the death."

"Would he help us fight the Brito?"

"I believe he would. And he is not alone." Orosius was getting excited about working with his old friend at purifying the church.

"Who else?" Jerome opened his eyes wide.

"You remember Lazarus, the Bishop of Aix?"

"He was accused of adultery."

"Falsely, by his enemies. There are many false believers who would do anything to keep good men from exposing them."

Jerome sighed, "Yes, it's sad, but true. Is he also in Palestine?"

"Yes, he is. The two of them could go directly to the Pope. With the bishops of Africa and with your friend Bishop Augustine the Pope would be forced to excommunicate this Pelagius. You wouldn't need to involve yourself."

"I want to meet these good men!" Jerome said.

That next afternoon in Jerome's home, Orosius brought Bishops Heros and Lazarus. Melania served them lunch as they talked.

"Orosius here has told me that both of you are at war with the poisonous beliefs in the church."

Heros smiled widely. "Yes and we are anxious to continue to be of service, especially to one like you who has such a reputation for purity in the church."

Jerome declared, "We need a larger gathering to override the bishop of Jerusalem. If you, as senior bishops call a synod of the entire Diospolis, we can let them all decide about the charges being made against Pelagius."

Melania nearly dropped the dish she was carrying.

Lazarus and Heros smiled, saying, "We are at your service."

A synod was declared in late December in Caesarea, and Pelagius was summoned.

Pelagius sighed deeply, his stomach hurt. He hadn't felt well since the meeting with the Bishop of Jerusalem. There was something about the look on Orosius' face that let him know that the matter was not finished.

His student Caelestius was now teaching as a priest in Ephesus. Fortunately, the church in Ephesus had not paid any attention to the condemnation that came from the bishops from Carthage. The Ephesians had ordained him.

There is nothing more frightening than knowing that an antagonist is after you and will not stop until you are destroyed. He didn't know who or why. He suspected Jerome, but did not want to believe that he would be so lacking in virtue.

He had more important work to do than constantly defending himself. He and Melania had set up a clinic to care for the poor in Jerusalem and Bethlehem. They traveled between the two places offering Christ's aid.

As he returned to his home on the evening before the synod meeting, he saw a letter on the table, placed carefully by a courier. It was from the Bishop Augustine. He knew the remarks he made about Augustine at the council meeting in Jerusalem had not gone over well. Bishop Augustine's opinion was powerful. He hoped these words were not words of condemnation. If they were, his days were done.

His hands shook as he opened the letter.

As he started to read, tears came to his eyes. Bishop Augustine had just finished reading the papers he had sent to the Bishop of Jerusalem. The letter began with the words that intended to assure him, and also to guide him in the next days defense. The letter praised him for his impeccable views about the life in Christ. The great bishop promised his enduring friendship.

A calm came over Pelagius as the members of the synod gathered. Orosius and Jerome sat in the audience. Heros and Lazarus were present as bishops of the region. Pelagius came into the hall and nodded to his antagonists, showing his Christian charity. He avoided the eye of Jerome who was sitting with Orosius.

All the bishops were staring at Pelagius.

As proceedings began Pelagius asked to speak. He read the letter from Bishop Augustine.

All were silent. After a moment he said, "Any doctrine that is alien to the church, I am also against."

He sat down. He was still shaking from the deep emotion of the last days.

Then the Bishop of Jerusalem stood and began to applaud. One by one the other bishops stood and joined in the applause. All, that is, but Heros and Lazarus. Orosius and Jerome left the synod hall quietly.

Jerome said bitterly, "Brother Augustine doesn't understand. I know this dog's thinking, he thinks nothing of lying to the synod."

Orosius put his hand on his shoulder saying, "That's why we have Brothers Heros and Lazarus. They'll do whatever you ask."

"Then send them to change the mind of Bishop Augustine," Jerome responded.

"The task is as good as done," Orosius assured him.

That night Orosius sent Bishops Heros and Lazarus to speak directly with Bishop Augustine.

Bishop Augustine asked for a transcript of the proceedings, but even after reading it, he continued to sing praises of Pelagius.

Several weeks later, Jerome wrote a personal letter to Bishop Augustine reminding him of their friendship. Augustine respected Jerome deeply but also admired Pelagius.

Why was Jerome was so adamant in his condemnation of Pelagius? The antagonists poison slowly began to work. Augustine began to question his positive judgment of Pelagius. He mentioned his doubts, informally, to a few of the other bishops in the region

IN ROME, WITHIN THE PAPAL CHAMBERS:

Shouting bishops filled the Papal meeting room. Pope Innocent was feeling weak and could barely stand.

Bishop Aurelius spoke first, "Your Holiness, there is a serious plague in the church. That is the teacher Pelagius and his student Caelestius who do not believe in prayer or grace. The exaltation of free will does away with the need for grace and recourse to prayer, and their attitude toward infant baptism condemns children to eternal death!"

Pope Innocent sighed deeply, saying, "I've read his words. They aren't as bad as that."

The bishops all began to speak at once.

Aurelius spoke above them, "Your Holiness, you've been ill. You haven't been able to pay attention. What he says could only mean that he is sending many to hell without God's saving grace. You must excommunicate him. We have tried to silence his student, but our brothers in Ephesus simply ignored us and ordained him. The church will be destroyed by this belief and many will be lost to the salvation offered in Christ Jesus."

Aurelius had tears streaming down his face. His fellow bishops nodded, murmuring to each other.

The Pope was dizzy from his own physical weakness and from the crowd in his chambers. "What does brother Augustine say; he has said he appreciates brother Pelagius?"

"Even he is admitting he has been wrong. He believes Pelagius has often lied at the hearings and then goes off to teach the poison."

There was silence in the Papal meeting rooms. Pope Innocent let out a groan. It was hard to tell whether it was his health or his decision that tortured him.

"Very well. I will send an order excommunicating both Pelagius and his student," he said softly.

The bishops all said soft words of affirmation for the victory in their midst.

Then the Pope added, "I will remove the action if they recant of the beliefs that do not fit with orthodoxy."

Bishop Aurelius sent word to Bishops Heros and Lazarus. They traveled to Palestine quickly to tell Jerome that they had been successful. There was a time to celebrate.

IN PALESTINE:

The excommunication came like a bolt out of the blue. Faced with excommunication by the Bishop of Rome, also called the Pope, Pelagius set to work on four books explaining his beliefs.

Then he went further into the desert for prayer.

IN ROME:

Within months Pope Innocent died. The newly elected Bishop of Rome, was from the eastern part of the church. He took the name Pope Zosimus.

IN ROME IN THE PAPAL CHAMBERS:

Before Pope Zosimus even made himself comfortable in his Papal rooms, he had callers.

An elderly priest known for his wisdom stood before him, saying, "Your Holiness, we celebrate your election. We know you are very busy but we come on an urgent matter. You need to overturn the ruling of your predecessor."

With him were several wealthy men of Rome, including the uncle of Demetria. "He has helped our family greatly by his counsel to my niece."

Demetria's uncle stepped forward with a stack of letters. "These are all the people who have found salvation through the teachings of brother Pelagius. They are from many of the influential families of Rome."

"I may be Pope now, but I can't easily overturn the rulings of His Holiness Innocent. He was a holy and wise man. We all grieve his passing."

"But we grieve the excommunication of Pelagius also," the priest said. "Many, who agree with him, fear that they are next." The old priest grimaced. "It is an ugly part of the church that a few angry bishops can have such a dangerous effect."

"Angry bishops?" Zosimus asked.

"Don't you know that the bishops of the North African provinces have wanted us all to agree with them? Except for Bishop Augustine, of Hippo, most of them want to stop all debate on issues of doctrine. Debate has been a crucial part of our church. Pelagius has been very much a part of that glorious debate. Even Bishop Augustine has expressed his appreciation of Pelagius."

Zosimus called to his assistant. "Where are the papers on Pelagius and Caelestius?"

While his assistant went off to find the papers, Zosimus nodded, "I have been irritated by the African bishops also. We in the eastern part of the church have our own ways of seeing Christ Jesus. We do not need their help."

"And," continued the old priest, "you should know that two of your bishops have been actively stirring the others against Pelagius, as though in a vendetta."

"Who would those be?" the Pope asked.

"You may remember Bishop Heros of Spain, who was unable to stand up to the Vandals."

"And he lost the territory for the church," Zosimus remembered.

"And Lazarus, the former Bishop of Aix."

"Who was forced to resign under accusation of adultery?" Zosimus asked, his voice wavering.

"The same one," the priest answered.

"They made their way to Palestine to team up, I'm sorry to say, with the great scholar Jerome," the priest said bowing his head. He did not look directly at Pope Zosimus.

"Brother Jerome is a good friend of Bishop Augustine. He wouldn't be involved with such plotting," Zosimus declared.

"He has a personal dislike of Pelagius. That I know," the priest responded.

"But these two bishops had a vendetta of their own it sounds like." Zosimus seemed to be moving toward action.

The priest was silent.

After a long silence Pope Zosimus said, "I'm sorry to hear that. What these two, Bishop Heros and Bishop Lazarus, have done is destroying the church. I have a mind to threaten them with excommunication if they do not stop their destructive activities. I also have a mind to censure the bishops of Africa for their lack of charity in dealing with Pelagius and his student

He turned back to the old priest who was looking now at the tiles on the Papal floor. "I thank you for your courage in coming forward. I ask you now to gather as many of the faithful as you can tomorrow. I will make an announcement."

Pope Zosimus went into his study with the papers, which included the defense Pelagius had written. He also read the glowing report from the Bishop of Jerusalem, and the letter from Bishop Augustine. As far as he could see, Pelagius' beliefs were fully orthodox and catholic. How could his predecessor have excommunicated him?

He sighed deeply. How could the church of the man of Nazareth have come to this? He needed to clean house.

Innocent's excommunication order could be rescinded if they returned to orthodoxy. Zosimus could, therefore honor Innocent's order by simply declaring that Pelagius and Caelestius had indeed returned to orthodoxy.

At the gathered assembly, the Pope made the declaration that as far as he could see the followers of Pelagius were men of unblemished faith. There were cheers and some even cried with joy.

Bishops Heros and Lazarus received papal letters threatening them with excommunication if they did not stop their vendetta against Pelagius. The troublesome bishops of Africa received letters of papal censure for their lack of charity and their divisiveness.

CHAPTER 21 – ESCAPE
CYMRU

"Both Augustus and his successor Tiberius published edicts against the Celtic priesthood. The ostensible reasons for the proscription hinged upon the barbarity of their sacrifices, but the real motives are likely to have been political. Despite the edicts, the pagan Celtic religion remained a powerful force throughout the Roman period and long afterward... The probability is that as the orders of Augustus and Tiberius were applied, surviving Druids would have fled from Gaul to Britain." [31]

A hawk flew over the three figures standing in the clearing outside the village. Suddenly the man in the white robes lifted his staff and struck the woman. The heavyset black bearded man grabbed him by the shoulders. He held him at a distance to calm him.

"May the curse of Dag be on you," Boandas yelled. "You have allowed us to be defiled!" Then more quietly, but pleading, he continued, "You put us at great risk. We may come to an end as a people if our gods are not appeased!"

Katika said, "Quiet Boandas, we are all filled with love for the gods and goddesses we have known, but our lands are making room for new gods, new goddesses, brought by new people. We must seek to understand them also."

"We must chase out the new gods. The danger is real. Why can't you see it!?" He was looking now at the man holding him.

There was silence. Then Boandas looked resigned and Torrida let him go.

Red faced, Boandas turned back to Katika, who was bleeding, and spit on her. "You are to be cursed and all your women with you if you do not do as I say," he said gritting his teeth as he moved away.

Torrida tried to reason with him. "And you, Boandas are not listening to your own gods. You are acting out of fear. The dark spirits have taken your mind. You will not take any of the youth in our care."

Boandas pleaded, "You know as I do that the seasons are changing. The rains are not coming regularly. The blight has stopped the fruit trees from bearing fruit. The darkness hangs over us. That's the voice of angry gods." Sweat was dripping from his forehead from the emotions that filled him.

As calmly as Boandas could, he continued speaking, "You have allowed the one with the blood of De Danaan to get close to the blood of the defiler. If this continues, we will have worse misery. We must do something. We must do it now. They will be taught well, they will be safe, trust me"

Torrida and Katika were silent.

Boandas walked up to Katika. "You women who live in the mountains, you have disappointed the gods. I forbid you to take any of our young women there." Looking up to the sky, he lifted his staff again. "The gods are waiting! We must give them a sign before the sun cycle is completed and the new sun is born. And so we are in such deep trouble. We must go back to the old ways. Many brothers agree."

Boandas, seeing that his powers of persuasion were not working concluded, "But I will not discuss this with you, I will take the youth I choose when the sun rises in the morning. You have no choice in this."

Torrida felt the heat of anger rising as he heard these words. He knew there was no arguing. He pretended to accept the idea. "So be it. Your words shall rule."

Torrida reached over and took Katika's arm and slowly they walked away from Boandas

The visit from Boandas puzzled Owain. It was strange that Boandas would come all the way to the island. He seemed to want to speak to him without Torrida present. Owain had been told many times that Boandas would not approve of his Greek blood and dark hair.

The old druid seemed open, even complementary. The boy felt flattered but uneasy. Owain noticed that as Boandas stood before him a chill seemed to fill the room. The holy man, Boandas, had told him that an important test was coming soon.

Owain had been studying the stories. He memorized the words exactly as Torrida recited them to him. Would that be a part of the test Boandas was going to give him? He was excited that maybe Boandas was going to accept him and he could have a relationship with Seabhac in the open.

He was filled with thoughts of Seabhac. She was now a woman, no longer a little girl. Torrida had talked to him about his responsibility to her. He wished he could be with her now and share what he was learning. He wanted to know what that first kiss would be like.

He was relieved to see Torrida come up the hill.

Owain left the hut to greet him.

"The Irish Druid came today!" Owain blurted out. He was anxious to have the words out and his questions answered.

Torrida looked at him with anger and fear. So, this young man was his choice.

"Boandas said there would be a test," Owain continued.

Torrida hesitated then said, "You must decide whether you will go with him or with me."

He wanted to grab this boy and protect him. But what if the god, Pallas, did want Owain in the divine realm? Maybe he had a purpose beyond what Torrida knew. It was not the way he understood the workings of Pallas. Who knows the thoughts of the gods?

Owain was looking deeply into Torrida's eyes, trying to read them for meaning. "If I go with the Irish druid would you still be my teacher?"

"No, you would not see me again. But you would be important and honored and do a great service for your people."

Owain felt paralyzed. He spoke weakly, "I will go with you." Tears formed in his eyes.

Torrida caught the look in his eyes then turned away. He could not bear to see the boy in such pain. "This may be your calling. Pray to Pallas about it. I will leave you while you do so."

A cold chill filled Torrida's body.

He shivered as he said, "I will be back at sundown and we will talk again. Whatever you decide, you will be leaving this place. You must pray. Will you go away with Boandas, or will you go away with me?"

Torrida's energy was drained as he went out of the room. He would wait. The boy would tell him tonight if the gods really wanted him.

Torrida quickly moved to the glade looking for the priestess Katika. As he approached her hut, Katika opened the door.

She looked drained and tired.

She whispered, "I don't know which of my girls he'll want." She sat on the mat and invited him to sit next to her, then added, "What can we do, my love?"

Not looking at her, he reported his news, "Boandas has already chosen for me. He wants Owain."

Katika stared at him as if trying to hear what he really said.

She exclaimed, "Owain? But he is Greek." She stared at Torrida, trying to pull it together.

"A good gift, don't you think, a fine joke? What a unique plaything for his gods!" said Torrida sarcastically.

"How do you know this?" Katika asked

"Owain told me. Boandas came to the island. I told Owain he must consider it prayerfully."

"But that would mean. . ." Katika stopped

"Maybe it is the god's choice," Torrida responded.

"And so the girl chosen. . ." Katika started to make the connection.

She stopped talking and for a moment looked into Torrida's eyes. She put her hands over her face. She moaned.

Katika looked into the fire. Then she said with resolve, "She will not go. We will leave before dawn for the caves of Ana."

Torrida breathed deeply and responded, "And Owain and I will go to the sea tonight also."

Katika embraced him.

He returned the embrace. Touching her hair, he said softly, "We will meet you in the mountains as soon as we can."

Laughter filled the small room. For a moment, the fire seemed peaceful and calming. They would make a tea to both calm them and give strength. They would go in opposite directions to save these young people. They were uncertain what Boandas would do. They did not know how many priests of the order of druids were part of the Brothers of Fireantachd. They did not know who would side with Boandas rather than them.

She moved to the doorway and watched the sun set. The days were getting so short. The sun was dying. Boandas would become desperate soon.

Torrida and Katika made tender love, knowing that the next year might be filled with danger. The work they did was fed by the passion of their god and goddess and of their love for each other. It was for the protection they gave each other. It was for the ecstasy found in evoking the gods and goddesses perfectly together. A priest for the priestess. Their life had been filled with beauty. They fell onto the mat and shared of the abundance of life that lay within them. Remembering laughing, kissing. Tonight they would go into danger separately.

The room was filled with a rainbow of colors that swirled until it became a white light and then a pale yellow glow. The glow softened as they emerged from their reverie. Strengthened, they knew what they needed to do. They embraced and Torrida left Katika for the work of the night.

Earlier that day Seabhac had been working at the laundry by the creek when her grandmother approached, "Come granddaughter, your father and mother must talk to you."

As she arrived at the family hut, she saw Boandas next to her father and mother. They were looking solemn.

Her grandmother startled her as she hissed, "Where is the red cloak I gave to you?"

"I..." Seabhac could not find the words to speak.

Her eyes were hard, "You have almost done as your aunt did but we have caught it in time. You have been secretly seeing a Roman and appeasing his gods and angering ours!"

"Is this true?" Finn said softly.

"I have a friend. He rescued me .. " Seabhac was shaking, but ready to confess.

"So you did lie to us," Boandas boomed out from behind the family.

"Yes, but...he is only a friend," she said softly.

"He cannot be a friend. You are an Eogan! Daughter, what have you been plotting?" M'alda sounded near tears.

"He has just been a friend!" she defended herself.

She saw her mother grab her father's hand. She froze. She looked into Boandas eyes and saw a look of hatred mixed with something else. It was fear. His eyes were hard.

He spoke now, "You must be punished and trained in the ways of a daughter of Eogan. You must go away with me!"

"No!" Seabhac heard herself say from a place deep inside her.

Her grandmother said softly, "If you do not go with the Holy One you are not welcome among us. It will be because of you that we don't climb to the heights of Shreedrum." Her words felt like a bludgeon. Seabhac's knees began to shake.

Boandas was still standing at a distance behind her family as he said, "Say good bye to your family and to all your friends. Your actions have been of a woman. You have made your choice. We must make ours. We will leave tomorrow morning at the first call of the birds."

She turned to her father. His eyes were hard and cold. His voice was as cold as he said, "You are not my daughter unless you go with Boandas. You must leave!" She looked at her mother.

M'alda turned away at first, but then mouthed the words, "Bridey be with you."

Seabhac was wordless through the rest of the day. No one came to her. She imagined what it would be like to go with Boandas. He had always frightened her. She had always felt that her family protected her from him. Now she was to be his alone. She shivered at the thought. She packed her cloaks and some of her amber. She put the red cloak of Iolaire in last.

Her girlfriend Elihf came into the hut.

She blurted out, "Seabhac! Is it true?" She sat down on the mat.

"That I am going away?" Seabhac responded, "Yes, with Boandas." She sounded matter of fact with her friend.

"People are saying that you have chosen a husband who is Roman and Boandas is angry."

Seabhac stared at her. She stammered out, "I haven't chosen a husband..." She hesitated.

"Is it that handsome young man in our circle in the grove?" Elihf laughed. "He was so wonderful. We all wanted him."

"Boandas wouldn't let me..." she muttered, surprised by Elihf's response.

"Oh," Elihf said, looking down at her hand, "I thought," her voice cracked as she continued, "You're in trouble aren't you?"

"I think so. . ."

"You'll always be my friend. I always thought we'd raise our children together." She stood up, embraced Seabhac, and kissed her on the cheek, and added, "Go with Bridey."

As night fell, she could not sleep. She did not want to wake up and find Boandas at her door. She drifted into a fitful sleep in spite of herself.

Torrida entered the hut and saw Owain was packing his few belongings. "So you have heard the gods speak to you. I'm proud of you Owain." The boy looked back at him uncertain whether the pride would last.

"The gods say I should go with you, and not Boandas." Owain said with a look of defiance.

Torrida laughed in a low booming guttural laugh and he embraced him. "Well then, fine. We will be great merchants together."

Owain was confused, but relieved and began to laugh also, like rain falling after a great deal of rumbling in the clouds.

They built up the fire with the sticks saved for winter. They would not be on this island this winter.

There was a strange ray of hope that lit the room that night. Torrida gathered whatever they would need for the years of journeying. He did not ever expect to return. This might be his last journey. So be it.

They both left the small house. Owain looked back one last time with a young man's mind. His mind was now set on the future. Torrida looked with an old man's mind. It was set on the memories. Torrida closed the door. They would travel by curragh around the peninsula. A merchant ship had been seen nearby. Boandas would not expect them to go in that direction.

Seabhac was startled to hear a rustling outside. She pulled her cloak on and went to check on the noise, trying not to wake her parents. In the dark, she saw the figure of Katika.

"Come!" Katika held out her hand.

"Don't speak," Katika was whispering, but there was urgency in the whisper. "Get all the belongings you can find in the dark. You will not be returning."

She collected the bag she had packed to go with Boandas.

"Take extra cloaks, it will be very cold," Katika whispered. Seabhac had all she could carry. They headed off only by the light of the near full moon.

"We must travel quickly."

Seabhac's stomach was tight. She was frightened, but relieved to be going off with Katika instead of Boandas.

She followed in silence, not daring to ask any questions. There seemed to be an envelope of safety in the silence. An owl called from a tree above. A thousand friendly eyes seemed to watch them. Seabhac knew that all the creatures enjoyed Katika's presence and made way for her. She longed to have that same sense of beauty and grace about her.

They were traveling inland. After several miles, she could make out the sound of a horse. She saw figures moving. Then she saw small horses attached to a wagon. A man was sitting there waiting for them. She drew in her breath as she put her belongings into the back of the cart.

She knew her life was out of her control. She would trust Katika and accept her fate.

They traveled inland until the light of the moon faded. It set behind them. The dawn began to show itself on the horizon in front of them. Seabhac pulled the cloak tightly around her, as a cold wind began to blow. She was glad for its warmth. It had been the robe of her exiled aunt. It served her well now. She felt sad as she remembered the story.

"Iolaire," Seabhac whispered. The memory of her aunt belonged on this journey of womanhood.

As the sun rose, color came to the world around her. A soft red glow bathed the sky and hills. It was an unfamiliar landscape. Rolling hills gave way to rocky crags. They gave way to high mountains in the distance. She gasped.

Katika spoke, "Seabhac, these mountains hold strong and powerful spirits. They will make us strong and protect us. "

Seabhac paused, "I've never seen mountains like this."

"They will be your home. You will learn from them."

They left the wagon and began carrying all their belongings on their backs. Katika blessed the cart driver and he turned the cart around and began the journey back to his home.

They began walking uphill through beech trees. Seabhac could hear the laughter of a stream to her left. The ground below was black rock. They turned. The path took them up a steep hill, leaving trees behind. The rock was hard and slippery, unlike her soft sandy stone of home.

The spirits must be different here, she thought.

They came to a rocky clearing. They both stood for a moment to see a panorama of mountains as far as the eye could see. A soft breeze blew.

It was evening again. Seabhac was exhausted from the night of traveling and the day of walking and from the thousand different emotions coursing through her. She and Katika found a shelter of piled rocks left by previous climbers. Katika lit a fire as Seabhac collected old wood from the sparse vegetation.

They huddled by the fire. Katika began to sing. Seabhac

remembered the songs from the early days in the sacred glade.

This new vista of mountain ranges gave her a sense of the earth's vastness.

They looked at the stars. The fire was sending out sparks that seemed to be rising to meet them.

"There is a long climb ahead of us. Sleep now," Katika said.

Seabhac was glad that she brought heavy woolens. She slept on the open rock with the wind howling over them. In her dreamworld, the fire flared. She heard women singing. She did not understand their language. She knew they were singing a song of welcome.

When Boandas found Seabhac and Katika were gone he sent word to the Brothers of Fireantachd. He was filled with fear and fury. He was afraid of the damage Katika might do if he allowed her to go off on her own with the girl. He would set out with a few of the men of the clan. He knew that Katika had been trained in the high mountains with the daughters of Ana. He did not know exactly where the caves were. He would find them.

Wisdom's Price

Part 2

CHAPTER 22 – THE SISTERS OF ANA CYMRU: FROM THE COAST TO THE EASTERN MOUNTAINS

"The Creatrix of our world is the Mother Goddess of birth, nature and death, whose mythical name is the first Sound on the outward human breathe – Aaaa... In time, She became known as Aaaa-na: Ana, Anu, Anna, Amma, An and Ann. She is the Great Grand Mother Ancestor of us all, who gave birth from Her cosmic Womb to a daughter – Planet Earth and to the Primal Ancestors – the great energy beings who underlie the natural elements and the forces of nature."[32]

As dawn approached, Seabhac awakened to find the world covered with a white icy coating. Her cloak was hard with the frozen dew. That was all that was keeping her from being chilled completely. She pulled it closer to her as she looked for Katika. She found her facing the dawn with her arms lifted in reverence, intoning a chant that Seabhac had never heard before. Seabhac watched her for a few moments. She looked around the rocky terrain. The higher hills around them were white with snow.

During her dreams she had been surrounded by women, some short, some tall, some light skinned and blonder than any she had ever seen, some were dark and short. They were all talking among themselves and they suddenly turned toward her and seemed delighted to see her. Then she woke up. She was alone with Katika in this strange world.

Katika was standing, arms outstretched, facing the rising sun.

As she moved toward Katika's place of prayer, still wrapped in the cloak, she was surprised by the brilliant red glow on the mountain before her. The sun rose, all was bathed in light. She was transfixed. Seabhac forgot the cold. She let her cloak fall as she also lifted her arms in praise.

Katika had kept the fire from the night before going with moss and twigs protected by a mound of rocks. They were able to get it burning quickly. Water from the nearby stream was nearly frozen but thawed and heated quickly. The last of the oats were thrown into the water.

As they stood waiting for the fire to flare up, Katika noticed that Seabhac was shivering. She smiled, saying, "I pulled you from the ocean to the mountains. You are now closer than you have ever been to Ana, Mother of All. You'll get used to Her chill and Her power. We'll be warm by this evening. There is a bright flame out there." She pointed toward the mountain. "In the mountain there is the great power."

They ate the cereal in silence.

Seabhac was beginning to feel warmer as the sun bathed the ridge.

"Pack up! There is a long way to travel." Katika pointed into the distance. "We'll go to the base of that mountain. Be silent as you go and you'll hear the sounds of Ana instructing you."

Seabhac excitedly, but carefully, packed all she had brought. A euphoria that came over her had little to do with the rising sun and more to do with the strength of the mountains they were walking through. She listened for the sounds of Ana.

The next hour was spent walking along a deer trail that headed along a ridge and down into a valley. The cold breeze blew, but the sun warmed the earth. The many birds began to sing in celebration.

At the bottom of the ridge, they found a thick grove of trees and a creek in the middle. The water glittered and splashed. It gave a ringing sound as it formed eddies and waterfalls on the shale below. They wordlessly traveled up the stream on the bank. They crossed over at a narrow spot. They then left the stream and found another animal path up the opposite ridge. There were occasional shale outcroppings. The rocks had broken away in places to reveal small caves covered by ferns and lichens. A squirrel followed along with them for a while. She saw two deer on the path that bolted in the other direction as they came toward them. The deer later reconsidered their danger, stopped, and stared at them.

Seabhac felt her legs get weak as they continued up the ridge. They reached a level spot and stopped for a moment. Katika seemed to be listening. She then pointed to a talus slope with its pile of rocks. It went straight up the mountain. Seabhac thought she could see the top.

They clamored up the rocks, seeing an occasional lizard and snake. A badger came out to watch them. As the slope grew steeper, they needed to use feet and hands for the sure footing. Seabhac carefully watched for the rocks and footings that Katika chose. When she tried to go her own way, she was stranded by a gap between the boulders that she couldn't leap. Katika would wait for her to backtrack and come up the correct way.

The trail became steep. After a long time of silence and steady uphill movement through trees, they broke out into a meadow. The suddenness of it shocked Seabhac. A cloud chased them from behind. It was dark and black as it covered the sun, now midway up the sky. It chilled them both. It blew by.

The valley was wide and filled with frost-covered shrubs with a glint of blue from the flowers hiding among the branches. Katika said, "As we move into this valley take in the fragrance of these herbs. They're placed here so that your spirit can be cleansed just by walking through. We'll have a midday meal here."

Seabhac was overwhelmed by the sweet pungent smell that surrounded her.

Katika set out her cape to cover the ground and opened a pack to reveal more bread. She then began to pick the tiny blue flowers, putting them in a pouch on her belt.

Katika laughed, "The sisters would be angry if I traveled through this valley without collecting these soothing flowers."

"What are they good for?" Seabhac asked remembering that every herb and flower had its purpose.

Katika looked at her thoughtfully, "Just lay back and listen. Ana will tell you. The plants themselves will tell you." Katika lit a fire and heated some water, putting the flowers into the hot water to steep. She offered a cup to Seabhac, and took one herself. They sat gazing at the mountains in the distance.

Seabhac lay back on the cape and watched the clouds roll by. She tried to listen. She tried to drink in all the sounds, the smells, the feel of the world of these mountains. Seabhac felt drawn deep into the earth she was resting on. She drifted into a wonder-filled sleep. The sun, now fully in the sky, warmed her.

Both she and Katika were sleeping as a dark cloud moved slowly over the ridges they had crossed. It covered the sun. The two women, still sleeping, pulled their cloaks over themselves. The cloud stopped as if watching them. The squirrels that had come to investigate any left over crumbs cleared away. Suddenly the cloud let go of its icy pellets.

Seabhac and Katika shrieked as they jumped up and pulled their belongings together. The ice turned to cold rain.

Laughing, they bundled themselves against it. As they ran toward the nearest tree, they were cold and shivering. Katika had her bag of herbs and flowers. She tucked them deeper into the bag she was carrying.

They watched the rain form rivulets on the meadow they had occupied.

"Let's go," was all Katika said. They moved through the trees avoiding the rain as much as they could. They traveled along the edge of the mountain.

Seabhac heard the ringing of a distant bell. As she followed Katika, the ringing became louder and more insistent.

"We are home now," said Katika. Seabhac looked around. All she saw were black boulders and a high cliff above them. They were out of the storm.

Katika let out a loud whistle. From within the rock, there was a return whistle. Katika pulled away a pile of rocks. In a few minutes, a stone was removed from the inside. A narrow passageway was revealed.

A woman's voice from within the cave said warmly, "Welcome to the womb of the Mother Ana." She could just see a face in the flickering candlelight.

A sheep fleece was pushed out through the opening. Katika touched Seahbac's shoulder. "Take off your clothes and wrap yourself in this fleece. Seabhac did as she was told, although she was shivering from the cold.

"Now go head first into the cave, stretching your arms out."

Seabhac hesitated. Then wrapped in only the soft fleece, she flung herself into the opening headfirst. She slid easily, with the fleece around her, along the rocks. Hands grasped her and carefully pulled her through. She could see nothing in the darkness. She felt the arms lift her and place her, standing, on a cold stone floor.

She took a few minutes to get used to the darkness, even with the torch lights all around her. Then she began to see figures and faces of women young and old. Some of them she had seen in the glade.

She saw the face of Amala smiling broadly. "Welcome sister," Amala said as she kissed her cheek.

The women started chanting as they led her to the center of the room where a fire was burning.

The fire was wonderfully warm against her chilled body. The smoke of the fire traveled up a chimney-like part of the cave. It would get lost in the clouds outside the mountain. Someone wrapped her in a simple brown robe.

In a pot by the flame was porridge of grains, berries and honey. Amala brought her a full steaming bowl. She ate quickly. She suddenly missed her family and the sound of the sea. As she ate, tears silently streamed down her face. It was as if the joy of arrival, and grief over what she left behind, were one.

An older woman sat by her as she ate. "Your task now is to learn the rituals. Rituals help your spirit grow beyond what your mind knows." She looked at the woman whose skin was wrinkled but whose eyes glowed with wisdom. "My name is Llakino. I have probably lived here the longest." She looked around and all nodded in agreement. They looked at her with reverence. "Memorize the stories and serve all who are here as you would serve the Mother Ana herself. They are women of wisdom. Live by their teachings and you will travel sweetly on the earth and go swiftly to the land of joy in your death."

Now Seabhac could look around and see the faces. She had dreamed about these women.

"You must be tired," Amala said, approaching her, with an outstretched hand. Seabhac took her hand and Amala led her down a passageway with rooms carved out of the rock. In one of the rooms, the torch revealed a series of shelves carved in the wall. They stopped at one of the shelves, with a pile of folded blankets.

"This place has been reserved for you," Amala said. "Sleep well and dream well," Amala whispered. Amala walked a short distance away to her own shelf and put out the torch. There was the sound of other women finding their way to bed.

There was only the glow of the eternal flame and the sound of water echoing from deep in the earth. She drifted off to sleep.

As she slept, she saw faces of women coming and smiling. She heard singing. Then she felt a hand shaking her. She awakened to find herself in the cave on her first morning.

Breakfast was nearly ready. Women began emerging from many passageways.

The sun began to shine through holes in the ceiling of the cave.

One of the women emerged with a fresh gathering of herbs and fruits from outside. Apparently, there was an easier way to emerge from the cave.

They ate breakfast together, sharing the dreams of the night.

Katika approached with a tall woman with short white hair. She said, "Seabhac, this is Seallam, your teacher. Listen carefully to everything she tells you."

"Come," said Scallam, with an outstretched hand. She led Seabhac into a small side room.

This room had a waterfall trickling down the side. Fleece covered the floor and a raised platform in the center held a bowl with a small flame in it. They sat facing the flame.

"Do you know why you are called here?"

Seabhac shrugged, saying, "I want to study the ways of Ana. Also, we are running from Boandas"

"There is that. Many of us have run from Boandas and those like him."

They were silent for a moment. Seabhac heard the steady dripping of water.

Seallam continued, "The best way to learn about Ana is to learn about all of us." She pointed out the doorway.

"We are women alone here. Although there are women here who have partners, they will spend this time apart from them. Women who have children must move out because a cave is not a place to raise a child. You may stay with us a long time, Katika tells me that you will not have children."

"But I would like a partner," Seabhac said, thinking of Owain.

"Of course you will chose a partner," Seallam said. "But that you will not have children means that Ana has special work for you." She paused for a moment, "Giving birth can be joyful, but it can also break your heart." She was silent and looked as though she were near tears.

Seallam continued, "You will learn your relationship with us, and we with you. You will learn about your depths, which you have not yet discovered."

Seabhac looking at her questioningly, asked, "How could there be something I don't know about myself?"

Seallam responded, "Your true self is as deep and mysterious as this cavern. There are still depths I have not discovered. In this cave we have sometimes come across a new room and found old pottery that would tell us that it is simply a forgotten place."

"So there are parts of me that I have forgotten?"

Seallam nodded, adding, "And parts you have yet to discover. You have been in many bodies. Just as you were born anew as you entered this cavern, you have been a baby, a mother, an old woman in other times. You are relearning the wisdom of Ana."

"I've never been in this cave before," Seabhac said.

"I don't know if you have or not, but I would suspect that you have been in the mind of Ana."

"The mind of Ana?"

"In Her mind you can be in this place, or by the shore near your people, or on the holy hill of Shreedrum, or in deserts of the south or on tiny islands surrounded by water. We can visit people in distant places. Silence and vision is a doorway to Her mind. We are always crossing over and greeting others and returning. There are women in our sisterhood who we cannot touch physically. We can only touch them through the mind of Ana. We hear their music and their laughter and their tears. Sometimes a woman who has seen us in the mind will travel for years to join us in this cave."

Sealllam continued, "You will then learn to tend the fire within you, the flame of inspiration. If you are patient enough, you will discover the flash of fire which stimulates the germ of life in the earth. It is within seeds hidden beneath the earth. It brings the return of new life from the depths of cold and ice. It is a power that is also in your deepest spirit."

She added, "It is what we all aspire to. You will become that energy. That is the Greenfire, the most sacred fire of Ana."

Seallam's voice grew more intense, "There are some who will try to put out the fire in you. You must be strong enough that the fire can be eternal."

Seabhac shivered. "What about Boandas? I had an aunt who was destroyed by him. Did he put out her fire? I just learned about her. They say she died after Boandas sent her away into exile."

"She didn't die. She almost did, but the sisters saved her, as they saved you."

Seabhac looked at her startled to hear that her aunt was alive.

She said softly, "How do you know about her? Do you know where she is?"

The woman sitting before her was silent for a moment. Then she said slowly. "I am your aunt, I was once Iolaire."

Seabhac stared at her in shock. After what seemed like an eternal silence, she whispered, "I have a cloak to return to you." Her aunt smiled and held up her hand. "I have no need of it, it is yours now."

Boandas was furious that he couldn't find the two women in the mountains, even with a group of five men, including Ciallach. They headed out into the mountains, but were blocked by the cliffs and steep drop-offs. They found no clues along the way. Then they saw two women hiking in the hills. As they approached they saw it was not Katika and Seabhac. After talking to the women for a moment they pretended to leave but assuming the women were heading for the caves of Ana, followed at a distance.

After a week of following the women, Boandas realized they were being led in a circle. It started to snow heavily, the women disappeared into a blizzard.

CHAPTER 23 – THE DRUID

I have made an assumption in this story that druids were a diverse group. They were serious in their study of nature and the gods and goddesses. They had all the difficulties that any other human groups have with religion.

There have been, in history, those who use religion to free themselves and others to explore the world within and around them. There have also been those who use religion to contain and control themselves and others. One comes from joy, the other from fear. When times are full of chaos and disorder the fear based, controlling religion becomes powerful.

My story has also assumed that Katika and Anaias were both initiated into a druid order of women. The cave of the daughters of Ana was like a college for women of the order. Were there women druids?

Philip Carr-Gomm assures us, "It is a common misperception of druidry that it is patriarchal. This came out of an eighteenth century revival, a neo-druid masonic movement. Both classical and Celtic accounts show that male and female druids existed. Celtic law gave equality to women – allowing them to choose their own husbands, divorce, own and inherit property, do battle and ascend to chieftainship."[33]

The problem of studying the druid beliefs and culture is the limited source material. We have quotes from Julius Caesar. We have the archeological analysis by Stuart Piggott. More recently, we have many writings, including Philip Carr-Gomm's.

The word Druid is *druidai* in Greek and *druidae* or *druides* in Latin. In old Irish texts druid is plural of *drui*. We don't know what the ancient people called themselves. As with so much of our written history, it comes from the vanquishing chroniclers. Scholars agree that it derives from 'one with knowledge of the oak'. If one knows the oak tree, one knows all trees. The oak symbolized ancient wisdom and strength.

According to Philip Carr-Gomm, there were three distinct groupings. He quotes Strabo in the Geographica, written at the end of the first century, "Among all the Gallic peoples, generally speaking, there are three sets of men who are held in exceptional honor: the bards, the vates and the druids. The bards are singers and poets, the vates are diviners and natural philosophers, and the druids, in addition to natural philosophy, study also moral philosophy."[34]

We can examine each of these groups. I will refer to each of them as a type of 'druid'.

The Bard – Diodorus Siculus in eight B. C. said, "And there are among them composers of verses whome they call Bards; these singing to instruments similar to a lyre, applaud some, while they vituperate others." Bards told the story of the people. A lot of training went into being a bard because they had to tell the story exactly as it had been handed down. It was said that it sometimes took twelve years to prepare as a bard.[35]

The Ovate – The ovates, or 'vates', understood the mysteries of death and rebirth, divining the future, conversing with the ancestors. The ovate needed to be able to travel through the realms of time. They believed in the cyclicity of life and believed in reincarnation.[36] This is the shaman of the druid orders.

Druid as Judge – Strabo in Geographica says: "The druids are considered the most just of men, and on this account they are entrusted with the decisions, not only of the private disputes, but the public disputes as well, so that, in former times, they ever arbitrated cases of war."[37]

Druid as Teacher – Caesar in De Bello Gallico describes them: "A great number of young men gather about them for the sake of instruction and hold them in great honor..."[38] Carr-Gomm states that some druids may have had one or two students living with them, others had what would amount to a college. Like monastic orders, the 'druid colleges' had a spectrum of education.[39] Torrida and Owain were teacher and student. The same is true of the women of the caves of Ana.

Druid as king and adviser to kings – they were the first to speak at official functions, no one had the right to speak before the druid had spoken. Boandas considered himself responsible for the royal family of Eogan.

Druid as scientist and inventor – there are accounts that the druids studied the stars and astrology. They certainly knew the seasons. There were those who did important work with fire and with metals. Fire and water are considered sacred to all druidry.

According to Carr-Gomm, 'The Welsh tradition states that a branch of druids, known as the Pherylit, worked as metallurgist and alchemists in the magical city of Emrya in Snowdonia. The Druid as metal-worker would have forged the swords for kings and nobles.[40]

CHAPTER 24 – EXPERIENCING THE GREENFIRE
EAST OF CYMRU – THE MOUNTAINS

"Even astronauts do not perceive the true solar colors. White is merely the retina's response to being bombarded by all the colors of the rainbow. Rather than debating the apparent color of the sun, we might be better off asking: 'Of all the colors in sunlight, which one does the sun emit most intensely?'
The answer shows up clearly in the spectrum cast by a prism of cut glass and in the arc of a natural rainbow. The brightest color is green, because green is where the sun's energy output is strongest." [41]

Seabhac spent the first few weeks learning about her aunt. Iolaire had wandered toward the mountains. She was found, by accident, by one of the sisters who was heading back to the caves. After her initiation, she had taken the name of light, Seallam.

Seabhac learned the routine of the place. Then she shared the loss of the oldest of the sisters.

Llakino died in her sleep. Drums beat steadily as the women gathered in the center meeting room of the cavern. The body of Llakino was wrapped in blue woolen cloth. It had been covered with herbs and oils. It would be taken to a room with an opening to the outside. It was called the traveling room. When her spirit had left the body, it would be given to the creatures, so that it could complete the cycle of creation.

They sat in a circle and spoke of her life. Each person who had a story, a memory, shared it with the others. They talked about her connection with them, with the earth, with the mind of Ana.

Seabhac remembered Llakino's words to her the night she arrived, "Live by these teachings and life and death will be sweet."

Seabhac was grateful when Seallam gave her a basket and told her to help work the gardens. The next morning she got up at the sound of the bells. She was excited about the new day.

One of the women, short with curly brown hair, brought her a bowl of cooked barley. She said, "Eat well, you'll need good food to do your day's work." They smiled at each other.

After eating, that same woman held out her hand. "Come, let's see the sky. I'm Luann, welcome. I'll introduce you to our gardens."

They headed out though a passageway that Seabhac had not noticed before.

They walked down the narrow hallway, single file. They went up a few steps and pushed aside a bush. She was assaulted by the brisk morning air. The sun had not yet come up. The brightness of the dawn was already affecting her eyes. She had grown accustomed to the darkness of the cave.

Luann said as she saw her squinting, "You'll notice that it is difficult to go in and out. Your eyes will learn to adjust quickly." Luann said, "It is good to come out before sunrise, so you can adjust with the birds."

They reached the edge of a cliff and began making the long journey down into the valley below. Seabhac could see the green rows of vegetables. They could see trees and a few grazing cattle.

They walked down a staircase. As the sun rose, they headed out to a field planted with oats, rye and barley, beans and fruits of all sorts.

Luann pointed toward the oats, "We harvest and tend these fields. First, we will harvest the morning plants. Then we will do whatever tending is necessary."

Luann said, "You'll get plenty of fresh air and blue sky now, and your body will remember how to sweat." She smiled.

"So this is why there's always enough food!" Seabhac looked around. "You've planted a beautiful garden."

"Thank you!" Luann blushed saying, "It seems to be my gift to make the plants want to bear their fruit."

"What a wonderful gift that is," Seabhac said.

"And yours will be to lead others," Luann responded.

"Why would you think that?" asked Seabhac.

"Because we've all seen you in a dream surrounded by people. They were looking to you for guidance." They continued plucking the grain. Luann wordlessly moved to the barley.

Seabhac said, "But I'd rather plant and harvest."

Laughing in a friendly way, Luann patted her. "So, here you are!" Then she turned away with a full load.

Seabhac asked, "Have you spent very much time here?"

"Years. For many of those years I've been seeking the vision of Ana," Luann answered.

Seabhac responded, "Seeking visions requires time and silence according to Seallam."

Luann was quiet for a moment, and then said, "Only through silence and vision can I understand the needs of all these creatures I care for. But I've always felt I needed to do something more."

"There are so many women here. Are they all seeking visions?" Seabhac changed the subject slightly.

"Yes. Some have come from very far away and may find visions on their journey. Some will go back to their villages and give their new wisdom back to their people. Some will go to new places. It will all unfold and surprise us," Luann said.

Luann talked as they worked. "Another gift of Ana is her daughter Bridey. The green of the plants is Bridey's fire. The plants need the fire of the sun to grow. The fire goes deep into the earth into the roots of the plants. Then we consume them and they give us energy to live. We know plants have the power to heal us. Which plant to use is a riddle given us by Ana. Her daughter, Bridey, whispers the solution to us."

"One plant may be poisonous. The plant next to it may be the cure." She busily picked herbs and sorted them. "Just listen to the spirit of the plant."

As they walked through the garden, they came to a stone enclosure. There was a bellow on the other side. Luann lifted the latch to a gate and went around the wall. There were two cows with three calves. Off in the distance Seabhac saw a lone bull. The calves pushed against her.

Luann laughed, "If you had joined me a month ago, you might have been a part of the birth of these fellows and the little girl. It was difficult when I realized one would have twins, especially as the cold season is coming soon." Luann left some of the grain for the cows. She pushed the calves away so she could get to the tits.

"She's filled with milk," said Luann. "Milk is the perfect gift of Bridey's fire. It keeps us strong."

The cow and her calves continued to bellow. "We must milk her quickly now or she'll become louder. There is more than enough milk for the little ones, and for us." Luann leaned down with a clay bowl, with a rope attached. She began to pump the tits until the milk started to spurt out. Seabhac watched her. She had done this a few times as a child, but these cows were larger than the ones at home.

Luann looked back to Seabhac. "Here, can you take her and fill this bowl while I take food to the poor lonely bull?" She gave the tit to Seahbac and stood for a moment watching Seabhac. When all seemed to be going well, Luann headed across the field.

When Luann returned, Seabhac had a full bucket. Delighted, Luann said, "There will be plenty of cheese this season."

Seeing her questioning look, Luann explained, "We are famous even among the Romans for our cheese. I will introduce you to our cheese maker."

They climbed back up to the cave entrance with the day's harvest. Seabhac felt satisfied by all she had learned and by the day outside. She had remembered how to sweat. It took several trips up the cliff-side to get all the produce and milk to the door of the cave. They piled it at the entrance.

By the entrance, Luann grabbed her. "Have you felt the fire of Ana that burns deep in the earth?"

Seabhac shook her head. Luann took her, along with one of the buckets of milk, through another entrance and down a cave passageway. They climbed down a wide stairway carved in the rock. The heat rose as they descended.

Luann whispered, "This is from the core of Ana's fire." When the heat became too intense, they paused. "We can't go further."

They turned to a room off to the side. Moira, the cheese maker, was waiting for them.

"What a good harvest!" she said when she saw the full bucket.

She poured the milk into empty pots. She dropped a mixture into it and stirred. There was a row of pots set in the room near the heat of the passageway. Moira took a bowl and ladled some soft cheese from one of the older pots. "This will be delicious tonight." she said, handing the bowl to Luann to take to the eating room.

Moira smiled at Seabhac, "Next week a group of us will go to the market, a week-long walk away, to exchange our cheese for other necessities that we need in this community."

Seabhac gasped, "Oh I'd love to go."

Luann touched her arm, saying, "Unfortunately you're in danger. If priest Boandas or any of his brothers saw you..."

There was silence. Seabhac forgot the danger outside of this community.

Then, it was time to prepare the gardens and the animals for the cold season. Seeds needed to be collected for replanting crops, when the earth warmed again. The cattle were guided to a protective shelter.

Seallam taught her that it is important to have a dormant season. All living things need to rest. Only then can new life explode into the world with the fire of Bride. Plants, animals and people all need to be silent for a time. Seabhac resisted the idea. She had experienced the cold season at home, but the sea air kept the earth from freezing. There was always plenty to do even then. She dreaded the time when the gardens would sleep. She dreaded silence.

She and Luann daily and carefully moved down the icy cliff to care for the animals. The plants, though, were asleep. It was in this season that the warmth of the cheese-makers room felt good. She visited Moira often.

Seallam's lessons turned to the spiritual discipline of silence in thought and action. During the dark, cold season, she said, human's should learn from the plants and animals. Be dormant and let your energy grow deep.

It had always been a hard season for Seabhac. She enjoyed the long sunny days and dreaded the short cold ones. At home there were always torches lit against the dark days. The homes were decorated with the trees and bushes that stayed green all year.

Some of the plants had bright red berries that decorated the doors of the huts. All this was to compensate for the long dark cold days. There were special stories told only at this time of year, saved for the times when everyone had to huddle around the fire for any warmth.

The cave was the same in some ways, but different. The greens were brought in, torches were lit all day, since the light rarely reached the cave openings. The warmth of the fire of Ana, though, kept the cave warm and cozy even when there was snow falling outside.

The women of the cave spent more time in silence, as if searching for some wisdom deep inside them.

After a few seemingly long months of darkness the season of new life exploded again into the world. The days were longer and finally it was the season of Bride.

The dormant seeds in the earth sprung forth with green shoots. Luann taught her how to plant the seeds and wait. They then watched them spout from the newly thawed ground. Trees suddenly came to life with leaves. They buzzed with the new life of insects. Birds of all sorts migrated through in crowds, landing in the trees, chatting noisily, planning nest building.

Luann was proud of her bee hives. She and Seabhac would set them near the fruit trees to help with pollination. They moved some to the upper meadows so they would make the honey from the flowers of Ana. She slept well after the hard physical labor.

The day of the full sun came and the women celebrated with a fire on the top of a nearby hill. The celebration lasted from full moon before to full moon after the longest day of the year.

The men of Pallas came to the hills surrounding the caves. They protected the women during the long warm months. They celebrated with honey-wine and dancing. They had to be careful not to gain attention. The place of the cave was best kept a secret.

Katika was disappointed, though, that Torrida and Owain were not able to make it to the caves this year. She had not heard from Torrida since their escape.

Boandas had been seen by several women on pilgrimage to the cave. They reported a druid who had lurked in the background and tried to follow them. He seemed to be alone in his search for the hidden caves of Ana. The women changed their route to confuse him.

Katika and Seallam did not tell Seabhac of the sightings. They decided it was better for her to learn the lessons of the daughters of Ana then dwell on the fear from the past.

The season of the sun turned again into the season of the harvest. They remembered the ancestors as all the sisters expressed gratitude for the fruits of the garden. Seabhac had been in the caves for one full year.

One morning she woke with intense anxiety. She felt a deep rumbling fear within her. It started in her stomach and crept up her back and down her arms. Of what was she afraid?

She went with Luann out into the fields, she hoped the work would calm her, but she could not shake the feeling. She wandered away from Luann into the orchard.

Beechna sat on a tree branch above her. She called out, "The fire of Ana is calling. That's the fear you feel. I've seen it before."

Her eyes grew big as she continued, "Ana Herself wants to talk to you. You must be important."

Beechna jumped down to the next branch. "You'll meet my cousins. I've told them about you. Sometimes they don't pay attention though."

She then jumped to a branch close to Seabhac's ear and whispered, "You must be careful, he is still searching for you. We've been trying to follow him."

Luann came up behind her. "There is a storm coming. We need to lead the cows into the grove for shelter." Seabhac stood up and headed out with Luann. Beechna became a sparrow and flew away.

The fear went with Seabhac. It was calling her. It was not about the storm or the cattle. Should she still be afraid of Boandas? She wondered about Beechna's words.

She had forgotten about Boandas during her months in the cave. Would he still be searching for her? A strange chill went through her body. She had never before thought of this beautiful garden as a place of danger. She wondered if Owain was in danger. She wondered if Owain, her dear friend, could ever come to her again.

Suddenly the rain started to fall. She saw a cow in the thicket. As she reached for her, the cow backed away. Seabhac looked up to see Beechna giggling.

"Help me, why don't you?"

"What a frightened cow! Wet cow!" Beechna taunted while dancing in the tree. Then she turned into a squirrel and jumped onto the back of the stuck cow. The cow's eyes opened wide and it sprung forward freeing itself from the thicket. The squirrel disappeared. Seabhac laughed as she grabbed the cow's halter and pulled it to dry safety.

Luann laughed, "Well, we've received enough of the god Lugh's laughter. You're sopping wet! We should go to the passageway of fire and get warm."

"Come on." Luann took her hand and took her back to the spot where the rocks were hot. They sat, talked, and laughed. Their clothing dried quickly.

Seabhac's curiosity grew as she came close to the fire in the center of Ana. She kept pausing at the passageway and felt the heat coming at her in waves. What was the source of the heat? What did Beechna mean about the fire of Ana calling to her?

Seallam had seen Seabhac gazing down the passageway. Today she approached her, "It is Ana's creative and destructive power. You must be strong enough to approach it. You must go with our direction." Seallam put her arm around her, "Maybe it is time for your initiation as our sister."

"Oh, I am ready to be a sister!" She gazed down the passageway, saying, "I'm not sure if I am ready to approach the power of Ana." Seabhac continued to feel the anxiety of the previous months.

"I think you're ready," Seallam said softly, "Come with me."

Seabhac followed her into the main room. Seallam gathered a pile of blankets and handed them to her, saying, "This is all you need."

Seallam then lit a torch from the main fire and led Seabhac down the passageway. A small carved out room was waiting. Seallam lit a fire in the corner of the room. She sat in silence. Seabhac placed a blanket on the straw mat in the other corner, and sat feeling the energy of the stillness.

After several minutes of silence, Seallam said, "You will learn to fight through the fear and sadness and anger that speaks from within you. You will learn to hear the strong voice of Ana. She is both fear and courage."

Amala brought in fruits, vegetables, bread and milk. Katika joined them with several other women, including Tinai and Moira.

Seallam continued, "Now your true initiation will begin. Turn to the deep darkness of the cavern. Discover the true fullness of the connection of Ana."

Tinai began to play her flute. It was a light tune. The women began to clap and sing softly about the journey.

Katika began to speak, "You will seek the mind of Ana. And when you find it, you will find us also, but you will see us as we truly are."

Amala spoke, "We will leave you here for a complete moon's cycle. Someone will come a few times each day to bring you food and to take care of your needs. Don't speak to us unless you have an emergency. We will not speak to you. It is more important that you speak to, and listen only to Ana now."

Seallam added, "We have all been through this time of entering Ana's mind and we know that you will emerge with great wisdom." She continued, "You will find that each time you have a question, you can go apart from others and find the same clarity that you will find in this moon cycle. It will be the beginning of all you are as a sister of Ana."

"Goodbye, good journey," each woman said as they left her. She was alone. There was a light in the room so that she could find all the gifts the women had left for her.

She was unsure what she was supposed to do now. There was warm tea in a cup by the fire. She tasted it. It was the soothing taste of the blue flower tea. She remembered the first time she had tasted it in the meadow on the way to the caves.

She sipped the tea and sat quietly and examined the gifts.

There were brilliant red flowers and sparkling stones. One stone was carved into the shape of a turtle, another into the shape of a bird. She was examining them as Seallam returned with a large hand-drum.

"I will launch you on your journey," Seallam said. She sat across from Seabhac and began to beat the drum slowly. Seabhac listened to the steady rhythm until it filled her thoughts.

Soon the drumming stopped and Seallam left her.

Seabhac heard the dripping of water in the room. Then she heard a rumbling. The rumbling became a voice. It barely sounded human as it hissed, "You will die."

There was silence. Fear gripped her.

This time the voice rumbled more loudly, "You will die"

"Who are you?" she whispered.

"You will die!" the voice kept repeating.

"Who are you?" she asked again, her voice wavering.

She could barely make out the whispered words. "You aren't brave enough to serve the goddess." the voice hissed, "You ran from Boandas. You are not brave enough to save yourself."

Seabhac pulled the blankets around her. She started shivering and curled herself into a ball. She fell into a deep sleep. Her dreams were filled with those same accusations and fears.

When she woke up, she did not know if it was night or day. The lamp was lit. Someone had left food. She was hungry. The bread was a heavy honey loaf, with coarse chewy grains. It tasted good. There was a jug of water.

"Thank you, Mother Ana, for your care," she whispered. She listened for the taunting voice but heard nothing.

She curled up on the mat again and slept. When she woke, the lamp was burned out. She tried to sleep but her head hurt.

It was dark in the room as she heard footsteps. Someone entered without a light. She could not see who it was. They left wordlessly. She could smell the warm oats and sweet honey they left. She felt her way to the food and ate in the darkness.

She began to remember her village in Cymru. She saw her sister Geanta and her mother coming to pick her up. It had been over a year since she had been home. She ached to be with her mother. Her aunts came in and began joking and laughing. The waves crashed on the shore.

She saw her father come in. A heavy cloud came over.

The scene shifted to her grandmother sitting before her with the red cape. Her grandmother said, glaring at her, "Be careful how you act. You must not bring shame on our family!"

Boandas appeared and pointed at her accusingly. He bellowed, "You have disgraced the family."

She turned to where her father was. He turned away. She felt sobs welling up from deep inside.

She decided to find happier thoughts and tried to picture Luann wandering in the gardens alone. She longed to be there with her. Then she imagined Boandas lurking on the far ridge above the gardens looking for her. Nothing felt safe. She curled up again in the darkness to try to sleep.

She heard footsteps coming toward her room. Suddenly there was light. Squinting, she looked toward the doorway.

Seallam stood there bathed in light from the lamp she carried. As she stepped into the room, the space was brilliant.

Seallam said sitting down on a cushion ready to talk, "So, what voices have you heard?" Seabhac was not sure she wanted to share the accusations and the shame. "You've heard the many voices within you. They make you afraid, don't they?"

"Yes, and sad," Seabhac replied quietly.

Seallam touched her hand. "You needed to experience that outer fear. Now you must go a deeper place. Let me lead you there." She began to drum again.

As she drummed, Seallam said, "You must go down deep into the earth. Your body would not survive there, but your spirit will."

Seabhac closed her eyes. She was breathing deeply. Her heart was now beating strongly and slowly. She could hear the thumping. She felt the blood flowing through her body. She felt the warmth within her.

All she heard was the drumming keeping time with her heartbeat.

She was moving down a passageway that was narrow and smelled like warm soil. It was as if she was without a body. The soil moved aside before her. She could see a red glow in the distance. She moved closer to the glow. It turned into a wall of fire. She felt a sharp pang of the fire burning her. She jumped and let out a cry.

She heard Seallam's voice saying, "Careful, little one. Simply explore, slowly and carefully. You may use the flame and not be hurt by it." She paused. "Let Ana see who you are in spirit," Seallam whispered.

In her imagination, Seabhac moved away from the molten red fire. She moved down another dark passageway that smelled of humus and soil. It was growing cooler. She could feel the molten core of the fire at her back.

"Look!" she heard a woman's voice say. It was no longer

Seallam's voice.

She saw before her the roots of the plants above. They intertwined beneath the ground. They glowed and sparkled. There seemed to be fire around them. There were colors: red, blue and yellow.

"This, daughter, is your task," she heard a voice say, "To know that this fire beneath the ground feeds the fire above the ground. This life brings life."

"Eat and grow wise." A shimmering figure stood before her holding a red root. Seabhac took it and bit into it. It tasted sweet. Suddenly Seabhac saw shimmering figures all around her.

"My soil heals and cleanses. It gives birth. See its fire. Only my daughters can see the fire. Through the soil you can be cleansed and strengthened."

Seabhac moved again through the earth. She came to a deep cavernous opening. She saw hundreds of Tywa, like Beechna. They were doing some sort of work; she could not recognize what they were doing. They were surrounded by a brilliant light. She could not tell the source. They smiled and waved as she continued to move beyond them.

She emerged into another huge underground room. She heard singing and chanting that seemed to come from the walls. She did not see any people.

The voice said, "These voices are lifting my energies to the surface. They have become part of my Mind."

She began to move up quickly and suddenly broke through the earth into the open air. She gasped for breath and spread her arms. Some force propelled her up into the sky. She looked down as she traveled quickly across the earth.

Below her, the earth was dry and sandy. She saw men and women below her with camels by their side. She kept moving. The earth became colder. Soon it was covered with ice. She was lifted up and seemed to fly across mountains until she emerged in a mountain temple. A bell was ringing. Next to it was a woman in robes on a windy mountainside.

She heard the chanting again. She felt herself flying down until the air around her became warm and wet. She emerged into a humid dark jungle. She heard songs in another sort of rhythm. Women were holding babies and singing together. Their feet were moving and their hands were clapping. Men were in the fields singing.

"Ana, who are they?" she whispered.

"They are your sisters and brothers, the creators."

She traveled across a sea to women in robes on a high rocky mountain. They were dressed in bright colors. Gold jewelry glimmered on their bodies. She saw a woman weaving in a field by her hut.

Then she shot straight up toward the stars. She traveled until the earth was tiny and blue. She moved past the planets and saw the light of an exploding star. The light of the star was so bright and the heat so intense, she seemed to disappear into it.

Suddenly, Seabhac was in the darkened room alone. She heard the drip of the water.

There was still a little light as the fire had burned down. The smell of incense was heavy in the air. She was overwhelmed by the number of sisters she had.

She knew she needed to keep the fire, in her body, alive. She was exhausted, even though she had not moved from this place.

She reached for the table and found the bread and a flask of fresh water. On the table were roots, parsnip and beets. She nibbled at them, remembering the vision and the fire that was in them.

She sat again and closed her eyes. The journey began again.

She found herself traveling down the passageway toward the molten rock.

It was so hot! She backed away. She heard a scream. It came from her.

A voice said, "This is life! Feel its heat!"

Seabhac backed away from it.

There was laughter all around her.

"Are you afraid!?" a voice said.

Unexpectedly, the fire engulfed her. She felt her body burning. She tried to scream. She could not breathe. "Seallam, Ana, save me!" she faintly heard herself cry.

Her spirit propelled her toward the intense heat. She was consumed by the fear. She saw swords coming at her. In the flame, she heard thunder. The face of Boandas appeared. A wild beast with horns came at her. Her fear was intense. She felt her body begin to burn. She looked down to see her hand turning to black char. The fire was all around her.

She pushed though the flame and the intense pain, determined to get through. She reminded herself that this was her spirit traveling. Her body was not destroyed. She pushed onward, away from the creatures. Suddenly she broke through the flame.

Rushing water swirled around her, cooling her body. An eddy brought her to an underground lagoon and a waterfall and ferns. She was exhausted but joyful.

A woman's voice said softly, "You are born." In front of her was a woman with long red-blonde hair and deep blue eyes. Seabhac knew instantly that this was Bridey, the keeper of the fire.

Seabhac was in a large room of the cavern. It was very warm. She smelled the fragrance of flowers and the green plants. She was lying in a bed of ferns. Sunlight was pouring through an opening in the rocks above. Steam came off the pool of water, heated gently by the fire of Ana.

She saw women in long robes wandering alone or gathering in groups. They had not seen her yet.

A familiar woman's voice said, "Congratulations, you made it into Ana's garden!" She turned to see Katika up the hill behind her. Katika was shimmering with light that seemed to emanate from her white gown. She signaled to the others who slowly wandered over.

Seallam was there, "You are a new woman. What name would you give yourself?"

Seabhac thought for a moment. "I'll call myself Anaias. I want to always remember I am a daughter of Ana."

One of them said, "Enjoy yourself here for the day, Anaias." Someone put a green blanket over her, woven of soft wool.

Was this a vision, or real? She drifted into a delicious sleep and woke up in the tiny room in the cave, covered with the green blanket.

Her visions continued until Seallam came to tell her that her initiation was almost complete.

She had been on her vision journey for a full moon cycle. She felt a deep sense of purpose and strength. She looked around the room in the dim light of the torch burning down. She pulled the green woolen blanket over her. She smiled and slept again. She felt a deep fire burning within her. The season of Bride was bringing life to the earth. The sisters would come soon, there would be a celebration.

IN THE HIGHER MOUNTAINS – TODAY'S SNOWDONIA:

Boandas was in despair. Caillach and the other Eogan men had deserted him when they first went after Seabhac. He had to turn back. The other brothers had also been frustrated in their ability to find youth for the ritual of renewal. The rains had come and the blight had gone away, but Boandas and the brothers knew this was just temporary. The gods and goddesses of the land were still angry.

His waking and sleeping dreams were about how he had been betrayed by Torrida and Katika. He would have his revenge. Maybe it would not be this year, but next. His brothers would not betray him, they acted together to purify the lands.

Boandas traveled north into the high snowy mountains. The season of Bride, the time of the quickening of life, was melting the snow on the mountains, causing raging streams and waterfalls where there would be none in a few months. The ground was soggy and he was cold. At night, in the distance, he could see a red glow against the sky. The fire melted the ore. His brother in Dag, Llocan, was growing in this skill.

As dawn came, he continued following the path that grew steeper than he had remembered. After a day, he began to hear the heavy pounding. Many people were required to pound the ore into the strong metal that would make a sword. In his younger years, he had been invited to join in the task; but now he merely watched. By evening, he came to the top of one ridge and started to make camp.

He was alarmed when two men with huge horses rode toward him. He jumped up with his tiny dagger held ominously. The men arrived at his side laughing. "Ah, brother Boandas! Have you seen such great horses? We found them wandering around the abandoned Roman garrison. These, with the swords Llocan is making for us, will scare anyone into right thinking."

Boandas was relieved and laughed, "If it isn't Broynas! You've made it here before me."

Broynas put out his hand, "Come with us brother, this horse has room for two."

Boandas nervously approached the huge animal. Broynas reached down and told him where to put his feet to be pulled up onto its back.

"Brother Boandas." The other man simply nodded to him. "We are glad you'll be with us."

"Brother Dignas, it is my fervent wish that we make the lands peaceful and fertile again," Boandas said as he settled near the horse's tail.

Suddenly both horses moved forward. First they trotted, and then sped up to a gallop. Boandas put his arms around Broynas hoping he would not be knocked off the back of the animal.

It was dark as they reached the metallurgy caves. The red glow filled the sky. Everything was covered with a black dust. A continuous pounding shook the air and the ground.

Llocan, a huge man, wearing a heavy woolen garment, with bare arms came to greet them. "You found Boandas. Good, we need more workers." Llocan helped them off the horses.

Llocan gave each of them a heavy garment including a leather shield. They entered the caves. The sound was deafening, the heat nearly unbearable. This was the land of Dag. In order to be a priest of Dag a man had to be able to withstand it. The heat led to a great transformation. They watched him take the red hot iron and hammer it into what looked like a blade.

Then he lead them outside, taking their protective garments, he said, "Come to my rooms and have dinner."

They left the noise and heat and walked down a path, over a stream and into a glade to his hut. It was quiet and cool. They entered the hut. A woman was stirring a pot of delicious smelling stew and two children were playing on the floor beside her.

As they sat on stools, she brought bowls of stew to each of them.

"Notice the pot and these bowls." Llocan said, "They are unlike any you have seen. They are iron. They are strong and able to take great heat." He enjoyed their appreciative gaze at the pot over the fire. "But the iron is nothing like it is after it has been heated and pounded by my workers. That is the iron of the finest swords."

Llocan slowly lifted a beautiful sleek sword and swung it in the air. It whistled as it swished near Boandas' head. He jumped.

"Just a view of these will bring our brothers and sisters back to following the way of Dagda," Llocan laughed.

CHAPTER 25 – PATRICK, AGAIN
THE WESTERN MEDITERRANEAN COAST, POSSIBLY NEAR MARSEILLE, FRANCE

The sailors who had rescued him made their way to a coastline by a sea whose waters were silken. Patrick wanted to stay as far away from his captors in Ireland as he could. The seaport seemed to have an abundance of fish. There were gardens on the cliff side. Patrick's plan was to stay until the God of Christ Jesus called him to move on.

The peace did not last very long. The village was invaded by Goths on their way to Spain. Once again Patrick found himself bound and blindfolded in a cart heading to an unknown location. He could feel the bruises and he could tell there was bleeding, but he did not think there were broken bones. He knew, though, in spite of his faith, prayers and fasting, he was a slave again.

"What have I done, Lord Almighty, to anger you again?"

An inner voice came to him. "You will be free in sixty days."

Paying attention to the voice, Patrick avoided despair about being captured twice in his young life.

He was once again put to keeping sheep, this time on a hillside in Spain.

Sure enough, after two months, the attention of his captors was turned elsewhere. He slipped away, down the hill and along the coast.

He collapsed by the shore. When he woke, there were two men in monk's robes standing over him. They spoke a foreign language. Seeing their robes he said in his best Latin, "I am a follower of Christ Jesus. Help me."

In Latin the monks responded, "Let us take you to safety."

They took him by boat to the monastery on the Island of Lerins off the coast of southern France.

CHAPTER 26 – PELAGIUS THE SNAKE
PALESTINE

It was a rare rainy April day in Palestine. Jerome was still causing trouble by spreading rumors about Pelagius, even accusing him of vandalizing his villa. Ridiculous! Pelagius admired the man's work but did not want any personal contact with him.

Pelagius had been cleared by Pope Zosimus. In fact he received a flow of letters congratulating him for 'living a blameless moral life and having an unimpeachable zeal for the cause of Christ.' Many letters recounted the standing ovation he had received because of his strong views on the grace of God. Paulus Orosius was silent now and had returned to Spain to write history. Pelagius reveled in the sound of the rain on his roof.

What he didn't know was that the African bishops had appealed the decision of Pope Zosimus to the Emperor Honorius. The emperor was impressed by all the attention and chose to overturn the Pope's ruling.

There was a knock on the door.

As he opened it he saw Caelestius, sopping wet and wide eyed. "Teacher!" was all he said as he collapsed into the room from exhaustion and hunger.

Pelagius pulled him inside the door and laid him on the bed. He went to the stove and made some porridge, like the kind that revived him in Britain.

Caelestius regained his strength enough to speak slowly, "The emperor...is against us."

Pelagius helped him, "Honorius?"

"They got to him," Caelestius cried out softly. "He has banned us both from Rome."

Pelagius thought for moment. He had not been in Rome for years, but this was serious. When the imperial arm crashes down on you, it is over. "But Pope Zosimus..."

"I received this, just before I fled to warn you..." Caelestius held out a crumpled paper. He explained, "The African bishops, the same ones who tried to excommunicate me, surrounded the emperor with their lies. The church apparently means nothing to them. The emperor has threatened Pope Zosimus. He has no choice...but to turn away from us."

Pelagius' heart began to thump as he took the paper. It was a summons from Pope Zosimus for Caelestius to appear before him to answer to new charges of heresy.

It was obvious what was happening. The bishops of Africa could not accept the ruling of Pope Zosimus and their rebuke by him. Had Augustine also been part of this power struggle? How would this action build up the church of Christ Jesus?

Weakly Pelagius tried to comfort his friend, "We'll find a way to change their minds."

Caelestius touched his arm, and with tears said, "It's too late. I'm going to Egypt. Please come with me. Save yourself. They mean to kill us."

Pelagius tried to hide his own fear by saying gently, "Stay with me a while. Let me at least get your strength back." For now, Pelagius knew, Jerusalem was safe.

Caelestius left for Egypt after a month.

Now Pelagius was alone. He began to write letters. There were at least eighteen bishops in Italy, including Julian, bishop of Eclanum in Campania who continued to support him.

By the middle of summer, it was obvious that Pope Zosimus, who had been so supportive of him, had been forced by the emperor to send a letter of excommunication. He had been banned from Rome, yet summoned to come from Rome. Going to Rome now would be suicide.

Sure enough, by Christmas the Pope had sent out a letter declaring that Pelagius and Caelestius had transgressed the central tenets of Christian doctrine of redemption. He not only excommunicated them but also sent a letter to Constantinople and the other major cities of the empire that any that supported or comforted them would also be excommunicated.

A priest in Bethlehem was the first to share the news with Pelagius. The old priest hugged Pelagius and wept as they shared mass together.

Pelagius went to his home and barred the door. For the first time in his life, he began to doubt the work he was doing. Maybe he should try to make it to Egypt. Caelestius had written that the bishop there has not accepted the Pope's letter. Pelagius had received an earlier letter from Isidore of Pelusium condemning the actions of Orosius. For now, that was the only safe place in the Mediterranean. He began to pack.

There was a knock at his door. He hesitated, but heard a woman's voice. "Pelagius are you in there? Please let us in."

As he unlatched and opened the door, he saw Melania and Paulina wrapped in their traveling shawls. Melania was carrying a huge satchel. "We've fled from Jerome. He was celebrating that the Synod of Jerusalem has banned you from all holy places. He went into a rage about my friendship with you."

Melania turned to Paulina. "I didn't feel that she was safe with Jerome. He is old and weak, but still has a temper. Demetrias has gone to live with her mother." Melania sat down at the table. "We must leave Palestine."

"You can't stay in my home tonight," he said gently. "If Jerome is angry with you now, he'll be angrier if the rumors tell him you're here. You know how the rumors travel."

"I don't plan on staying here with you!" Melania said tears streaming down her face. "Don't you understand? We are leaving with you."

"If I go into hiding, it will not be a place for two women." Pelagius felt fear rise up. "Egypt is my probable destination. I don't know how you would make it in Egypt."

Melania said brightly, "Could we go toward your home?"

"Britain?" Pelagius was shocked that she would think such a thing.

"Well, you have said it was lush and beautiful. I know God is calling us to go there. God is for certain telling us to leave here." Melania was said emphatically.

"It may be hard to get there," Pelagius said, his mind whirring with possibilities

"You said there were traders that could guide us." Melania looked determined.

He knew she was right. They would go to Britain.

CHAPTER 27 – IN SEARCH OF PELAGIUS

Anaias has said to me, "Even as I am a daughter of Ana, I am a follow of Christ Jesus; who I also called Rabboni Yesua. I was baptized before my family returned to Shreedrum. Bishop Patrick rejected my belief. I found, in my time, that the church is dangerous."

With these words, I started to search for an unnamed, unorthodox Christian missionary. A little research into the events of the 5th century led me to Pelagius.

Pelagius was excommunicated in around 418. Recent historians claim that he simply disappeared into the deserts of Egypt.

But his teaching suddenly appeared in Wales. There are arguments about the place of his birth. Some scholars, such as Heinrich Zimmer thought he was likely Irish since his teachings were so popular among the Irish. J.B. Bury suggested that Pelagius was "an Irishman who came from a family which had settled in western Britain." Another historian suggests that "Britain is by far the strongest candidate for the honour, if such it be...at different times the main contenders have emerged as the southwest, southeast, and north of England and, of course, Wales, that traditional stronghold of dissent." [42]

Historians shy away from traditions not backed up with factual proof. Because I am an intuitive historian I get to explore the stories. One tradition claims that rather than going into the Egyptian desert he ended his days as a wise man at the monastery of Bangor Yscoed near Caerleon, Wales. Another story even makes him a Professor of Cambridge University for years after his disappearance from the Mediterranean.[43] Other stories say that he traveled to Ireland, or an Irish settlement in south-west Britain.[44] These stories, rejected by academic historians, fit right into my 'intuitive history.'

Historians tend to 'jump on board' with one another. When an idea is rejected by the historical community it is then professionally dangerous for an academic historian to explore it. That was true with the idea that Pelagius may have returned to Britain. A more recent historian, though, admits, "From this standpoint there is nothing inherently impossible in the idea of a Pelagian influence ... in southwest Wales... If there was such an influence, then we should look for its source not on the continent but in Ireland, since there had long been a two-way traffic between Wales and Ireland."[45]

Pelagius could have been in Wales the place of Exile for the Eogan family. Anaias said he was.

Legend says that Aengus was the Eogan king who was baptized

by Patrick in the early 400's. Pelagius disappeared around 418. Aengus, Anaias (unnamed in history of course, as women tend to be) and Pelagius and Patrick all lived at about the same time. Time and dates were not recorded as accurately as they are today, so we can play with the dates.

If Pelagius was not in Britain why was there such an excitement about his beliefs in that region? Why was the hatred of him centered on the regions on Wales and south West Britain? Venerable Bede, a sixth century historian claimed that the Briton Pelagius "spread far and wide his noxious and abominable teaching that man had no need of God's grace."[46] Venerable Bede is vehement in his hatred of the Pelagian heresy in Britain. He said, "The Pelagian heresy...had seriously infected the faith of the British Church."[47] It might have been that missionaries brought his beliefs to Britain, but there is nothing like the preaching first-hand by a gifted teacher.

Most of what we know about Pelagius is from his arguments with Augustine.

He stood over against Augustine in the debate on the subject of original sin and free will. He stressed free will as a route to moral integrity. To him this was more important than espoused doctrine. Free will did not suggest a lack of God, it suggested a wonderful gift from God. Church tradition, though, has had little mercy on him or on his beliefs. Until recently, we have not heard his actual words. In the last century, scholars have found many of his letters tucked in with the writings of Augustine. Now we can know what he actually taught.

Up until the time of his condemnation, debate was lively and energizing around the Mediterranean. Pelagius, trained as a lawyer as well as a theologian, was a great debater. Pelagius believed that Adam's sin injured himself only, not the whole human race; that every child is born as free as Adam before the fall and can do right and keep God's commandments if he chooses. Some people, like Noah and Job, who lived before the time of Christ were sinless.[48] Love and compassion were an attributes available to humans because God, the creator, put it into us at creation. Many bishops and scholars at the time agreed with him and celebrated his views. For whatever reason debate was cut off and those outside the narrow belief system were accused of heresy.

Many of us, today, would face the same charge of heresy. The idea of 'original sin' does not fit with a concept of the loving God. Matthew Fox, in the creation spirituality tradition, says for many of us, "Saint Augustine said that Adam's sin was an original sin due to pride. I say no! It was not about pride. It was about {a lack of} creativity."[49] Pelagius talks about action and choice. Like Pelagius, Matthew Fox calls creation an 'original blessing'. From that blessing come other blessings including 'those we give our loved ones, and those we struggle to bring about by healing, celebration, and justice-making."[50] According to Pelagius and Matthew Fox we are given, at our birth, the ability to make choices that will lead to a more loving and compassionate human community.

He was accused of not believing in human's need for God's grace for salvation. He, though, said things like, "When he walked from village to village speaking to the ordinary people he met, Jesus did not ask people to accept high-flown doctrines. Instead he asked them to enter into a relationship with God. He told them that if they prayed to God as a loving father, God would fill them with wisdom and strength."[51]

Despite the charges that Pelagius didn't believe in grace his teachings seem to abound with it. For him grace allowed people to do works of love and compassion.

This heretic, Pelagius, argued with those who lived by the letter, not the heart, of scripture, "There are people who eat little, who live simply and who are celibate; yet show no love and compassion toward their neighbor."[52] To Pelagius Jesus' teachings were primarily about how you act toward others.

Rosemary Radford Ruether, the ecofeminist theologian, writes, "Pelagius was a Christian teacher who was primarily concerned with strengthening his students in their capacity to 'do good and avoid evil.' He grounded his anthropology in a firm affirmation of the essential goodness of human nature as 'image of God.'"[53] She continues, "Pelagius' teachings seemed quite unexceptional to most of the Eastern teachers of Christianity, according, as it did, with their own concepts of free will and of Christ as the renewer of creation."[54]

His condemnation in the western church was an overt decision to move away from lessons from Jesus to doctrines about Jesus. The church moved away from the 'sermon on the mount' and more toward the Pauline teachings.

Mary Aileen Schmiel gives further insights, "Pelagius came under Jerome's censure of...his peripatetic teaching methods and association with 'unclean types'." She quotes Jerome, "How can he claim any moral purity for himself, he who is in the midst of the crowd and a man of the people?"[55] Jerome criticizes Pelagius' many friendships with 'mere women' and he writes scornfully of the 'Amazons who attach themselves to the Celtic master.' The church was moving from an anthropology that accepted all people, to one with clear hierarchy and exclusion.

For centuries now, the adjective 'Pelagian' has been used to discredit theologians who want to talk about the importance of right action in the world over right doctrine. Great thinkers like John Cassian, Vincent of Lerins and Faustus of Riez in the fifth century, Erigena in the ninth, Alexander of Hales, Peter Abelard, Duns Scotus and Thomas Aquinas in the twelfth and thirteenth, William of Ockham in the fourteenth, Melanchthon and Arminius in the sixteenth, John Wesley in the eighteenth and Teilhard de Chardin in the twentieth have been condemned for being 'Pelagian.'[56] In the 20th century Reinhold Niebuhr saw Pelagians in every pew.[57]

As an intuitive historian, I want to look at Pelagius with new eyes. Looking at the smear of the centuries, what was he trying to say? Why did it seem dangerous to the theologians of his time? Why does he still seem dangerous to theologians of our time?

Once someone is labeled a saint or a heretic all discussion stops.

Patrick drove the snakes out of Ireland. Pelagius was called vile, a snake, a wicked deceiver.

It is interesting to me that the formative church, as it tried to set out its beliefs, gave us the Nicean Creed and the Apostle's creed. Neither one of those had a social justice component. Pelagius seemed to be deeply concerned about social justice, and the call from Jesus to ascribe to that and to care for the least of these.

The fourth century church, under Augustine and those who followed him, was kept busy narrowing down the tenets of the faith. To some, at the time, it seemed noble to restrict what could be considered right belief. For them right belief and purity went hand in hand. Their attempt, however, to seek purity in belief over compassion in action, led to an increasingly cruel approach to what was called 'heresy'. Seeking heretics became a obsession that was becoming increasingly violent.

To many on the outside looking in at Christianity during the 5th century the question might have been, "Why do they hate each other so much?"

CHAPTER 28 – WELCOME ANAIAS
IN HER WORDS
THE MOUNTAINS

My initiation as a daughter of Ana was complete.
The table was piled high with fruits, cheese, and bread. We all ate and laughed and talked.
Luann cried when she saw me. "Oh, I've missed you."
I said, hugging Luann, "I often imagined you in that garden and longed to be there."
Luann added, "The men are tending it now."
My heart beat faster as I asked, "Which men?"
Hearing the tone in my voice, Katika said, "Yes, Owain is here. Now they call him Papallas. He has been initiated into his order."
The women continued eating and talking. As they gathered around in the main hall for singing and playing instruments, I felt I had left someone behind. I would never be the same little girl who had arrived in the caves of Ana.
The women gathered around and with the dyes and needles renewed the colors on woman-body tattoos. They added the green spiral symbol of Ana. Tinai's flute and Seallam's drum played as my body received the colors.

Seallam called everyone to silence. She held a white shimmering gown.
She looked at me. "You have emerged from your initiation journey as a priestess of Ana." She touched my shoulder. "Because you have entered the mind of Ana you can stand before any destructive enemy and terrify them with your very life spirit. You have been through the fire and emerged unscathed. There is nothing for you to fear. Your name is no longer Seabhac for the hawk that flies only over this dimension of earth. Your name is Anaias. You are a daughter of the Goddess. With her, your spirit will fly the depths and heights of the divine and eternal one. You live now in the mind of Ana."
Several women took the white gown and put it on me. I felt the softness of the fabric as it glided over my skin.
"Welcome Anaias," said the women.
I bowed at their greeting and took a moment to dance in the great hall of the cave with my sisters. Awareness came over me that I didn't need to look back, but only forward.
Suddenly I remembered Owain, now Papallas, was in the

garden. As the women were eating, I slipped up the path to the cave exit to the outside.

I quickly ran down the cliff side stairs to the gardens below.

Papallas was on his knees working the ground. I approached him quietly and knelt beside him, getting my gown muddy. I reached for his hand.

Our eyes met. Papallas grinned.

"I am now Anaias, daughter of Ana. I need a companion. I would choose you, Papallas, son of Pallas."

Tears filled his eyes as he gazed into mine. He looked as though he would say something in response to me, but instead he reached over to me, put his hand behind my head, and kissed me gently on the lips.

The next day the women of the order of Ana and the men of the order of Pallas gathered around Papallas and me as they led us up the hill to a place set with a temporary tent and piled with food.

With everyone gathered around, Katika and Torrida led us in a ritual of companionship. Both Papallas and I dipped our fingers into the pot of honey offered us as a symbol of the sweet mystery of life. We stayed together on that hill, under that tent for an entire moon cycle as we discovered the depths and heights of our bodies and our souls.

The men stayed until long after the season of the full sun. We celebrated together and then Papallas, my partner, and Torrida left again. It was a good time for the ships to travel south.

With my new status as a priestess of Ana, I still followed Luann into the gardens and helped Moira with her tasks. I had lived in this community of Ana for two years. I forgot any dangers in the world outside. I only knew that Papallas was out there traveling the seas. He'd bring home many exciting stories.

The time of harvest came, and again the season of cold and dormancy.

They returned just as the earth was quickening with new life. It is the season of Bridey. She brings the green out of the gray and brown. She brings flowers and the flowers bring the bees. The bees bring the honey.

This year Katika announced that Papallas and I would bring in the season of the sun at the ancient center stones. Katika and Torrida would present us to the council of druids. The preparations began as the new moon before the full sun began to show itself.

The journey to the great stone circle would take several weeks.

CHAPTER 29 – THE STONE CIRCLE GATHERING
SALISBURY PLAIN – STONEHENGE

"They have many discussions about the stars and their movement, the size of the universe and of the earth, the order of nature, the strength and the powers of the immortal gods, and they hand down their lore to the young men."[58]

After the long journey through the marshes, Anaias and Papallas, Katika and Torrida arrived on the shore. They joined the crowd of druid celebrants for the walk to the large stone circle.

As they walked, the crowd grew larger. People were arriving from hundreds of miles around. They were coming from the continent as well as the northern regions of Britain.

Occasionally Katika would wave at someone, who would wave back. Torrida would see someone and run over and slap him on the back. They would embrace, talk for a few minutes. Then Torrida returned to Katika saying only a word or two.

Anaias and Papallas knew none of these people, but were overwhelmed by the numbers of brothers and sisters of the sacred orders.

Suddenly, out of the mist, the huge stone circle emerged before them.

"Oh!" Anaias said involuntarily.

Papallas smiled and took her hand as they walked with the crowd.

Katika turned to Anaias, sensing her excitement. "The stones seem alive, don't they?"

Torrida said as he slowed to walk next to them, "And when you actually walk on the ground around them you will feel the power of all the gods and goddesses of the world." He added, "Such a feeling is only available to those who have studied, as you have, to be in the order." He stopped talking for a moment. He said softly, "Others would go mad, from the divine chaos."

"What is divine chaos?" Papallas asked. He had not heard his teacher use this term.

"With all the gods and goddesses, from all the lands, here together, their wisdom is greater than any human mind can absorb," Torrida responded.

"But the gods have the same truth, don't they?" Papallas questioned.

"Maybe they do, but it is sometimes not obvious. We memorize the prayers, rituals and visions of one god. Another god has different rituals, is it the same truth?" He looked at Papallas. "There are some gods who no person has yet discovered. That god is here, whether we know that god or not. Some of us want to continue discovering new gods and goddesses. Some of us are afraid of that."

They were silent as they pondered this possibility. Anaias gazed at the stones before them.

Beechna, Rodnic, and their cousins, crowds of Tywa, had arrived.

A dog Anaias had not seen before licked her hand. She noticed that many of those gathering had friendly dogs with them.

As they approached an outer circle far from the stones, a group of druid officers stood by the road. Katika and Torrida motioned to Anaias and Papallas to follow them, and walked over to one of them.

Katika spoke, "Anyllad, may the sun shine brightly! We have brought two who have just been initiated in the orders."

Anyllad was an older man, "Welcome to the celebration! Welcome brother and sister!" He looked like her father with bushy red hair. His eyes caught hers and held them for a moment. "You are needed in times like this." He extended his hands and took both of Anaias' hands in his. He continued to look into her eyes as though he were reading deeply.

Then he broke the stare and turned to Papallas. "And you, brother, I think we have met before!"

Torrida stepped up, "Yes, I have been taking him on journeys since he was quite young."

Anyllad said, "Ah yes, an eager young man, who will keep our trade routes open! It is good to see you Torrida! I've missed you at the new sun meetings."

"Do you know what the rumors are?" Anyllad said quietly to Torrida.

Torrida said, "I have heard some of them. We can talk later." He turned to Katika and took her hand.

Katika asked, "May we pass into the circle?"

Anyllad motioned them on, saying, "Go forth!' He stepped aside and moved his hand toward the stones in the distance in a sweeping gesture.

A man in white robes with a white beard came quickly toward them. As he got within talking distance, he opened his arms as if to embrace them all. "Ah yes! You are here! And you have brought the new ones."

Without embracing, as they had done with the others they met, they stopped before this man with reverence. Anaias had never seen such kind eyes gaze at her. As the man stood before them, a light seemed to surround them. Everyone around them became a blur.

His eyes stared into hers. "And this is the descendent of the ancient ones, I can tell." He bowed deeply to her. Tears came to her eyes. Why would he bow to her?

He then looked at Papallas, "You have an important charge here! You must keep her safe so she can do her work!"

Papallas seemed as stunned as she was at the friendliness of the arch-druid. "Yes," he said clearing his voice. "I am ready for the task." Papallas looked at Anaias and smiled shyly.

Torrida stepped forward and held his hands out. He said formally, "Hail, Cearnan, we come to celebrate."

Cearnan turned to him and to Katika next to him. He took both their hands, saying, "And so we shall celebrate the fullness of the sun. There is little to celebrate for some though."

Katika asked, "What do you hear from the south?"

"It is not good. There is famine. Too many people have pushed their way into the land. The trade routes have been broken. Many of our brothers and sisters are blaming the new gods and goddesses the strangers are bringing for the great hunger and the disease. Most of us simply want to decide how we can reopen the routes.

"The way by sea is still open," Papallas blurted out.

Cearnan gazing at him, responded, "Yes, you and your teacher and many others have been able to keep the routes open by sea and on the far southern routes. That gives us the supplies we need." He looked at Torrida and added, "It is the territories just out of range of your ships that suffer."

Cearnan motioned them on, concluding, "But we will have many sessions discussing these matters. Go now and enjoy the celebration."

They continued to move closer to the stones. The crowds of robed druids began to jostle one another.

"Seabhac, little one! Is that you?!"

She looked over to see Cormonthuc, the bard, with his harp, pushing through the crowd toward her. When he got to her, he carefully put the harp on the ground, opened his arms wide, and embraced her. Before she knew it, his lips were on hers and he kissed her.

Then he pulled back and looked at the dark eyes of Papallas. "Sorry lad, she is just so beautiful!" He put his hands out and grasped Papallas' hands. He added, jokingly, "So you are the one who has caused all the trouble for the Eogan clan."

Anaias was still recovering from the kiss and remembering all the feelings she had had for this bard as a child. She was overjoyed that he was standing before her now.

Cormonthuc said to Papallas, "I've heard your god takes you on merchant ships. We will be talking about places you have traveled. I need to hear some of your stories." He put his arm around him.

Papallas said, "Maybe we will find a place to talk tonight after the festivities have started."

"Yes!" Cormonthuc laughed, "If we haven't had too much honey-wine and ale." He smiled and began to look around. "I need to find stories for my songs."

Anaias looked at him longingly. He seemed to know what she wanted to ask, "Little one, we will talk. Your family was well last I saw. They miss you terribly, though your grandmother would not admit it. You should see Aengus; he has grown into quite a leader!' He picked up his harp and left them.

Anaias looked around for Katika and Torrida. They were at a distance talking with another man and woman. Anaias took Papallas' hand and they joined them.

"Ah, here they are," Torrida said. "I have been telling, Darida and Pacora about the two of you."

"Welcome, Anaias and Papallas," the man, Pacora, said in a thick accent. "We have come across the sea to be here." He laughed, "It will be good to eat well finally, and to have some good ale."

Darida said, "Katika tells me that you, Anaias, have studied to be a healer. She says that you, though, will have the power to advise kings."

Anaias responded, "If we ever return, I suppose I can advise my uncle, should he ask." Then she looked embarrassed. "But it may be that I'll never see my family again."

Darida looked at Katika and spoke angrily, "I suppose it is Boandas and his group that makes her doubt herself!"

Katika spoke, "Yes, he's threatened her. He even chased us, trying to find the cave of Ana."

Darida threw her hands into the air. "How terrible! How does he have the right to interfere with his sisters?! How does he have the right to interfere with the goddess?!"

Pacora interjected, "He and those around him seem to think they know the gods and goddesses personally, and the rest of us don't know them at all."

A familiar booming voice came from behind, "Ah, there you are. The little hawk." The group snapped to attention, turning toward the voice.

Boandas stood, smiling,

"Good to see you brother and sister from Gaul," Boandas said to Darida and Pacora. He continued, "You have met the little girl who kept falling down cliffs, and couldn't seem to stop her flights of fancy."

He smiled at Anaias, saying teasingly, "I am surprised that

you've been admitted to the company of the druids."

Ignoring everyone else, he looked into her eyes. She blinked and turned away.

He came closer, saying softly to her, "We will talk about your failures before the festivities are through."

As he disappeared into the crowd, she remembered the fire of the cave and tried to bring forth her courage.

The six of them now moved toward the stones and reached the outer circle.

Anaias and Papallas both reached out to touch one of the stones to feel its power. They grinned at each other. They were filled with wonder at being in this place.

A voice called from the very center of the stones, "Gods, goddesses! Brothers, sisters, ancient ones, those of all races come!"

It was Cearnan. He was standing on a large center stone. Next to him was his companion. She had long, dark curly hair with flecks of grey. She lifted a cup. She spoke the ancient language of the high order druids. Lights seem to flicker around her. In the crowd, drums started beating. Someone began to play a flute. Several others joined in. Others clapped. At first, it was chaos with everyone playing their own tune and rhythm, as Torrida had warned. Then they created one rhythm and tune together. For several minutes the music flowed over them and through them.

Anaias looked around her and where she thought Papallas was standing she saw a bright light, and within that light, she saw a tall red-blonde woman in a light blue robe. The woman was clapping and swaying with the music. She turned and looked at Anaias. Their eyes met. Anaias felt herself pulled into the deep blue eyes. The woman seemed to be saying something that Anaias could not understand. Then she smiled, and put her finger over her lips and faded away. Anaias felt dizzy for a moment.

Papallas was standing where the woman had stood. Looking over to her, he took her hand.

The music stopped. Cearnan and his companion each took a drink from the cup. The cup was offered to whoever wanted to speak. A druid stepped onto the stone and took a drink from the cup. He spoke in an unfamiliar language but seemed to be introducing himself. Then he offered the cup to a woman who also took a drink and introduced herself. The cup was offered from druid to druid. Each addressed the crowd. Katika grabbed Anaias' hand and pulled her through the crowd, toward the stone. Anaias felt fear. She remembered Katika pulling her into the forest, into the unknown. There was chaos around her and Katika was going to make her a part of it. She was afraid of standing before all of these wise people.

Holding Anaias' hand, Katika came close to the center stone. A man in a red robe jumped up to speak. "I am Corcran; I come from the far north. We were spoiled by Romans. We befriended them and they fed us and left us alone with our beliefs." Several booed. "But now they are gone." A cheer was heard. "As they have gone, we have grown hungry. Perhaps the generations before us were wrong to have joined with these people from the south. We forgot how to eat. We are learning to eat off the land again. The gods and goddesses of the land are growing stronger."

He handed the cup to Katika. She took it and jumped up on the stone. She took a sip from the cup. "You know me as Katika. I am a child of Cymru. I am a daughter of Ana." Many cheered. "In the caves of the mountains we see many visions. We see gods and goddesses of distant places. We see changes taking place. We can endure those changes." There was murmuring in the crowd. "I will introduce a new daughter of Ana. I believe she will be great in the midst of those changes. Come, Anaias, speak to all your brothers and sisters." Katika reached down for her and helped her onto the rock. She handed her the cup.

Anaias heard a thundering cheer and applause and a cheer from the back of the crowd, "Hail, Ana! Hail, Ana!"

She took a sip from the cup as she had seen others do. She tasted honey-wine smoother and sweeter than she had ever tasted before. All eyes were on her,

"I was born on the shores of Cymru but my people long to return to their lands in Eire." She paused, "I have recently been in the mountain cave of Ana where I received my initiation." She saw Papallas in the crowd. "My companion travels by the seas. I have traveled in spirit to distant places. All is well. The gods and goddesses celebrate. There is life. We need to seek it."

She lifted the cup and continued. "I long for the island that my people call home. I ask the goddess of that land to lead my people home safely."

Her eyes met Boandas' eyes. Someone yelled, "May we all find safety."

The crowd yelled, "Welcome, Anaias!"

As she stepped down from the stone, she saw Boandas reaching for her hand. She had no choice but to give it to him. She handed him the cup as she stepped down.

Boandas held up the cup of honey-wine as he jumped up, spilling some of it. As he stood, he sipped from the cup. "I come from the same shore that the young woman spoke of." His voice was gruff. "All is not going well. The gods are angry. There are those present who have caused that anger." There was booing.

He pulled a shining dagger from his cloak and lifted it. "We cannot ignore our gods and goddesses, and let others take their place."

He kept talking over the boos. "There is ruin before us unless we take action now." He lifted the cup. "In this gathering I will gain allies. Join me if you want to save our lands." The boos were deafening. There were also cheers.

The speeches went on throughout the afternoon. One of the last to speak was Torrida. He spoke of the sea routes and the health of the people he had met. He introduced Papallas who had little to say but his name. He seemed to want to pass the cup to someone else quickly to avoid speaking.

When they were done, Cormonthuc came and began to sing. Cups of honey-wine were offered to everyone, and that was replaced with ale. Food was brought out and shared by the travelers. Anaias and Papallas drank and laughed with the others and fell asleep wrapped in blankets they had brought in their satchel.

The dogs that had joined them came to eat scraps. They carefully avoided any of the meat. They curled up to sleep against the warm human bodies by the stones.

Anaias awakened to drums and a loud ringing of bells. There were shouts. "The Sun comes. Awaken! Greet him! Awaken! Bel come! Bel come." Bel was the ancient name of the sun in this region. The fullness of the sun was anticipated. The fires in the circle would now be lit. This would be followed by a lighting of fires in all the villages in the lands of the druids. Sentinels were on hills throughout the lands giving the signal for the lighting of those fires.

People began to move to the fires and cook their breakfast. Katika was busy at one of the fires. She saw Anaias and said, "Come, eat. It will be a busy day. Come, Papallas." Papallas was behind her looking as disheveled as Anaias felt.

They ate the oat porridge and drank the tea. Anaias began to awaken to the scene before her. She was overwhelmed by the number of people gathered, and all the languages spoken. She remembered that she had spoken to them last night

Suddenly the quiet of the morning was shattered. From the distant hill beyond the stone circle, they heard screaming and shouting.

Horses larger than any had seen before galloped over the hill with riders in white robes, carrying glimmering swords held high to glisten in the morning sun. They heard a booming voice shout, "The appeasers must die!" The riders disappeared over the hill. Everything was silent.

Torrida grabbed Papallas' arm. "That is the show of the Brothers of Fireantachd."

"Are we in danger? I believe Boandas was with them," Papallas responded.

"We've been in danger ever since we took you and Anaias in the night," Torrida said grimly. "I'm sure his hurt pride has translated into righteous anger." He turned toward their cookfire. Torrida snarled, "That one brother would threaten to injure another at these sacred stones is a sacrilege."

Papallas grimaced, "I think we need to continue watching Boandas. We're certainly appeasers to him."

Torrida laughed, "And you, young one, are the result of appeasement; which is why I'm for it."

The people gathered again at the stones. People were shouting the names of those they thought were on the horses. Cearnan called them to order. There was heated discussion about what to do in the various lands. There were theories on what it meant to accept new gods and new people. Boandas and the Brothers of Fireantachd were not present for the discussion.

Cearnan kept the discussion calm, even though voices were strained at the points of disagreement.

As the discussion continued, the horsemen appeared again on the horizon; but this time held their horses still, as if watching.

CHAPTER 30 – THE BROTHERS' RIDE AROUND STONEHENGE – DAY OF THE FULL SUN – OUR MONTH OF JUNE AROUND THE 21ST

That afternoon the druid brothers and sisters were preparing to return to their homes.

Suddenly horses plowed into the crowd. People began screaming and shouting.

There was chaos and surprise as horse hooves and people made contact.

Two dogs appeared and stood growling next to Anaias. The dog began to snarl and bark as one of the horsemen galloped toward her. She ran, but the horse followed her. Papallas, seeing what was happening ran to shield Anaias. Torrida also ran toward both of them and put his body between them and the horse.

As the horseman came down on them, the rider swung his sword down and struck Torrida's side.

"No-o-o!" Katika screamed as she saw her companion fall under the horse. She saw his blood spurting onto the ground.

The horseman turned around for another run. Suddenly the horse was surrounded by snarling dogs and a bright light. Through the light was an army of tall redheaded men guiding the horse away from Torrida. All around the stones was this same light surrounding each horse and rider.

The horses galloped away with dogs snarling at their heels.

As the dust settled, Anaias gasped to see Katika kneeling, covered with blood, holding Torrida on her lap.

Anaias tore a strip from her under-gown in hopes of stopping the bleeding. She ran over to Katika and Torrida.

Papallas was shouting, "We can save him. He taught me healing." He knelt down to check the wounds on Torrida and cried out. "Teacher!! I will save you! I will avenge you!" Tears began to stream down Papallas' face as he knelt over Torrida's body.

Katika held up one hand to stop them from offering aid. "There is nothing to be done. Let us have this moment," she said.

Torrida opened his mouth to speak, but could not. His eyes were trying to make a connection with Katika's.

Katika, covered with his blood, rested his head in her arms and kissed him.

"Good-bye for now, my love," he whispered, barely audibly.

"I'll follow soon," Katika whispered back.

The life went out of Torrida's body and Katika collapsed into it. Anaias embraced Katika. She saw what Katika had seen. The left side of the body had been crushed by the horse's hoofs. There was a deep gash, from the sword in his shoulder.

Papallas stood protectively watching for the riders return. Tears still streaming down his face, he cried, "I will destroy them!!"

Five other druid leaders lay bleeding on the ground around the stones.

Several of the friends of Katika and Torrida gathered around them and began to pray for the spirit of Torrida.

Cearnan, who had not been injured, though one horse had aimed for him, approached, "We were helped by the Tuatha de Danaan and by the little people; but not soon enough for this great leader."

Covered with blood, Katika stood up. She made a bow toward Cearnan.

"I will go to the island now. I'll take the shell of this man; who has my heart; with me."

Cearnan responded, "You are right that you must go. The Tuatha will be protecting you and all of the others who are grieving this day."

He had seen Darida also killed as well as Anyllad.

Cearnan turned to Papallas and gently said, "I believe they were aiming also for Anaias and for you. You must find safety. We will use the power of the gods and goddesses to stop the Brothers of Fireantachd. They have betrayed their oath of brotherhood and desecrated this holy ground. We will stop them. You leave the vengeance to us, and live for the work you are called to do." Cearnan extended his hand to Papallas who could barely stand for the weight of his grief at Torrida's death.

Katika embraced Anaias, who was stunned and crying.

Katika reached into her carrying bag and pulled out her jewel encrusted ritual cup. Anaias had remembered the times, as a child, that Katika used this cup to serve the holy honey-wine. She remembered how when it was lifted, the spirits of all the creatures around made it glisten. "This is yours now."

"I can't..." Anaias started to say, feeling she could never have the powers of Katika. She also realized what it meant that Katika was giving up the cup. Fear invaded her grief.

"Holy One, don't leave us," Anaias whimpered.

Katika, her teacher, suddenly looked very old, as if the life had left her as it had left Torrida.

Katika said softly, "You must find safety. I will go with Torrida.

You will not see me again in this life." She touched Anaias' hand, the one that held the cup. "You have extraordinary work to do. You must find safety now."

Several of their friends helped her prepare the body of Torrida for burial. They helped Katika put the body into one of the boats.

As Cearnan led the chant, the bodies of Torrida, Darida and Anyllad and the other bodies of those killed were placed into the boats. Katika and Pecora would accompany them to the island. The drumming and chanting grew louder. Papallas and Anaias became a part of it. An energy field formed around the grieving druids. The sky changed and a rainbow of colors swirled around them. The boats began to move on the water. Suddenly Anaias saw the island she had seen as a child. It was shining in the distance. The boat carrying the dead, and carrying Katika and Pecora moved toward it. In a flash, they all disappeared.

Anaias turned to Cearnan in shock, she whispered, "That island..." She stopped not knowing what more to say, but feeling a strange peace in the middle of her grief.

Cearnan, the arch-druid, smiled, saying softly to both Anaias and Papallas, "The island is in a realm of mystery. Only those who are invited can enter that realm. Katika and Pecora and the spirits of those who died are now safe, that we know. We also know that they can never again return to this place."

Cearnan blessed them and walked away slowly, bent over, like a man who was carrying a heavy burden.

CHAPTER 31 – THE REFUGE ON TODAY'S DEVON COAST

"Many other Christians came hither, especially into the Northern parts, and lands, with Saint Joseph of Aramathia besides them which continued with him at Glastenbury, and many of them married with Britans continuing Christianitie heare in their children and posteritie, untill the generall Conversion of Britaine." [59]

"When it was evening, there came a rich man from Arimathea, named Joseph, who also was a disciple of Jesus. He went to Pilate and asked for the body of Jesus. Then Pilate ordered it to be given to him. And Joseph took the body, and wrapped it in a clean linen shroud, and laid it in his own new tomb, which he had hewn in the rock; and he rolled a great stone to the door of the tomb. Mary Magdalene and the other Mary were there, sitting opposite the sepulchre." Matthew 27:57-61 [60]

The tide moved the boat out of the marshy region north of the stones.

Papallas and Anaias were exhausted and in shock by the closing events of the last days. They fell asleep as the boat drifted onto the muddy shoal and lodged against a flat rock. Two seagulls took the ride with them. A voice awakened them.

A man said in a thick accent, "Are you hurt?" Anaias and Papallas opened their eyes and tried to jump up but the soreness of their bodies kept them from moving quickly.

Seeing their fear, the man held his hand out to them. He talked slowly as though trying to find the words, "Don't move! We can help you."

He reached into a pack on his back. He set out a cloth on the rock and piled food on it. "Here is bread. I have apples. There is cheese. We have dried some fish."

Papallas spoke first, "Thank you for your help."

Papallas took some of the bread. It was flat and chewy. It reminded him of the bread he purchased in Rome. He looked at the man's dark eyes and dark curly hair.

Papallas asked, "Are you a stranger here?"

The man pointed up the hill. "I am Jacob. I was born nearby." There was a stone stairway that led to the top of the cliff.

Anaias reached over to the rock with the food. She took a piece of the apple. "Thank you," she said.

Jacob saw the blood on Papallas' cloak. "If you are injured, we have healers."

Papallas said, pointing north, "Our wounds will heal. We need help getting across the channel."

Jacob shook his head, "No, not for several hours, the tide is only coming in now. You cannot travel until the waters can pull you out."

He sighed and stood up. "I will get my sister Susanna. She can talk better than me."

Jacob climbed up the side of the cliff, using the staircase. The dawn was breaking. A wind was blowing from the sea.

Anaias and Papallas were exhausted from the grief and lack of sleep. They fell asleep again.

A woman's voice awakened them, "Hello, are you well?" Her accent was not as strong as her brother's was. "I am Susanna Miraham. My brother Jacob has told me that you are lost and maybe injured. I have brought a torch for fire to warm you while you wait for the tide to change." She lit a fire for them.

Anaias stood and extended her hand. Susanna Miraham took her hand in both of hers and smiled warmly. Susanna was tall with olive skin. She wore a dress of blue and a headscarf. Her dark curly hair flowed down her back.

She saw the blood on Papallas clothing. "You are in trouble?" she asked.

Anaias answered, "Some of our people were killed in a battle. I think we're safe now." Anaias felt a sob welling up as she spoke. She had not wanted to speak about yesterday and the death of Torrida and loss of Katika.

Susanna Miraham continued, "Do you have a place to go?"

"We do," Papallas said, without certainty.

"If you have lost your people, we have a safe place for you." Susanna looked back at Jacob who was returning down the hill with a collecting bucket for mussels. "Although we do not invite local people to come to our refuge, God has called us to invite you."

Anaias responded, "We thank you for your invitation. We need to go to the mountains across the water to tell them of the deaths." She wondered about Susanna Miraham's reference to a nameless god. These people did not seem to be followers of the druids. To what god were they referring? Maybe it was one of the invader gods Boandas was worried about.

Susanna looked saddened by the words. "I am so sorry at your sad task." She looked at their damp clothing. "Can we do anything for you while you wait for the tides?"

Papallas was silent for a moment, as if composing his next statement. Slowly, he said, "Would you let us return to this refuge, after our trip north?"

Anaias looked startled.

Papallas noticed her reaction and put his hand on her arm, saying, "It's not safe for my companion to return permanently to the mountains. She needs a safe place to live."

He said to Anaias, "I need to travel south on the merchant ship soon and you need to be safe." He paused, then added, "I trust these strangers. I have met people like them in the south. I think I have even brought some people fleeing from Rome to their refuge. They seem like strangers, but they are good people."

"Oh!" Jacob injected, "I knew I recognized you." He said smiling, "You are one of those on the ship that brings many of our refugees from the south." He frowned, "We have seen you often with the older man, the druid."

Papallas could barely speak, "That was Torrida, my teacher, who was killed."

"I am sorry," Jacob said softly. "More than ever we invite you to join our refuge until it is safe for you to travel on."

Susanna Miraham said, "The only thing we ask is that you tell no one about us. We have lived here for many generations only because few people know about our community."

"That's what keeps us safe," Jacob added.

"Why would you help strangers like us?" Anaias asked.

Susanna Miraham sat, eager to tell the story, "Because of the Rabboni Yesua. God shines through him. He taught us to help all people."

Susanna Miraham lifted her hand, saying, "The legend says that Rabboni Yesua had an uncle who was a merchant of tin. His name was Joseph from the town of Arimathia far south of here. He brought the child Yesua on a merchant trip with him. It was on this very spot that the ship was grounded. It was not unlike what happened to you. Theirs was a large ship that tipped over." She continued, "The local people recognized Joseph, and when they saw the child Yesua, they felt they were seeing a god. They brought them to safety."

Jacob added, "Joseph returned to the south with the child. When the Rabboni Yesua grew into manhood he taught people about God. He healed people, and told them to heal others. He taught that God was love. This message of love enraged the people in control. He was killed. He was nailed to boards and left to die. It is what the Roman Empire has done to people who anger them."

Papallas nodded, saying, "Yes, the Romans have been very cruel. We are glad they are leaving our lands."

Jacob continued, "This Joseph was there when he died and took him and buried him in a cave. Something wonderful happened though. Our God reached into that cave and brought Rabboni Yesua back to life.

He is with us now with a great and powerful love." Jacob blushed as he grew passionate in this story telling.

Susanna continued, "Rabboni Yesua's followers were threatened. Joseph rescued them by bringing many of the followers to live here. He brought many women, including the companion of Rabboni Yesua whose name was Miraham from Magda."

Jacob now took over the storytelling, "Then Joseph created this refuge on the moors, and hid us from the Romans. He was old, but Miraham was young and began to teach about Rabboni Yesua." He pointed to Susanna, "My sister and I are descendants of Joseph. We are distant cousins of the Rabboni Yesua. What we know about him, we know from Miraham of Magda. She told our ancestors how much he loved people and called all people to care for one another, even the stranger and the enemy," he said proudly.

Susanna Miraham added, "So we have kept this place open to those who need refuge." She looked skyward and lifted her hands. "Our God tells us who to invite. We invite you!"

Anaias listened to this story with fascination. She liked Susanna. She was different from any person she had met. She felt Ana's voice within her telling her that she needed to come to the refuge and live for a while.

Anaias responded, "We will return then, and try to be helpful in your refuge."

Jacob spoke to Papallas, "When you come, it is important that you come to the cove with this symbol." He drew the sign of a fish in the sand. "It will be carved into a wooden marker."

Susanna added, "Be careful in the cove as you land. The people who live on the hill above are wild and dangerous. Don't attract their attention."

Jacob continued, "Walk up the path by the river until you find the place of the meeting of two rivers. Follow the river to your right, up stream, until you find a large meadow there. Wait there until we come to guide you."

Papallas stood up and embraced Jacob. "Thank you, we don't know your god, but he gives us gifts. Thank him through your rituals." He stepped back. "We will return in a few weeks."

Jacob and Susanna left them and walked up the hill. Anaias and Papallas gratefully built up the fire. They set out their clothing to dry. Jacob had left a few mussels for them. They set them on the fire to cook and ate them in the shell. Papallas found a flask of ale in the boat. They drank to this new life, as strange as it might be.

They waited until the tide was high and loaded the boat. Anaias took the leftover bread, cheese, and fruit and tucked it into her cloak pocket. The outgoing tide took them quickly to the other side of the channel. Papallas was able to navigate them to the trail that would lead to the mountain caves.

They took several days to move up the steep path. When they came to the gardens of the cave, tears came into Anaias' eyes. She remembered the joy she had felt here. She had been so innocent. She huddled into Papallas arms and wept.

After a few moments, they climbed up the cliff-side. At the top, they were met by Seallam. She had been crying. "We have heard of the sorrow." She embraced Anaias. Then she took Papallas' hand.

Anaias spoke, "We can't stay. We wanted to tell you about Torrida and Katika. We wanted to say good-bye."

Seallam took both of Anaias hands, "Don't let fear stop you from the work you must do," she said fiercely.

Luann came out. "We were so worried about you, sister." She hugged Anaias.

Luann continued, "Moira, Tinai and I have been talking. Wherever you and Papallas go, we want to go with you."

Anaias stepped back and let go of her hands, "I can't let you leave the safety of the cave. You know what happened to Katika and Torrida. That may well happen to Papallas and me."

Luann stamped her foot, saying, "There's no room for argument. We're coming with you."

Papallas and Anaias spent the next few nights under the stars on the rocks above the cave. The sky was beautiful. They remembered the first night they spent together as companions. They made love, like that, under the stars.

They woke early in the morning and headed out with full supplies for a life on their own. Luann, Moira, and Tinai went with them. They were given two calves, male and female. A small dog also insisted on going with them.

CHAPTER 32 – IN SEARCH OF THE REFUGE
SEASIDE, CALIFORNIA – 1997

May 13 1997 – I took a year long sabbatical to pay complete attention to the unfolding of the story. I moved to a cottage in Seaside, California. I rented it from a writer who had gone off on a sailing ship around the world. He had a writing shed in the back yard. I spent my time there, listening, researching, taking long walks and writing. As a single woman I enjoyed the company of my mother, who has an ability to see the beauty in nature, wherever she looks. I also had a dog who loved to run on the beach while I walked and thought.

During the sabbatical I became co-chair of the Sierra Club chapter; intensely wanting to get out the word about the fragility and beauty of the planet earth. To make a little income to support my writing, I decided it would be fun to try my hand as a travel agent in a small office in Carmel, California. I discovered that I like to travel, not necessarily plan other people's trips. Very few people like to be surprised on their journeys. Surprise is what I look for. My kind of travel, as an intuitive historian was, and is, unique.

A new location had suddenly appeared in my story – the refuge of the Rabboni Yesua and Miraham. Could I find it geographically?
It was not just a geographical location, it was a cultural shift. This was a Jewish-Christian community. How would a Jewish community find it's way to Britain? What would the 5th century Jewish-Christian be like? What would they have believed?
Library research reminded me of the story of Joseph of Arimathea and the Holy Grail. Who was he, what did he believe? What would those around him have believed? In the first century the followers of Jesus still considered themselves Jewish. What would a group, separated from the influences of the early church formation of Rome and Greece be like? What would followers of Jesus, who had never heard the teaching of leaders like Paul, believe? What would followers of Jesus who heard the teachings of Mary Magdalene, rather than Peter, believe?

I got out my map of Britain and tacked it to the wall of the shed. I found an area along the Bristol Channel, close enough to the shores of Wales (Cymru) for a small boat to travel with the tides. I needed an area with high cliffs, coves and protection. The boat carrying Papallas and the women had come into a cove. On the cliff above was a war-like community. Anaias described the refuge as on a flat plain, between two rivers. Anaias and her group had come to a grassy meadow and camped next to a wide river.

As I looked on the map, I saw two possible locations on the edge of the Bristol Channel, Minehead to the north and Lynmouth further south. Both had rivers coming down from Exmoor and emptying into the bay. Both seemed to have cliffs and coves.

By this time, I was becoming confident that I would discover the location of the story she was telling. I was confident that I was actually doing 'intuitive history'. Since there is absolutely no historical legend of an early Christian refuge in the region, I was a little embarrassed to bring it up on my journey.

Again, I flew to London. Again, I left it open to Anaias to guide me on this journey. I had no reservations beyond London. I carried a backpack and a raincoat and new boots.

My first direction was decided as I emerged onto the platform for buses. One bus was leaving immediately for the Reading train station. Decided. But what train would I take?

As I stepped off the bus, a conductor yelled at me to hurry up if this was the train I wanted. It was going to Taunton. Decided.

Now I had to decide whether my destination was Minehead or Lynmouth. I asked the conductor if he knew about Minehead. He said he vacationed there once. It was crowded in summer. This was spring, it should be nice.

As I arrived in Taunton I had to make the decision, I was disoriented and suffering from jetlag. There would probably be more buses to Minehead. I wandered out to the bus stop with its many confusing signs. All of them said Minehead, none said Lynmouth.

While I was reading the signs, a bus driver approached me. "We've got a space in our commuter bus. If you're by yourself, we can take you. Are you going to Minehead or Lynmouth?"

"Um, I'm not sure which one I'm going to," I said. He didn't seem surprised by my indecision. "Well come on then. I'll see if my people can decide for you."

The bus driver told the bus riders my dilemma and asked for a show of hands. It was unanimous, I'd go to Lynmouth. They all agreed the town was hard to get to, and definitely worth seeing.

CHAPTER 33 – A SAFE PLACE
FROM THE MOUNTAINS OF CYMRU,
TODAY'S WALES, TO THE EXMOOR PLAIN

"St. Joseph of Aramathia, was dispatched... to introduce in the place of barbarous and bloody rites, long exercised by the bigotted and besotted druids, the meek and gentle system of Christianity."[61]

The heavy load slowed them down as they made their way down the trail. The small boat was waiting. They crowded the man, four women, two calves, the dog and belongings on-board. They waited for the tide to take them across the channel. Papallas guided the boat down the coast until they found the cove with the wooden sign of a fish.

They pulled the boat onto the beach. Papallas hid it in the bushes.

To the north, they made out huts on the hills above. They heard dogs barking but no people emerged. They saw a stone wall partway down the cliff.

"Let's get everything up the hill," said Papallas.

Anaias and the women helped Papallas haul their belongings up the steep sandstone path away from the huts. Anaias remembered Susanna's warnings. In a meadow surrounded by trees, they set up camp. They could now hear the sounds of children laughing.

They set out small stones in a small protective circle and built a fire in the center. Anaias blessed the area and invoked the name of Ana. She pulled from her pouch the blessing herbs and began to make a tea potion to protect them from dangers in this strange area. Two squirrels came down a tree to add their blessings.

She took a deep drink of the fresh stream water. The sun was warm and the water of the stream formed a pool that was inviting. Anaias took off her cloak and placed it on a rock. She then removed her undergown and dipped her brilliantly tattooed body into the water. The chill surprised her. The fresh flowing water felt wonderful on her body. Then Luann, Tinai and Moira, seeing her obvious delight, joined her. They splashed each other in the sunlight. Finally, Papallas jumped in, making a huge splash.

After the swim, Luann and the women went out to see what might be available in the way of herbs in this new land. Papallas went out to find game for an evening meal.

Later, Luann found Anaias by the fire. "It's wonderful. These people haven't harvested in this area recently. There is sweet grass and berries for dinner cakes tonight".

Moira exclaimed, "It's so beautiful here. The sun shines like a blessing."

"Well maybe," said Tinai. "I don't like being so close to those strangers."

Anaias felt uneasy too, "I agree, but these are risks we need to take in a new land."

"It's good you don't like them," Papallas added as he approached the fire. "They might, indeed, be dangerous."

Just then, the dog nuzzled Anaias. She was glad he would be guarding them. Certainly he would warn them with his barking.

Papallas laid a large rabbit carcass on the rock within the circle. It would be large enough to feed them all well. Anaias asked its spirit's forgiveness. Beechna, hidden in the trees was seething. She turned into a crow and squawked at them.

Moira prepared the rabbit. They would feast in this new land.

They had a glorious meal of roast rabbit and oatcakes with berries and cheese from the caves. They sang familiar songs and forgot, for a moment, the sorrow and fear that sent them to this place at the edge of a refuge of strangers, with a strange god.

Anaias stood up. "I'm going to bed. We have a long day tomorrow."

Papallas warned them, "We should take turns watching tonight. The dog will warn us if any strangers get curious. One of us, though, should be awake at all times."

The dog wagged its tail and looked up at Papallas with reverence. He smiled and patted his head.

Papallas would take the first watch. Anaias went into her tent alone. The night was filled with the sounds of frogs and the distant howl of the dogs from the nearby fort. Anaias shivered. The excitement of the day had worn her out. She fell asleep quickly.

After a few hours, Papallas came in. She reluctantly left the promise of his warm, ready body. She went into the cold damp unfamiliar night. The stars had come out. The moon was full and lit the trees around them. Silhouettes of strange rock formations appeared in the distance. The wind had stilled. The rain had not come. The night seemed wonderfully peaceful. The time went quickly. The moon moved closer to the west. Anaias went to Luann's tent to tell her that it was her turn at watch.

Anaias' cold body moved eagerly under the covers and met the warmth of the sleeping Papallas. She wrapped around him, feeling the wonder of his presence. He turned to her and embraced her in his muscular frame. They made love with a quiet passion.

The dog began to bark furiously. A scream tore through the night. Anaias and Papallas broke from a tight embrace and dashed out of the tent. Two figures were struggling by the fire. The dog continued his barking and was nipping at the intruder.

"Aneis git yog," Papallas shouted. The language was strange. The figure seemed to respond.

In the fire flicker, Anaias saw an adolescent boy with a knife to Tinai's throat. He had wrapped her hair around his hand and was using that to drag her. Seeing them startled him, but did not make him drop his prey.

Anaias lunged for him. The dog, snarling, jumped on him. As the boy ran to escape, he loosened his grip enough for Tinai to squirm away. Papallas slammed him with a fist across the ear. Papallas was careful not to seriously injure the boy. He wanted to send a message to the fort that this was an dangerous camp of strangers.

The boy disappeared into the woods, with the dog chasing him, barking wildly. They all decided to double the watch for the rest of the night. Dawn would not be far away now.

When they woke, they were surrounded by a foggy mist. They pulled their belongings up the path by a stream. By mid-day, they began to hear the thundering of water. They came to the place where two rivers met. The roar of the waters meeting was deafening and exhilarating. They sat and had lunch.

They followed the one river upstream and came to a clearing. The river was smooth and glassy but wide. On the opposite bank was a tree-covered hill.

"Make the circle here," said Papallas standing in the middle of the meadow.

Anaias was unsure. "There is a strange energy here, Papa. Do we want to sleep with it?"

"You are not used to being a stranger. I forgot about that," Papallas laughed. "That's my career. When you travel the land always seems strange. You learn new lessons from new lands."

Anaias looked around her and she felt the earth below her. She looked up and studied the sky for a moment. There was definitely a strange energy coming from this field.

"Okay," she said, "I'll try". She kissed him on the cheek.

They set the stones in a circle and made camp within it. Luann lit the fire and began to prepare the evening meal. They continued the evening with ancient songs and stories of Papallas' journeys. There was a rustling in the branches nearby. Only a slight breeze was evident.

They took turns guarding the encampment.

The next morning, Anaias got up as the sun was just rising but hidden by fog. The birds had just begun the morning song. She had not slept well. She felt darkness around her. The earth still did not speak to her. She felt a disturbing chaotic fear-filled energy. What was lurking in this land? In her sleep, she had seen shadowy figures and heard weeping and shouting in another language. Hands touched her shoulders. She jumped in terror and turned.

She saw Papallas' figure in the predawn darkness. "Why aren't you still sleeping?" he asked her.

"This isn't a land for sleep," Anaias spoke sharply, feeling her nerves frazzled. She felt Papallas' arm closing around her as they both looked across the river.

Papallas reminded Anaias that he could not join her in the refuge. He had work to do. He needed to make a last trading run now that it was time of the full sun. He was concerned about the changes that might have taken place. Some of the trade routes might be blocked. If ships were going, they would go now. He needed to catch one of them.

Papallas looked forward to seeing Rome when the weather was be warm and mild. He would have to travel alone, without Torrida. it would be strange to be without his teacher Torrida. It was his duty to go. At the druid gathering he heard a disturbing rumor that Rome had been invaded and strangers were controlling it. The ships might have more refugees to bring to this place.

Papallas built up the fire.

The fog lifted, the sun began to show itself, and Anaias began her morning chant and ritual.

Luann appeared from her tent looking disheveled and lost. She shuffled to the center of the stone circle and warmed herself in the fire Papallas had built.

"Bridey, warm our bodies," Luann said as she added a few twigs to the fire. She added, "Thank you Bridey for your gift of flame." Then she added branches to build the fire.

When the fire grew large enough, Moira made porridge with the addition of last night's berries. While it was cooking she and Tinai began to discuss how difficult the night had been. The meadow was hate-filled and damp. "I hope there is something better across the river," Tinai said.

They heard a woman's voice calling from the hill. It was an unfamiliar language. They saw two figures up the hill through the trees.

Anaias was relieved as she saw two women and three men emerge from the thicket and launch a raft.

It was time now to break camp. These would be their people. The first meeting was the most important. They were strangers with a strange tongue and strange customs. Ana was with her. She saw two squirrels watching the small raft from the streams edge, chattering to each other. She smiled. Her dog came and nuzzled her robes. His tail began to wag furiously.

The men used long poles to propel the raft across the river. The raft slowly made its way. The river was wide and moved slowly at this spot. The raft was catching the small amount of current. As it reached the shore, the men jumped into the shallow water and secured it by ropes to a post set in the riverbank.

Susanna Miraham, the woman who had met them on the beach over a week ago, stepped off the raft. The woman's eyes grew suddenly bright. She threw off her head covering and laughed in delight. "Sister!" she shouted. Susanna's accent was so strong that at first it seemed to be a foreign word, but Anaias recognized it was her language.

Susanna Miraham smiled at Anaias and put her arm around her. Lifting her other arm to signify a reason for celebration, she exclaimed, "She is here! Our sister! She has made it to us!" She then reached out for Luann, Moira and Tinai. "We now have more sisters." She turned and embraced each of them.

Nervously, Tinai helped put their belongings onto the raft. Moira tended the calves. Anaias sensed their reluctance to follow this woman with a strange accent.

Dogs were easier. He simply followed, wagging his tail. The squirrels changed into frogs and jumped on to the raft for the ride.

Before the launch, Papallas and Anaias embraced. He said, "I won't be crossing with you. I need to find a ship that is going south. I will return before the season changes."

She turned her eyes across the river to the unfamiliar community. She needed him to be here as she met these strangers. He understood strangers, how to be open and flowing with them. She knew Susanna was right, they were sisters, but it would be hard work getting to know her and her culture.

Anaias knew that she had to let him go, that was a part of their relationship. He followed Pallas, the god of the sea.

She said, "I only hope that Ana and Pallas have a reason for keeping us apart."

Papallas said nothing but kissed her lightly and pulled away from her reluctantly. She stepped onto the raft. He watched the crowded raft as it crossed the river. They climbed off the raft on the other side of the river and started the climb up the hill. They were now part of the refuge.

Susanna Miraham and Anaias began to talk.

"Did you sleep well in the meadow?" asked Susanna Miraham in broken Cymru.

"We couldn't sleep last night," Anaias responded slowly.

Susanna Miraham explained, "I suppose you saw the people. Some say they still walk this land. The tribes never come here, because they believe there is a curse. They call it 'crying meadow'. That is why we use it as a staging ground for our refugees. They won't be bothered."

She added, "Rabboni Yesua protects us all."

Susanna continued. "Even then, the curse is not meant for us. There was a massacre there. The spirits cry for vengeance. The curse is for the descendants on the hill you first camped by. Their great-grandfathers slaughtered many women and children in this meadow in order to conquer it and settle it. Now they are afraid of the land they conquered."

"We hope to never have to sleep there again," Anaias added.

"Good," Susanna Miraham said, "you will not have to sleep there. You are home here. Rabboni Yesua protects you." She said thoughtfully, "Most people are not so spiritually sensitive".

They continued pulling their belongings up the hill. Her dog trotted along beside her. Luann pulled the animals up the hill though they stopped to eat nearby branches. A dense forest was ahead of them. Anaias saw the men moving toward a barely visible trail that led through the brambles and disappeared into a forest of pine trees.

As they reached the top of the ridge, they suddenly came to a clearing. They were surrounded by giggling children. One of the little girls took Anaias' hand and looked into her eyes. Beyond the children she saw a crowd of fifty or more men and women. They applauded as Anaias and the women appeared up the hill.

Susanna Miraham took her by the arm. "They applaud for each one who makes it out of danger, to this refuge," she said.

They turned to a young woman with light brown hair. "Deidre speaks your language well. It will be easier to learn about us from her."

Deidre smiled shyly, "Hail, Anaias," she said with a slight bow. "We are glad you are here. We will make you welcome." She spoke with an accent similar to Papallas', "I will translate so you and teacher Susanna can talk."

"Thank you so much," said Anaias, relieved. She reached back to find Luann, saying, "This is Luann; I hope you will be friends. And here is Moira and Tinai."

"You are all welcome." Deidre said to them all. She suddenly seemed less shy. "I will show you where you can make your own home." She pointed up the hill. "We all have our own communities within one community."

Anaias followed her up the hill. She was sad to leave Susanna, who had disappeared into the crowd, but glad was she could relax with someone who understood their culture.

A new life was beginning. The clearing extended as far as the eye could see. They were on the top of a flat mountain. She could look down and see the ocean in the distance. The sun warmed them. There were purple, yellow, and red flowers painting the landscape.

As they walked, carrying their belongings and herding the animals, Deidre explained that she was from northern Cymru, "I learned about the Rabboni Yesua from my cousin Morgan, he called him Christ Jesus. It is the same wondrous teacher, whatever name you give." She continued to talk in a thick northern native accent. "He had become so intrigued with the teachings that he often talked to the Romans and traders." She looked out to the distant sea. "He disappeared on a ship like the ones your companion leaves on."

They found a clearing against a rock cliff. There was an oak grove on one side. "This can be your new home." Deidre pointed around her.

"Oh," said Luann with excitement. "The herbs here are so rich and lush!"

Deidre smiled, "The community, though they've lived in this land for hundreds of years, has been very careful about the use of the land. They will not overuse the growth of any one spot."

They put down their belongings and found a protected place to build the fire against a rock outcropping. Deidre continued to tell her story. "I became an outcast of my family because I spoke well of my cousin. The druid priests said I angered the goddess." She looked sad. "I was so scared."

"I ran away and traveled south for several days. Some kind people took me by boat to this side of the waters." Looking to the sky, "I tried praying to the goddesses of the place, but they did not answer." She continued, "Then I prayed to the Rabboni that my cousin had told me about. I kept walking. I was without food and near death. When I woke, Susanna Miraham was over me. She had food and water."

Deidre stopped talking for a moment as they helped Tinai with the tent.

She continued, "So I had found my way to this place between the rivers."

They set out a small stone circle around the encampment for protection. Each woman would have a tent. They set the tents within the circle. The dog set about marking each rock to declare his presence, two wrens began to sing above this new home. Tinai took the calves a little ways off to a good field for grazing.

As the sun reached a high point in the sky, Susanna Miraham approached. She invited them to an afternoon of feasting and celebrating.

All of the houses built by the people of the refuge had sharp corners and straight lines, rather than being round. They were like the Roman buildings, now ruins, that Anaias had seen. Anaias wondered what it was like to live in a home that wasn't round, it would seem uncomfortable and against nature.

As Anaias and Susanna approached the center of the community, there was music. Anaias thought that the rhythms of the singing were different, but pleasant. Someone played a stringed instrument and a flute. There was an instrument of clattering metal.

Hands reached out from a circle of people dancing; Luann, Moira and Tinai joined them; trying to move their feet like the others.

They ate and danced until they were exhausted. They slept well that night.

CHAPTER 34 – IN SEARCH OF THE REFUGE: EXMOOR, THE NORTHERN DEVON TOWN OF LYNMOUTH AND LYNTON – 1997

May 15 1997 – So there I was in Lynmouth, a beautiful seaside village with very few tourists. I found a b&b with a deep bathtub and skylight over it. As I soaked in the hot, soapy water, a warbler sang outside my window. I took a walk along the shoreline. For dinner I bought fish and chips from a seaside stand, I went back to the room and fell into a deep, jetlag sleep, missing breakfast the next morning. The hostess was aware I might, and saved some bread and butter and coffee for me.

Lynmouth is on the shore of Bristol Channel, with its extreme tides. The town of Lynton is a water-powered tram ride (or a stiff walk) up the side of a cliff. That morning I chose the tram.

The surprising discovery came in a museum in Lynton. An old guidebook there told a little known story of how Joseph of Arimathea and his grand-nephew, Jesus, ran aground on the cliffs near Lynmouth. The local people rescued them, then took them into their homes and fed them. This was the town. Jesus had walked here![62] It's just a legend, but then, it also fits into the story Anaias was telling me.

I talked to a few locals about a possible community in the fifth century. Even historical experts shrugged but told me about the story of Lorna Doone set in the Exmoor hills. The legend of King Arthur took place further south of Exmoor. There were stories of prehistoric villages. Nothing about the community in my story, except in the legend of Arimathea.

The town of Lynton is on the shore of the west Lyn River. The river became wide and meandering near a picnic area. There was a bridge leading to the other side of the river. Then a public foot path led me up the bank on the other side that was steep and wooded. I climbed up through the woods and suddenly came upon the wide expansive tableland of Exmoor, rising 1500 feet above the sea below. The public path took me through a sheep ranch. The sheep came to greet me, hoping I was going to feed them. There were old stone walls and a marker indicating a prehistoric village on the spot.

As I crossed the moors, the sun came out and I was able to look down to the Bristol Channel. If there had been a community here, the inhabitants could definitely see ships coming.

Walking to the other side of the moor you could also look out on a low flat landscape toward Glastonbury, thought to be the legendary Isle of Avalon of the King Arthur legends. Writings in the museum indicated that until recent times Bristol Channel had widened out into a tidal sea. There were tribes that lived there on islands traveling only by boat.

In ancient times, at high tide the sea would flood these lowlands. It would surround Glastonbury, the isle of Avalon, on the north. It lapped up onto the edge of the Salisbury Plain, several miles from Stonehenge. Today it has been drained for farmland and towns.

Standing on the heights of Exmoor I imagined that it might have been a very safe and hidden place for a refuge.

As I came down the other side, I heard the thundering of the waterfall. The east and west Lyn rivers came together in a little town called Watersmeet. There was a coffee house and park for lingering near the rapids.

The view from the trail became less scenic as it took me by the hydroelectric plant and back into the town of Lynmouth.

The next day I wandered along the coastline, through an area of strange rock formations in the middle of the sandstone cliffs called 'Valley of the Rocks.. I discovered a small cove just as Susanna had described it. It was sandy, with shrubs around. A high promontory next to the cove had a castle ruin on it. I sat in the cove and imagined Papallas, Anaias, Tinai, Moira and Luann with all the animals coming onto shore here with their small boat.

My time in Exmoor was done. I took a bus back to the town of Taunton to catch the train. The main church in Taunton was dedicated to Mary Magdalene. I didn't really expect much, but went inside. There was a statue of Mary Magdalene and a modern painting of her. I sat and prayed for a few moments.

May 20th, 1997 – I was curious about the Isle of Avalon, now Glastonbury. I wanted to find out more about the legend of Joseph of Arimathea. I took the train to Wells, then the bus to Glastonbury. Legend says that Joseph arrived in Glastonbury and founded a church 63 CE years after Jesus birth, or 30 years after his crucifixion. That would have made him a very old man. There would be nothing to have stopped him though, from coming earlier, as my story says, right after Jesus' death and resurrection with those fleeing for their lives.

He is said to have planted a thorn tree brought from Jerusalem on a hill. It is said to bloom every year on Christmas day. Even today people are invited to write prayers on cloth and tie the cloth to the thorn tree that is still on the historic spot. Legend tells us that Joseph also brought the cup Jesus used at the last supper, that had been once filled with the blood of the crucifixion. He threw it down a well. You can find the supposed well in the chalice garden. The waters of that well are healing. I filled a water bottle.

At the edge of the town is the magical Tor, or hill. Though there was constant rain and thunder, I climbed the long labyrinth path to the top. I listened for the fairies who are said to live and ring bells within the hollow hill. I didn't hear anything but my breath and heartbeat and the wind, as I climbed. I was drenched by the time I reached the top of the hill. Suddenly the clouds cleared and the sun came out. I explored the ruins of a church dedicated to Saint Michael. It had a stone carving of Bridey milking her traditional cow. I sat and looked at the view wondering at all the legends surrounding this sacred place.

Faith in the goddess is still very powerful in this place. It is said that the island is the very body of the goddess Ana. I walked gently.

The stories of Joseph of Arimathea, though discounted by historians, fit into my story. The legends say that Joseph of Arimathea, the man who gave his tomb for Jesus' body, came to Glastonbury after Jesus' death, escaping with several women. He was familiar with the area. As a tin merchant, legend says, he often brought family members with him, including Mary the mother of Jesus, his niece, and Jesus himself, his great nephew.

Was Mary Magdalene one of this group of women?

CHAPTER 35 – MIRAHAM OF MAGDA, TEACHER
THE REFUGE – TODAY'S EXMOOR PLAIN

"Jesus said to her, "Mary". She turned and said to him in Hebrew, "Rabboni" (which means Teacher)". John 20:16

"Miraham, thou blessed one, whom I will complete in all the mysteries of the heights, speak openly, thou art she whose heart is more directed to the Kingdom of Heaven than all thy brothers". Pistis Sophia Chapter 17[63]

Peter leapt forward, he said to Jesus: "My Lord, we are not able to suffer this woman who takes the opportunity from us, and does not allow anyone of us to speak, but she speaks many times"
Pistis Sophia, Chapter 36[64]

"It happened however when Jesus finished hearing these words which Mariam spoke, he said; "Excellent, Mariam, thou inheritor of the light"
Pistis Sophia Chapter 62[65]

"And they remembered his words, and returning from the tomb they told all this to the eleven and to all the rest. Now it was Mary Magdalene and Joanna and Mary the mother of James ... but these words seemed to them an idle tale, and they did not believe them."
Luke 24:8-11[66]

Susanna explained through Deidre, "Miraham of Magda had been silenced because women were not allowed to teach about God."

Anaias was surprised and responded, "But women are so close to the sacred. They give birth and know about life and its source."

Susanna continued, "But in the south it's true, women cannot teach men about God. Miraham of Magda had learned so much from Rabboni Yesua that people needed to learn. She gathered those, who would listen, around her, mostly women. When her life seemed to be in danger, Joseph brought her here with many others. Most of those who fled to this area were men and women who wanted to hear the teachings of Miraham. She eventually left us and traveled to the south to teach others about the Rabboni Yesua."

Anaias exclaimed, "So that's why your name has her name in it." She added "So was she a goddess?"

"No!" Susanna said, "She was a person just like us, a follower of the Rabboni Yesua. She was his best student."

She continued, "Then the Rabboni Yesua was killed by enemies, but the power of his life and love was so great that he came to life again. Miraham was the first to see him!"

Susanna continued, "So Miraham went to the others and told them. They didn't believe her. Since they refused to hear her explanation they were afraid and they ran and hid."

Anaias was trying to understand, "So they never knew the healing of your god?!"

Susanna Miraham said, looking at the ground, "They only knew because the Rabboni Yesua appeared to them alive." She paused, then continued, "If they hadn't had the rules about not listening to women they would have known sooner."

"After the Rabboni stopped appearing, the male followers became very angry every time Miraham spoke. They began telling lies about her. And this is why Miraham had to leave her land."

Susanna reached into her bag and brought out a scroll. "We have her words on these pages."

Anaias recoiled, "How can her words be there?"

Susanna was surprised, "Through writing. You don't have writing?"

Anaias was silent, and shook her head.

Susanna explained, "These marks on the paper are writing. Because of it we can remember the words of the ancient ones."

Anaias responded, "It seems dangerous to freeze words like that! In our world the druid, especially the bard, learns from the teacher. They spend years memorizing the words of our ancient ones."

"To us, it is good that we have writing. Some words we memorize. If our ancestors die without telling us, or if there is a disaster, we still have the words. The words remind us of the truth. I will tell you about the Torah."

"What is the Torah?" Anaias asked

"I will begin to read it to you." Susanna responded. "They are words about the relationship our people have had with God."

Just then Susanna's son and daughter appeared. The small girl and boy insisted on her attention.

Susanna laughed, "This is Mary and Mark, my children."

A tall light haired man walked into the room, "And this is my husband, David."

Anaias greeted these members of Susanna's family and excused herself.

Anaias returned to her camp. She would be interested in this thing called writing. It was amazing that sacred words could be captured on this thing called paper. She was sure Ana was blessing her curiosity.

Later that evening Deidre appeared, saying, "You are all invited to the ritual of the Rabboni. Come!"

They followed her.

As they approached the larger community, there seemed to be a strange cacophony of devotion. Men and women and children, sat in a circle with heads bowed, speaking prayers in many languages. It sounded like a familiar dream.

As Anaias and her women entered the circle, the prayers stopped. Everyone looked at Susanna.

Susanna stood in the middle of the circle. "Each family now wants to give an offering to our new community members." She turned to Anaias and the women and smiled. "Please receive our gifts of love."

Each family brought something forward and placed their gift in front of Anaias. There were several blankets, shawls, loaves of bread. apples, herbs and firewood piled up.

When they were done, Anaias said softly, "Why do you give us these things? We have given you nothing."

Susanna said, "You come in need, we give to you. The Rabboni Yesua taught this. This is the way we thank God, by giving to others."

Before Anaias and the women could thank them again, Susanna interrupted.

"But we are here to celebrate God's gift in the new moon! Susanna pointed to the sky at midday. The thin line of the moon was visible.

Deidre whispered to Anaias, "The moon reminds us of wisdom and our journey of growth. It is a good time for you sisters to start a life in a new place."

Anaias whispered back, "We also celebrate the moon as daughters of Ana."

Susanna called out, looking toward the moon, "Wisdom, come and speak. We dance to you!"

Several women began to rattle the unfamiliar musical instrument, called a tambourine. One woman and two men set the beat with drums. There were a few dozen men and women, young and old. They moved in a circle with arms outstretched.

The movement stopped the women lifted their arms to the moon. The women shouted,

"I am sent forth from the power."

Moving again, they chanted,

*"reflect upon me,
seek after me.*

*look upon me,
you hearers, hear me.*

The women repeated the words. The tambourines clattered. The drummers pounded with the sound of thunder. There was silence.

The women continued moving slowly in the inner circle chanting,

*"I am the silence that is mystery,
I am the idea that keeps recurring.
I am the voice whose sound is manifold
I am the word whose appearance is multiple.
I am the utterance of my name.*

The women were silent and stood still.

The men formed a circle and shouted,
"One power divided above and below,!"

Moving they chanted,
*"generating itself,
growing itself,
seeking itself,
finding itself,"*

The men repeated the words. Men and women together took hands and slowly moved in one circle:
*"being mother of itself,
father of itself
sister of itself,
spouse of itself,
daughter of itself,
son of itself,
mother, father unity,
being a source of the entire circle of existence.
We are one.
We are one.
We are one.
We are one..."*[67]

They kept beat around the circle. The steps were slow and measured. Anaias, Luann, Moira and Tinai danced with them trying to keep in step. In her family and among the sisters the dance would be wilder, freer. She remembered these were different people. Same moon, different dances, different god.

The next day Deidre came to the camp as the women were making breakfast. "We wanted to know if you are sleeping better."

"Very much better!" Luann exclaimed, remembering the sleepless nights on the journey here.

Deidre said, "Susanna would like to give you more knowledge of our God." They followed her to the central fire circle.

Susanna read the words from the paper she called the Torah. They were in a strange language. Then Susanna translated, telling them about the story of God guiding the people out of slavery in Egypt. They wandered in the desert. Susanna had to explain what a desert was.

Anaias and Luann couldn't help laughing at the thought of living in a hot place with no trees and few plants. Imagine having to eat the morning frost called manna? Susanna stressed that the God of the Rabboni pulled people out of danger.

Anaias was on guard about having this strange god pushed on her. Did they expect her to leave Ana for this god?

This was a god without enough to do. Ana had to care for the trees, the grass, the birds, the seasons, she didn't have time to worry about people who got themselves into trouble. She smiled, maybe a god who lives in sand is less busy.

Later she thought about the lessons. Maybe her goddess did lead her people in the same way as the god of the Torah. She thought about Danaa throughout the day, about the story of the migration of the Tuatha de Danaan. Danaa used the bees to lead them. She fed them honey, like the sweet Manna of the people in sand. Ana had led Anaias to this place. She felt that strongly.

That night she came to the ritual. The Torah was brought out in a case encrusted with jewels.

Jacob and the other men chanted to the stringed instrument, a little like Cormonthuc's harp. Deidre said it was called a Psalm. She translated the words for the women.

"Praise the Lord!
Praise the Lord form the heavens, praise him in the heights!
Praise him, all his angels, praise him, all his host!
Praise him sun and moon, praise him, all you shining stars!
Praise him, you highest heavens, and you waters above the heavens.
Praise the Lord from the earth, you sea monsters and all deeps, fire and hail, snow and frost, stormy wind fulfilling his command!
Mountains and all hills, fruit trees and add cedars! Beasts and all cattle, creeping things and flying birds!
Kings of the earth and all peoples, princes and all rulers of earth
Praise the Lord!"[68]

Then Susanna took a loaf and cup. She lifted the cup skyward and spoke in Hebrew.

Deidre whispered, "She thanks God for the fruit of the vine, for our life"

Susanna lifted the bread and spoke.

Deidre whispered, "She thanks God for the daily bread."

This reminded Anaias of the cup of honey-wine lifted at celebrations to call forth the sacred creatures. She was so excited she found herself standing as if to speak. Everyone looked at her. Suddenly she realized that she had gotten in the way and it was not her ritual. She sat down.

Each person was invited to eat the bread and drink the wine in thanks to God.

Anaias and the women had never tasted wine before. As Luann took a drink, she nearly spit it out from the bitter taste. Anaias took a moment before she tasted a different sort of sweetness.

Then Jacob spoke about Rabboni Yesua's teachings. Deidre tried to translate as he spoke. He said that the hardest word to translate was love.

It was the reason the group always welcomed new people. It was why they gave the gifts to Anaias and Luann, Moira and Tinai. Every week they gave gifts to someone who was sick or in need. Sometimes they even crossed the river "to the Gentile", that is, to the wild tribes near the cove.

As Anaias listened to Deidre's translation, she thought this love was ridiculously dangerous.

Jacob continued, "Here is what love is like. We all care for the child. Rabboni Yesua cares for us like we are children."

Anaias, wondered about this teaching. Was her beloved Ana here? She saw two ants crawling along the ground moving their antennae toward her in greeting. She smiled.

The lecture ended and Anaias and the women returned to their camp silently.

Anaias missed her community of women and the rituals to Ana. They were so familiar. She could do them without thinking. The rituals moved her toward Ana. Anaias was beginning to feel she did not belong with Deidre and Susanna, learning about this strange god of the desert sand.

She began to prepare the herbs that Luann had collected and placed in her tent. The smell was pungent. It took over her thoughts. She would be ready for any who needed healing in their body. Ana had given that gift to her.

As the months wore on, she and her women joined in the rituals and festivities of the camp. People came with many languages, and seemed to have one god but many opinions about that god. Anaias grew weary of the language differences.

The community seemed to be more interested in teaching her their language and about their god, than learning about hers. So much of who she was could only be spoken in her language. So much of who she was was expressed in her goddess. She was not willing to leave that behind.

Tinai began to spend time with one of the single men. He has apparently a recent refugee. She came back at night with more stories of the desert.

"Jeremiah said that Rabboni Yesua, who he calls Jesus the Christ, was killed because people were proclaiming him king of Israel," Tinai shared. "But after he was killed he came back to life. So Rabboni Yesua is a king of the universe, forever and ever!"

Luann appeared up the hill with a basket of apples. She sat with them as they continued talking. A cloud blew by, covering the sun for a moment and then moved on its way.

Anaias was interested. She asked, "He was a king? I wonder if he is like the kings and queens of the Tuatha de Danaan."

Luann speculated on this new religion, "Then would his companion, Miraham, be his queen?"

Anaias said thoughtfully, "The Tuatha de Danaan didn't die and return to life; they simply live long lives."

Tinai explained, "Jeremiah said that Rabboni Yesua is alive forever and can help anyone who asks with anything they need."

Anaias laughed, "Ah. If this king and queen could return us to Eire, I'd worship them as I do Ana." Then she realized this was exactly the thinking that made Boandas want to kill her.

A cold breeze blew across the moors. They pulled their cloaks tighter and clinging to each other for warmth ran toward the warmth of the fire. They laughed at their newfound understanding.

Moira cooked a dinner of roots and mussels. They enjoyed the savory flavors of the dinner together. Anaias watched the sparks of the night fire shoot into the sky. She thought about the sisters of Ana in the caves. She wondered if Torrida and Katika were together somewhere. She wondered if Papallas was warm somewhere at sea. She wondered if her family had heard word from Sheedrum.

As dawn broke the next morning, the skies were cloudy. Anaias walked to the edge of the moors. On the one side, she could see out to the bay she and Papallas had crossed. The other way was onto the endless rolling green hills and the ancient stone circle of the druid gathering. Her heart ached as she remembered the violence.

She turned back to the sea and wondered why her time of death had not yet come. The land of Eire waited. It was the land of her dreams.

"Oh, Ana, great one, allow me to live long enough to see my people restored to the throne of Sheedrum. If this new god can help, don't be angry at me for turning to him. Rabboni Yesua, the healer, and Miraham, the teacher; help us."

The winds began to blow and rain started to fall.

CHAPTER 36 – IN SEARCH OF THE FOLLOWERS OF MARY MAGDALENE

I've always been moved by the Resurrection story in the gospel according to John. Mary stays in the garden after the others have gone. She is weeping and she encounters one who she supposes is the gardener. It is Jesus. All he needs to say is her name and she recognizes him. In this story, Mary is obviously the first to know of the resurrection. She is a student. She refers to Jesus as Rabboni or teacher.[69]

The translation of the *Gospel of Mary*, from the *Nag Hammadi* texts, gives clues about Mary's position beside Jesus. It also gives clues about the beginning of problems for Mary of Magdala.

The disciples grieve at the huge and frightening task of preaching the gospel to the gentiles. They ask the question, "If they did not spare him, how will they spare us?"

Mary responds with comforting words, she says, "Do not weep, and do not grieve nor be irresolute, for his grace will be entirely with you and will protect you."

Then Peter says to Mary, "Sister, we know that the Savior loved you more than the rest of the women. Tell us the words of the Savior which you remember – which you know."

After Mary tells them, in words lost to us, because a part of the text is missing, Peter responds, "Did he really speak privately with a woman and not openly to us? Are we to turn about and all listen to her? Did he prefer her to us?"

The text then tells us that Mary wept at Peter's response. Levi comes to her defense in a startling admission, "Peter, you have always been hot-tempered. Now I see you contending against the woman like the adversaries. But if the Savior made her worthy, who are you indeed to reject her? Surely the Savior knows her very well. That is why he loved her more than us."[70]

More clues come from the *Sophia Pistis* [wisdom faith], discovered as a Coptic text, copied from a Greek text. It was probably written in the 1st or 2nd century but was not translated until the last century.

In it there are long conversations between the resurrected Jesus and the disciples. Continually, Mary, called Miraham, asks the questions. Jesus likes her questions. It means she has understood his teachings. He calls her, 'The inheritor of light.'[71]

Peter complains, "My Lord, we will not endure this woman, for she takes the opportunity from us and has let none of us speak, but she discourses many times.[72]

Jesus simply comforts him and asks him for his thoughts.

The *Gospel of Philip* also includes the sense of dissension. We read, "And the companion of the [savior is] Mary Magdalene. [But Christ loved] her more than [all] the disciples [and used to] kiss her [often] on her [mouth]. The rest of [the disciples were offended] by it [and expressed disapproval]. They said to him, 'Why do you love her more than all of us?' The Savior answered and said to them, 'Why do I not love you like her?'"[73]

Where did Mary Magdalene go after the ascension of Jesus? A strong tradition says that Mary Magdalene went to southern France.

As I've mentioned before, Joseph of Arimathia may have brought Mary Magdalene with him to Glastonbury.

Legend says that Mary Magdalene spent the last thirty-three years of her life preaching in southern France. She is said to have spent her last days in a large cave, called La Sainte-Baume in Provence, near Marseilles.

The merchant route to Britain started in the coastal regions of France around Marseilles in Provence. She might have traveled to Britain at some time in the thirty-three years of her ministry after Jesus' death.

Jesus was, in so many of his teachings, a revolutionary. His relationships with women were revolutionary. He may have formed a relationship with Mary Magdalene that was so surprising that we can't understand it, even today.

Her followers would certainly have been aware of the relationship, as they listened to her teachings about Jesus.

In writing this story I felt honored to simply indicate that there was an important and powerful relationship between Miraham of Magda and Rabboni Yesua, and that Miraham was a great teacher.

CHAPTER 37 – ANAIAS AND PELAGIUS MEET THE REFUGE

The rain-drenched earth was covered with mist, as she took her morning walk. She carried the basket in case she found any herbs for her collection. She knelt down at the stream that had just formed from the rain. She dipped her hand in it for the new water blessing. A squirrel chattered to her from an oak tree.

A voice boomed behind her, "Ani!" She jumped up and turned around. Papallas stood behind her grinning.

"Papa!" she shrieked and hugged him smothering him with kisses. She saw three people behind him.

One was a silver haired woman with her hair swept up on her head. She wore a blue gown and head covering like Susanna's. There was kindness in her eyes. Beside her was a very large man.

Papallas introduced them, "Anaias, daughter of the goddess Ana, may I present Melania of Rome and Pelagius, also know as Morgan."

Papallas extended his hands in presentation, bowing slightly between them. "I also present Melania's niece, Paulina."

Melania extended her hand. She spoke a foreign language, even different from Susanna's. Papallas was able to speak easily to Melania.

Papallas translated, "She says you are quite beautiful with a gentle spirit."

Anaias smiled and asked Papallas to thank her for the complement.

Without need for introduction, Pelagius-Morgan stepped forward.

He said in Cyrman, with a thick accent similar to Deidre's, "I am looking forward to hearing of your goddess." He took her hand in both of his huge hands and kissed it.

Her eyes met his. His were light blue with laughter in them. He added, "I hope you will also learn about my God."

The young woman, Paulina, hung back staring at Anaias warily, saying nothing.

Papallas continued, "Pelagius is Deidre's cousin. His local name is Morgan, but he changed it to be accepted by Rome." He turned toward Pelagius, saying, "He has been a great teacher in Rome."

Pelagius interrupted him, "Now I'm back home, after causing a bit of a debate among my friends in the south. I have come here to let them cool off."

He looked back at Anaias, saying, "And you, you are honored by your people as a holy woman. Have you heard enough of Christ Jesus?" He seemed serious now.

"I have heard of Rabboni Yesua and his companion Miraham," Anaias responded.

"Yes. He is the same person," Pelagius-Morgan said, smiling. "I'm tired now, but later, holy woman, talk to me of your goddess and I will talk to you of God."

He looked around, and asked, "Where's my cousin? I've heard she's here?"

Suddenly Deidre appeared at the top of the hill. She called out, "Is he here? Is he really here?"

Deidre ran over to Pelagius-Morgan. She stopped for moment, realizing that she did not really know him well, even though they were cousins.

She cried, "Morgan, I've longed to see you again."

Pelagius reached out to her and embraced her tenderly. "Where is our home? We need some food and some sleep."

They walked off together. Anaias noticed what a large man he was next to Deidre. Her hand seemed lost in his. Melania and Paulina followed them at a distance.

Anaias could not believe that Papallas was standing before her. He had kept his promise of arriving before the full change of seasons. The long warm days were not quite over. She had so much to tell him about the refuge and the work of Luann, Moira and Tinai.

As they approached the camp, Luann shrieked, "Papallas, you've actually come!"

The dog, jumped on him trying to lick his face."

Tinai said, "Here is some honeycake and tea."

"It's good to be home." Papallas sat down on a wooden bench. They ate together and drank the tea. He looked around, saying, "This looks like a home we can be happy in for a long time."

Anaias beamed with joy and leaned over whispering, "For a very long time. Until Eire calls."

He pulled her down to kiss her. Laughing, they rolled off the bench onto the ground. They moved into the hut. Throughout the afternoon they made long and passionate love. Afterwards Papallas fell asleep, exhausted from the journey.

He woke up several hours later. There was still time to give him a tour. Papallas was impressed with the round hut Anaias had built, with the help of the men in the community. It was not built of the materials that he and Torrida would have used, but it was adequate.

"We will need to add straw and mud to the walls before the cold season comes," he said, examining the room. Anaias appreciated his need to add his own touches. She knew she would lose him during the day to the group of men who enjoyed repairing and assisting each other in building.

She took him to the edge of the woods where she proudly showed him the hives that were humming with bees. This was the culmination of the honey harvesting. Together they tasted the product. Luann was collecting the honey, a little every day in the ceramic jars provided by Susanna. Jacob and Susanna would come by every few days to sample some of the sweetness. They were excited about having the expert beekeepers in the community.

With Moira, they went out into the fields and found that the two cows had joined a small herd. There was milk available from the older cows for drinking. Tinai also discovered the milk of goats. It was pungent. Moira did not have the heat of the caves to make the cheese of Ana, but Susanna and Jacob introduced her to the process of making cheese with goat's milk. Moira experimented with various methods of making cheeses.

The sun was lower in the sky and set earlier in the day. From now on, the days would be colder. The festival of harvest had been celebrated in her home village. Papallas and the women built a fire and sang some of the songs of their childhood. Luann had brewed honey-wine.

They stayed up late around the fire, talked, and laughed about times when they were young.

Before dawn, Papallas was awake. He woke Anaias with fresh brewed tea. He said, "Pelagius-Morgan was telling me how he used to catch salmon in the rivers when he was a boy. He said he would meet me on the edge of the community at daybreak." He kissed her sleepy forehead. "Would you want to join us?"

Anaias sleepily responded, "I've never gone fishing in a river. In my village it was only my father and brothers who caught the salmon and it was in the ocean."

Papallas laughed, "And now you are in the refuge and there are new rules. You can be the expert fisher-woman!"

Anaias jumped from the bed. "Well, okay, that sounds like fun." She pulled on her heavy cloak. She continued drinking her tea and waking up.

"Is there breakfast here?" Papallas and Anaias heard a laughing voice. Pelagius came into their camp ready for a day of adventure. They had pulled out a loaf of bread and cut him a piece. He ate it quickly.

Pelagius showed them the net on a pole. "I borrowed this from Latanai's husband."

They walked down the hill to the river.

"Talk to me of your gods and goddesses," Pelagius said as they walked down the hill.

Anaias, surprised by his direct question, answered, "There's much about Ana that a man would never understand."

"Then tell me only what you can," Pelagius responded.

"She is not one to be talked of, but to be experienced." Anaias tried to think how she would talk about Ana.

"Help me experience this Ana." Pelagius Morgan continued to push her.

She nervously began, "Ana is part of everything that you see here. She makes the grasses grow and the trees to drop their leaves. She makes the oaks grow strong. She makes certain herbs to heal us. That reminds us of her presence. When we do not honor her well enough, we become ill, or problems come into our communities."

They continued down the hill. "Sounds very fearful," he responded.

Anaias continued, "She can be if you don't pay attention. We need to learn her ways. We learn from the animals. Each creature has certain lessons to teach us. The bird can tell us that wings are nice for flight, but they must also risk all in building a nest on the ground or in a tree. A bird with newborn chicks cannot just fly away, but must protect the young. The wings are not for freedom but for the work of caring for the young."

She and Papallas sat by the river as Pelagius positioned himself to catch a salmon. Papallas held the basket to hold the fish they would catch.

Anaias began remembering, "When I was a child, I would climb down the side of the sandstone cliff to steal the eggs." She smiled at the memory. "Some nests you could get close to, but couldn't steal the eggs because the parent swooped in and attacked your hand."

Pelagius Morgan interjected, "That could be dangerous for a child hanging on with one hand"

"Yes, and that is the point," she said thoughtfully, "Other nests could be easily approached, and the eggs taken. Ana is protecting both; but requires the poor nest builder to pay the price."

"Like the person who doesn't take their responsibility to family seriously, versus the one who is willing to give up her life for family." Pelagius summed up what he thought she was saying.

"Yes, my Ana calls us to take responsibility for all our lives," Anaias said, appreciating his understanding.

She looked up to see Beechna sitting in the tree watching them. Beechna was yawning as if bored by the conversation.

"And then there are my ancestors." She looked at him as though her next words were very important. "The Tuatha De Danaan no longer live in the regular sense. They live as a magical race underground in another dimension. In humans though, only the blood exists. I am said to have some of the blood in my veins. Then there are the little people who live around us. Some of us see them and some of us do not."

He chuckled softly, saying, "Ah yes, I know the little people well from my childhood." Pelagius added, "In my part of the country we were only occasionally bothered by the tricks and practical jokes."

Just then, Pelagius pulled out a medium sized fish and placed it still leaping in the basket. He commented, "Christ Jesus said that we are all like fishermen. We are to catch people by telling them about God's love."

He talked as the net again waited in the water. Suddenly the net started to snap back. He reached in and pulled out another salmon. "Is this too small for us?" he said to them both.

"We take what we can get," said Papallas, holding a basket out to catch the fish.

"Christ Jesus said that too." Pelagius laughed uproariously at his own joke.

After catching a few more fish, they headed back up the hill.

CHAPTER 38 – ANAIAS' DREAM
THE REFUGE

The morning sun was glinting off the distant bay. Last night's dream had startled her. Two figures, a man and a woman, had appeared, surrounded by light. The woman said, "Don't be afraid." The man had simply extended his hand and said, "Come, follow me."

She woke up thinking about Pelagius. She needed to talk to him. Was this Miraham of Magda and Rabboni Yesua? Could they really come into her dreams? Why would they? They were the gods of strangers. Why would they care about her?

Her world was in chaos. She and Papallas still grieved for Katika and Torrida. With all the gods and goddesses there at the druid gathering, none had stopped Torrida's death. She and Papallas had talked about revenge.

Susanna had said that Miraham taught that all people were to forgive. Miraham had learned this from Rabboni Yesua. Anaias did not feel that Ana would call on her to forgive. Ana calls for balance and harmony. Sometimes that called for vengeance.

The world was changing for everyone. No doubt the lesser gods were as confused as the people they sometimes cared for. The people got little satisfaction or relief through their rituals. She understood the fear that filled Boandas' heart. Even though she felt he sought the wrong solution, preserving the stories of the gods and goddesses was what gave the people life.

Maybe Pelagius could help her with the dream. She walked close to his camp. Suddenly he emerged from one of the tents and looked in her direction. It was as if he sensed her presence.

Pelagius said softly, "Anaias, daughter of Ana! How good it is for you to come. Melania has made some cakes for the morning meal and you must be hungry."

"I am hungry, more for your thoughts than for food," Anaias responded.

She hesitated for a moment, then said, "There were so many gods and goddesses at the meeting of the druids. You bring new gods. I try to find wisdom but all I find is sleepless nights."

"Ani, stop troubling yourself with the crowd of gods and goddesses. It's not about what the name of your goddess is, or your god, it is about you and how you are living your life. Christ Jesus has told us we are to love God with all our heart and mind and strength and our neighbor as ourselves. Our God calls us to do something for love. We respond by living a different way because of that."

Anaias thought for a moment, then responded, "As a daughter of Ana, I live a different way from before I was initiated. I know that all creation is filled with the fire that is life. We are all interconnected in that life. We act toward each other with an awareness of the interconnection."

Pelagius responded, "Christ Jesus simply says to love, your neighbor, your enemy. I imagine the meaning behind this love is that we are all indeed one. The apostle, whom we call Paul, even tells us that we are one, not Jew or Gentile. . .maybe he would add. . .not daughter of Ana . . . not teacher of God's love in Christ Jesus, . . . not male or female. We are one."

Anaias softly shared, "I had a dream last night. Two figures appeared to me. One was a woman, like the Miraham of Susanna's lessons. The other seemed to be like a god, surrounded by light, I think he was Rabboni Yesua; the one you call Christ Jesus. In the dream he said, 'Follow me!' I've heard the stories of him and those he called who caught fish. Why would he say that to me?"

Pelagius felt tears coming into his eyes. "What a glorious dream! You are truly blessed. Christ Jesus calls us all to follow. We don't all have dreams like you had."

He looked lovingly at Anaias. "You are being called to live a life of love. If you follow Christ Jesus, Rabboni Yesua, he will enter your life, as he did your dream. We call it God's grace and with that you will find it easier than you ever imagined to live a life of love."

Anaias looked at her hands, daring not to look at Pelagius. She said quietly, "I live a life of what you call love as a follower of Ana."

"Yes you do," Pelagius responded. "I often said this to my students in Palestine. Those who are not followers of Christ Jesus often are tolerant, temperate, generous and kind. People with other gods and goddesses are able to reject the pleasures and honors of this world. Even they can chose the way of simplicity and humility. That is the teaching of Christ Jesus and is the way that Christians are called to act. It is also the way of human beings because God made you. He put goodness in your heart."

"Why then would I follow Christ Jesus?" Anaias asked softly.

He answered, "Ah, this was often part of my debates in Palestine. It is easier to do good when you are being touched by and led by Christ Jesus. We have free will to do good, or to do evil. The apostle Paul tells us that there is no power greater than the power of the God of Christ Jesus. When Christ Jesus is your Lord, there is a constant joy in your heart even when difficulty and danger surround you."

Anaias breathed deeply, as she collected her thoughts. "I've been told that I have an important task to perform. I was supposed to be with my family when they return to Eire. However, right now, I am here, in this refuge, hiding. I wonder if your God in Rabboni Yesua can guide me to take my people home."

Pelagius said seriously, "Pray to God and then do what you need to do. You know through your initiation that the world is complex. It is not only your desires and needs and decisions. There are many decisions being made right now connected to you and your family returning to Eire. You can trust that the God of Christ Jesus will be working with you for good, because of, over against, or in spite of the many other decisions people are making."

He was quiet as Anaias was gazing at him.

She responded, "I know through my visions that all life, humans and all creatures are connected like to a spider's web. If you touch one part, the shape of the web changes. It is hard to even imagine the complexity."

Pelagius said, "That's why it's so important for us to choose to do good. Good can change that spider's web of human decisions so that even evil can be transformed."

"How do I decide to follow your Christ Jesus?" she asked.

He answered, "You must first decide not to worship all these other spirits. The God of all creation, the God of Rabboni Yesua must be your only God."

Anaias responded, "But isn't it dangerous not to pay attention to the gods and goddesses of a certain place, a stream, a hill. They've sought revenge many times. Our local priest Boandas is always warning us of the danger of ignoring the local gods. Floods, storms and disease can come." She shuddered at the thought of angry gods and goddesses.

"Are these spirits really that powerful? As for the spirits of a place, you can recognize them and honor them, but it is different to worship them." Pelagius scratched his forehead and stroked his chin, then said, "The unseen force you acknowledge may be worthy of your attention. In the same way, you might pay attention to the time of sunrise or the migration of the birds. You might notice the planting of the particular crop in full sun and not during the cold season." He looked at her and made sure he had her attention.

She smiled, appreciating his point.

He said, "Attention, however, is not adoration." He lifted the water jug, saying, "Do you adore the river god of this region?"

Anaias shuddered at the thought of saying words that might be overheard by the mischievous little people around. "Not adore. Appreciation is a word I might use. Vigilance is perhaps more like it, especially after a heavy rain, as he decides whether to overflow his banks."

She looked up to the treetops. A hawk was flying. "I do however, adore the Mother, Ana. She has woven all things together. As a daughter of Ana, I and my sisters are called to watch over Ana's creation."

Melania brought the cakes and tea. Anaias automatically made the gesture of thanks, lifting her hands up and outward, a symbol of giving herself back to the One who gave this good food.

Pelagius bowed his head in thanks and began to eat the cake and drink the tea, dipping the cake into it as he ate. There was silence for a moment. "The gestures you made, are they to little gods?" he asked.

Startled at having to think through what she did automatically and without thought, Anaias stared at her lap for a moment, as if asking her hands what they did and why. "I did it for Ana, the Mother of all, the One who brings us this food"

"The one Mother?"

"Yes, Ana, who my people have worshiped. She has many names, she has been called Danaa. She brought my ancestors to the land of Eire. She protected my family in exile, helping us find shelter among strangers in Cymru." She looked at Pelagius waiting for his response.

He asked, "She is not like those little gods and goddesses we were talking about?".

"No! They are to be watched out for. . .and don't always have our best interest in mind. Ana is different."

Pelagius's eyes started to dance and he clapped his hands together. "So she is great. She is One?"

Anaias stared at him unsure whether to walk into his trap, "Absolutely, She is great."

"Would you want others to give their lives to her?" Pelagius asked enthusiastically

"I believe that others do worship the one I call Ana but may call Her by another name. They have their own divine ones, some are good, and some are not. I don't understand other people's gods and goddesses, and they don't understand mine." Anaias checked to see if this made sense to him. "At the gathering of the druids, there were many gods and goddesses, even gods with no worshipers."

"With all those gods and goddesses, could you drop your belief in your goddess and chose a better one?"

He continued, "A better way to ask might be, can you move beyond your Goddess?"

Anaias stopped. She was trying to catch the thoughts and implications floating in the air. Were we free to choose our gods and goddesses or did they choose and own us from our birth? She had chosen to be a priestess of Ana, but she hadn't chosen Ana. Ana would have been a part of her life even if she had stayed in her village and lived as her mother and sister did, keeping a home and having children. Ana, Danaa, Bridey, had just been a part of her birth, childhood and adult understanding of the world. Ana gave order to her world. Even thinking the name caused her to imagine the smell of a sweet flower, hear the buzzing of Her bees. It was healing to remember the stories of her ancestors and how Ana had led and protected them.

"Who would do that?" she asked. "Who would decide to leave the gods and goddesses of their childhood and accept a strange god belonging to other people?"

Pelagius stood up; his huge body lumbered a few steps away from her. He said emphatically, "I have left them." He was silent, "They were too small."

He looked at the ground, saying, "The people of the south worship a god without a name, an unknown god. It is a God of honor and logic and order." He paused, "And beauty and laughter and birth. Most importantly, the God of Christ Jesus is Love."

He concluded, "That God is neither male nor female. It may be that the one you call Ana, who calls you to love all creation, is also within the God of Christ Jesus."

She decided to change the subject. "Were we going to fish today? The salmon are running and I saw them in the water, they're big and fat." She laughed and stood up, extending her hand to him.

They walked together back to her camp. There was a scuffle of tiny feet and the sound of laughter. Maybe it was the gust of wind. The clouds were staccato against the brilliant blue sky. A lonely hawk was flying in circles a little way from where they walked. The dog was busy finding bugs below the rowan tree by the house. A squirrel was collecting acorns. A deer was foraging, well hidden from any roving eyes.

She and Pelagius went back to her camp where she found Papallas cutting wood. Together they all headed down to the river to try out their skills in catching salmon for dinner.

That evening they all sat around the central fire.

Papallas began to tell his story, "The merchant ship took me as far south as it could go. I then needed to travel overland. Torrida and I have made this trip together many times. I travel with the other merchants, but it is not the same as having a close friend with you. It is necessary to be vigilant. There are many robbers on the road now.

The grand estates that used to be along the way, with the servants that would welcome me into their homes, are abandoned. There are strangers, speaking strange tongues. I have found, though, that if you approach people in peace, they know it. So, I made my way."

Pelagius listened with interest, "It is through God's grace that you came to the seaport on the coast of Gaul when you did."

Papallas explained to everyone, "It was on my way back, after trading in Rome, that I was told through whispers that a family in the port town was looking for a merchant from Britain."

Pelagius said soberly, "We had made it as far as the outskirts of Rome. The emperor had banned me from the city, but I still had many friends there. It was in the winter that we started our journey. We couldn't go far over the mountains, so we stayed with friends for several months. When Spring came we started out again and made our way to the sea port in Gaul, well away from the danger of Rome. The God of Christ Jesus protected the three of us on our way."

Melania nodded thoughtfully, and added, "It has been a long journey."

Papallas continued, "So, I found them and led them by land across Gaul to the waiting ships."

Pelagius was silent. Everyone's attention was pulled toward him.

Jacob broke the silence. He said to Pelagius, "You seem less than jovial this evening?"

Pelagius responded, "I'm remembering the good days in Rome and Palestine."

Melania smiled, saying, "It can be a beautiful land. The buildings are huge and the ceremonies are beautiful. There are discussions, arguments, and parties. That is, there were until Christians began to turn on one another and threaten one another.

"They didn't turn on one another," Paulina interjected. "Father Jerome and Bishop Augustine are trying to protect the true faith, so we would not all burn in hell."

Melania responded, "There are many ways to understand the teachings of scripture that do not lead to hell, Paulina!' She was obviously embarrassed by Paulina's outburst.

Paulina sighed, "Father Jerome would disagree." She turned to Melania and whined, "I miss Father Jerome so much!"

Pelagius looked at Paulina and said, "We probably should not have brought you with us. Jerome might have continued being kind to you. He was not kind to your aunt, Melania, or to me."

Anaias responded perplexed, "I thought you said that followers of Christ Jesus, the Rabboni Yesua, were always kind and loving?"

Pelagius responded, "Oh, if it were only so easy. We work to love. Something in our nature wants to love others. In the same way something in our nature wants to hate others. The church, like every group of people, struggles with human nature."

Papallas added, "The church is like our clans. We quarrel with each other."

Melania added, "The quarrels in the church are worse. They are supposed to be followers of Christ Jesus who taught of love, but they try to destroy one another. I suppose they are trying to make up for the chaos around Rome, by building a tightly ordered, rigid system. They do it on the backs of good men like Pelagius."

Papallas said firmly, "We're glad you're here!"

Pelagius responded, "I thank you for the transportation through dangerous territory." He looked around saying with an ominous sound in his voice, "I don't know if my condemners will continue looking for me. I don't want to put all of you in danger." Pelagius Morgan took a sweeping looked each person in the firelight.

Papallas shook his head, "Even without your condemners, safety is not easy to come by. The world we have known is crumbling fast."

David said, "We are here to protect you, as we have protected people for generations. We accept the danger."

Jacob added, "It was the Roman empire that protected this refuge, even as they ignored us."

Papallas nodded, saying, "That protection is gone now. It's replaced with chaos and people moving, and being pushed out of their homes and moving again." He was silent, then continued, "Every time I go to the south I find new people, something different. Sometimes it is devastation. Sometimes it's new people eager to trade goods for food."

Pelagius stood up. Yawning he said, "And I believe God commands us to go to sleep now. Thank you all for listening."

He extended his hand to Melania. She took it and they walked off into the darkness toward Deidre's camp. Paulina, her arms still folded, followed at a distance.

As Pelagius and Melania walked off, Paulina turned around. She stopped for a moment and looked back at Anaias. She walked back and sat next to her in the circle.

Her accent was hard to understand but her tone was not, "If you want to know Christ Jesus you must not listen to Pelagius. His words will send you to a fiery hell."

Anaias engaged her, "In my initiation I went through the fire and survived. I do not know this word hell."

Paulina continued, "I need to warn you. You are in danger of hell now. It is a place of eternal torment and fire."

Paulina took her hand and held it tightly. Anaias winced at the tightness of her hold. Paulina looked at her intensely. "You must give up your gods and goddesses and all the rituals, they are demons, and they are evil. Let me be your teacher and you will find salvation."

Sensing a danger from Paulina more than from her words, Anaias said, "Thank you for your warning."

Then Anaias stretched her arms out and yawned then said gently, "We must sleep also. Good night, Paulina."

CHAPTER 39 – CHAOS: THE LATE EMPIRE AND THE BARBARIANS

Many of the doctrines of Christianity, born in the 5th century, came as a response to chaos, fear, and a need to find control in a world that seemed to be spiraling apart.

For unknown reasons, during the year 376 CE, the tribes living in the north beyond the Danube started to flood across the borders of the Roman Empire. They seemed to be fleeing from the Huns, the most terrible of the barbarian peoples. Why were the Huns in motion?
In south-eastern Europe, there were two 'barbarian' confederations. The Ostrogoths occupied the steppe-lands between Crimea and rivers Don and Dniester. The Visigoths occupied the land between rivers Dniester and Danube. They regularly traded with the Roman Empire.[74]

In the east were the Vandals, the Burgundians, the Gepids and the Lombards. In the west, there were the Franks, the Alamans, Saxons, Frisians and Thuringians.

When the Asiatic Huns broke loose, thousands were on the move looking for safety, food and shelter. It was beyond the ability of the Roman leaders to control.

The empire had always had an amiable relationship with tribes on the borders. Rome needed workers to maintain the massive infrastructure of roads and walls. People on the borders could be hired for their labor. There were few enough of them to be able to sort out who was of the empire, and who was simply a visitor. With the flood of new people the governmental system of Rome, with its strict and anxious state supervision and its strong sense of the rightness of social hierarchy began to break down.

The Roman empire also suffered from epidemics. Because of them, large areas of agricultural land went out of production.

The changing social structure forced Rome to use barbarian tribes to defend against barbarian tribes, but they were never completely trusted. One example is the greatest of barbarian chieftains, the Vandal Stilicho. He even married the niece of Emperor Theodosius I. At the death of Theodosius in 395, the Roman Empire was divided between two sons. Arcadius took the eastern empire, including Constantinople and Honorius took the western empire including Rome. Stilicho was made protector of Honorius and Rome. His tactic was to use the Goths, with their chieftain Alaric, to hold back other tribes invading from the east. When he failed to stop the encroachment of Alaric and the Goths he was executed.

In 409 Alaric, the Visigoth warned the Emperor that he was about to sack Rome. Every wealthy person was given the opportunity to flee with their wealth. When citizens saw that the attack was not as violent as expected, they returned. Alaric repeated the sacking of Rome, this time more effectly in 413.

The Goths and Vandals tended to be Christian, having been converted in the 340's by Ulfilas, a Greek. It was, though, the organizing church's worst nightmare. Ulfilas was an 'Arian' Christian. Arian Christianity was one of the great heresies fought by western church. Arians believed that in the Trinity, the Son was less than the Father. By the end of the 5th century Aquitaine, Gascony, Narbonne, Provence and the greater part of Spain was Gothic and therefore Arian. If the empire wanted to befriend the invader, it still needed to fight the heresy.

Constantine declared the empire Christian in 312. The church had several million adherents and was able to use the civil machinery of the Roman provincial government.[75] They didn't have the hearts and minds of the people of Rome. The people of city of Rome were not excited about embracing Christianity. Romans tended to believe less in the deities than in philosophy of skepticism and personal communion with the divine. Mystery cults of Thrace, Egypt, Syria and Persia were popular.

To win the Roman, the theology had to include the popular ideas and philosophies. The Christianity of Bishop Augustine of Hippo, later a Saint, came through the filter the philosophical thought of the neo-Platonists. Neo-Platonism had a mystic cosmology that included asceticism, fasts, vigils, ritual, saints, angels, demons, reliance on visions and sorties. There was a need to purify ones-self of worldly influences.[76] The spirit was good. The world was evil. When good fights evil it is natural to assume that good humans must fight evil humans.

During the early years of Christianity most converts were against fighting and war. Christ Jesus' teachings of love and forgiveness were powerful. Christianity as an imperial religion had different requirements. Christianity under the spiritual leadership of Saint Augustine grew more and more militaristic. He perfected the idea of the 'just war'. It was clear that if everyone was Christian and no one was willing to be a soldier, who would defend the empire?

With the many invasions, including the sacking of Rome, imperial Christians needed to be encouraged to be warriors. The invaders were bringing chaos, destroying the well ordered empire. That chaos was in itself evil and needed a clear unified response.

The theologian with a dissenting opinion was seen as one w was tearing down the structure that was needed to repair the breach in t empire. That dissenting theologian seemed to be the evil siding with chaos. In the church of the 5th century it seemed you were either for the dogma of the unified church or you were one with the enemy of the empire.

The 5th century west was trapped in despair, and deep, all-encompassing grief. The world they had known and loved was gone. The sacking of Rome, the invasions of strangers, the breakdown of authority must have been a shock to people like Augustine and Jerome and the many others who had grown up with the order of the Empire.

How does despair influence history? How did it shape the decisions made in the 5th century. There was a need to set rigid rules within the church. There was a tendency to lash out with more and more violence.

That despair certainly reached to Britain. The strong civilization they had known had crumbled. They were now at the mercy of invading tribes. The fragile Romano-British community was visited by Germanus, Bishop of Auxerre in 429. He was apparently invited to Britain by a group within the British Church who wanted to overcome the teaching of Pelagius.[77] Augustine Germanus had control of the British soldiers. He reports that most of the soldiers were new baptized: "Strong in faith and fresh from the waters of baptism, the army advanced: and whereas they had formerly despaired of human strength, all now trusted in the power of God."[78] This was the power of the Christianity of the empire. Correct belief and the sword would save them. That is the way to move through chaos; through love, through violence.

This was the Christianity that came with the missionaries into Britain and with Patrick into Ireland.

CHAPTER 40 – PATRICK THE DEACON
ISLE OF LERINS OFF THE FRENCH COAST, NEAR CANNES

The monastery on the island of Lerins was filled with ancient books. Patrick was learning to read them. It was slow going for him. He was more a man of action than of ideas.

The island was filled with beauty. The pines, rosemary, thyme, wild honeysuckle filled the air with fragrance. The white rock cliffs and secluded lagoons offered space for contemplation. There was plenty of food. The monks worked together in the gardens below the main building.

Patrick learned what he needed to learn. He memorized the creeds of the church. He learned about the heresies that had tried to ravage Christianity.

He especially studied the writings of the great Augustine. He learned how important it was that we totally give ourselves to God. We needed to recognize our total depravity as human beings. As Adam and Eve had disobeyed God, we all have inherited their great Sin. Only through Christ Jesus and his death is that sin forgiven. Only by accepting the death of Christ Jesus as the payment for your sin could a person avoid hell. Then the soul needed to be washed in the waters of baptism.

The task of a missionary was to go out into the world and save souls of those who would otherwise burn eternally.

It made Patrick shake to think of how God had punished him. God had led him to this place now, so that he could receive the training and authority to save others.

Patrick knew that the world was filled with snakes, sorcerers, and murderers. Liars and perjurers deserved only the lake of everlasting fire.

One thing he knew was that you needed to avoid those who did not repent, or who acted in a sinful manner, in spite of claiming to be Christian. You must not court favor with them by taking food or drink with them or even accepting their offerings. Sinners must come in floods of tears in order to be freed as servants of God and baptized as handmaids of Christ, for whom He was crucified.

CHAPTER 41 – ANAIAS' VISION
IN HER OWN WORDS
THE REFUGE

That night, I had the same dream about Rabboni Yesua and Miraham of Magda. Again, he looked at me and said, "Follow me."

The dog barked and I woke up. Papallas was sleeping soundly next to me. The air was crisp and cold.

I pulled my cloak over my shoulders and left the bed and its warmth. I walked out into the darkness. There was mist over the ground. I looked up for the stars, but the fog covered them. "People of De Danaa, Mother, Ana, I can't leave you for another god. Guide me."

I knew what I needed to do. I filled my backpack with food and blankets and a woven mat. When Papallas woke up, I whispered to him, "I need to search for a vision. I need to talk to Ana, if she will talk to me. I'll be back after the full moon."

He made a sound indicating he had heard me.

As I started up the path I reached a rock outcropping and both the dog and I were startled to see a hawk sitting in a mangled tree starring at us. The dog started barking furiously. The hawk spread its wings, flew toward us and then up skyward and continued to circle overhead.

As I watched the hawk soar, the dog began to bark more fanatically. I looked at him beside me and saw Beechna standing with a wild grin.

"Welcome back!" Beechna said to me.

"I haven't been gone," I responded. "But I haven't seen you for a while."

She laughed, saying, "You're always gone when you are in those deep thoughts and conversations about the divine ones." She leaped, "Just be here, that's all you need!"

I responded, "Help me find a place of vision."

I followed Beechna. Sometimes I lost sight of her as she jumped through the trees branches, but Beechna always got my attention. We were going up the bank of the river that protected the refuge.

We traveled up stream, fighting through brambles. The nettles burned my skin. We then found a flat pathway that followed the upper stream. As the stream got narrower, we came to the source. There was a pool created by an underground spring. This was the place, filled with sacred energy. There were ferns, on the pond bank, for a soft bed under my mat.

I tied the ends of the blanket with cord to the four trees that seemed to stand together in a perfect square. There were several oaks and a yew tree that gave a powerful energy. The energy of the trees would also help me as they held the blanket for a rain-roof.

Just in case the rain was hard, I built a lean-to out of fallen logs and bark. I set it against a rock outcropping. I would prefer to stay under the open sky and would use it only in emergencies.

I lit a small fire then removed my heavy cloak and then my clothing to reveal my colorful nakedness. I sat with my face and hands uplifted. "Ana come!" I repeated this chant. Beechna sat at a reverent distance from me. The steady flickering of the fire mesmerized me.

I heard and saw the hawk as it circled overhead. As quickly as I looked, I was the hawk. I soared over the refuge, huts and tents. I began crossing the bay to my home on the coast of Cymru.

I came to a landing on a treetop near my birth home. I saw my mother looking older now.

My grandmother was moving very slowly. She said, "Where is my son!? He should be home now!"

M'alda looked sullen, "It's been several weeks mother. The boat has been lost in the storm."

My grandmother spoke angrily, "He will return. He is strong! He will return!"

I flew to the other side of the village and saw my cousin Aengus. He didn't look like the boy I played with anymore. He was tall and lean but muscular, with a beard. He was pulling a small boat onto the shore.

Aengus called out, "Who will go out with me again tomorrow to search for my father?"

The others were silent.

My brother, Ciallach, said, "Cousin, we must accept that he is lost."

Aengus flared, "I will never accept it."

Suddenly, my heart began to ache for my family back home. Something terrible had happened to the Eogan king, my uncle, Nad Fraich. Tears came to my eyes as I realized I would not be there to comfort my mother who had lost a brother and my grandmother who had lost a son, my cousin who had lost a father.

The hawk took wing and skimmed across the surface of a red, red cliff. I landed on a rock. From that perch, I looked out at the sea.

As I came out of the vision, I felt the discomfort of the ground I was sitting on. I stood up and found some bread in the bag and some of the cheese. I drank deeply of the water from the pool. I washed my face and splashed the water over my head.

"My daughter, don't be afraid of my water however it comes to cleanse you!" I heard the voice behind me.

I turned and saw the speaker. It was a tall woman with reddish blond air and deep blue eyes. Instantly I knew it was Bridey, the goddess daughter of Danaa. I knelt before her. The woman touched my head. "You are born for this moment. You must help bring the family of the earth together."

I said in despair, thinking of my family in exile, "How can I do that, if they don't want to see me?"

"That is not your whole family." The woman waved her arm. "These are your family. There are those in your family who are not born yet. You have people in distant places who you will meet only in dreams."

She touched my head. "I am not just goddess of this place; I am a part of the great One who creates all."

"I have been hearing of the teachings of the one God and the Rabboni Yesua," I said.

"We are one," she smiled as she spoke. "You do not need to leave Ana by going to the One they call the God of the Rabboni Yesua. All creation is sacred, even though it shows itself in many ways. We are One. Listen also to the teachings of Miraham of Magda. She is our sister. She knew and knows now how to travel through the dimensions of time and space."

The woman vanished. I stood by the pond staring at the spot to see a trace of her divine presence. I sat and gazed through the trees to the sky.

Unexpectedly, in my vision, there was a crowd of young girls and boys around me. I saw women weaving, cooking, washing, and laughing as if it were the teaching village of Katika. The figures were not solid. I could see them, but could see through them. A hawk then began to fly between them. Again, I became the hawk. As I flew, a ribbon of gold seemed to trail behind me, binding them. All was bound together loosely, all hawk, women, earth. I flew to where the men were working and worked the ribbon of gold through them.

Then the hawk with its trailing golden ribbon flew into a dark tunnel. In my vision, I began to hear other voices of women down the tunnel. I let myself fall. There was a new voice of chanting and bells. I saw women sitting cross-legged facing a statue holding a knotted rope. Outside were bells tinkling in the gentle breeze that, was blowing away the mists of morning on the high mountain cliffs.

Quickly I moved through the tunnel again and found myself in the midst of a field with waving maize being harvested by women with infants on their backs. The women called to each other and laughed. The sun beat down making the shadows crisp and clear. Around were deep canyons and distant mesas. The women's hands moved quickly as they picked the corn and placed it into a pouch and then unloaded it into a basket. The maize was treated with reverence.

Brilliant colors appeared and the husks were removed, blue, red, yellow, and white. The women placed each color in a separate basket. One woman was removing the kernels from the blue maize that had been dried in the sun and began to grind it into a fine powder.

She put the blue finely ground meal into the clay mixing bowl. She pushed a third to the back and added boiling water to the rest and stirred it. The dough was heavy and stiff. She had ash set aside and strained it into the dough. After kneading, she added water, making a thin batter. She turned to a large stone that was red hot from a flame underneath.

She dipped her hands into the batter and with a curve of her fingers; she covered the stone with a thin layer of batter, moving her fingers quickly across the stone. She then lifted the tissue thin bread off the stone and began to roll it into a cylinder. She continued the process. She muttered to the stone asking it to do its work and not be lazy.

I saw an old man in a kiva weaving cotton threads, moving his fingers quickly. He spoke the name of his granddaughter. He was weaving her wedding dress.

Other men outside a kiva were gathering weapons for hunting. They repaired any that were broken. One man looked up at me, sitting on a tree branch. He smiled as though he recognized me.

I entered the tunnel again and emerged on a steep hillside on the brow of the rainforest. I saw sharp snow-covered peaks in the distance. Baskets of potatoes of all colors were in the main square. Around me were women and men standing before a sundial. Incense was burning in a bowl. The season had been declared. A woman stood before them in brightly colored robes lifting the incense-filled bowl to the sun. She was one of the Chosen Women of the Inca. Her head and arms were adorned with shimmering gold and crystal that caught the light of the sun. The men and women chanted. The haunting sound of a flute came from the valley below. There was anticipation of a ceremony about to begin.

I swooped across the tops of trees and then miles of ocean. I could hear the women and men calling. There was the steady thump of a hollow log turned into a drum. A monkey looked down at me from a tree above and a young child looked up at me and grinned happily. A young mother came out of the village and grabbed the child. She didn't see me standing before her, but the child looked back and waved at me. I followed the woman into the village. It was smoky from the many fires. In the distance, I heard the laughter of children and women singing.

The voices were of the people chanting, praying, cajoling, laughing, singing, and intermingled. I woke up to find myself lying by the pond..

I smelled the sweetness of the crushed ferns beneath my body. A spider crawled across me. I heard the rustling of the squirrel and the branches crackling under hoofs. A doe and fawn came into the clearing. The doe nibbled on the tender vine a foot away.

I whispered, "Mother of the doe and fowl, thank you for bringing me into community.' The deer then settled down and began nuzzling its fawn. The baby occasionally nibbled at a fresh vine following its mother, then returned to suckling.

Clearly seeing signs of safety, a family of squirrel came down from the nearest tree and began teaching its young to forage across my mat. I lay still as they began to sniff around my feet. Even the flowers in my tattooed body seem to gather their attention.

I suddenly sat up. Around me a mist appeared. There were human figures. I couldn't tell if they were male or female. They were just forms kneeling, barely touching, and walking between the deer. They seemed surprised at seeing each other, and embraced. Beechna jumped up and disappeared into them. The dog wagged his tail in excitement.

As if on cue, each lifted an arm and a gossamer ribbon appeared between them and beyond them. As they began to move in a slow stately dance, the ribbon touched each creature and began to include the trees. They moved slowly around me as I was seated.

As the ribbon touched me, I felt suddenly powerful and joy filled. I no longer felt a separation from the creatures around me. I felt myself rise up and become like mist and dance among them far from the ground, yet connected with the sky and the earth. I was no longer a woman but was one with them.

As the ribbon was woven, music was heard from the creatures, birds, wolves, and crickets. The ribbon, which might have bound us, was setting us free.

Suddenly it started to rain. I was startled by the cold downpour that awakened, or brought me back. I rushed under the lean-to that I had created up the hill.

The rain fell hard as I looked out the opening. I saw none of the creatures who had been gathered there. I saw none of the gossamer ribbon. I saw none of the figures who had wrapped me in their dance. I heard a bird singing a melody to the new rain.

Beechna and the dog joined me in the lean-to. Beechna peered out the door.

The dog began to whine. Beechna looked disgusted.

I reached into my pack and pulled out a piece of dried bread and gave it do the dog. He grabbed it, put it between his paws, and began to chew on it.

"I saw him chasing a rabbit!" she said accusingly.

"Well yes, he is a friend and a hunter"

"But I might be that rabbit!'

I was both serious and amused, "If you are going to be a rabbit around my dog, Beechna, learn to run fast, every rabbit knows that!!"

Beechna began to giggle. She became a rabbit and began to hop around the tent. The dog ignored her. Finally she ran out the door and then the dog couldn't resist the chase. Before he caught her she became a bird again and flew to a tree. The dog barked furiously.

I thought of Beechna's fluidity. She lived off that same life force that caused the perennial flower to die back and bloom again. It was the force that kept the pine green in the cold winter, that cleansed the earth after disease and death. I knew some of that connection; but a simple rainfall could distract me.

Beechna flew back and landed in the tent, becoming herself again, "You can see a little of our world, can't you?"

Beechna read my thoughts, knowing the answer, that sometimes I could and sometimes I couldn't. She continued, "That's why you have to remember and believe what you see when you see it."

Beechna, having made her pronouncement, was now out of the tent prancing about in the rain lifting her arms and splashing. The dog braved the wetness to join her, putting his front paws down and wagging his tail calling her to play with him. He ran in circles to her rain dance. I sat, laughed, and watched from my dry spot.

I stayed in this place for seven days. I had brought more than enough food to eat for that period. I offered the extra bread I had brought to Beechna. What she didn't eat I gave to the dog.. He also supplemented his meal in ways known only to him. Beechna and I did not want to know who he ate.

The last night had been a full moon and it was time to return to the refuge. I had much to carry in my spirit.

Wisdom's Gifts

Part 3

CHAPTER 42 – HONEY AND WINE – TWO SACRED CUPS
THE REFUGE

WISDOM'S GIFT 1 – KEEP WATCHING FOR THE UNEXPECTED JOY

The season of cold came. The chill and the fog shrouded the huts and seemed to hide the surroundings. Anaias and Papallas spent the cold months together in the refuge. As the months wore on, the sun slowly returned and began to warm the earth. Tinai and Jeremiah announced that they planned to be married.

Tinai came to Anaias, "Can you bless our wedding with the honey-wine cup? Pelagius will give us the blessing of the Rabboni."

She smiled, "Jeremiah says that Rabboni Yesua turned water into wine at a wedding." She continued, "And so Jeremiah has asked that we also be blessed with the wine cup and the bread."

There were many ritual reasons to lift the cup of wine in the refuge. There was the Hebrew blessing ceremony, that went back far into Jewish tradition, that included the cup and loaf, acknowledging God as the giver of blessings. Susanna Miraham often shared this cup and loaf.

There was the ritual only for baptized Christians, taking the cup and loaf as a symbol of Christ Jesus' sacrifice of body and blood.

There was the cup that celebrated community by acknowledging Christ Jesus' presence there. This included the remembrance of Jesus turning water into wine at the wedding in Canaa in Galilee. Christ Jesus is the giver of miracles whether you acknowledge his God or not.

The cup of wine and loaf of bread at this wedding would be the third, a cup and loaf simply acknowledging Christ Jesus' continuing presence in community.

In anticipation, Anaias brought out the cup of Ana, the one that Katika had used. She held it up to the noon day light. The jewels and enamel were bright. The engravings told the story of the earth and all living things.

She pulled out the red cloak of Seallam and smelled the fragrance of all the places it had been. It still smelled of the incense of the cave of the sisters. Now she had it again in this new place.

She would wear it for this ceremony. Red was the color of life. It was the color of birth. It is the reminder of the fertility of women. In both men and women the blood flowed mysteriously in our veins unseen, but without it we could not live. Wearing the red robe was a declaration of the importance of the human creature, with all its passion and creative power. Pelagius said that God has given potential to human beings. It is for us to give it the shape and form. It would also be to honor Seallam and Katika.

The women of the refuge fashioned a dress for Tinai that had a look of many cultures. Jeremiah wore his finest robe.

Pelagius came forward and held the scroll. He read of Jesus' turning water into wine. He also read about the blessings that came from the life of those who were willing to be poor in spirit, pure in heart and merciful. He asked Tinai and Jeremiah if they promised to be faithful to one another for the rest of their lives. Each of them spoke of their love and commitment. They agreed to a life of faithfulness.

Pelagius said, "Then live together in Christ Jesus. To remember that miracle of love of Christ Jesus, take this cup."

The bride and groom drank from the cup of wine. They offered the cup to everyone present.

Pelagius turned back to everyone gathered, and preached, "A holy mind is a sacred temple for God, and the best altar for God is a heart pure and sinless."

"In Christ we are given freedom. We have freedom to live in a condition of spontaneous goodness. That goodness is implanted in all of us. We may choose it and obey the will of God and be without sin."

"May this marriage of Jeremiah and Tinai be fruitful and reveal that goodness in the love of Christ Jesus to the world," Pelagius concluded.

Anaias stepped forward and lifted the cup of honey-wine. "The custom of my people is to recognize the sweetness of the creation of Ana. Love is the sweetest of gifts for our world. Honey is created in the deep mystery of the hive. Your love was created in the deep mystery of that spirit that is within each of you that is eternal."

She looked at the couple in front of her, "Tinai and Jeremiah will you always acknowledge the deep wisdom of all creation?"

"We will." They said together.

"Then drink of the cup of Ana's sweet gift." Tinai and Jeremiah drank the honey-wine in the cup. "Now all may drink!" Anaias said. She took a drink and offered it to Papallas. Then Moira and Luann brought out flasks of honey-wine for everyone.

Tinai and Jeremiah kissed. Everyone began laughing and shouting good wishes to them.

Paulina angrily returned to her camp.

When the festivities were over, Melania met Paulina in the doorway of the hut.

"How could you join in such a sacrilege?!" Paulina's face was red with anger.

"It was a celebration, a marriage. Dear Paulina, what is so wrong?" Melania asked, disappointed to have her joy crushed by this anger.

"First, the pagans were given the cup of Christ. That is a sacrilege. Then you all drank the honey-wine. The honey-wine was offered to a different god, a goddess, a demon, Melania!"

Melania responded, perplexed, "It was a time of joy, Paulina. The cup was to celebrate the wedding. The message of Christ Jesus is a message of joy. Where is your joy?"

Paulina was screaming, "It's like those going after the graven images in Canaan. God's punishment will be swift and I don't want to be part of it!! I followed you, since you have been like my mother. You have always been an upright woman of God."

"And now I am not?" Melania responded.

Paulina shouted, "I don't know what you are now! You are living with heathens. You are heathen. I am afraid for your soul!" Tears started to stream down her face.

Melania said calmly, "Your words have hurt me deeply. You know that I'm a follower of Christ Jesus. I was before you were born. I have lived more years than you. I have spent time in the wilderness questioning the God of Christ Jesus. I believe that He celebrates even with pagans. God has shown me many faces. We must not limit the ways that God will come to us. Christ Jesus himself told us simply to seek God."

Paulina quieted herself, "I worry for your soul and because of you I worry for mine. I believe God is testing me. You may be lost, and I am certain he is lost," she pointed at Pelagius, coming down the path.

Paulina turned away from Melania and was silent.

CHAPTER 43 – REJECTION AND ACCEPTANCE
THE REFUGE

A week later Papallas came to Melania and Pelagius saying, "Paulina insists she must go back to the Mediterranean. She says she would rather perish at sea or by pirates than have her soul perish by staying here."

"Let me talk to her," Pelagius said, wanting to help.

Melania responded, "No, you especially must not, I'm afraid. The same ones who condemn you have her heart." She took his big hand in hers.

Papallas gathered as many young single men as he could get for the journey to the south. They would travel across land to the south and catch a ship in the port there. It would be safer for Paulina not to have to be on the open sea for too long.

He was anxious about the state of Gaul since his last journey. With luck, he would bring back new fabrics, incense, and foods from the Mediterranean. By now, the new inhabitants might be settled enough to have items to trade.

Anaias was deep in her own thoughts, "Papa, while you are out, on the sea, if you happen to hear of Aengus and the end of exile . . ."

"If I can, I'll find out."

He put his hands on her shoulders and touched the nape of her neck. They gazed at each other. "You deserve your place in the family of Eogan, to be their priestess, to serve them the cup." He kissed her gently.

Tears streamed down her face. She was surprised by the deep emotion that filled her. She missed her family.

Four young men decided to go with Papallas. They were eager for adventure and discovery. Most of them were born in the refuge and they hoped to catch a glimpse of the land of their parents who came as refugees. Maybe they would even see the land of Miraham and Rabboni Yesua.

Papallas collected items for trade, finely spun lamb's wool, herbs and Luann's honey. He would collect minerals and tin as he traveled inland toward the southern coast.

Anaias, Susanna and Melania walked with them to the southern edge of the moor. Melania had tried to end the silence and convince Paulina to stay. It would be dangerous for her to return to Rome and even more dangerous to go back to Palestine.

"Stay with your father in Africa. Don't return to Palestine," she begged.

"I'll be okay, Melania. I'll visit Carthage, but my father's ways are not mine. I'll find Master Jerome," Paulina responded.

"Good-bye sweet Paulina." She embraced her for a long time. Tears were in Paulina's eyes.

Paulina said softly, "You can come with me."

Melania shook her head, "May God bless this journey, and take you safely home."

The carts started down the hill to the south, rather than to the cove.

As Melania turned around, she saw Pelagius on the hill above, watching the group leave. She walked up the hill to meet him. He put his arms out to embrace her.

He softly said, "God will be with her. Our God is strong and good."

Anaias listened, wondered about the God of the Rabboni Yesua. Why would teachings of love cause such hardness in the soul? She silently said a prayer to Ana and the god of the sea to watch over those on the journey.

"I want to be baptized into the faith of my husband," Tinai said to Anaias. "Jeremiah has been patient with me, but we can do so much more when we share the same God. Pelagius said we can meet at the river next week. He will teach me what I don't know yet. Jeremiah has been teaching me a lot."

Anaias wasn't sure what to say at this announcement. "We will all be there to celebrate with you."

"Will you be baptized with me?" Tinai asked

"No, I am a daughter of Ana and don't understand this god of sand," Anaias said softly. "I'm happy for you and for Jeremiah."

The next week the whole community went to the spot where the two rivers meet. The rapids roared and Anaias felt the power of the mist. The community climbed down the hill. They could feel the energy of the falls. Some of them brought musical instruments with them. They sang songs.

Anaias, Luann and Moira were standing with them as they sang.

They walked down river and found a calm pool. Tinai waded into the water with Pelagius. Pelagius reached into the river, brought out handfuls of water, and baptized her in the name of the Creator, the Teacher and the Spirit. Beechna couldn't help herself. She became a white dove and flew over the scene. Tinai hugged Pelagius.

Pelagius looked up at Anaias. She flinched as she remembered the dream and the man who reached out saying, 'Follow me.' She couldn't, not yet.

Jeremiah met Tinai at the water's edge and hugged her. Susanna laughed and then hugged them both. Then Tinai turned to Deidre and hugged her. "I'm so happy for you." Deidre said.

Luann and Moira went down to the riverbank with dry clothes to greet Tinai. Anaias left for her hut.

CHAPTER 44 – THE CURSE
THE REFUGE

WISDOM'S GIFT 2 – BE READY FOR DARKNESS

Beechna's heart raced. Anaias needed to go back home. She had heard from her flying messengers that Aengus was fully-grown. There was also a feeling of restlessness that he was ready to leave for Ireland to reclaim the throne. Oh, she thought, how much he would need that magic of Anaias for that deed. Did he even know?

Beechna wished she could talk to Anaias. Throughout history, the Tywa had rarely held Torca attention. Beechna was irritated. Anaias needed to hear her and needed to hear her now.

Beechna had tried to get her attention by playing tricks on her. Maybe Beechna would sneak into the hut and hide items. Anaias would then have to interrupt her work to search for it, until she caught on. Once acknowledged, Beechna would return it.

This morning her amber robe pin was missing. After searching the hut for a few moments Anaias stormed outside.

"What do you want?" Anaias she said sharply, her hands on her hips. She was looking in the wrong direction.

Beechna shook her head quickly to clear her thoughts. "What I want to tell you is that you must go home. Aengus your cousin needs you now."

"I've been feeling that. But I can't, not yet." Anaias reached for her cloak, she was cold, even though the day was warm.

Beechna whined, "It's time for you do go home now! Go home now!"

"I can't just go home. I have people here who are important," Anaias responded.

Suddenly Beechna began to scream, "No!!! No!!" She seemed to be looking at something invisible to Anaias.

She looked around, "It's here, a curse!! It is here!"

She took Anaias' hand, "I think you are sick!"

Suddenly every bone in Anaias' body hurt as though it was being crushed. Her stomach spasmed and she bent down to her knees and began to vomit violently. She crumpled to the ground. Beechna saw her fall and ran to her side. "My friend be strong. It is a curse!"

She woke up in a panic. She was hot!! She looked for flames but saw darkness. She remembered the wall of fire in her initiation vision. She remembered Paulina's eyes and her warning of hellfire. Fire was all around her.

A wave of chill blew over her. She began to shudder. The pain!! She remembered doubling over with a stomach pain as she was talking to Beechna. Her whole body felt like it was being crushed. She needed air. She tried to stand but her legs would not hold her. She started shaking intensely.

In a vision, she saw her father, his eyes were glowing with love and longing. He reached out his hand to her and seemed to be trying to say words to her. Then the flames came and devoured him. She saw flickering lights continue. They turned into snarling wolves and hissing snakes. They came running at her and started gnawing at her skin. She tried to scream and run but she fell. The vision stopped.

Her father; she had seen her father! He was calling to her.

"Sister, are you awake?" Anaias heard the voice as if down a dark tunnel. It was Luann. Anaias recognized the voice.

She tried to feel her body but could not. It was as if she was under a heavy blanket. Any attempt to move caused intense pain in her head and in every joint.

She moved her lips but no sound came out, "Ana, Ana, Ana," she repeated, soundlessly, calling on a vision of her sisters in the cool darkness of the cave. It was a curse around her. She needed strong power to release it. "Rabboni Yesua, Miraham, heal me!" she said, in her mind.

In the distance, she felt the coolness of a rag put on her forehead. She heard unfamiliar chanting. It was as though it was far away.

"Has she opened her eyes?" She heard a man's voice. It was a familiar voice. She tried to open her eyes but they did not respond.

She felt a cool hand on her arm. Suddenly she was calm. It was as though, from the touch of this hand, a joyful blue light had filled her. Just the touch gave her healing. She wanted to open her eyes to see the face attached to the arm.

She drifted into a peaceful sleep.

When she awoke again, she heard the birds chirping outside the hut. There was the sound of sheep calling. She was still unable to open her eyes. She heard that same man speaking softly in a strange language. His voice was solemn as he chanted prayers in Latin. She recognized it as Pelagius.

He had been teaching her a few of the words in Latin, but the sounds were so different from her own language. She wanted to reach out to him and reassure him that she was there in this deadweight body.

She put her mind on Ana. She tried to discipline her mind to concentrate on Ana's beauty. She imagined Her as She was in the earth beneath. She imagined Her in the sound of the birds. She listened for Her in the distant roar of the waves. She even heard Her in the sound of Pelagius praying in Latin.

She tried to open her eyes. They were heavy. She saw around her in the darkness, a light, a red pinkish glow. She relaxed into it. She knew she was basking in the power of Ana. The earth was healing. Now, she felt as if she were under the healing power of the sun.

She wanted Papallas there with her. She remembered that he had just left a few weeks ago.

She drifted off to sleep, awoke, and again heard Pelagius praying. She continued to listen to the rhythm of the prayers and felt peace. A change must have taken place in her outward features.

"Ah, you are there my friend. I can feel you returning to us," he said softly. "Thanks be to God!" he said. He held her hand in both of his. With her mind, she smiled and reached out toward the feel of his hands, but still could not move.

She fell again into sleep. This time she was surrounded by a deep calm sense of peace. She fell into a dream

In her dream, she was at the edge of a waterfall. Suddenly, instead of down, the water started up the cliff. She rode the wave higher and higher to the top. She went still higher until she saw in the shimmering light, a castle on a hill.

Around it were beautiful tall men and women with bright auburn hair. The women were dressed in blue velvet with jewels adorning their necks and hair. The men wore multicolored cloaks over brown. They were smiling, laughing, and singing an ancient song that she felt she should know.

She moved into the castle and found a table filled with honeycakes, berries and honeycombs dripping with the sacred sweet liquid. The bees still hovered around the comb. There were plates of laver and oats. There were no people. It was as though everyone was waiting for the occupants of the castle to return and expected them to come soon.

In another room, people, of the same race, were dressed in work clothes scrubbing the walls and sweeping the floors. Anaias felt herself walking into the room. She was startled to see herself in a mirror on the wall. She was like them, tall and slender with long red hair and fair complexion. She had a light blue gown on, made of a silk-like fabric, soft to the touch. On her head was a tiara with rubies and emeralds. She reached up to touch it.

"Beautiful isn't it?" a gentle voice said from behind her. She turned and tried to speak. The beauty of the woman who spoke dazzled her.

The woman did not seem to notice her difficulty. "You don't need to help us, you know, we're doing this for you! You are returning soon and we will celebrate when you arrive!"

She went on talking, not even looking at Anaias' confusion, "It's been so long since we've had you in this place."

The woman stopped and looked at her, saying, "You are coming aren't you!?"

Then as if looking at her complexion and sensing her illness said, "You won't die first will you? All the others like you have died first before they gain their rightful place."

She shook her head, "It's hard on you mortals. You just get burned up by our immortal fire that's still in your veins."

She took Anaias' hand in both of hers. There was a tingling feeling from the touch, "You must strengthen yourself. You must be strong enough to contain our fire."

A beautiful man with a red beard and deep blue eyes came over and touched her face, as if testing her. "No, she'll be all right," he said.

In her vision, Anaias wandered away from this man and women. She was drawn back outside. She saw a staircase and a grassy plateau covered with beautiful flowers. There were Bridey's flowers, glistening gold, interspersed with violets and asters. A group of these welcoming people was collecting armfuls of flowers. As they picked the flowers more bloomed instantaneously.

Anaias looked out at the rolling hills covered with forests. She saw the sweeping valleys.

Suddenly, as the dream continued, she was a child holding hands with her cousin Aengus. They were running through the fields picking the flowers and throwing them into the air laughing with glee.

"Bridey, Bridey, maid of Imbolg, bless us in this fertile time of year." Crowds of children were running around with them now. The sound of laughter echoed and drifted away.

Her dream continued. It changed course.

She was lifted up from the hill and by some unseen force, she flew over water. In the distance, she saw a green island. It was the island she saw when she was a child.

A female voice called, "Come, Come and I will give you a new life." She was curious about the island. She started to move toward it. The dream ended.

"Anaias ...are you there?! Can you open your eyes?" She heard a woman.

Suddenly the pain hit her again in her head, her legs, and her stomach. She felt the cool cloth on her head. She tried again to move and this time she did ever so slightly. She struggled to open her eyes. She saw the blur of a gray-haired woman. The light hurt her eyes. She shut them. "Praise God, you're waking up," she said with a heavy accent.

"How long," she tried to say. Her lips were thick and dry.

"From the full moon to the new moon."

Now she tried again to open her eyes. She saw Melania smile. "Welcome back. It's so good to see you!" Melania took her hand in both of hers.

Anaias tried to focus her eyes. "I must go! My father ... dying." She struggled to move from the bed.

Melania gently pushed her back, saying, "No child, you're not going anywhere. You almost died yourself. You need rest so that the good Lord can be convinced to keep you among us."

There was no use struggling anyway. Her body did not respond. Pain shot through her muscles. They were not strong enough to let her move. She was glad Melania was there.

"I must go to him..."

"But your father is very far away. It will take weeks for you to be well enough"

"Get me well," Anaias whispered, smiling weakly, "and then I will go."

"Pelagius and I will go with you..." Melania responded, "We must wait for your husband to return."

Anaias felt a deep longing for Papallas. She wanted to tell him all she had seen. Maybe he would have word about her family. She drifted again into a deep sleep.

She awakened to see Moira sitting by her bed. When she opened her eyes, Moira jumped up and brought her a steaming cup of broth. It smelled delicious and she recognized the smell of herbs that she herself would have prescribed. Her stomach awakened to an intense hunger. The pain was gone. She was cautious, though, remembering the intensity of it.

"It will settle your stomach," Moira said. "You need it to build strength."

"Thank you, Moira." Anaias took the cup and drank the broth.

She noticed a soft golden blanket that was covering her. Moira said, "I wanted to surround you with the sun." Anaias smiled. Her checks hurt from the effort. It was the color of healing. It was like the golden Bridey flower on the hill in her vision.

"Oh, we have been so afraid...so many have died," Moira said.

Suddenly Anaias realized how dangerous her pain was.

"Who?!" she asked cautiously.

"Susanna's son, Mark. Some of the older people – and the new baby..." she slowed, and began to fight tears, "and our close friend, Deidre, Pelagius' cousin."

Anaias' mind reeled at the thought of the loss. She cried out, "Oh no...and Susanna?"

"She's okay. She thinks the disease came in through from the village market at the base our hill. Deidre had gone to sell some goat's milk just before she became ill."

Anaias knew that Katika would say it was a dark, evil spirit. Beechna had felt it as a curse. Sometimes curses were free floating, without a target.

She said to Moira, "We must leave this place. I have to go home!"

Her family needed her. The people of de Danaa needed her. She had to get hold of Aengus. But how could she?

"Luann and I will go with you when you are strong enough," Moira answered.

Anaias remembered her father's eyes in the vision. How had he found her? She had traveled so much since she had fled from them. She knew the family would have no idea where she was, especially in this place of refuge.

Somehow, his spirit found her. Had the druid powers helped? Was it the death goddess Keridwen giving him this last wish before he died?

Could it be that Papallas told her father where she was? But if Boandas was there, ruling over the village, they would not have let Papallas in.

One thing was true. Her father's spirit was barely hanging on to its body. She must go to him. She needed to hear his voice again.

It did not make any difference what she wanted. Her body was so weak. It had been almost a month now. The moon was coming full again. Healing came with the waxing moon. Luann and the other women looked worn from caring for her. Susanna, in black, had come to sit with her. She sang Hebrew tunes.

Pelagius and Melania prayed at her side in Latin. Her dog licked her hand or just curled up at her side. Beechna sat passively on a shelf watching.

It was the full moon and Anaias felt her strength returning. She felt absolute joy in being able to walk in the sunshine. It felt good to get back to her daily rituals.

She was shocked to discover how the epidemic had struck the refuge. Altogether, of the two hundred inhabitants, seventy of them had suffered with the illness. Thirteen had died, including several children, Susanna's son and Deidre. Those who survived were exhausted from caring for those who all seemed near death.

Susanna came to her with a bouquet of fragrant fresh flowers.

She was wearing a black robe and head covering. Her eyes were red from crying. "We have lost so many. But we thank God for your return to us."

"Is the curse gone?" Anaias asked. "Among my people we would leave this place and burn everything to get rid of the curse."

"We have been praying. Rabboni Yesua has brought us through this terrible time," Susanna responded. "We have also burned the clothing of those who died. We buried them quickly." Susanna looked down, "Our scripture tells us many things we can do to stop disease like this from spreading."

"I'm so sorry for your grief. Whatever your people believe about this curse I know that I must leave this place." Anaias said.

"Yes, I know," Susanna responded. She paused and made a choking sound as if she were holding back a sob.

Anaias continued, "It is time for me to return to my family and find out if they will receive me." Her voice was raspy from her exhaustion.

"But you will wait for your husband Papallas, won't you?" Susanna asked,

"Yes, I'll wait," Anaias said reluctantly. She longed for Papallas to be by her side now. She wanted to know what he had heard about her family.

As she got her strength back, she began to visit homes of those affected by the illness.

Jacob left the refuge to find out whether the illness had affected other parts of the region. There was a old Roman town to the east of them. It was not as wealthy as it had been before the Roman troops left, but usually he could find good trading. There were fruits and squashes he could purchase here that they could not grow on the moors.

A man grabbed him by the arm, saying, "Are you a follower of Christ Jesus?" The man was large and carried a sword.

Jacob hesitated, the responded, "My people are followers of Jesus, yes."

"We are looking for a dangerous man. He pretends to be a follower of Christ Jesus, but he is a snake who preaches what can only cause damnation to the listener." Jacob listened but backed away as the man's vehemence spewed out.

"How would we know this man?" Jacob asked.

"He fled like a coward from Palestine. And we think the snake may have returned to Britain because it is his home. We believe that some unknowing good folk may have taken him in. They called him Pelagius in the south. Do you know of a refuge for heretic Christians in these hills?" the man spit out.

"And if you find this man?" Jacob responded, ignoring the second part of the question.

"If he is preaching still, we have no choice but to cut out his tongue, or maybe cut off his whole evil head," the man laughed.

"Thank you for the warning." Jacob moved quickly away from the man. He knew he needed to get back to the refuge. Never before had anyone actually wanted to search for the refuge.

As he visited the market, he found that the disease had hit in many other villages. Some of the island people had come there for medicine. There were fewer people at the market to buy and sell goods

He also noticed that there were strangers crowded outside the town. They spoke a strange language and a strange odor came from their cooking pots. He quickly took the road home.

Jacob looked over his shoulder to make sure no one was following him. Camps with tents filled with new people were dotted all along the road to the upper moors. The land, and its population, was changing.

As he arrived within the safety of the community, he gathered several of the men together. They agreed to stand guard at the eastern entrance to the refuge.

Jacob spoke to Susanna's husband David, "We have been here for many generations. We had the protection of the Roman soldiers, even though they never knew they were protecting us." He furrowed his brow, saying, "I am afraid now. We can no longer call ourselves a refuge."

Pelagius wandered by as they talked. He said, "I heard they're looking for me."

David held up his hand, "You'll be safe. We'll keep you safe."

Pelagius responded, "It is not for you to keep me safe. I shouldn't have stayed so long. I need to trust in God to lead me where I'm to go. I'm sorry I've brought danger to you."

Jacob stood next to him. "It is not just the soldiers looking for you. There is a crowd of people pushing into our lands. The world has been changing. You've seen that. Now the change is going to affect us."

Susanna arrived to hear these words, "We need to assemble a council to make a decision on whether to move the refuge and where to move it."

The refuge was awakened by dogs barking and men bellowing, "We demand the snake of the devil, Pelagius, and his followers!! Bring him out!"

Anaias heard men of the refuge shouting at them to leave. She heard a woman scream in fear. She jumped off her mat and ran towards the screams and shouts. As she approached, she pictured the wall of fire of the cave. She felt the power welling up within her.

She set forth the scream of Ana. "A-a-a-a-a-a-a!"

She turned around to see Luann, Moira and Tinai joining her in the aural fight.

The scream of Ana was a sound that could shatter the nervous system of any warrior. It was said it could stop the blood's flow. It had stopped Caesar's armies without any loss of life. They had retreated instantly, never to return to the lands they sought to invade.

The refuge invaders turned white. They turned and ran down the hill carrying their swords.

Everyone was starring at Anaias.

Then they all began to laugh. Anaias said simply, "Ana has weapons greater than swords."

Jacob grew serious, "We can't stay here any longer. We can't wait for your husband. They've found us."

Pelagius said softly, "Let us pray about this and gather this afternoon."

CHAPTER 45 – LEAVING MEANS RETURNING THE REFUGE

WISDOM'S GIFT 3 – OUT OF DARKNESS COMES THE SWEETEST AWAKENINGS

Susanna and Jacob appeared at Anaias' hut, "We've met as a council of the refuge and have voted. We need to disband the refuge. Many of us would like to follow you to the west. We believe we can find another place of safety."

"You would follow me?" Anaias asked.

Susanna added, "Not all of us. Some will go home to the distant south. They want to return to the land of our ancestors. There are others that just want to head out to the north or east. They've heard about settlements that might welcome them."

Jacob continued Susanna's thoughts, "The east and south are the direction of the empire and the new invaders." He hesitated, then said, "We thought, with the friendship of your family in the west, we might find unused land."

Behind Susanna, Beechna was still sitting on the shelf. She was dressed in a garland of the flowers. Anaias had remembered her dream. She had important work to do. Beechna was making faces at her, trying to get her attention. She seemed to be anticipating a celebration.

Anaias laughed and caught herself.

She looked back at Susanna and Jacob, "I may not even be welcome in my land. It wouldn't be fair to take so many of you into another dangerous place."

"We feel we'll be safe negotiating with your people," Jacob said. "God is guiding us."

Anaias was silent for several minutes, and then spoke slowly, "It's true that we must leave here. It is also true that I must return to my family, no matter what their feelings are toward me. I need to be at my father's side."

Both Susanna and Jacob were staring at her, waiting. She continued, "I will agree to lead you to a place where you might recreate your refuge, a place near my people."

"Thank you!" They both hugged her and walked out of the hut.

Anaias stood on her weak legs to watch Susanna and Jacob leave. She was shaking uncontrollably as she turned back onto her mat.

She felt relieved to be going home and overwhelmed by the

burden of all these people who needed to find a new place of safety. She felt a knot in her chest that was a sob ready to come out. It was also a longing and a hope.

"Papallas, please come home," she said to the walls.

Papallas was the one who took people on journeys. How could she do it?

The thought of going home made her feel very much like Seabhac, the little hawk-girl. Memories flooded her mind. She remembered the carefree days of her childhood.

"So, are we going home now?" Beechna jumped in front of her. "I will send word to my people."

"Yes, we're going home!" Anaias said softly.

Beechna lifted her arms and danced around singing, "Going home, going home." The dog started barking and pranced with her.

Anaias laughed realizing how much she needed this Tywa friend and the dog friend to help her see the celebration within her decision.

Anaias watched Beechna dance, wishing she had the strength to dance also.

Seabhac was the hawk that hovered high in the sky and could see prey from hundreds of feet up. The hawk could see danger ahead. She needed to remember what she had learned as a child. She had memorized every inch of the cliffs and shoreline near her family's place of exile. She remembered the red cliffs overlooking the sea. The earth was as red as mother's blood. Anaias knew it was sacred land.

The land was fertile and available for grazing and planting. There were eggs that she had gathered from the plentiful sea birds and the seaweed that could be collected from the rocks at the shoreline. This was the place she would take them.

She opened her hands upward. She closed her eyes and waited for Ana to speak. The great Mother seemed to be putting it all in motion. She needed divine help to make it all safe and successful. They would go to the land of Bridey. She added a prayer to Rabboni Yesua and Miraham.

Throughout the morning, they prayed and planned. It was now time to meet.

"What information do we have?" Anaias asked.

One of the men said, "I was down at the shore yesterday. A merchant with a good size ship will have no cargo as he travels through the bay. He can take all of us to south Cymru."

"When would we have to go?" she asked.

"He is coming back through in a week."

David reminded them, "It may not be safe going in a merchant ship. They'll tell the story of our journey."

All nodded. There was a long silence.

An old man said softly, "We need to make small curraghs that will make the crossing at the narrow part of the channel. They can be made fairly easily." He continued, "I have made boats in the past. I'll direct the construction. If we have four persons per boat, we need ten boats. That way we can carry any belongings that we need."

It started to rain. They all ran toward their huts.

Everyone was excited about the move and the leadership of Anaias. Those who were grieving the loss of a child or spouse or sister or brother could think for a moment about the journey, a new land.

The rain stopped and everyone returned to the fire circle. Five of the families voted to take the merchants offer and travel to Palestine. They weren't certain whether the merchant would take them that far. They were willing to go as far as the merchant would take them.

About six families choose to head to the east to the islands in the swampy country. Many good settlements had been left behind by Romans. The area was considered sacred by followers of Miraham.

Two families chose to move a few miles inland away from the place of the curse, but still remaining on the fertile land of the moors.

The day came. The small boats had been constructed. Everyone was packed to leave this sacred place.

Everyone made a vow that they would never tell about the refuge. No one would ever know where it was, or where it was moving.

As each hut was torn down, the extended family of each was responsible for destroying the evidence.

In a solemn ceremony, bread was broken and the two cups were offered to all the members of the refuge. The one cup had the wine from grapes, the other the sweet wine from honey.

There were many tearful farewells. There was also a sense of joy. Tinai started to play the flute in a lilting dance tune. Pelagius began to dance slowly to the music. His huge body seemed graceful as he reached out to Melania. Then he turned to Anaias and she followed his dance steps. Jeremiah joined them. Susanna, David and their daughter Mary danced together. Eventually all were dancing and laughing.

CHAPTER 46 – HOME WHERE THEY HAD NEVER BEEN TO THE CYMRUN (WELSH) COAST

Ten small boats were waiting for them in the cove. They took turns taking their belongings across the river on the raft. Then they made their way down the trail, watching carefully for signs of the local tribe people. They all looked back in gratitude to the place of refuge, its forests, its cliffs, and its sometimes treacherous coastline. For so many years, it had kept so many safe and hidden.

The crossing was uneventful. They emerged on a bank that looked vaguely familiar to Anaias.

"We'll set up camp here," Anaias said, remembering that this was the spot where she and Papallas had anticipated the move to the refuge.

"There should be good fishing," she said to the men eager to get started.

The women dug for mussels and collected seaweed. There was laughter and conversation into the night.

As the others headed to their tents, Anaias was alone with her memories and thoughts of Papallas. He had not returned in time. Would he know where they were headed?

Pelagius approached her in the dark. "You are very brave," he said softly.

"Or just crazy," she laughed.

Pelagius responded, "Yes, we all are." He was silent.

He said warmly, "Your husband will find you."

She said softly, "Yes, he will."

The next morning at highest tide, they headed out again in the boats, staying close to the shore. They camped further up the coast and could see the lights of distant fires on the hills above them but saw no people.

On the third day, they were just miles from Anaias' family. She breathed deeply as they set up camp. Pelagius was standing nearby. She said as she smiled at him, "I can almost smell the salt air of my childhood."

He responded, "Thank you for bringing the refuge to this place."

There was a knot in her stomach at the thought of returning to her home. She remembered how she had left in the dark so many years ago.

A gull flew over and landed next to her. Suddenly Beechna was there. "I told my friends you were coming home. They told the healer, Shrigan. She is the only one who listens. Most don't listen!"

Beechna seemed to pout for a moment. Then she giggled and waved her arms. "You're home!!! You're home!" She put her tiny arms around Anaias and hugged her.

They climbed to the top of the sandstone cliff to make their camp. Jeremiah helped Tinai climb. She had discovered she was pregnant just as they began the journey.

In spite of her excitement, Anaias fell asleep quickly.

Anaias awoke to her dog's bark. It was morning again. The dog's tail started to wag. She crawled out of her tent. As her eyes focused in the early morning light, she realized it was her cousin, Aengus.

He laughed, "Welcome home, Seabhac. We thought you might have gone off to find a husband, but we didn't expect such a large family."

"Aengus!" she cried. She jumped up and embraced him.

Aengus grinned. He pointed to the wagon he came in. "Your sisters and mother sent bread for all of you. There is salmon from yesterday's catch."

Anaias felt a sense of confidence as she saw her cousin's smile, she said, "We're going to settle all of these people on the cliffs above the village." She gave him a familiar look, and continued, "Where we used to play."

She was silent as she searched his eyes for the answer to the next question, "I have a lot to tell you, but first I want to see my father. He came to me in a dream..."

Aengus eyes grew large as he gently said, "He died a month ago, Seabhac. He called for you as he was dying. He must have found you. "

Tears filled her eyes, "But I thought..."

"That you could be here to nurse him." Aengus looked at her with softness, "Your mother and sisters were with him."

Aengus thought for a moment and added, "No one knew where you were. Now we're filled with joy."

Aengus embraced Anaias as she wept with grief and relief.

The encampment had been on silent alert since the stranger entered. Susanna, Pelagius, Melania and the others were standing together watching from a distance.

Anaias walked over to them holding Aengus' hand. "May I introduce you to Aengus, my cousin. He has brought food from the family."

Jacob and Pelagius stepped forward first. The men of the community joined in greeting Aengus.

They helped unload the food from the waiting wagon. They built a fire. The group of travelers realized how hungry they were and ate well.

When he was alone with Anaias, Aengus said, "I want you to tell me about the gods and goddesses that you met along the way and that you bring with you. We can always use powerful divine ones as long as they are friendly to us."

Aengus got back into the unloaded wagon and disappeared over the hill.

That afternoon, he came back with five wagons driven by her brothers, Ciallach and Giosai and two other young men she did not recognize. The four men stood at a distance, studying her and looking afraid of the refugees. Finally Giosai approached them.

It was now that Anaias really looked at the wagons Aengus had brought. "I don't remember that we were so wealthy." She stroked the wagons. "And the horses are beautiful."

Giosai said as he approached her, "The larger wagons are better for the bumpy paths. The wheels are sturdy."

Aengus walked up behind them, "We gained a lot when the Roman garrisons to the East were deserted. They left the wagons and horses. We helped ourselves." Aengus gave a boyish smile.

Giosai took Anaias' hand, "We've missed you."

The moment Giosai said those words his eyes left hers and he saw Luann. He said nothing but Anaias saw a light shining in him.

Her brother Ciallach stood in the distance and said nothing.

As Aengus pulled her up onto the seat next to him, he whispered to her, "It is time that you are finally home, cousin. You're needed here."

The land looked unfamiliar. Anaias looked across the sweeping landscape of Cymru. She was no longer looking through the eyes of a child.

The wagons stopped on the cliffs above her family's village. She could now, once again, see the ocean of her childhood. It was all that separated them from Eire. There was the smoke from the fires around the seaside village. Aengus, Ciallach and Giosai helped unload the wagons and set up tents.

She was silent as she remembered the night she left. She had felt her family would never forgive her. At the time, she had felt afraid and alone. A chill ran through her, knowing that she was still that frightened child even as she was the grown woman. Ana had taken her away to teach her what she needed to know. Ana had brought her back to do the work she needed to do.

In the distance, she saw a group of women emerge from outside the village carrying baskets and pots. There were six to seven of them all wearing shawls of varying shades of the village yellow.

Anaias' stomach began to rumble in response to her memory of the settlement's delicacies. She had forgotten after all these years, but now remembered. She remembered the breads and stews, the prepared laver and the eggs from the cliff edges. It was also the season of the berries, sweeter than anywhere else she had visited.

As the group of women moved slowly up the steep hillside trail, she began to see their faces. She saw Morganna and one who looked vaguely familiar. Suddenly she realized that it was her little sister, Geanta. She was a child when she left, now she was a woman of the village. Could it be?!

A cape hid the woman behind Geanta. Anaias' heart raced. She let out a cry without intending to. She ran to the edge of the path and stopped. She waited until the women arrived at the top of the clay path.

She had eyes for no one but the woman in the cape, "Mother!" Anaias cried.

M'alda looked up, pulled back the cape. Their eyes locked. They were searching for the old bond of mother and daughter. Immediately they found it. M'alda put down her pots and embraced Anaias.

Anaias looked at the face of this woman who had given her birth, who had celebrated her first steps and drilled into her the lessons of rudimentary survival.

Now Anaias was an adult looking at her mother through adult eyes. This woman had lost her husband, her brother and her father.

M'alda said simply, "You look strong and healthy, Seabhac."

Anaias' eyes then traveled to the young woman she had seen from the cliff-top.

"Are you. . .really...?" Anaias approached her.

"I am Geanta, yes," said the young woman, in a cold distant tone. "Welcome sister, it has been many years."

There was a chill in the voice, but Anaias remembered that her sister had always been shy. How can you get close to a sister you have never really known?

Geanta continued with the cold tone, "Aengus is our leader now and he has told us to welcome all these who you've brought."

Morganna pushed past them all and embraced her, "Seabhac, you are needed. We want you here. We've heard that you have a deep magic that you have learned from the caves of Ana. We've heard that the ones you bring have a powerful god. Our gods have apparently grown tired of us. They've left us to languish with the lesser spirits."

"Thank you for the welcome," Anaias said smiling at Morganna, who now talked to her as an equal. Anaias took the basket that her mother had put down. Luann had taken the pot of stew.

As she turned, she saw Pelagius and Melania at the top of the hill.

"We mustn't stay," said her mother. Quickly they put down the baskets and pots and turned to go down the hill. Each nodded to the assembled refugees. They each gave a shy smile to Anaias, once Seabhac.

Anaias was wounded by the quick departure. There was a surprise in each smile, though. There was shyness, which gave her some hope of reconciliation. Whether her younger sister looked at her with fear, shyness, or anger, she could not tell.

Anaias watched them go down the limestone cliff trail, now empty-handed. She pictured Seabhac running down behind them, scrambling to be surrounded by these women of strength and beauty. These women did magic with food, shelter, and clothing. All she knew about simple survival came from them. Survival of the body and of the heart was the magic of women.

The knowledge she gained in the caves of Ana and through the teachings of the Rabboni Yesua complicated her life. It seemed that as you dug deeper to find the power of the gods, your life became more intense. These women held the secret of simplicity

Suddenly Anaias smelled the fresh baked bread in the baskets...and oh, the stew! She became very hungry. Everyone from the refuge started to gather around and collect the food. Tomorrow they would travel to the red cliffs of her childhood. It would be a new place of refuge for these people. She was excited and filled with hope. It all seemed right and good. Joy filled her.

They ate the meal and set up the camp. They were ready for an afternoon of laughter and storytelling. Suddenly a gale force wind gusted in from the sea. It carried ice crystals and hard pelting rain.

Everyone screamed and ran for cover. Anaias hoped the tents they set up would withstand the winds and keep out the horizontal rain. She had grown up with this kind of weather. Storms that came with no warning were as familiar as the land, the laver, and the stews.

Anaias pulled a dry cloak around her. She was in her tent listening to the rain, and pulled the cloak around her more tightly as the sides of the tent bent in the wind.

A high-pitched taunting voice came from outside the tent. It was a childhood verse, "Rain, Bridey, rain! Give me a husband, give me grain, and make me fat with babies."

She flung back the flap and with rain pelting in, she saw a figure wrapped in black flax. A face peeped through.

She cried, "Elihf!"

"Seabhac! It is you, girly! No one would let me near. I took advantage of the storm. Nobody was paying attention, so I could sneak up here"

"How did you get up the slippery path?"

"I've lived here all the years you haven't." Elihf's face appeared now as she pushed her way into the tent, water dripping everywhere. She threw off the heavy cloak and flung her arms around Anaias. Elihf held Anaias in a tight embrace.

"Girly, it's so good to see you. When I heard you were alive and coming back to us, I could barely contain myself." Elihf pushed Anaias back and smiled as she searched her eyes.

Elihf laughed, "You're the same one all right. You're all grown up but I see the impish one in there. They said you were a priestess of Ana. Some are saying you are almost a goddess! Have you really seen Bridey?" She looked at Anaias' wide-eyed. "They say the women of the caves of Ana talk directly to Bridey?"

Elihf paused, but not long enough for Anaias to speak. She continued, "But then some say you have been cavorting with brownies and trolls and Romans and other folk to do us in. Boandas says you will want revenge." She took a breath.

Anaias responded, "I want only to be with my family and protect my new friends and serve Ana. Oh Elihf, it's so good to see you. You look so healthy."

Elihf responded, "I'm not only healthy, but I have two healthy sons and a good man to keep me warm at night. My man would be furious that I climbed here to see you. He's away now. You know they go out to sea quite often. I suppose he is getting food and exploring, and finding all sorts of wonderful treasures. Oh his stories . . . "

She stopped, "Oh Seabhac! I've missed you! It tore my heart out when my best friend just disappeared. And Boandas sent a curse behind you. The others spoke only ill of you. They wouldn't even let me talk about you."

Elihf sat closer to Anaias, "I wished you had been there at my wedding and when my sons were born. I thought about how much we could share together."

She looked at Anaias' face, saying, "How are you really girl? Have you had fruit from your womb? They say you came with many people, but no man!!"

Anaias took her hand, "Owain, now called Papallas is my companion. We have no children."

"So you've been able to be with that dreamy man? He appeared to be strong and smart! I imagine you've had such joy. There's such pain in giving birth. I guess it's a gift that you didn't go through it. But I love my boys. Where is Owain?"

"He is called Papallas now, and he is at sea as a druid

merchant."

"So we have that in common. We both yearn for strong arms and a warm body?!"

Anaias laughed, "Sometimes I wonder. I ache to be with him. Just the way you and I used to imagine it would be."

"But we've both shared the fury of life's storms, haven't we, girl?" said Elihf.

As they embraced, she remembered all the fears that had been a part of her life. She wondered if Elihf was still afraid of the ocean, rocks, and trees. She didn't appear to be.

Elihf took Anaias' hand and held it tightly, "This storm is fearsome. It's like a rage coming from Eire. Do you suppose that the gods of the EiNeill are angry because you and your magic have returned to us?"

Anaias laughed, "Oh that's just bluster. It's the winds that always blow. The people I came with have a god who calms storms."

Elihf brightened, "So the gods of EiNeill know they don't have a chance to stop the Eogan from returning soon." She stood and hugged Anaias, "Oh, I'm so glad you're home!"

The storm began to subside. Elihf picked up the tent flap, "I'd better get back. I'll be stewed if they find that I've been your official emissary. Many claim to have forgotten you. I surely never could. You're my same friend always." She hugged her, again, tightly. Then she pulled on her wet, heavy cloak and was gone.

As suddenly as it had started, the storm ended. The clouds were gone, the blue sky returned. The sun shone. Anaias emerged from the tent.

Pelagius smiled as Melania also emerged with Susanna. Pelagius asked, laughing, "Does this happen often? I might think that as cordial as the welcome of your people, they secretly tried to blow us off the cliff."

"I forgot to tell you. The ancient stories were that the gods of Eire have an ancient grievance against the gods of Cymru. They're always fighting and blowing." Anaias smiled to show that she was being light-hearted. "And I'm waiting for your Rabboni Yesua to bring calm."

"Ah yes, he will." Pelagius laughed.

Luann and Moira were busy cleaning the mess created by the storm. She had known them so long she only suddenly realized that they were not from here either.

Melania looked down on the village. "It is good of your people to feed us. We need to find a way to help them."

Anaias responded, "They are always ready for refugees, but usually they come from the sea. They expected us." She followed their gaze into the village below.

Just as she finished speaking the rest of the people gathered around, huddling and shivering, in the newly emerged sun.

They took a rope and strung it between two beech trees. The sopping wet capes and undergarments were left to dry in the sun.

She looked out at the sea and wondered if Papallas was on his way.

There were no ships on the horizon as the sun set. There was, however a beautiful red glow, set off by the clouds from the passing storm.

As she drifted off to sleep, she was reassured by the night song of the crickets and the sound of frogs. That was always a good sign, she mused.

She had come without her familiar collection of herbs but she was in the place that had been her home throughout her childhood. She pleasantly thought of how she would spend the morning gathering medicines before the first dew left the leaves. It was then that the spirit of the plant was most active and so its medicine was more potent. If Luann was awake, she might take her and show her all the possibilities. The spirit of this land was so strong.

In her dream, Ana brushed against her as a hot, invisible spirit. Anaias knew, though, who it was and followed her into the dark soils of the land. She had known this land throughout her childhood. She had never known it as Ana did. Beneath the earth, she saw the flickering lights of the energized roots. The animals and insects emanated their own energy.

Still dreaming they emerged from the earth. She saw, in her vision, the night forest she thought she knew, filled with flickering lights of all the life that was there. These were lights only visible to those who were willing to open themselves.

Suddenly the scene changed. Creatures appeared on horses whose teeth were flashing. They were like the horses of Boandas and the Brothers of Fireantachd. A loud whistling noise pierced the air. The horses and creatures whirled around each other. Anaias was uncertain whether they were locked in battle or in dance. The figures turned and rushed toward her. One was surrounded by a yellow light that became brighter as it approached until it was blinding. The horse came so close; she felt its breath and jumped out of the way. The horse road on. She knew who this was. Instantly she recognized the spirit of the Eogan, her ancestor. Behind him, glowing red was Neill. His horse, chasing Eogan also galloped toward her, then stopped where she stood. Neill looked directly at her with shock.

She screamed the blood curdling war scream of Ana. The dream ended.

She awoke to the calm of the night. Her body was drenched in perspiration and her heart was racing.

She heard footsteps stopping outside her tent. She held her breath and reached for her knife.

"Seabhac!" It was a raspy whisper.

It was a vaguely familiar male voice. She had been unnerved by the dream. Now she was frightened by whatever emergency required someone to awaken her.

"Seabhac!" The voice whispered again.

She pulled on her cloak and combed her hair. "Ana, Rabboni Yesua, Miraham, watch over me," she whispered to herself.

"Who is it this late?" she said testily.

"It's your brother," the voice said.

She opened the flap just enough to see out into the darkness. She saw a tall figure holding a torch.

"Seabhac, sister, it's good to see you." As her eyes focused, she saw her brother Ciallach. She remembered his look of hostility earlier. She was wary.

"May we talk, sister?"

"Can't it wait until morning?" she yawned.

"What I have to say to you is for you alone. It's for our family," Ciallach said.

To hear the words 'our family' include her was unfamiliar. She opened the tent to him. "Come in, Ciallach, it's been a long time since you called me sister." She opened the flap completely and didn't close it again, tying the flap open. The night air was mild.

"Seabhac, little sister, I hope you haven't been hurt by my silence to you. It was necessary." He walked back to where she had the flap tied open and untied it letting it fall closed.

He took both her hands in his. He looked tall, charming, and brotherly. "You look as though you have been strengthened by the years away," he said softly. He kissed her on the forehead.

She said nothing.

"We heard you were protected by the Roman you left with," he continued.

She felt the anger rising in her, "I did not leave with Romans. They were Greek, Cymru, and strangers to you, but friends to me. In my travels, I have learned a lot about the world. I've learned to be open to the ways of other peoples."

"Seabhac, you are obviously a woman of power and wisdom." He still held her hands. He let go of her hands and sat down on her mat. He patted it, as if asking her to sit next to him. She continued to stand.

"Please, sister, trust me. I'm your brother and I care very much for your welfare and that of our mother and brother and sisters." He patted the mat again. "Please sit and listen to what I have to say."

"We've never been close, Ciallach," she said gently. "But I'll listen to you." She sat next to him.

He made sure that he was looking directly into her eyes as he spoke. "Your cousin Aengus appears to be your friend." He steadied the gaze. "You need to know, though, that he has worked against our family. He has worked against your family."

"But he's our cousin. He is our family," she broke in.

"Don't interrupt me. You don't know what has been happening here." He raised his voice slightly. "Our uncle, Nad Fraich, spoke to me several times before he was lost at sea. He declared that I should be king if he should die. He didn't trust his own son. He thought he was weak."

"Why would he turn against his son?" she responded incredulously.

"That demonstrates the deep lack of faith he had in him," Ciallach said.

"Was anyone else present for this declaration?"

"Our grandmother was there."

"She is willing to declare you king?" she asked.

"We've not spoken about it. It is obvious, though, that I am the stronger person," he whispered emphatically.

"I don't know that that's true, Ciallach!" she said sharply.

"You are my sister. You must stand by me!" He raised his voice. He was no longer whispering.

"What could I do for you? Why are you telling me this? I'm almost a stranger to you." She continued her sharp tone.

He took her hand again. She started to pull it back, but he grabbed it. "I thought that when I first saw you. But then I realized that you've returned for a purpose. You are stronger and wiser than any other woman I have known."

He held her hand tightly. "If I am king in Eire, you will be very wealthy and powerful."

"Who else is part of this plan?" She was shaking.

"Many have grown dissatisfied with our cousin. He has led them into the land of the Romans and has obviously angered the old gods. His lack of desire for blood and battle is cowardly to say the least. He will disgrace our lineage. The Eogan dynasty deserves so much more."

"But what am I. . ." she said hesitating.

"You have brought people with you. Would they not like you to have all the power and wealth?"

"You would provide for them?" She doubted it even as she asked.

"I will give you land." He dropped her hands and stood up. Then he hesitated.

He tried to reassure her, saying, "You're strong. I will make you my adviser."

Anaias said sharply, "And you are therefore suggesting that I turn against Aengus and support you."

"Not openly. I'll tell you when." He turned from her. "When the time is right and he is off guard, thinking he can trust you, we'll act." He raised his hands and brought them down in a cutting action.

He did not see her shudder at his threat of violence.

He turned back to her, "Together we will return to Sheedrum. When the throne is in sight, we will topple the false one."

"Brother, I will not topple my cousin," she said firmly.

He was obviously shocked. He stopped talking and looked at her for a few moments as if assessing how to continue.

Softly he said, "You've been flattered by his attention. You're living in your memories. You remember him as a playmate." He smiled. He sat on the mat again. He tried to take her hand but this time she kept it firmly on her lap. "Things are different Seabhac! You will see! He may have been a great playmate. He must not be king." His voice was deliberate and controlled.

"But Ciallach. . ." she started to speak but knowing that more conversation was useless, she stopped.

He smiled as a co-conspirator. He patted her hand, "Keep making him think you are his old playmate. That's good. He'll not suspect a thing."

Her skin prickled at his words and manner.

"You go back to sleep now, little sister!" He stood up, as though he had accomplished his purpose. She stood up with him this time.

He kissed her forehead again, saying, "Dream of gold and fine cloth and amber stones adorning your red hair." He brushed her hair with his hand.

He embraced her and then kept his mouth close to her ear as he whispered, "Think about being called 'Your highness' and the men of the Eire bowing to you. It's within our grasp. You've been brought back for that." He turned and left silently.

His heavy energy remained in the tent after he left.

The morning thrush was beginning its song. It was time to search for herbs. Even if the sun didn't come up for a while, she would never get back to sleep. In spite of her conversation with her brother, her dream gave her strength. She knew the return to Eire was soon. The EiNeill ancestors were aware of her presence and it shocked them. In the meantime, she would care for the people here.

She stepped out of her tent. She turned to the east to look for the rising of the sun. There were no clouds, only a mist. It was very dark. It was the time of the new moon. It was a good time for beginnings.

In the darkness, she could hear the waves of the incoming tide crashing on the beach and nearby cliffs. The sparrows were each lending a verse to the morning song. She could feel the mist on her skin. She could smell and taste the salt air. It was a dance of the senses. She remembered again that she was finally home with her family.

Anaias headed out of the tent with her cloak pulled tightly around her. It was cold. She would find her way to the stream.

"Guide my steps, Ana," she whispered, wanting help scrambling down the hillside in the dark. She also needed help sorting out her dreams and the messages of the night.

"Why have you brought me here, Mother Ana?" She slipped on the muddy hillside. The rising sun hit her face. It warmed her.

"I have walked through fire..." She remembered the sisters. "for this."

A patch of herbs with the tiny red flowers was at her feet. She had her collecting bag open and began carefully pulling the plant up by the root. It was the root that soothed the spirit.

CHAPTER 47 – ALL IS WELL
CYMRU – IN TODAY'S PEMBROKESHIRE ON ST. BRIDE'S BAY

The sun warmed the earth. Beechna walked beside her with a glow surrounding them both. Beechna was glad to be back at her familiar tree home. It was like she had never left it, except for the tree being a bit taller and wider.

With Beechna's help, Anaias was able to find many of the familiar herbs. Some she had not seen since she left. Some only grew in this place. She would have to return to the tent and prepare them quickly before the full energy that they had collected during the night dissipated.

Anaias remembered the dance of the spirits. As a child, she heard a lot of the chattering of the non-human creatures, now the chatter of adulthood distracted her.

She scrambled down the side of the hill, blocked by a heavy growth of brambles. Obviously, no one had been this way for years. It had been a familiar path to her as a child, but now she could barely find it. Sliding down the hill, there was a break in the brush. There was the sound of lapping of water. This was her spring.

She knelt in the green ferny growth, risking the thorns. Pushing the overgrowth aside, she found a tender leafy plant with white flowers still clinging to life. She pulled up the unwanted plants so that this one could flourish. She continued to find and collect the plants and roots she needed.

She climbed back to the top of the ridge and turned toward the rising sun offering thanks to Ana. She stood silently absorbing the rays. A chorus of joy rose from the earth, Anaias added to it by asking for blessings upon all the people she had brought for refuge. She asked for blessings for her family, including Ciallach, and for Elihf who had silently stood by her. She asked for blessing and understanding for Pelagius, Melania and Susanna. She asked blessing for and from the holy friends Rabboni Yesua and Miraham of Magda. She asked for blessings for Boandas, where-ever he was. She asked for blessings for Papallas and for all who were to be a part of the new-born refuge. She asked a blessing for Katika and the spirit of Torrida.

She looked over at Beechna who had become a thrush greeting the morning with song. She remembered Ciallach's late night visit. Rabboni Yesua seemed to understand humans and what Pelagius called sin. Humans seemed to need the most help being what they were created to be. The other creatures seem to do well on their own.

She saw smoke from a fire coming from the center of the camp and smelled the fragrance of cooking oats that filled the air. She heard laughter and male voices.

She recognized Aengus' laugh, then she realized the second voice was that of Papallas.

Aengus, Papallas and Pelagius stood to receive her. All she saw was Papallas.

She put down her harvest and walked to him, embracing him wordlessly. They kissed long and tenderly. "Thank you," she whispered.

She remembered the others.

Anaias greeted them, "The morning is beautiful and fresh. Ana be praised! Rabboni Yesua be praised." She smiled at Pelagius, but continued to hold Papallas' hand.

"Thank you for the breakfast cousin." She gave the contents of the kettle a stir, sniffing at the oats and honey.

"I was awakened by your companion. He came up the cove at high tide," Aengus said.

"I was glad Aengus was standing watch." Papallas stood close to Anaias. "I wasn't sure if this was where you had gone. Fortunately some of the refugees were by the shore near the refuge and told me your plan."

He hesitated, then said, "I went to the refuge and was shocked to find it full of soldiers. They seemed furious. When I appeared, they started to rough me up." He acted out the treatment. "I acted like I couldn't speak their language." He looked at Pelagius. "They were looking for you. Apparently Paulina found that Jerome had died and went to live in Carthage. She told the bishop there where you were and that you were still preaching heresy."

All were silent for a while.

Pelagius spoke, "We are glad Christ Jesus has led you safely to us."

Anaias added, "How was your journey? Were you able to trade?"

Aengus was eager for information, "Tell me about Rome."

Papallas sat and remembered, "It is just a shadow of what it was when I arrived so many years ago. It has changed in just a short time," he said thoughtfully. "I found many Roman supplies abandoned on the roads. If you see something you need, you just take it. When we have time, we can explore the remains of an old Roman ship that I saw in the cove of the island where Torrida and I used to live. We may use it for the crossing back to Eire." Now he was looking at Aengus.

Papallas added, laughing, "The new tribes are coming in, but are more concerned about food and shelter than about traveling long distances in wagons or recovering old ships." Looking out to the sea, he said, "Every time I go south, the landscape and people change."

At that moment Aengus jumped up, ready for the day, saying, "I have seen all that you've brought. It will be useful for setting up your new refuge. We will check out the ship later." He turned to Anaias, "We need to get you to the more permanent settlement so your sheep can graze and your cattle will begin to give milk."

Anaias looked at him questioningly.

"Certainly you know that your share of the flock was kept safe for you, in case you did return." Aengus smiled at her, but turned away quickly to tend to business.

She thought about how many times she had wanted to come home but had assumed that she would be rejected. Now the reality was that at least some had been holding a place for her.

"We'll have to travel by the inland route. The wagons will be too heavy for the coast route," Aengus said thoughtfully.

Anaias was still amazed to see Papallas and Aengus side by side planning. She would never have thought this would be possible. There was the powerful hand of the gods and goddesses in this. Bridey and Pallas had always been close. Now Rabboni Yesua of the God of love also guided events.

Her heart felt that it would burst with love as she saw the men loading the wagons. They continued to talk about the trip up and over the hill. They planned how the trail could be cleared. They were discussing the spot Anaias envisioned for the new refuge.

Giosai, her brother, helped. Her older brother, Ciallach, stood off at a distance with a dozen men. His stares unnerved her. His hatred of Aengus cut like a knife though the joy of the occasion.

"Come and help," shouted Aengus.

"I'll help. Sure, I'll help," Ciallach yelled back, with sarcasm in his voice.

One of the friends with Ciallach came walking slowly toward them. Suddenly he turned and spit on Papallas, hissing, "You are Roman and are scum." His fist slammed into Papallas' stomach.

Papallas recovered quickly and swung his fist knocking him to the ground. Three other men came running over ready to join the fight.

Pelagius appeared between them, his huge body stopping them. "There will be no violence," he shouted. "There is a God of love who commands you to stop." Everyone stood still and starred at him. Then they turned and saw Ciallach who held a dagger in his hand.

Ciallach left the encampment with his friends. The work continued silently.

Anaias' sisters, mother, and aunts started measuring the women and men to make clothes for them to replace the old and worn ones they were wearing. Anaias marveled that they had really accepted these refugees as if they were her kinfolk. She smiled as she thought of how

Susanna and Melania would look in Eogan colors.

The clothing would be made from the woolen fabric dyed in the local lichens which gave a rich color using the right mordant.

She and her mother and sisters were talking as though no time had gone by. She met Pa'abhallia's children who were born while she was gone.

"You collected quite a few herbs this morning," her mother exclaimed.

"We left it all behind. I had to refresh my supplies for healing and well-being."

"And cooking too." Her mother picked up the savory weeds and sniffed them.

Anaias laughed, "Some have a double purpose."

M'alda looked at her and touched her arm gently. "I'm glad you were willing to come home,"

"I never stopped wanting to come home, mother." Anaias warmed to her mother's touch.

M'alda looked hard into her eyes. "Have the years been difficult, daughter?"

"Some were, mother, as for us all." Tears filled her eyes. "But you know that Ana watched over us so that this day might come."

"And this dark man, who made Boandas so angry, does he make you happy?"

"Very happy." Anaias smiled. She gazed off to the horizon. "Where is Boandas?"

Looking down and shaking her head, M`alda answered, "He was quite insane after you left with priestess Katika. He purged our camp to make sure that no one else would go against his rule. Your father plotted to have him replaced, but your uncle stayed by him believing that he wasn't just mad." She sighed, "My brother was afraid that Boandas had the gods obeying him."

"Is he here now?" Anaias felt a chill.

"He left us six months ago to meet with the council. He hasn't returned yet." M`alda answered.

"So you've been without a religious leader?"

"We have the wisdom of our old people. And Aengus has been very wise."

Listening, Anaias started to ask, "Did Aengus . . . ?"

M'alda interrupted, "You know your cousin, always curious, always breaking the chief druid's rules, always being punished."

"But never banished, like me," Anaias said softly

"He is the future king. . ." M'alda responded.

"But I heard that his father. . ." Anaias stopped.

"Didn't want that for him?" Her mother began to mix the dough for the cakes. "It was hard to tell what your uncle thought at the end. The end came too soon for him." She looked toward her oldest son in the distance. "I know that your brother has big plans because of a blessing he said he received."

"That would be good for our family," Anaias said testing her brother's powers over his mother.

Her mother searched her face. "I've never thought of your brother as one who could rule." She sighed, "To rule you have to care about people, not just having wealth and power."

"He asked me to help him." Anaias confided

"Of course he did, as he has promised me great things." M'alda began to knead the dough with hard pounding. "I used to think he was simply silly, but his talk is now dangerous."

Anaias felt relief. She was also beginning to see a growing picture of the future. "So he doesn't have the family's support."

"He has his friends," her mother said softly. "They are trouble. There is not an ounce of wisdom among them. You saw the way they acted with Papallas. They'll bring Ciallach down further."

M'alda put the dough in the pot, covered it, and built up the fire. "But I love him. My only task is to control him enough that we can get the rightful heir on the throne, your cousin. Then hopefully Aengus will make sure he is kept busy with a large bit of land." She smiled and laughed as if to cut the tension.

"And wealth," Anaias said as gaily.

"Yes, and what does your brother know of wealth?" She wiped her hands on her skirt and she stoked the fire. "I imagine he'll be happy with just a bit of the great wealth we will all have as the royal family. I remember my childhood, the jewels, the feasts, the castle with it's many rooms and the carriages." Her eyes were filled with delight at the memories.

Her mother turned her gaze to the Irish Sea. Then she turned quickly to Anaias. "We won't let you get away again." She smiled at her daughter. "We must make your huge family safe and happy."

Anaias said softly, "Thank you for being so accepting mother."

M'alda checked the fire again. "You've chosen the red rocks for them. I always thought it would be a good place to live. I once saw Bridey herself hovering over the place and felt blessed by her."

Pointing to the fields, she said, "We'll give you some of the new lambs. Oh, Seabhac their wool is so soft. We've mixed them with new breeds from the south. You can have a few of the milk cows," she continued talking as she cut the herbs.

Anaias responded, "I could barely believe it when Aengus told me that my portion had been saved for me."

M'alda looked surprised, "Of course we saved it! We couldn't stop hoping that you'd come back."

Tears filled Anaias eyes, "I never knew..."

M'alda gently said, "Of course we've always longed for your return. I'm so sorry you doubted that. But now you're home."

M'alda looked at her little redheaded girl. She was grown now. To M'alda she was still tiny and in need of protection. Of course Bridey will come. Who would not desire to be near this beautiful daughter? And she was home to stay!! How often she and her husband had talked of their longing to see her again. He had promised to search for her after his death if the spirit flight would allow it. She wordlessly reached up and touched her daughter's cheek.

They packed the wagons with food for the journey and new supplies for building. The large Roman wagons carried the heavy materials and refugees. They needed the larger horse to pull them. A few smaller wagons were also used. Smaller Cymran horses were sufficient.

They moved slowly up the chosen path.

The crows yelled at the procession as it moved slowly through the beech and alder. Out of the stream valley, the path leveled out and the trees changed to oaks. Sunlight filtered through the trees.

After an hour, they were at the top of a plateau and a wide wild-flowered expanse of limestone. A stiff breeze blew. An occasional outcropping showed a yellowish white stone. The caravan came upon a family of rabbits feeding who scurried out of the way of the intruders.

To the west, the terrain would be more difficult. The interface of the different rock outcroppings caused more hills and canyons.

The wagons stopped. They needed to leave the larger Roman wagons behind and load everything, through several trips, into the smaller wagons. Two of the smaller wagons were loaded with as many of the essential items as they could hold.

Anaias was looking forward to visiting this land of her childhood. She could almost see the young goddess Bridey dancing, swaying in the wind with the branches of the yew trees and oak trees that dotted the landscape.

All the spirits were alerted. Every creature shouted out to the others along the way. From birds to foxes to squirrels to rabbits, the reception committee prepared the way and discussed the possibilities. The winds awakened, the clouds gathered and drew near. Bridey herself awakened and stood tall in anticipation of this group of strangers settling on her land.

They came to a creek surrounded by berry bushes. A thrush sang brightly as Aengus navigated along the side of the stream searching for a way over.

Finding no obvious route, they got out. They pulled the horse into the stream at a wide shallow spot. Papallas and Anaias on either side steadied the load as they bounced it over the slick algae covered rocks.

As they reached the opposite bank, it was lush with gentian

blooming. A family of frogs leapt out of their way. The bank was steep. A group of lilies greeted them as they pulled from the front and pushed from behind. Anaias was assaulted by the fragrance of the fresh green leaves being crushed below the wheels and under their feet.

They bounced over the flat field avoiding the holes left by the many creatures that made their home there already. They were silent as they moved along.

Suddenly, in front of them was an outcropping of blood red stone.

Bridey sent a beam of sunlight as if pointing the way. She sent the songbirds to sing entry and called forth a whole gathering of the gannets to fly overhead. She sent a hawk for the little Seabhac. It circled the place over and over again in gentle circles. The rabbits and squirrels, excited by the energy of the arrival, scampered to, around, and before the wagons. The small wagons were moving slowly over the muddy, soft ground. The foxes and bobcats forgot their shyness and came out to watch.

Anaias got out and walked to the cliff's edge. She could see a potential path to the sea below but it was far beneath. The pathway she remembered as a child were now so narrow to her as an adult. The waves crashed on the rocks below. "Bridey, come now, greet your guests, fill us with your blessings," she whispered.

She turned around and looked back from the cliff.

"Grandmother Ana, by whose blood all creatures are born, give birth to a new community in this place," Anaias called out.

Quickly Anaias now named each place. The kitchen and the temple would be on the ocean side of the flame. The community room and the place of worship for Rabboni Yesua would be on other side of the flame toward the open fields.

The wagons were unloaded and the men headed back for the next loads. The people waiting on the road would come last.

Beechna came up over the hill and swooped down as a gull. It was smooth flying as she followed the breezes above the wagons. In the distance, she saw Rodnic, her brother, now a stag. She landed next to him. They took Tywa form to talk.

Rodnic grumbled, frowning, "Can't you stop them from building on our land!"

Beechna smiled at Rodnic's displeasure. She responded, "Bridey seems to be allowing it. I can't stop it."

"Torca have enough land. This has been ours for always," Rodnic complained.

"They're coming brother, lots of them. At least with these strangers, Anaias and Papallas are with them to teach them to respect our ways," Beechna said.

"Well..." Rodnic looked in their direction for a long time. Then he shrugged and said, "Let's play." He turned again into a stag and bounded across the field.

Papallas stood next to Anaias as they gazed out to the island he and Torrida had called home.

She asked him, "Will you return to visit to your small island, now that we have come this far?"

He responded, "No there is nothing for me there." He held her hand tightly thinking of Torrida and his days as a student. "Let the birds and the little people have that space."

Anaias stood gazing off at the sea. She thought about the power of the God who Pelagius and Melania had talked so much about. The teachings of Rabboni Yesua and Miriam of Magda did not seem to her to argue with the teachings of Ana. Ana was a creator who wanted all creatures to know of their oneness. Humans seemed to have the most problem with this. It made sense that the creator would send a human as a teacher.

She turned to see Susanna walking up behind her wearing her blue shawl. Susanna said softly, "Will you join us in the prayer?"

Anaias responded, "Of course."

They walked together to the makeshift village.

Pelagius started the prayer, "We thank you God for delivering us from danger and bringing us to this place of light. We thank you for your daughter Anaias and son Papallas who have led us to this place. Help us live gently upon this land." Pelagius then sprinkled water on the space around them, letting some of it fall on the refugees.

Anaias added a prayer, "Thank you Ana for your continued care. Teach us to care for one another."

Pelagius lifted the cup of wine. Anaias lifted the cup of honey. Everyone drank from both.

CHAPTER 48 – OPENINGS
CYMRU – PEMBROKESHIRE, WALES

"The man who really put the Eogan on their feet in Cashel and indeed in north Munster was Oengus son of Nad Fraich,"[79]

As Aengus cleared the edge of the forest by the stream, he heard Boandas shouting, "So he has finally defiled the goddess. We shall be ruined for sure!"

So Boandas is finally home, he thought. He saw him talking to Ciallach, his cousin. There was a knot in his stomach. What plot were they hatching now?

He rode past them and stopped the wagons in front of M`alda's hut. She came out and took charge of the horses.

M'alda rubbed the horses with a cloth. "Did they all settle in safely?"

"Yes, and it looked like the weather would be warm and dry for the building of their huts," Aengus said smiling.

M'alda sighed, "It's good to have Seabhac back among us."

Aengus added, "I'm not sure that is Seabhac. They call her Anaias now. She's changed so much."

M'alda smiled. "She's not a child anymore. But she's the woman that was always in that child."

Aengus said, "But she's so serious. She has a large family of strangers for her to care for now. There is an intensity about her. She seems to be attached to another world."

M`alda touched his shoulder. "And it's that intensity and attachment that will help you when you become king."

"But your son wants to be king. Why don't you support him?"

"Because he's not wise enough. A mother knows her own child." She looked in the direction of Ciallach who was still talking to Boandas. "My daughter Seabhac-Anaias and you are the only children wise enough to rule the Eogan lands."

Aengus responded, "And so you would insist that your daughter sit by my side?"

M'alda looked out to the sea, "You need to listen to her. Her journeys and ordeals have made her very wise." She added, "That wisdom will be necessary when we return." She sighed, "I think that great damage has been done to our people back in Eire. You need to be the healers as well as the leaders."

Ciallach was calling from the ridge, "Mother! Come quickly, the priest wants to talk to you."

M'alda had tied up the horse. She handed the cloth to Aengus and headed up the hill.

Aengus thought that he was also glad that Anaias was home. He enjoyed talking to Papallas and was curious about Pelagius and his god. It would be important to have ties with the riches of the southern lands. While the EiNeills attacked and plundered from the north, it would always be the strength of alliances from the south that would keep the Eogan family and the kings of Munster strong. It was trade and the strength of ideas and people that would help them hold the line. The god of Pelagius might give that strength. Certainly, Papallas assured him of the trade that was possible.

Geanta came down the hill from her morning tasks. She approached Aengus and said, "Has my sister been settled then?"

"Yes, she'll come to visit us in a few weeks."

Geanta sighed, "I don't remember her, only the grief that she caused when she left. Now it seems she's made Boandas angry again, not just at her but at all of us."

Aengus put his arm around her. "Her return, with these strangers, is his worst nightmare. It's said he tried to kill her. You need to help me protect her. We're glad she's home, we need her." He kissed her cheek.

Aengus headed up the hill to his hut. As he entered, Boandas, in his white robes, was waiting inside. Aengus was silent. As he hung up his cloak, he turned his back to him.

Boandas said harshly, "You put us all in danger."

"I don't think so," Aengus replied his back still to him.

"What you think is not important. You're foolish. It is what the gods think. You are not fit to be king of Munster." Boandas was hissing the words.

"Your task, holy one, is to support the king." He turned to him now. "I am to be the king and you must support my actions with your blessings and prayers and sacrifices to the gods."

Boandas said harshly, "Those you have brought onto our soil have defiled the whole meaning of sacrifice!"

Face to face now, Aengus looked into his eyes, "They have, I believe, brought greater blessings than you will ever understand!"

Boandas moved toward the door. Before he left, he turned back. "You will come to me weeping and begging for my blessings. It shall be soon!"

Aengus felt a chill in the hut as the priest left. He was uncertain. The gods of Boandas were old and familiar. His rituals had been so comforting to Aengus in his childhood. He had always wondered about the condemning words Boandas used towards Seabhac. He had, though, as a child trusted that Boandas knew something he didn't know.

Now he felt such joy at her return. Papallas was a friend with knowledge of the world outside. These were not enemies. Any gods that did not welcome these people did not deserve to be worshiped. At this thought, Aengus shivered. He could not be without gods. He would need to talk to Papallas and Anaias soon. He was curious about what Pelagius would say.

The refugees grew a taste for oats, seaweed, and the trout that swam in the upper streams. Anaias introduced them to the local vegetation and mushrooms.

Aengus and M'alda visited often. At first, they worshiped separately. Daily they found, though, that they gained more by sharing together. To speak of different gods seemed senseless since they were all being blessed equally.

Jeremiah came shouting and running through the new village toward Anaias' tent. "Someone, quick! Help! Tinai is calling for you."

All the women heard and put on their cloaks and ran toward Tinai. By morning, a new infant's cry was heard. It was like a blessing. Tinai and Jeremiah named their new son, Morgan. It was the birth name of Pelagius. The baby was surrounded by the blessings of Susanna, Melania and Anaias. The baby's cry was heard by all the creatures, as well as by the members of the Eogan clan down below. A baby's cry gives hope to all creation.

The red soil was said to be stained with the birthing blood of the goddess. So, of course, there was a lot of talk about blood. There was the blood of Rabboni Yesua's sacrifice. There was the blood of the persecution. It was the blood of courage. It was also the blood of the promise. The promise was life and the blood of the heart that continued to pump through their veins.

Anaias thought of the blood of her people, the blood of De Danaan said to be in her veins. There was the blood that her ancestors had shed to become the kings of Munster. There was the blood they had shed when they were sent into exile. There was the blood that would need to be shed before Aengus could ascend the royal hill.

She prayed to the Ana and to the God of the Rabboni Yesua and Miraham that her brother would not cause blood of the family to be shed for his schemes. He visited her regularly to remind her of those schemes.

The bard came. Cormonthuc was now married to one of the villagers that Anaias had seen in his lap, teasing him, that day so long ago when she had been a jealous child. He had ten children, all girls, who gathered around him adoringly.

He began to strum the harp and sing of the refuge and of the journey Anaias made.

Anaias held her hand up, saying, "Stop...we can't spread word of our refuge. It's a place where many people go and hide. Some adventures are best not told."

"But how will future generations know?" he asked.

"They'll know...somehow." Anaias thought about this and wondered. There was an ache in her heart that no song would tell the story. But then, she thought, maybe the story will somehow be told. She knew, for certain, that the goddess was with her. She was beginning to think that there was also the strong presence of the holy couple, Rabboni Yesua and Miraham of Magda. Somehow, she would just trust.

Papallas did not go on any journeys for several turns of the seasons. They tended the sheep and harvested the wool. They lived on eggs and goat's milk and seaweed and oats and honey. Whatever other herbs and roots they could harvest, they added to the diet and used for healing.

Every morning she woke with his embrace and in joy, they made love.

Anaias and Papallas were fascinated with the writings on the scrolls read by Pelagius and Susanna. Pelagius worked with Aengus to translate their sacred 'line and slash' writing called Ogham into Latin so it could record the words of their god and goddesses. At first, they felt nervous about writing the wisdom of the gods and goddesses. Then they understood that this was a way of communicating to those you may never meet in another generation.

Anaias stood by the cliff side holding the baby, Morgan. He was a toddler now. She was filled with delight that this child was growing in this new place. He would be a part of the earth here.

She was learning more about the god of the Rabboni Yesua. He cared how people acted toward one another. Her training about Ana was that all life was connected. She would, Anaias was sure, agree that it mattered very much how we cared for each other.

Most of the many gods and goddesses of the lands, rivers and streams did not worry about humans, though, except as humans touched their realm.

Humans certainly did need help. Rabboni Yesua came from God but was a human being. It was good that he was, he could help other human beings become what they were created to be. Pelagius reminded her how much wisdom people had, if they only used it. It was like Seallam's teaching about growing in the mind of Ana.

But then Pelagius had tried to explain that although Rabboni Yesua was human he was also a god. That confused her. He healed people who were sick, as Anaias tried to do. He seemed to understand, as the goddess Ana did, that the power of healing was within the person being healed as much as it was in the herbs.

It was much easier to identify with Miraham, his companion. She was human, but was his perfect student. Anaias thought she could try to be a perfect student of Pelagius and therefore of Rabboni Yesua, as she tried to be the perfect student of Ana. She prayed for Miraham's of Magda's guidance. Miraham would understand a woman's heart more than Rabboni Yesua and Pelagius would.

Through Rabboni Yesua, she heard that there was a powerful energy. She had heard a story of a time when he glowed like the sun. Rabboni Yesua taught Miraham that this same energy came to us when we were open to the fire of god and were within the mind of god. He called Miraham the 'inheritor of light.'

Anaias remembered the fire of the caves. She wanted to glow like the light of the sun to all the people. That glow would be what Pelagius called love.

Rabboni Yesua's god called on all to love, even your enemies, and to forgive and to walk even an extra mile. This god wanted you to give water to the thirsty and food to the hungry and clothing to the naked.

Pelagius explained that if you were a follower of Yesua, who he called Christ Jesus, you would be able to find in yourself the ability to heal people and to stop violence and bloodshed, and guide others to a new understanding of themselves.

Pelagius explained that the ritual, the initiation for opening your soul to this power of love and forgiveness, was baptism. Even a small amount of water given in the name of God as creator, would lift the heavy weight of the anger and sorrow of life and let you live in love.

CHAPTER 49 – EIRE CALLING CYMRU

WISDOM'S GIFT 4 -WHEN CALLED, MAKE CERTAIN IT IS A SACRED CALLING, THEN GO.

Anaias remembered the baptism of Tinai, and how her face had glowed as if God were really inside of her. She and Papallas decided they would be baptized. Luann and Moira also agreed. Tinai was excited and asked that her baby Morgan be baptized that same day.

The community walked down the cliff-side. There was a pool where the waters collected before thundering down the side of the sheer limestone rocks and entering the ocean. They waded into the pool with Pelagius-Morgan and Susanna Miraham and promised themselves to Rabboni Yesua, who is Christ Jesus, and the realm of love. They celebrated afterward with the two cups, of wine and honey.

Everyone who had been baptized also shared in new meaning for the loaf of bread and the cup of wine. Pelagius explained that this cup and loaf represented Christ Jesus' sacrifice for all. It was his blood and his body. It was only for those who were baptized.

Anaias pondered this ritual and its meaning. She would continue to offer the cup of honey-wine as a symbol of the joy in the dark deep mystery of creation.

The night after the baptism, Anaias had a dream. In it, there were old women on their knees reaching to the soil and wailing. There were no crops. She dreamed about babies dying in their mothers' arms. She heard the words, "Go home. Take the king and return to the throne."

She woke abruptly from the dream and got up in the night. She walked to the edge of the cliff and looked out at the glassy sea. Eire was calling. The full moon reflected off water. She was mesmerized by the iridescence of the moon against the white of the waves breaking on the cliffs below.

The next day she went down to the cove to talk to Aengus. As she arrived, she saw Boandas talking to Ciallach. She had lost her fear of Boandas and she had lost her desire to avenge the death of Torrida. Her heart opened in sadness for him. This must be the power of my baptism in Rabboni Yesua, she thought to herself.

"Hail Boandas," was all she said. "Have you seen the king?'

"Ha!' he snarled, "Not a king yet!!" Boandas pointed, "Your cousin, Aengus, is up the hill."

Anaias felt a gnawing in her stomach, realizing that she still disliked Boandas. Rabboni Yesua could not seem to end the power of those feelings. She continued through the village until she found Aengus.

"Cousin, we can't wait any longer, we need to return to Eire. I've heard them calling to me. We have to pack all the food we have available to us and load the ships and be ready to feed your people."

"Why haven't I had this dream?" Aengus asked.

She laughed, "Maybe I'm chosen to be your dreamer!"

"I'll call the leaders together and we'll decide." Aengus looked out to the sea. "You must meet with us and tell us your plan."

"I will." She bowed slightly.

As the people of the Eogan clan met, they expressed shock at the idea of returning to Eire without encouragement from any allies.

Ciallach was the first to stand and speak, "I agree with my sister. We need to return to Eire now, and be ready to fight for our rightful place on Shreedrum."

M'alda stood, saying, "I remember when my father was slaughtered on a field below the hill of Shreedrum. If the clan of EiNeill still has a grip on the land, they'll make our blood flow. It is better for us to wait and let our generations grow in peace here in Cymru."

Ciallach responded, "Mother, those are the sentiments I'd expect from you. Nevertheless, we've grown strong in exile and we have tools from the Roman Empire that will help us in an invasion. Our priest Boandas has brought us swords crafted by druids in the high mountains."

Anaias stood, saying, "My mother speaks as one with children who she wants to protect; but I speak as a follower of Rabboni Yesua. Rabboni Yesua' taught we must love our enemy not slaughter him. He also taught that we must feed those who are hungry if we can. There is a famine in Eire, we must get food to the people of our country, before there is any thought of battle."

Ciallach laughed, "How do you propose we feed the people without slaughtering the tyrants?"

Boandas said as he slowly walked around to the front of Ciallach, "We must not be timid. That our child Seabhac, once a daughter of Ana, now a follower of a stranger god, has had a dream is a strong omen. Bad or good, we can only guess. It may also be a trick of the gods. The druids of the EiNeill clan may have placed a spell on her. She is no longer pure. She has angered the gods. We may listen to her at our peril."

Several people rose to speak. Boandas held up his hand to stop them. "But, I like the idea of returning to Eire. The EiNeill clan is so used to us being gone. They would not expect us to return. We can sneak up to the hill of Shreedrum and slit the throats of the tyrants in their sleep. I can give a spell that will deaden them to our coming."

Anaias turned to Boandas, "But don't you see, if we draw the sword and kill an EiNeill, the monster will awaken and all the northern tribes will declare war on us." She turned to Aengus, saying, "Instead of feeding a starving people we'll bring a long and bloody war to them. That is no way to begin your reign."

Aengus was silent for a moment. "I don't see how we can return, cousin, without bloodshed," he responded.

"We have allies," Anaias said. "A small group of us could arrive with food at one of the ports of the Muscraige. The EiNeill clan will, as Priest Boandas said, not be expecting us. If we bring food to those who are willing to protect us, we can strengthen them. We can then grow our influence until we are able to verbally convince the EiNeills to leave Shreedrum."

Giosai stood, saying, "How do we even know if the EiNeills are still at Shreedrum. They may have already abandoned the place because of the famine."

Aengus turned to him, "You're right. We don't know." He turned to look at the group assembled, and said, "We need to send our own spies."

Anaias interjected, "We need to send food and healing."

Boandas stood up and shouted thunderously waving his staff, "This is absurd. Our gods require that we avenge the deaths of the parents and grandparents. We will not regain the throne of Shreedrum unless the gods see that we are willing to pay the price for it in our blood. If we return, we must fight our way to the holy hill. Only then can the rightful Eogan king find his way to the throne. Only then will the people follow his rule."

Ciallach jumped up in agreement, and pointing to the men around the room, shouted, "I'm brave enough to shed EiNeill blood. Who else is?"

All of the men in the room shouted that they were brave.

Anaias, standing next to Boandas throughout it all, held up her hand. She said, "While it's true that the gods may ask us to gain revenge, my training as priestess of Ana, and my training as a follower of Rabboni Yesua has taught me that all life is precious. Our cousins in Eire are starving and babies are dying of diseases. Right now, we must find a way to bring food and healing to them. We can win their hearts because they will see that we care for them. The teacher from the refuge, Pelagius, has told me of the words of Rabboni Yesua. He tells us that the power of love and compassion is greater than the power of hate and revenge."

Ciallach hissed, "That sounds like the words of a woman caring for her children or a man afraid to fight. We can bring food and we can also bring swords."

Aengus had been listening silently to the discussion. Now he stood, saying, "I hear my cousin's words, and they have extra power because they come from a dream. I don't understand the god she refers to, but I know it is a god of the powerful southern people. We will collect the grains and herbs, whatever beasts we can spare, and send a small group to the shores of the clans of the Muscraige. Our kinfolk are hungry and we must feed them." The room was silent as he spoke. "We will meet tomorrow, after we've brought the food to the shore. We'll prepare one of the Muscraige boats to be sea worthy."

Anaias added, "It needs to be a group that comes in peace, so that the children can be fed."

Everyone in the hut stood and prepared to leave the meeting. Most were stunned that the return to Eire was actually going to happen.

As the day progressed, Aengus decided that one of the Muscraige refugees, Ailill, would be part of the returning party. Anaias convinced him that she and Papallas would not raise suspicion. Later that day Giosai silently approached Aengus with a desire to go.

Papallas, Giosai and Aengus and several Muscraige clansmen repaired one of the ships that had brought them to Cymru years ago. They loaded it with grain and fresh herbs. Each family brought a pair of sheep. Several who could afford it offered a milk cow. As Anaias saw the food being put on the little ship she wondered just how severe the famine was. How many could be fed? Would they be overwhelmed by the need?

The village was filled with excitement. Even though it was just a small party of people going, everyone knew that this was going to be the beginning of the regaining of the throne of Eogan.

There was a lot of discussion about Anaias' dream. She had brought the interpretation of Ana and the teachings of Rabboni Yesua together in a way that people could understand. Of course, it made sense. If you fed a hungry enemy, you might gain their trust. But there was also a healthy discussion on the need for revenge and appeasing the gods of the land.

Anaias and Papallas prepared what they needed for the journey. She knew that she was now following the teachings of Rabboni Yesua and needed the help of his god, whose name was simply God.

She approached Pelagius' hut. He anticipated her coming, and came out, "You're doing the good work as a follower of the Christ Jesus. You're putting the words of his teachings to work. God's blessings will be with you."

"Will you come with us, as a teacher?" Anaias asked, almost pleading. She knew so little about this God she was following.

Pelagius smiled and gently said, "No, you're the one to teach the ways of Christ Jesus through your actions. The Spirit of God will help you."

Giosai was especially interested in making an inventory of the food and supplies; anticipating how many people could be fed and for how long. Anaias approached him.

Giosai was thoughtful, "This is a strange god Pelagius talks about. To give people we don't know a cow and sheep without requiring any payment or promise is odd."

Anaias wasn't surprised. She had been confused by the generosity of the refuge when she arrived there. She knew Giosai as a deep thinker. She answered, "But when you think about it, it makes more sense for our creator to want to feed us all; rather than wanting us to harm each other."

Giosai stopped and looked at her, "Yes, but I don't believe we can regain the throne without killing some EiNeills."

Anaias smiled, "Go talk to Pelagius. He'll tell you even more that makes sense about our creator."

Giosai stared at her, "Maybe I'll talk to Luann. She is also baptized, as you call it, in honor of this new god."

She laughed wordlessly and hugged her little brother.

On the other side of the beach Ciallach and Boandas were working on another Muscraige boat. Ciallach had his friends helping.

Papallas laughed, "It looks like theirs needs even more work."

Anaias said frowning, "We may need to leave in the night, so they can't follow us with their swords and talk of revenge."

Anaias packed work clothes, but she also packed her green ceremonial robe just in case it came time to approach the EiNeill brother who sat on the throne in Shreedrum. She shivered at the thought of the reality of approaching that Holy Hill.

It was late that night that the group of people, sheep, cows and pushed off from the shore. Beechna, and Rodnic climbed aboard excited about seeing their distant cousins. Beechna left everything behind except her amulet bag and the feather robe her grandmother had worn in Tuatha de Danaan banquets. She expected that she and Rodnic would be invited often, now that they were returning to Eire.

Aengus was not aware that they had left until morning.

Anaias stayed awake on the boat all night, gazing out at the sea. It was a storm-less night, which was unusual. It was the season of the sun and the days were warm and the nights short. She felt Ana guiding her; she felt Rabboni Yesua and Miraham; she felt Bride. She felt the stars dancing. She saw three shooting stars in a row. She pulled her cloak around her as the chill of the night grew.

The current was strong and all of them had to take turns rowing. By morning, exhausted, they saw land. The Muscraige, Ailill, guided them south to avoid the unfriendly tribes of the EiCeinnselaigh.

They launched a curragh from the boat and rowed to the shore, landing on a peaceful beach. Tears sprung into Anaias eyes as she stepped on Irish soil for the first time in her life.

She hugged Papallas and then turned to Ailill, saying, "Thank you for bringing us here."

Looking up the hill Anaias asked, "Are there any villages near here?"

"Just over the ridge, is my family home," he said looking worried. Usually his people were out on the beach in the morning. What had happened to them over these years?

Suddenly a group of giggling children appeared on the hill above. They ran off.

Anaias laughed, "Well I guess the adults will know soon that we're here."

They began to unload the animals and grains.

A group of men with spears appeared on the same cliff above. Ailill shouted in his Muscraige dialect, "We bring food for you!"

"Why are you here?" came the shouted reply.

"I am a cousin. I've been gone for many years and now return with food. We heard you were hungry," Ailill answered.

There was silence. One man came down from the cliff-side still holding his spear.

He stood at a distance staring at Ailill and then looking at the small group gathered around him. He stared for a long time at Papallas with his dark curly hair. Everyone was silent, allowing him to decide for himself whether they were friendly.

"You are kinfolk?" he said to Ailill.

"Yes many years ago I left with my family to go to the kings refuge in Cymru, across the sea." He pointed toward the waters.

"Have you seen our king?" the man asked.

"Yes, King Aengus sent this food. He wants to strengthen you and then he'll return." Ailill added.

Papallas knew that they came in peace, but he was nervous about the intentions of this man who held the spear.

The man lowered his weapon and extended his hand. Ailill told him the whole story of the dream and their purpose in bringing food. The man turned and walked back up the hill.

As they started a fire to cook the noon meal, a woman appeared with a basket. She didn't seem to be as afraid as the others.

She called as she approached, "We heard Ailill has come home and that our prayers to Danaa might have been answered."

Ailill stood and embraced her as a cousin.

She opened the basket to reveal dried salmon, turnips and a flask.

She saw Papallas looking at the flask. She asked, "Have you had the ale of Danaa?" She smiled, "If you are not of our land it might have an odd effect on you."

She offered the flask to Papallas. He took it answering, "Thank you, I'll try it after this long journey."

The woman turned to Anaias, "I'm Fiona and I heard that you're a healer who heard our prayers in your dreams."

Anaias blushed, "I've longed to be here all my life. If I can also heal your people and feed your hungry, it would bring me happiness beyond my wildest dreams."

Fiona responded, "We lost many of our healers. The gods and goddesses of this land have deserted us for some reason. Our animals have died and our crops have failed. It rains too much and the sun rarely shines. There is little for the cattle to eat. There's no milk for the children. The EiNeill king then demands a part of the nothing we have."

"We've come to help," said Anaias bowing to her.

Fiona fell to her knees and took Anaias hand. "We were the ones praying. We didn't know you would hear them in your dreams. You are an answer to our prayers."

Anaias eyes filled with tears. "It is not me. It's the teachings of the God of Rabboni Yesua, who teaches about how we should care for one another."

Fiona was still on her knees as she said, "Whoever your god is, if he sends you to bring food, I'll follow him also. I guess he's the one who answers our prayers now."

Several other women appeared on the horizon.

CHAPTER 50 – EIRE UNDER FOOT SOUTHERN IRISH COAST NEAR TODAY'S WEXFORD

WISDOM'S GIFT 5 – TREASURE THE CONNECTIONS THAT ARE GIVEN TO YOU.

Ailill was surrounded by women hugging him. Some were distant cousins. Some were just friends that had known him since he was a child. They asked about the family he'd taken with him to Cymru. They were healthy, he said.

Fiona turned to Anaias and Papallas. "You're welcome in our village. We accept this gift of cattle and lambs. We'll share them with other villages. We'll also ration the grains and herbs carefully."

Anaias could tell that Fiona was the leader in her village. She said to her, "We need to know from you how much food is needed. We can return to Cymru for more."

Fiona looked startled, "But you must stay. The next ship we see must be the king coming home."

They headed toward the village with the animals and other food. Children began to crowd around them. Their faces appeared sunken and yellow. They were children, though, and they jumped and laughed.

A very old man came out of the hut with a flute. Several other men came out with drums to celebrate this small group's arrival.

The man with the flute stopped playing. He took Anaias' hand, "My name is Brion. I fought with your grandfather. Welcome home."

A woman walked up behind Anaias and stood silently. Anaias turned around to see her holding a young boy. His arm had a large oozing wound. "Can you heal him with your powers?" She looked at her wide eyed. "We've tried remedies and none has worked to get the wound to heal."

Anaias walked off alone with the woman and boy. She found her pack with the healing salves. As she looked at the wound, the boy screamed. It was infected. She took out her blade and cut away the infection. The boy screamed in pain and fear. She had the women boil some of the astringent herbs and placed a poultice on the wound. She put a bandage over it.

She said to the mother, "Tomorrow we'll let the wound be baked by the sun."

The boy continued to whimper as Anaias inspected his general health. She noticed that the boy's arm was just skin and bones. His face was sallow. She kissed the boy's head. Tears were streaming down his face from the pain she had caused. He was not sure if he wanted her kiss.

"He needs something to eat," Anaias said softly to the mother. "The cows we brought are full of enough milk for all the children. We should start with the children."

The people in the Muscraige village brought out the meager food supplies they had stored. Fiona tried to feed Anaias and Papallas extra because they were guests, but they refused it.

In the meantime Beechna and Rodnic were wandering over the countryside. They were amazed by the lightness they felt in this land. "It's like we were born to be here!" Rodnic said to Beechna, "The Tuatha de Danaan can't be far away."

Beechna lifted her arms, "I think they know that Anaias is here, and they're celebrating also."

Rodnic looked at her wide eyed, "Let's go to Shreedrum and see who's there."

Beechna put out her hands, "Shall we join the crows?" Rodnic took her hand, turned feathered and black and they both flew off to the south west.

That night they returned and found Anaias awake next to Papallas in the tent.

Rodnic jumped to where her face was on the ground, and waved his feathered arms.

Anaias yawned, "I wondered where you'd gone."

Rodnic was breathless as he turned back into his Tywa form, "We've been to Shreedrum. You've got to go there with your message of helpfulness. The prince of EiNeill is Conal Err Breg. He is almost ready to pack and leave."

Beechna appeared behind him, "We heard his wife yelling at him."

Anaias asked, "Why would he want to leave?"

Rodnic responded, "I think he feels betrayed by his father, that his brothers received more prosperous lands."

Rodnic added, "He can't get enough to eat, even when he holds hostages and demands food from the people."

Anaias frowned, "Well of course he can't. There is not enough food here to feed the people, let alone one who thinks he should eat well as king."

Beechna nodded, "From what we saw he eats well. His platter was filled with salmon, beef, carrots, and turnips. He had the finest honey-wine." She frowned, saying, "He has a wife and daughter that eat well too, even though they were yelling and complaining."

Anaias sat up on her mat, saying, "It's too early for me to go to

Shreedrum." Somehow, though, her heart told her it was time. Rodnic and Beechna disappeared. Anaias went to sleep.

In her dream, she became the hawk, she saw the castle on the hill. She flew above Conal Err Breg as he slept. She saw a group of the Tuatha de Danaan, surrounded with light, tall and red-haired with shimmering robes massed like an army around the base of Shreedrum.

One of the men turned to Anaias in her dream and said, "You alone can talk them into leaving." She woke up. Anaias could hear the crickets outside the tent. She remembered the dream she had had years ago when the Tuatha de Danaan were preparing the hill of Shreedrum. She was now in Eire. She was home. Everything was moving so fast. She fell asleep again.

In her dream, the women of the cave of Ana appeared to her. She saw Katika, her eyes filled with tears, and Llakino, the old woman of the cave who had died, and Seallam her aunt and teacher of Ana. Seallam stepped forward, "Go to Shreedrum. It's time. You were born for this." They disappeared.

She woke up to the bird's morning song. She found the ceremonial cloak.

Fiona was cooking the porridge in the central kitchen. Anaias asked her, "How far is Shreedrum from here?"

Fiona looked at her wide eyed, "It is a half day's ride in one of our carts, two days walk. But it's a dangerous road."

Anaias responded, "I need to go talk to Conal Err Breg. He's ready to leave on his own."

Papallas was coming to the fire as he heard the conversation. "That's not your work. Only a man with a sword should talk to an EiNeill. They won't understand your talk of forgiveness and love."

Anaias turned to Papallas, "I believe he will respond, not because it's forgiveness and love, but because he knows there is nothing here for him. The people are too poor for his lavish lifestyle. I will simply tell him what he knows already."

Papallas looked grim, "You need a group of men to go with you to protect you."

Anaias said softly, "No, it is better if I go alone. But with your prayers."

Brion fixed a small cart pulled by an Irish horse. He looked at her wistfully, "I'm not a young man anymore. I wish I could go and defend you." He looked into her eyes for a moment, "But you are not an ordinary woman. I don't think I need to worry about you."

She headed down the path in the cart. It was not a large Roman road, but more like a narrow trail just big enough for the cart and horse. She was a woman alone wrapped in a green cape. For those who could see it, she was not alone. A crowd of Tuatha de Danaan and a cloud of Tywa surrounded her. As she traveled down the road, most people did not observe her. The most important thing was that she arrive at Shreedrum.

As the hill appeared before her, she let out a gasp. She wished she could share this first sighting with Aengus and Papallas. Her eyes were the first of her family, born in exile, to see this holy hill, Shreedrum, this rightful home of the Eogan clan, the Kings of Munster. On this hill, her cousin Aengus would rule as king. The words she would speak today would clear the way. She prayed for the wisdom of Ana, of Rabboni Yesua, of Miraham of Magda.

She stopped the cart in the village below the hill. There were merchants trying to sell chickens and lambs and vegetables. The chickens and lambs were skinny and the vegetables were wilted. No one appeared to be buying.

Anaias began to walk up the steep hill.

She kept the green robe pulled tightly around her. As she reached the top of the hill, she entered a dark room. She was surprised there were no guards.

As her eyes got used to the darkness, she saw a heavyset, short man sitting at a table. She assumed it was Conal. "Hail Conal Err Breg, son of EiNeill; I come from the cave of the daughters of Ana."

He looked surprised to see her. He stood and approached her. "You do me honor. We've often heard of the exploits of the daughters of Ana as they fought off the armies of Caesar," Conal said laughing.

Anaias smiled, "So you know more about the world than I thought."

"We take slaves and the slaves talk. But why are you here?"

"I come to talk about the great work you might do with your brothers to the north"

"They're fully occupied."

"Maybe they are, but there is more to be done because the lands there are fertile and full of promise."

"Why are you concerned?"

"Because you're not of these people and you never can be."

"My father would disagree with you."

"But your father has died. It is only you brothers that divide the land."

Conal came close to her, saying menacingly, "I think you've come because you've heard of my prowess as a man. I have a wife and daughter in the castle, but many sons in the village below. Would you like to take off your priestess robe and ...?"

Anaias stepped back, saying sharply, "Please, I've come to talk sense to you. I've come in peace."

He moved toward her menacing, "I'm not a peaceful man. You

are a lone woman and you can do nothing to stop me. What if I take you as my hostage and use you when I want to..."

He put his arm around her body and pulled her close. He then pushed her up against the wall. She could smell his strong odor and began to feel sick. He tried to find the opening in her cape. She struggled but could not break free of the grip of his one arm. She felt his rough hand move to her naked skin and across her breast.

With his other arm, he pushed himself on her until she could feel the hardness of his groin protruding and pushing against her.

She suddenly found the strength to shove him away with a free arm and she kicked him in the swollen groin. He held her cloak and finally knocked her to the ground.

"Ah, you make me even more anxious to be inside you. He lunged down on her, as she scrambled out from under him and slammed the back of his head. She ran for the doorway. She screamed, "May the curse of Danaa be on you and your family."

She ran down the path from Shreedrum. Deep sobs came from within her. Why had she come? She was so stupid to come alone.

She did not dare look back to see whether he was chasing her.

She found the cart as she had left it. No one even looked at her as she headed the little horse and cart back toward the Muscraige village.

As she traveled she began to run though every movement. Why weren't there any guards? It was only because he was alone that she was able to run free. Why was he alone?

She continued to consider her stupidity, her embarrassment, as she let the horse take her to his home. She wondered at the teachings of Rabboni Yesua. She wanted this meeting to be peace filled and to show her forgiveness; but how could you forgive the foul EiNeill creatures. She failed Ana; now she failed Rabboni Yesua.

She heard a voice within, "You have done what needed to be done."

Whose voice was it? Was it from the Tuatha? What is Katika's voice? Was it the voice of Ana or of Miraham? Could it be her own voice of wisdom?

She had, after all, been through fire. Now she had faced down an EiNeill brother.

It was after dark when she and the horse pulled the cart into the village.

Papallas met her, "You're back quickly, I'm so glad. I was worried that the EiNeill brother would injure you."

She wordlessly got out of the cart and hugged Papallas. Trying to hold back her tears she did not say anything, but moved toward their tent and went inside.

She collapsed onto her mat sobbing. Luckily, Papallas did not follow her into the tent or ask her what was wrong. She had been stupid. She had failed in her task. The words of Pelagius were worthless. What was this 'love your enemy, forgive' all about? She had cursed Conall Err Breg not just for threatening her but for letting these people starve while he was living well. She would keep shouting curses at him. He had been a part of the family that killed her grandfather and uncles and put her family in exile. It had not gone well and she was filled with a heavy sinking feeling. She fell into a deep sleep.

Papallas awakened her later to give her broth. She woke and drank it, but her body felt heavy. Sorrow filled her. All her life she had dreamed of Eire and here she was, but she could not make their life better.

She was in a deep sleep all night. In the morning, she woke to the sound of a wren celebrating the sunrise. Papallas was on the mat with her, holding her gently. She quietly moved his arm and walked into the Irish sunrise.

She saw the cloak she had worn yesterday hanging in the sun. Someone had been thoughtful enough to wash it. Conal's touch was gone from the cloak, but she needed to wash her own body.

There was a chill in the air as she walked to the cliff by the shore. The tide was in. She walked down the steep path and took off her under-gown. Taking a deep breath, she stepped into the incoming wave walking further out and sinking down until the ocean water cleansed her skin and healed her spirit.

As she emerged, she sat in the warmth of the rising sun. The brilliance of the tattoos of her woman-body glistened on her wet body.

She said softly to the air, "Rabboni Yesua, Miraham his partner, your teachings are so entrancing, why don't they work?" She loved the sound of Pelagius' teachings. Everyone has good in them; talk to them; bring out their good; pray about it. Pelagius had said it was so much better then killing and being killed. Life was so precious, he said.

Ana would say the same thing. Life was precious. Ana, though, didn't require forgiveness.

"Miraham, you are a woman so maybe you understand more than the man Yesua. Were you able to live his message of love? After he died, where did you go? Did you stay faithful to all he said?" She sat silently waiting for some answer from Miraham of Magda.

The sun warmed her. She felt a euphoria welling up in her in spite of her sadness. She was home. This was Eire. She no longer needed to search the horizon looking for ships. She felt a joke welling up. So this was Eire? Did she expect a fairyland where the Tywa ruled with games and laughter? Hadn't she heard all her life that this was a land torn by war?

She heard a voice deep inside, "This is your work, Anaias, it is not easy. That's why I prepared you."

Who was speaking? Was it Ana or Rabboni Yesua or Miraham or just her deep wisdom? Pelagius said we all had deep wisdom.

She sat for a while longer until the sun was fully in the sky. Her skin was dry. She put on her under-gown and walked back to the village.

Fiona was at the village edge to greet her. "What did that Conal do to you? I was afraid for you. I've heard rumors of how crude and evil he is."

Anaias stopped before her. "He wasn't able to hurt me. I think I hurt him." She said as much as she could, considering the pain of the encounter. "But I failed in my talk with him. I don't know why my dream said I should go. It felt like the right thing, but..."

Fiona looked at her sympathetically. "We've all hoped the EiNeill family would just up and leave. What you did was no better but no worse than anyone else's attempts to convince him." She smiled, "But maybe you hurt him enough in the right places." She playfully grabbed her crotch. Fiona and Anaias started giggling like girls.

Papallas walked up when he saw the laughter. He was afraid for Anaias and was relieved to see her laugh.

Papallas said to Anaias, "We're glad you're back with us. There are several children in the next village that need your healing medicines."

Fiona responded, "So, let's feed you, and put you all to work." They walked over to the central fire where several women were cooking the morning porridge.

There was a bucket of fresh milk from the cows they had brought. The children were pouring it liberally on the porridge.

One of the young mothers, Brianne, sighed, "It's been a long time since we could let the children drink so much milk. Our cows stopped producing when the fields stopped growing the grass for feed."

Brianne turned to Anaias, "Thank you for saving our children."

When breakfast was over, Papallas and Anaias went with Ailill to another Muscraige village with one of the cows. Several of the children were weak and growing thin. Anaias gave them a tea to strengthen them and left the cow with the villagers.

A full cycle of the moon had gone by. It was the new moon. A runner from the Fir Maige came into the village shouting. "They're gone! Conal Err Breg and his family and his guards are gone!"

A crowd gathered around him, asking him what he meant.

"In the town around Shreedrum they saw him leaving in the night. A group went up to check the Holy Hill and found it empty."

He looked around as if figuring whatever question would be next. "And he took all the extra food and jewels with him."

There were cheers and Brion came out with his flute. The

drummers came out and several people started dancing in joy. The runner went on to the next village.

Fiona hugged Anaias, "I guess your talk with him worked!!" She looked into her eyes and laughed playfully.

Anaias was stunned. Had she heard right? Was it really over? Had the EiNeill clan really left Shreedrum?

Papallas came up behind her. She turned and sunk into his arms amazed, confused, and strangely wiser.

Papallas looked into her eyes, "I guess we should go back to Cymru and get our king."

CHAPTER 51- THE KING RETURNS
SOUTHERN IRISH COAST NEAR WATERFORD

This time, when someone of the Eogan clan saw a ship on the horizon, it was Anaias and Papallas. This time it was the news they had been awaiting for decades. It was time for the king to return to Shreedrum.

Aengus and a crew had salvaged the Roman ship. This ship would hold more people and supplies for the return journey of the royal family.

Pa'abhallia, her sister, would stay behind with her family. Geanta decided to stay with Pa'abhallia and her Cymru village.

Elihf hugged her, saying, "You go on ahead. My man, children and I will join you and the king soon. We're not really adventurers, you know."

Anaias looked deeply into the eyes of this friend and hugged her. Then she said, "I'll miss you. Come soon and join us."

Anaias and Papallas said good-bye to the people of the refuge.

Jacob, Susanna and David and the others would carry on their tradition of opening their hospitality to those needing safety. Jeremiah, Tinai, and the baby Morgan would stay in Cymru.

Luann and Moira decided to go with the family to Eire. They spent a few tearful moments saying goodbye to Tinai and the toddler Morgan.

Pelagius and Melania decided to continue their journey to his childhood home in northern Cymru, call Yscoed. In spite of the dangers, he wanted to see who in his family was still alive. He would once again use the name Morgan, and disappear into the crowds.

Pelagius said to Anaias, "You've heard my message, daughter of Ana, and I think you understand the teachings of Christ Jesus very well."

"They're hard words I've learned." Anaias responded. "I'm not sorry that I shouted curses at the EiNeill brother."

Pelagius laughed and responded, "Sometimes it is not wrong to call evil what it is. Love is not all about comforting people. Sometimes we need to challenge them to hear God's call to be better people. So for you I say, go with God!"

She hugged him. His huge body enveloped her for a long time.

Melania was standing behind them, and stepped forward and hugged Anaias. She said "Blessings to you, in your journeys. You'll learn to understand the power of the teachings of Christ Jesus. Keep telling people about him, maybe you'll awaken the spirit of love throughout Eire."

It was tedious getting everyone onto the ship. Once on the ship, all eyes turned west, to Eire. Anaias and Papallas were the last on, after all the farewells. When the sea was calm enough, Cormonthuc took out his harp and sang about the journey home.

He even sang about Anaias' visit to the EiNeill brother, and how he fled with his family soon after. The song included the gift of food taken to the people of Eire.

At dawn, someone shouted that land was appearing. Then they heard the music.

As they approached the shore, the sound of pipes and drums shook the silence of the long sea crossing.

Danathie, the former king's wife, stood at the bow, wearing her robes freshly dyed and repaired by Morganna. Boandas stood next to her in full white robe with gold belt and necklaces. Aengus wore the robes of his grandfather. Anaias wore the white gown from the caves of Ana. Papallas was beside her with the robes of Pallas.

Aengus turned to Anaias, "You didn't warn me about the brilliant green of the land." He took her hand. "This is the day we have waited for all our lives. Thank you for making it happen." He was silent, almost sad as he added, "I wish my father could be here, and my mother."

Anaias was silent as she realized that he rarely spoke of his mother who died when he was very young.

The boats came closer to the shore. The musicians were standing with family groups, dressed in similar colors. She felt the pure love that she had heard was in the Rabboni Yesua and was a part of the mind of Ana. That love filled her and reached out to all the people she saw.

Papallas walked up to her side.

"Do you feel it?" Anaias asked Papallas as he held her hand.

"I do," he said softly and kissed her cheek.

She could now hear the voices. There was cheering, laughter and women's voices from the shore. She heard children shouting.

They dropped anchor a distance out and lowered the curraghs into the shallow water. The royalty waited until last, so the others could prepare the way. As each curragh paddled to the shore, she saw a group of people run forward to pull it in. As the boats were unloaded, there were shrieks of joy and the music got louder for a while. The people then stood back to look for the next curragh that was coming in.

Danathie and M`alda were taken to shore by Ciallach and Giosai. Danathie was still considered queen. The people on the shore wrapped her in their capes as she walked into the center of the crowd. They bowed to her. Some of the older ones wept at her return after so many years.

The curragh carrying Aengus also included Boandas and Anaias. As it came to shore, a group ran forward to pull it in. The music was full volume now. Boandas was the first off the boat. As he arrived on the shore, he waved his staff. All the people gasped and stepped back.

Boandas shouted, "Be watchful of the gods and goddesses as they test you." He looked around at the people. "It has not been an accident that you've been miserable." He reached out to a child in the crowd. "Make sure that in the future you pay attention to the needs of the divine ones. I am here to help you. Do not be so sure about who the gods have chosen as your king."

Anaias was the second off the small boat. The people cleared the way for her. As she touched the sandy beach, the air seemed still. The light's danced. It seemed as if she were walking through another time and space, as if the Tuatha de Danaa had spun a spell. She had no words to speak.

Finally, Aengus came off the boat. Only Brion and the elder men of the clans stepped forward. There was silence and everyone present bowed to declare his or her loyalty.

Brion declared, "Welcome, son of Nad Fraich. Welcome, king of Munster."

As Aengus walked to where Boandas, Anaias, his grandmother and aunt stood, people began to applaud.

He said, "We had to leave, and we are sorry we left you in the hands of tyrants. We hope we have come back to you wiser. We know you have grown in wisdom and can teach us. If you will allow me to rule, I will rule with fairness. The divine realm will smile on us all."

An old woman and man emerged from the crowd offering a cup of honey-wine. "Weary travelers, it is time you shared the stuff of Ireland. It will mend your hearts so that your family can return to its former glory. The hives of this place, through the help of the goddess, have taken the light and heat of the Irish sun, gone into the heart of the brilliant Irish flower. It has been made in the darkness of the queen bee's cave, thinking of this day, and was taken only at peril of the sting by a brave keeper."

Boandas reached for the cup, but the woman pulled it back from him and offered it to Anaias.

The old woman smiled at Anaias, saying, "Yes, Danaa is strong here, as is her daughter Bridey!"

Anaias stepped forward and bowed as she took the cup. Anaias lifted the cup and asked for a blessing from the sacred presence around them. She took a sip and then she offered it to Aengus. She was amazed at the full quality of the honey-wine. It was sweet and fiery. It tasted like none she had drunk before. This was true honey-wine of the Tuatha De Danaan.

Aengus spoke, "The hives that led our people here eons ago have led us here again and offered us the sweet first fruits of their care." He sipped again. Then he emptied the cup.

A cheer went up. Then there was laughter as the old woman reached behind her and pulled out a flask tied to her waist. The king held out the empty cup and she filled it again.

"You will be our king for many decades to come!" she whispered to him.

He took the newly filled cup and offered it to Boandas and then his grandmother and all the mothers and brothers and sisters and cousins. As Ciallach took the cup his eyes met Anaias'. The anger in them cut through the light of the hope-filled moment.

She felt the cold chill. She remembered Pelagius warning to her that peace and joy was fragile. One should celebrate in it. All the while, we must expect the treachery of the stupid and greedy. Was her brother really just stupid?

Suddenly a hawk flew over and let out a cry. Everyone watched it circle in the sky. Flocks of gannets circled and were joined by gulls. Several people shouted that a school of dolphins had been spotted in the surf.

Anaias smiled at her fears. Whatever might happen, she and Aengus were here, and he was king.

As they moved up the shore, they found tables spread with food. They were hungry and thirsty. The food was welcome.

The table was piled high with salmon and mussels and greens and carrots and turnips. Cream cakes and berries were brought down the hill.

Anaias turned to Brion, "I thought you had a famine."

Brion winked at her, "Ah we did, for the brother EiNeill. For the real King of Munster we are wealthy."

They ate until they were stuffed.

After they had eaten, Cormonthuc silenced everyone. They gathered around as he sang the story of the time in exile. They cried as he sang of the death of the king in battle and his son in exile. They cheered as he added the words of the triumph and long life of the queen.

The pipers started to play. This time it was for dancing. Aengus and Anaias led the dancers. The others swayed for a while. One by one or two by two, they joined in the dancing, until all were part of it. The pace picked up and the frenzy of joy began. As it stopped suddenly, they were all in laughter. The rain began to fall in a mist. As it blew by, they were surrounded by rainbows. They continued to dance; a little Irish rain wouldn't slow the Eogans now that they were in Eire.

The new arrivals set up camp that night on the hills above the beach. Hearing the roar of the sea, Anaias looked back toward Cymru, and the land of her childhood. It was the land where she had learned hard lessons. She saw the crescent moon rising in the dark night. She was home, really home. She felt her feet firmly on the ground beneath her and sniffed in the fragrance. It was a pungent and strong smell of peat and salt air, flowers and pine.

She heard footsteps behind her.

A male voice said, "This land could clothe my sister in the finest fabrics and jewels!" She turned to see her brother.

"Aengus is king, brother. The sooner you accept that, the sooner you can gain your true power and wealth," she retorted.

"I'm surprised at how easily you turn away from your family, little sister." He gave her a reproachful look. "We're not kids in a game. You know that Aengus is not fit to rule."

"I know no such thing!" she spoke sharply.

"I know you claim to get your wisdom from the gods. I'm not sure they've given you any." He looked at her earnestly.

He continued, "They've filled your head with the story that the Tuatha de Danaan blood in your veins runs differently from mine. I was born in this land. I was present in Cymru when Aengus and you were born. I was there when you were a little baby. Why won't you be loyal to me, your older brother?"

Ciallach looked out at the landscape, "I know that we are descendent from a fighting people, who have always been victorious, who do not coddle the stranger. We know what it is to be an Eogan."

Anaias argued, "The teachings of Pelagius, and his teacher Rabboni Yesua, and the teachings from the caves of Ana are that victory can come through loving, and recognizing our oneness, not fighting and causing hatred."

Ciallach bristled, "Aengus is like you. He is afraid to fight. He agreed too quickly with your desire to feed the enemy. That's fine for a woman to feel that concern. However, a man must be willing to kill the enemy and be done with it. We need a strong warrior to bring the people of this land into submission." He winced, "Our cousin will give the land back to the EiNeill clan and we'll be sent running away again. He would have peace no matter what honor is lost."

"Peace allows children to grow and cattle to fatten," she countered. "So if you were king, would you not work for peace?" she asked softly.

"There would be a peaceful life for those who swore allegiance to me and lived by our family's rules. The others would be in fear of our family." He looked at her as if he had made a good point. "That's the only way to rule, little sister. Peace comes because some leader has supreme power."

She was silent before his logic. He continued, "You say that women want food and home and fire and health. The men do also. They will have it if they pledge their loyalty to us."

He said, encouraged by her silence, "But only if you and the others will come with me and declare our place. It must happen now!"

She replied calmly, "It's treason to be plotting against the king just as he reaches Shreedrum!"

"Aengus is not yet king." He speeded up his talk. "He is not king until he has been crowned in that spot of our grandfather's death."

"It is treason because I have sworn allegiance to our cousin as king."

Speaking harshly now, he said, "You're crazy sister. You are wrong, very wrong." He looked menacingly at her. "You will often look back at this conversation and wish it had ended differently."

"I'm sure that's true, brother. I will always be sad that you could not join us in celebrating with the son of Nad Fraich."

Ciallach disappeared into the night.

She looked back at the moon. It was still climbing in the sky. It was just a month ago that they had heard the hill of Shreedrum was empty. New creation needed to come as the moon was waxing. So much needed to be created in the days and seasons ahead. So much needed to be woven together. She listened to the waves crashing on the rocks below. The tide was at its highest. As the night grew darker, she was amazed at the brilliance of the stars.

As she headed for bed, she saw Papallas looking for her. They stood outside, absorbing the sounds of the night. They entered a tent with several couples. There was a straw mat set out for them. They wrapped each other in an embrace. Soon, all were asleep.

The next morning she heard the raucous sounds of birds singing the morning song. Anaias stepped outside, pulling her night cloak to her. She left Papallas sleeping.

"They've come to greet this new day." An old woman came to her side. "This is Eire. The birds are more excited here than anywhere you've been in your wanderings I'd imagine. Like you, they also wander. They know they are home now, like you are home now."

Anaias knew she had seen many beautiful and blessed places. Papallas, Pelagius and Torrida told her of beautiful lands to the south. There was a lot of beauty in this world. But she had always know that this was truly her home.

She responded, "My roots are once again growing in this land. The ancient roots of my soul have always been here. They are now spreading out!"

The woman said, "I should love to know you better. When your roots have fully drunk in the nourishment of this place, we'll talk again."

"Perhaps," Anaias said gazing at the sunrise. She glanced at the woman, "Come to king's hill in a year and test me!" she added smiling.

The old woman laughed, "Oh, who knows where the goddess will have taken me in a year, or what the little people might have teased me with! It's a long way from my tiny hut to the king's hill, but I'll come if I can."

Anaias laughed, "Yes, we'll both be taunted and teased a lot in the next days."

The woman responded, "This is just a beginning. It's one of many beginnings." The woman paused, and added, "We're glad you're here!"

Anaias turned to the woman and gave her a gentle hug.

At the precise moment, they both smelled fish frying at the central fire below.

The old woman said, "Let's dress for the day and get some of that before the crowd in this place gets it first. There is a lot of work to do today!"

They both returned to their tent to change for the day.

Papallas had seen that Anaias was out of bed. He had quickly dressed.

"Breakfast seems to be ready," she said cheerfully.

Papallas smiled at the joy of the whole Eogan family's first morning in Eire. He was not a blood member of the family, but had shared Anaias' hope for this day.

As they arrived at the central fire, Aengus was there. There was a man with him. Stones had been set out in a large circle. The larger fire was surrounded by several smaller hearths that came off that fire. Women were tending fires for their own family groups. Luann and Moira were tending a fire of their own. Giosai was getting firewood.

That morning's catch of fish was excellent. She was surprised at the presence of such wealth. She was given a silver plate, with two finger long fish, cooked in savory herbs. To the side was heavy bread with berry jam and butter.

A steaming hot cup of herb tea was given to her. They sat next to Aengus. Several men had obviously appointed themselves to be the king's cooks and servants.

"Welcome to Eire, Holy Ones," said one of the older men. "This is the wealth we've been saving for you. The silver platters and spoons were kept hidden until this day."

She looked over to see Ciallach being offered a similar silver plate, heaped high with fish and bread. What more could he want? This was more than either of them had ever known. This was home. She ate, savoring each bite of Ireland. Her roots sunk in.

Papallas ate quickly and went to join several of the men who were repairing the boats.

After breakfast, people gathered and introduced themselves to Aengus. They offered gifts to show their loyalty to him. She learned the colors of the Ciarrage, who lived in the far south west, of the EiFidgenti, just north of them, of the Fir Maige by the southeast shores, of the EiLiathain, of the Uaithne, and of the Orbraige. She listened carefully to their stories. One of the younger men drew a map in the sand to show the territories of their ancestors. They told of the tyranny of the EiNeills and explained why Aengus' coming would bring elation to their lands.

The crowds cleared away as Criomthann, King of EiCennselaign appeared. His territory was on the borders of the EiNeill lands and the Muscraige lands. No one had been able to conquer his territory and his people had been untouched by the sunless drought.

He bowed to Aengus saying, "I was waiting for the family Eogan to return; but did not think it would be in my lifetime, or the lifetime of my sons and daughters. That you have chased away the brother of EiNeill without bloodshed says you are a man of deep wisdom. I have heard how you brought food to the Muscraige just south of us. They have not been our friends, but their hunger worried us. I have kept my distance from the clans around us. I've found, however, that there are violent people to the north and west. I want to have strong and wise friends to the south. I want to make an alliance with you that we might quell the greed of the EiNeill brothers forever, or for as long as the great goddess allows it."

Aengus stood and extended his hands and said, "The family Eogan is honored that you will join with us. Let's continue to talk about the alliance."

Aengus eyes immediately left Criomthann. The most beautiful woman he had even seen stood behind him.

Criomthann followed his eyes and turned to see his sons and daughters standing there. "Ah, let me introduce my sons Fedelmid and Eochaid and my daughter Eithne. They've also been excited about your return and will be as eager as I am to make this alliance work for generations beyond us."

Eithne had locked eyes with Aengus and she bowed with her brothers.

The King of EiCennselaign and his family left. Aengus watched them leave. Anaias was standing behind him taking it all in.

"What do you think of them all Anaias?" he asked when the crowds had begun to clear as they headed for the afternoon rest.

"I believe they will serve you with loyalty cousin."

"And what about you? Will you serve me loyally?" Aengus asked, gazing at her for the answer.

"Why would you ask that? You've been my friend since childhood. The sisters of the cave, all my dreams, tell me that I am to serve you as king." Anaias tried not to sound as upset as she was over this question.

"Even though your brother offers you riches?" Aengus said

sharply. Anaias jumped at his knowledge. Then, of course, Aengus was aware of her brother's heart.

"You're my childhood playmate. More than that, you're my king. I have no doubt of that. Ana would remind me if I did doubt it. The creator, Ana or God of Rabboni Yesua, who are the same, calls you. Don't forget that!" She looked hard at him.

He took her hand tenderly and kissed it. He looked lovingly into her eyes. "Thank you."

They were silent for a moment.

Several women brought a lunch with heavy bread and cheese. As she ate, she remembered the women of the caves.

Aengus lifted the cheese, "We have not known wealth like this."

His grandmother was standing behind them now. "You are the king. You will get used to it."

Aengus said quietly, "As long as my people are hungry, I'll share my wealth."

"We have earned it, my grandson. Eat well and enjoy it," his grandmother said, remembering the years of her pain.

CHAPTER 52 – SHREEDRUM RECLAIMED
IRISH COAST TO SHREEDRUM, TODAY'S CASHEL

WISDOM'S GIFT 6 – BE PREPARED TO ACCEPT THE NEW.

Early the next morning, a storm blew over the camp rattling the tent flaps and waking everyone with the sound of ice pellets slapping the ground. A few birds, this morning, were struggling to find their song. Anaias stood at the tent flap looking out at the icy rain.

Just then, as if the skies were simply a stage, the storm was gone. As if holding their note for just this moment, the birds joined together for a loud chorus. The blue sky held only a few clouds, and the sun, now well above the horizon warmed them. Steam rose from the icy ground.

Papallas and Anaias were ready for the day's adventure.

The task today, was putting Aengus on the throne.

As the wagons arrived, Anaias eyes grew big. She saw the high gloss of the brightly painted carriages.

Ailill smiled. "They've kept these carriages hidden all the time the EiNeill's were in power. We kept the lineage of these horses going in a southern village. We weren't going to let those tyrants dirty them up."

The small horses were sleek and white with silken manes. Anaias had not seen anything like it. So, this was royalty? The seats inside were covered with a soft sheepskin and the inside of the coach was painted white.

She flashed on the faces of the sisters of the cave. She heard the drums and music of the women of the high hills, dark forests and vast plains. She thought of the women holding babies to the sun for naming. She saw the women from the cave with gray hair and wrinkled skin. For all of them she was taking the hand of the carriage man stepping up the gleaming steps. Papallas climbed in behind her. Aengus, Danathie and M'alda joined them.

Boandas and Ciallach and Giosai followed in the second carriage. Luann and Moira came with the rest of the family, in a long line of wagons.

The excitement grew as the wagons prepared to move. Crowds were gathered and with pipes and drums, took their place ahead. It would be a slow procession up the hills and through the valleys. Everyone, within visual or hearing distance, would know that the king was on his way. The word was out for them all to come now to greet the royal procession. As the road went by a homestead, the children would come and cheer and chase the carriages. The adults cheered or sang or played instruments.

They reached a crossroad. Anaias watched the driver suddenly become alert. He took hold of his spear as they moved slowly.

The driver said in explanation, "The tribes in this region have been subdued, but are always ready to make it rough on the new king."

"Who lives in this region?" Aengus asked.

"The Osraige live up these valleys. I think they go back to the Fir Bolg race. They are very rough and dumb," the first man added.

Anaias thought of what they must look like. She had heard of the ancient race. They were large, slow and violent. She shivered, and said a prayer, as she looked up the gentle valley.

The drivers relaxed as the valley broadened. Off ahead, to the northwest, they could barely see a rock rising high above the green valley. On that rock was a castle glimmering in the sunlight. The rock disappeared again behind the hills. She heard Aengus gasp at the sight.

They stopped abruptly by the river. Everyone got out of the carriages. Town folk appeared from all around bringing baskets of fruit, breads and trout. They brought cheese, milk and honey. One woman brought a barrel of ale she hoped would be useful in the king's household. Aengus accepted the gifts with thanks. Anaias thought he was taking well to being king.

The same people looked over at her with surprise. Some simply walked up to her and touched her, not speaking, as if to find out whether she was real. They gazed at Papallas with curiosity because of his dark features.

She said to Aengus, "We need to come back and be among these people."

Hearing them speak, the young driver said, "I'm sure it would be appreciated. People here need healing in their bodies for sure. More than that, they need healing in the spirit. They've lost the love of the goddess."

Anaias said softly, "I've heard about the famine. I'm sure the goddess still loves them."

The driver responded, "Tell them that then."

The caravan procession started up again. Aengus had been having a conversation with several men. He was in deep thought as they moved forward. The hill with its castle could no longer be seen from the road. The journey was in silence.

There were no more stops before late afternoon. They approached the holdings around king's hill.

The large rock and castle again loomed high above the valley.

The piping started. It was joined by cheers and drums as the crowds grew. Apparently, those who met them on the road had taken a short cut to reach this place, before them.

The cheering was intensified as the carriage and wagons moved through the village below the hill. People crowded onto the ramp road that led to the top of the hill.

Anaias' heart beat quickly. This was not the same Shreedrum she had ascended a month ago, that one was surrounded in darkness and fear. This Shreedrum was surrounded with light and joy.

Tears formed in her eyes as she realized that this was the moment of her dreams. This was the dream that she and Aengus had played out as children. This was not a game. The family of Eogan was home. The King, who would make the goddess sing, and the De Danaan People dance, was heading to his throne and would not leave again.

The carriages stopped. Slowly, the royal family, Aengus, Danathie, M'alda and Anaias emerged. Ciallach and Giosai gathered with them. They knelt on the sunny grass covered field on top of the hill. Each prayed silently to the sacred presence in the place.

The breeze blew. They could hear the drumming below, but the people did not follow. They could look out from any vantage point and see what seemed to be all of southern Eire.

To the east toward Cymru and the land of the refuge, Anaias saw the rainbow. To the west, she could see mountains and dark clouds.

In the forests and valleys, dancing was going on by the streambeds and in the treetops. The world glittered with lights. The squirrels, deer and all the creatures felt exceptionally playful. It was said that for the next month every flowering plant flowered whether it was its season or not. For the next year, there were more honeybees than anyone had remembered for decades and more honey.

As Aengus and Anaias moved into the castle, they discovered that it was larger than it appeared. Rooms had been built deep into the rock. It seemed to have been inhabited by generations beyond memory.

There were generous rooms for each family member. Everyone from the exile had a place on the hill. Danathie walked from room to room touching memories of her own. There was even a second story, Anaias and Papallas were given a room on the very top level with a window and a view of all the lands around.

They were exhausted and fell into a deep sleep immediately upon arriving in the room. Her dreams were filled with the sweetness of fulfillment. She dreamed of sitting at a long table piled high with cakes and pots of honey and berries and roots and the fragrance of the cooked pigeon and rabbits that had been offered. Her dreams were joyful.

CHAPTER 53 – ANAIAS' VISION – A DARK CLOUD IN HER WORDS ON SHREEDRUM

I awakened while it was still dark. I left Papallas' side and opened the window. I sat in silence as the winds of the pre-dawn blew. The crows were beginning to join the other birds in a morning song. The sky slowly reddened with the coming sunrise. A hawk appeared overhead and let out a scream. A second one appeared and together they circled the hill.

One of the hawks swooped to land on the windowsill. I stepped back in shock. It became Beechna.

"Come, join us, we have something to show you." Beechna pulled my hand with her tiny one. Beechna became the hawk again. I let my thoughts move to the circling hawks and soon found myself with them, soaring above the earth.

I saw the deer, foxes, I saw the tiniest creatures. Then I saw villages with women starting the cookfire from the central hearth, with thin hungry children clinging to them. The men were gathering separately in small circles, no doubt spreading the gossip of the previous day and trying to understand their place in the events.

I swooped down into the valley isolated from the rest and found a tiny village with one or two huts built of wood and covered with mud.

A boy emerged from the forest with a heavy limp and favoring his hand. He was struggling to collect twigs. He seemed to be alone. Then, I saw two other boys lying in the open, covered with rough woolen blankets. Their faces were twisted with pain.

As I flew to the west, I found that the sky began to darken. My wings labored and my forward movement was difficult. It felt dark and sticky, not a normal cloud. My wings became heavy, I closed my eyes and began to fall.

I opened my eyes again and was back by the window on Shreedrum. The sun was rising in the brilliant blue Irish sky, but I began to shiver. Beechna was there with me, "Did you see it? Did you feel it?" she asked me

"What was that?" I asked. "Where did we go?"

Beechna said solemnly, "The Tywa, in this land, say it's a heavy sorrow from generations of suffering."

Beechna added, "You must beware, it can effect everything that happens in these lands. It can turn into violence and hatreds. The EiNeill were not strong enough to resist it. The darkness may have defeated your grandfather."

"Who were those children?" I asked.

"There are many children trying to raise themselves. Conal Err Breg had their parents killed for disobedience and left the children to fend for themselves," Beechna answered.

"As these children grow in sorrow, the heavy, dark cloud grows in strength," she said.

Beechna once again became a hawk and flew away.

I felt weak from the encounter and my body wanted desperately to go back to my mat and sleep. Papallas was already up and dressed. In my mind, I was also eager to face this new day in Eire.

The rising sun began to warm the earth. I needed to place my feet firmly on the land of my ancestors. It had not been long enough ago that the EiNeills were on this spot. I felt their uneven fractured energy. Maybe that was some of the energy I felt in my flight.

Papallas came over to me and silently kissed me.

I dressed in a simple working gown. There was plenty of healing that needed to be done in these lands. I walked carefully down the narrow staircase that led to the main rooms of the castle. I stopped first at my brothers' room. Ciallach and Giosai were sharing the space. I heard loud snoring.

I continued down to the main hall. It was empty. I walked to an exit on the north of the king's hill. With a prayer of thanks to all the spirits and to Ana and the god of the Rabboni Yesua and Miraham of Magda, I stepped onto the earth. I felt the earth embrace my feet as I stepped. The field was covered with flowers in yellows, pinks and blues.

CHAPTER 54 – ROYAL LOVE ON SHREEDRUM

In the distance, Anaias saw Aengus and a young woman. She approached them and gently bowed, "My king, it is good to see you up so early."

Aengus blushed as he turned away from the young woman. She had curly blond hair and pink cheeks and was a good foot shorter than Aengus. She had intelligent eyes.

He said to her, "Anaias you may remember Eithne, the daughter of Criomthann, King of EiCennselaign. He and his daughter had traveled all yesterday to greet us again and arrived after we had gone to bed. They stayed in the village, but came back this morning. If I hadn't been restless, I would never have found her outside the gates."

He smiled shyly toward Eithne. "Eithne has been telling me all that's happened in the years we've been away."

Anaias saw the way Eithne was gazing lovingly at Aengus as he spoke.

She said to Eithne, "Thank you for coming again and offering us your assistance."

"I'm honored! We've needed you so!" Eithne responded joyfully.

Aengus smiled at Anaias and said, "I suppose you've soared over the lands in your dreams this morning."

"It's hard not to soar at delight in being so close to the land of our Bridey. I am sure that the God of Rabboni Yesua is blessing us."

"There are many sweet spirits here," he said, smiling at Anaias and then looking at the girl next to him.

"We'll talk later," Anaias said to Aengus.

Anaias said to Eithne, "I hope to be able to talk more with you." Anaias left them to continue their conversation.

Later Anaias found Aengus alone to report what she had seen, "There are fierce spirits with the sweet ones in Eire."

"What did you see in your flight?" he asked earnestly

"Darkness. It was in that direction." She pointed to the southwest. The sky was blue now. It looked quite bright as the sun spread its light.

"We'll start by consolidating the relationships of those who greeted us. After we have their allegiance, we can head on out to areas that have no intention of being friends to the family of Eogan," he said.

"It's good to keep an eye on the west"

Anaias sighed, "Must we celebrate the sunrise, but worry about the sunset?"

As they entered the eating hall, people were coming from all the doorways of the castle, finding their way to a table. Anaias saw her brothers and mother as well as her grandmother. Luann and the others were sitting at the far side of the hall.

The villagers had brought food in the morning. They piled the table high again with bread, cheese, and fish. Anaias wondered how a people who had suffered famine could continue to feed the royal family so well. Maybe the EiNeill brothers expected it; but, she thought, her family had been used to far less.

Aengus jumped up on the table, to get everyone's attention. "Good morning! May we all greet, with gratitude, this new morning. It is a dawn for our family and our land. May the ancestors and spirits in this place rejoice." As he said this, he looked at his grandmother.

He called on Boandas to bless the morning. The old druid stood and spoke in an ancient language. He seemed lost as he sat down again.

Anaias, Luann and Moira headed out into the village to find out the needs of the people around Shreedrum.

That afternoon, Anaias and Papallas traveled to the southwest.

They found many people wracked with illness that could be prevented, or healed, with the correct herbs. Anaias did not always understand the language, but she understood the symptoms. She found the children Beechna had shown her, whose parents had been killed. They were homeless and desperate.

In the days that followed, Luann and Moira found an old hut in the village below Shreedrum and decided to make a place for the homeless children that Anaias brought to them. Giosai was always there helping with any chores needed to fix the hut. He brought them firewood and meat for meals.

They let it be known in all the regions that Aengus would not rule with violence. If any clan leader had a grievance, that leader could bring it to the king without fear. There was no reason for more killing, grief and vengeance.

Ciallach rolled his eyes every time Aengus made an alliance speech. Ciallach rarely visited Anaias. When he did, it was to tell her that Aengus was weak and a coward and blind to the forces that were going to take down the dynasty.

Boandas was obviously jealous of Anaias' role as adviser to the king. She avoided him. He glared at her often. He spent a great deal of time with Ciallach. She was so busy she had little time to be concerned.

After a few months, she and Papallas decided to find a place for themselves off the hill. They found a forested area by the river. She could sense the goodness of the spirits in that place and often saw them peeking out from the trees. She had not seen Beechna for a while. She missed her.

The Eogan family spent their first cold season in Eire. The oak trees were bare; only the pines stood green against the darkened sky. It did not seem as bitterly cold as it often did in Cymru. Anaias and Papallas were able to continue traveling in the countryside healing people and encouraging them.

Criomthann, King of EiCennselaign had wanted the alliance and brought many gifts. He hoped that the King of Munster might choose his daughter as his wife. He did not need to push them together, though. The couple was obviously in love.

When the season of first growth came in Eire, Aengus announced that he would marry Eithne. Plans were made for the ceremony. Luann and M'alda joined to plan the feast. It was exciting to weave the families together and to insure the continuation of the Eogan dynasty.

The clan of the EiCennselaign arrived with music and cheers. Cormonthuc, the bard, sang of the young lovers and of the strength of the alliance. Boandas was asked to give his blessing in the ancient language.

Anaias was asked to give the blessing of Ana by lifting the cup of honey-wine and passing it to the bride and groom. They offered it to everyone present. Anaias also shared words about Rabboni Yesua and Miraham of Magda and their love for each other. Eithne had been listening to Anaias' stories about the holy couple and Rabboni's teachings. She wanted to learn more.

With all these blessings, the couple disappeared into the king's chamber.

The celebration lasted for several days. Aengus and Eithne appeared occasionally. Papallas and Anaias met many clan chiefs and kings of small regions. Danathie and M'alda, the former queen and princess, greeted old friends. There were many hugs, tears of sorrow and joy.

The celebrations ended with a feeling of happiness that had not been felt in Shreedrum for a long time.

Papallas and Anaias often returned to king's hill to dine with Aengus and Eithne.

Aengus was curious about Papallas' travels to the Mediterranean.

Papallas explained, "Traveling to the south is more dangerous then it was. Many are hungry. There are diseases that have never been in the land before. There are more robbers on the road."

"Would you go south again, given those dangers?" Eithne asked.

"Oh, yes! Trade is good," Papallas said with excitement. "The new inhabitants have brought goods with them that I've never seen before. The fruits and spices are wonderful."

Anaias began to go with Eithne into the village. As they traveled Anaias shared the stories she had heard about Rabboni Yesua and Miraham of Magda.

Eithne was impressed, "It makes sense that a god would want us to care for one another and for all living things."

Anaias commented, "The teachings of Rabboni Yesua are not that different from what I learned in the caves of Ana. Ana is creator of all and love is the fiber that holds us together; like a weaver and the yarn."

Eithne laughed, "I like that. But you know it is not so easy to love your enemy."

Anaias agreed, "You and I agree on that. My teacher, Pelagius said that that is the hardest lesson we have to learn. Forgiveness is the strangest rule of this God. It is hard to forgive, maybe even impossible, unless we know Christ Jesus. Pelagius taught that we aren't alone. There is deep within each of us knowledge of how to love and forgive like that. God's spirit is there to guide us."

Eithne breathed deeply, "Well, I'm ready for that guidance."

Anaias and Eithne spent the day with Luann, Moira and Giosai, working in the hut, caring for the crowds of children without parents.

CHAPTER 55 – PATRICK RETURNS HOME LERINS ISLE IN SOUTHERN FRANCE – TO BRITAIN

Patrick didn't do well among the monks. There were some who judged him harshly for his confessions of what he was forced to do as a slave. They hadn't understood his suffering and his conversion.

Besides, he felt called to return to whatever was left of his family. He left the little island on the Mediterranean after he had been ordained as a deacon. The bishop blessed him and assigned him to the people of Britain to bring them to Christ Jesus, saving them from certain hell.

He traveled more easily than he had after his escape from slavery. Patrick knew it was because God was with him. He arrived in the village of his youth and began to ask about his family.

Suddenly an older woman burst out of her hut. She cried, "Is that you, Sucat? Is this the son of my cousin Calpornius?" She threw her arms around him and wept.

She spoke through her tears, "May God be praised for keeping you safe."

He went into her house. She treated him as though he were her own son.

CHAPTER 56 – OPEN TO NEW WORLDS
SHREEDRUM, EIRE

WISDOM'S GIFT 7 – NOTHING IS FAMILIAR, NO MATTER HOW LONG YOU HAVE KNOWN IT.

The season of the sun had come again and Papallas decided it was time to travel south. Several of the Muscraige men wondered if they could pilot the Roman ship that had brought the exiles home and go with him.

Papallas directed them to collect jars of Irish honey and woven fabrics of the fine lamb's wool that grew in Eire for trade. With a crew of Muscraige and Fir Maige and the sons of EiCeinneselaigh, they headed off.

They returned a few months later with many stories and wonderful fruits and herbs. There were fabrics and jewelry that the people had not seen before.

Aengus invited Papallas to come to Shreedrum and share the stories of his journey.

Aengus said, as he took Eithne's hand in his, "Is there any way to form alliances with Rome? I have often thought that with Rome backing us we might not have been as vulnerable to the EiNeill clan."

Papallas shook his head, saying, "I don't know. There's little talk of trade with these islands." He added, "When Rome talks about Eire they think of the violent clans in the north. They don't think of trade. They think of defense."

Aengus sighed, "Again, we have to fight the EiNeill clan. This time it's their reputation."

Papallas stopped to collect his thoughts. "There is a possibility though. The followers of the religion of Christ Jesus are becoming more powerful than the empire. There is a one follower of Christ Jesus who might help us. The EiNeill clan kidnapped him when he was a child but he escaped. He studied his religion in the south. He has been sent back to Britain as a teacher."

"He is like Pelagius?" Anaias was hopeful.

Papallas responded, "I suppose he is a follower of the same God. But you remember that our Pelagius was in trouble." He paused, adding, "The similarities are great."

Aengus interrupted, "He was kidnapped by the EiNeill clan?"

Papallas answered, "The story I heard was that he was a slave for six years before he escaped. Then the Goths in the south captured him. He escaped to an island that has a school for followers of Christ Jesus. He was initiated as a priest on that island."

Aengus continued to follow this thinking, "Would he come to Eire again, do you think?"

Papallas responded, "I think he might. The rumors say he's filled with excitement about spreading the word of Christ Jesus."

Eithne asked wide-eyed, "Why would he return after he was treated so badly by the people of Eire? Would he know the difference between our people and those of the EiNeill?"

Anaias responded, "That's the kind of thing this God of the Rabboni Yesua asks people to do. This Patrick might want to come back to those who have wronged them, just so he can forgive them."

Aengus asked, "Do you think he would come to us?"

"We could get a message to him and invite him," Papallas suggested.

Anaias was silent. She felt a tug at her heart. She longed for the fellowship between Pelagius, Melania and Susanna. She missed the gentle people of the refuge. Maybe this Patrick was like them.

Anaias then added, "Perhaps this Patrick can be contacted through the 'mind of Rabboni Yesua', like I can contact sisters through the 'mind of Ana.' Like the old woman in the Muscraige village who called for us in her prayer when the people were hungry and I heard her in a dream."

"We can try," Aengus said, smiling at her excitement. It excited him also, to have this new door opened. "We can also send an emissary to lead him to our hill."

Aengus called all his leaders together, including Boandas and Ciallach. Boandas seemed amazingly open to the idea. Anaias and Papallas stood together with Boandas as they knelt in prayer that this Patrick might come to them.

Patrick, now called Sucat, was returning to the normal life that he had left behind in his youth. The Romans were gone from the village of his youth, but they had left the wide roads connecting villages. He was able to travel to other communities and spread his message of the saving grace of Christ Jesus. He helped his aunt keep the house, the chickens and the gardens.

One night he had a dream. People standing on a high hill in southern Ireland called to him, saying, "Come, Patrick, to our people."

All day he prayed about the dream. It excited him and scared him. Was he really being called to return to that land of his slavery?

That night at the evening meal, his aunt brought the stew to him. He held his breath for a moment and then blurted out, "I am called to return to Ireland!"

"No!" she shouted, "they're murderers. You can't go help them. You can't!!"

"This is different. God calls me to go. They're calling for me. They're ready for the salvation of Christ Jesus," Patrick answered.

"You promised never to leave me!!" she cried, "I have no family but you!"

"Aunt, I won't go unless the Bishop directs me to go," Sucat-Patrick assured her. He knew, in his heart, that the Bishop would be enthusiastic.

It took months for his letter to travel to the island of Lerins and months for a response to come. The Bishop's letter told Patrick that he would go not just as a missionary but as the Bishop of Ireland with powers to ordain priests and appoint regional bishops.

Patrick assembled a group of friends to help him. He left in spite of his aunt's tears.

He arrived by boat at a southern port of Ireland. He had heard that a new, friendlier dynasty had reasserted itself in that region.

It was several months before they learned that Patrick was arriving in a southern port. Aengus sent Giosai and Ciallach to meet him. They brought him, and his entourage in royal carriages to the gates at the edge of the hill of Shreedrum.

Aengus and Eithne were dressed in their royal robes. Boandas stood ready to greet him in the white robe of the druid. Anaias was in her shimmering gown of the caves of Ana.

She and Papallas, Luann and Moira were eager to greet him as baptized followers of Christ Jesus. They were eager to share with him all they knew about the stories and teachings of this man called both Rabboni Yesua and Christ Jesus. There were many in the village below ready to be baptized because of her work.

Anaias was there to greet him at the gate of Shreedrum. She said, "In the name of Christ Jesus, we welcome you!"

Patrick's eyes showed shock, then surprise. Then he broke into laughter, saying, "So you have already received salvation?"

Papallas stepped forward, "My wife and I are baptized in Christ Jesus. May we also introduce Luann and Moira, who have also been baptized?"

Patrick was shorter than Anaias expected. She had been so used to Pelagius' size. He was, though, full of energy. He came with an eager group of people serving his needs. The children of the village were gathered at the gates and danced around him. He seemed to enjoy their company. He laughed easily. She liked him. She knew he was filled with the spirit of the Rabboni Yesua or Christ Jesus whatever name he used.

Anaias walked with Patrick through the gates of Shreedrum. Boandas was just inside gate. She said simply, "I present to you the druid leader, Boandas." Patrick silently bowed to him, eyeing his golden chains, and the amulets that hung from them.

She moved past Boandas, to Aengus and Eithne.

She said, "Most importantly I present the Eogan king, Aengus, and his queen Eithne."

Anaias continued, "They've been learning of the teachings of Christ Jesus and are close to accepting him in baptism also."

Aengus said, "We're eager to hear of your journey. We imagine, though, that you're in need of food and drink." He ushered him into the great hall. Eithne followed.

Aengus continued, "I've invited my entire family, including our druid leader, Boandas, to hear your teachings."

The table was filled with the usually feast for a royal visitor and his entourage.

Patrick and the others ate well. Everyone was gathered, including Ciallach, Giosai. M'alda and Danathie.

Boandas was sitting across from Patrick. He seemed strangely nervous. Ciallach sat next to him. Boandas continued to glare at Anaias.

CHAPTER 57 – WHICH CHRIST JESUS DO YOU FOLLOW?

Bishop Patrick began, "I heard your call in a dream. It is your salvation in Christ Jesus that I bring. My heart is filled with happiness that you might accept it so easily."

He looked at Boandas, "You must turn away from the false gods and those you would call goddesses. There is just one God, our Father, and the Father of Christ Jesus."

Pointing to Boandas' staff and amulets, he said, "Any signs or symbols that point to those creatures are idols." Lifting his hand sharply, he said, "Throw them from you or burn in the everlasting fire."

Everyone gasped. Anaias had never heard Pelagius talk like this. She remembered the words of Paulina though.

Boandas was silent.

Patrick continued, "I come to rid the land of the power of the demons that you have, in your ignorance, worshiped." He spoke more softly, "The good news is that if you accept the power of Christ Jesus you are forgiven the sin that was with you at your birth."

He told them the story of Jesus' arrest and death on the cross. He slowly and in detail told them all of the torture of Christ Jesus. He looked into the eyes of Boandas as he talked about the nails that pierced the hands of Jesus and the pain of his death. He told of the soldiers at the base of the cross who bartered for his belongings. Everyone gasped at the story of the soldier who pierced his side to see if he was dead. Then there was silence.

"You all deserve to die that way. Christ Jesus died for you. You all hold unforgivable sin in you. God sent Christ Jesus, his son, as a substitute for you. Christ Jesus suffered and bled as a sacrifice to save you."

Boandas groaned, but was silent. His head was in his hands.

Patrick turned to Papallas and Anaias, "So you have accepted baptism. I am surprised. I didn't know that one of our missionaries had come to this place."

Anaias responded, "It was across the sea, while we were in exile, that we received the waters of baptism and accepted Christ Jesus."

Luann blurted out, "Our teacher was a learned man from the south, named Pelagius, and his partner Melania."

Patrick jumped from his seat and shouted, "Oh no, my dear children, you've been deceived. It is the devil himself who has taught you." His face was red. Everyone gasped.

Patrick continued, "You have not received the baptism that washes your sins away. You received the waters of hell that only seemed cool, but will burn you."

Anaias shaken by his words about Pelagius, responded, "But he was a follower of Christ Jesus like you, he glowed with the love of the One."

He walked over to Anaias and put his hand on her head and said, "I was sent to drive out snakes like him. My poor child, your immortal soul is in danger as long as you think he held the true faith." He knelt by her and looked into her eyes with sincerity, saying, "Satan comes to us as one who seems good and brings us pleasure."

Papallas countered, "He was truly a man of goodness and love."

Patrick said with deep feeling, "It is not about goodness! That is only a part of it. It is about salvation of your immortal soul. The great teacher named Augustine, who has recently died, taught that we have all been born with an inherited sin. From the moment of our birth, we are condemned to punishment. Only the waters of baptism can cleanse us from that sin. Augustine spoke harshly against the teachings of this teacher Pelagius. Pelagius didn't believe in our sin; he didn't believe in our need for God's grace. Without that belief, you cannot be saved. I'm sorry you encountered him."

Anaias spoke; she felt a power speaking though her, "Pelagius taught that it is our individual sin and our free will that must be cleansed. He taught that we're strengthened to do good works through Christ Jesus' presence in our baptism. The God of Christ Jesus is our loving creator and created us with all we need to be perfect. He said that Christ Jesus said, 'Be perfect as your Father in heaven is perfect.'"

Patrick said softly, "And the council condemned Pelagius for that teaching. You are going to eternal torment unless you leave his teachings behind."

Luann and Moira began weeping softly. These were not the words they expected to hear from this teacher of love. Giosai walked over to Luann to comfort her.

There was a deep nervous silence in the room.

Suddenly Boandas jumped up and shouted out, "Forgive me!!! I toss away my false gods and goddesses. Demons have tormented me and I have not known who they were."

Boandas began to fling off his gold necklace and belt. He threw his staff against the wall. Several ducked as it bounced back.

He tore off his robe. "Save me! Save me from the torment I have known, and the eternal torment."

Boandas came to Patrick and knelt at his feet.

Patrick said softly, as he touched Boandas head, "Alleluia! God is giving us miracles!"

Patrick turned to the gathered family, "Who else comes to the cleansing waters of baptism?"

Aengus and Eithne walked forward saying, "We would be baptized and all our family. We will invite all in the village to come to the waters."

Patrick looked back at Anaias, "Did the snake Pelagius teach them his vile lessons?"

She stared back at him, saying nothing. He continued, "They must be untaught."

Patrick proclaimed. "We will have lessons for all of you. Only after you learn the true teachings about Christ Jesus, about the Incarnation, about the Trinity, about Salvation, can you receive the waters of baptism. Only then, can you receive the body and blood of our Lord."

CHAPTER 58 – KNOWING THE TRUTH

Patrick stayed with them on Shreedrum for two months. In spite of the cruelty of some of his words he seemed to be a kind man. Anaias noticed how he treated the children in the house kept by Luann and Moira.

Anaias was confused, though. How could he and Pelagius both be followers of the same Christ Jesus? Their teachings seemed to go in different directions. With Pelagius, it was about acting in love. With Patrick, it was about the words you used. It was directed toward salvation from hellfire. With Pelagius, every creature was blessed by God; with Patrick, every creature started with a curse, which with humans could only be washed off with baptism.

She had to agree that people could be very wicked; but certainly, as Pelagius taught, their actions were their own choice, not that of these ancestors named Adam and Eve. Patrick's words did not make sense to her, yet Boandas seemed to be moved deeply by them.

Boandas was staying by Patrick's side. He had put aside his priestly robes. He wore a coarse brown wool smock. He listened carefully to everything Patrick said.

Anaias enjoyed listening to Patrick when he talked about Christ Jesus and his teachings about the kingdom of God, which was like a mustard seed, and a treasure in the field. She remembered those stories from her time with Pelagius and Melania. Then he would speak of the fiery punishment and she would recoil in confusion.

The day of the fire of the full sun was coming again. As people prepared for the celebration, Patrick saw his moment to change their hearts. He had been holding classes for a large group. Now they would be asked to decide between heaven or hell.

Patrick declared at breakfast, "Tomorrow we will call all who will come, to baptism."

He turned to Giosai and said, "Bring me water from the river. We will baptize all on this King's Hill. We will sanctify this place to Christ Jesus."

The next morning crowds gathered. The gates were opened and all were invited to come onto the Kings Hill. Many of the villagers from below just wanted to walk the grounds. They all wanted to hear the powerful preaching of Patrick.

Patrick was standing on the green grass of the high hill of Shreedrum. From this vantage point, the valleys and fields of distant mountains of Eire were visible. He wore a white robe and large cross around his neck. Next to him, Giosai held a basin of water from the river. Patrick had a long staff with a metal point.

Patrick touched the water in the basin and said, "Bless this water with your power, oh God of Abraham and Isaac. Bless this water by the power of the sacrificial blood of Christ Jesus who died that they may not receive everlasting punishment. Turn these people from their pagan ways and open them to your cleansing blood! Open them to the eternal love of the risen savior."

He carefully stepped up on the rock used for druid rituals of sacrificing animals. It was an ancient rock used at one time in ancient memory even for human sacrifice. Patrick wanted to symbolize its transformation to a Christian place of baptism.

The transformation was especially powerful to Boandas. He would normally be sacrificing a lamb in preparation for the celebration of fire.

Patrick shouted at the gathered crowd, "Who repents of their sin and accepts Christ Jesus as their savior? Come and die! Come and be reborn in Christ Jesus!"

Aengus stepped forward in the simple brown wool smock that Patrick had given them all for the purpose of repentance.

With his hand, Patrick sprinkled the water over Aengus' head and slammed his staff into the stone. "You are baptized in the name of the Father."

Aengus felt the sharp point of the staff cut through his foot. He was shocked at the pain, but had heard Patrick's words about Christ Jesus and blood. He did not want to appear weak. He did not flinch.

Again, Patrick reached into the bowl with water and repeated the ritual, "You are baptized in the name of the Son." He reached into the bowl, "You are baptized in the name of the Holy Spirit." He finished by shouting, "So help us God!!!"

Tears were coming down Patrick's cheeks. He embraced Aengus who was shaking with pain. Aengus was standing in a pool of his blood; everyone watched it drip from the sides of the sacrificial rock.

Patrick looked down at the blood, "Why didn't you stop me?"

Aengus responded, "With all your talk about God's hatred for us before baptism, and our death, I thought it was my final punishment before forgiveness."

Patrick put his hand on his shoulder and prayed. He wondered himself whether God might not want a final punishment of these people who had worshipped false gods and had almost embraced a false Christ..

Eithne came forward. As he baptized her, Patrick was careful with his staff. Giosai and Ciallach received baptism. M'alda and Danathie held back, praying to Danaa whose presence they felt even at this moment.

Boandas came forward with tears flowing, crying out, "Let me die! Forgive me! Cleanse me!"

Patrick baptized him. Boandas shuttered and fell to the ground. Several people helped move him away as Patrick baptized the rest of the Eogan family and many of the people from the village.

Patrick was careful only to baptize those who had come to his lessons.

Anaias and Papallas, Luann and Moira slipped back into the crowd. They felt their baptism was good enough. They did not want to accept the words Patrick spoke that condemned their teachers and friends, Pelagius and Melania. Hearing Patrick's view of the teachings of Christ Jesus, they did not dare mention the teachings about Rabboni Yesua and Miraham of Magda as taught by Susanna, David and Jacob in the refuge. Those teachings were so different from Patrick's, but also seemed so true and right.

They wandered down into the village and ended up in the hut filled with the homeless children. Four of the younger children came running up to them giggling as they arrived. Luann and Moira had become mothers to all these children because of the teachings of Pelagius and Melania. The four of them sat stunned at all they had seen on the hill. It was only the laughter of the children playing around them that pulled them out of their depression.

Anaias said, after a silence, "I'm glad that Aengus and Eithne have accepted Christ Jesus." After a pause she continued. "I think they understand the Rabboni Yesua as Pelagius and Melania did."

Luann added, "Aengus was affected by the teachings of Susanna, David and Jacob, as well as Pelagius."

Moira began to prepare a simple meal for all of them, including the children.

There would be a feast and festival on the hill. They would miss it. They were not sure when they could return to the hill considering the condemnation of Patrick.

Anaias said softly, "Maybe we should have let him baptize us."

Papallas said, his jaw clenched, "We are baptized."

That evening Aengus and Eithne came to the house. Aengus said, "Please don't be afraid to join us. As king, I accept your baptism. You and your teachings are welcome in my realm."

They all hugged each other. There was a joy and radiance that had come over Aengus and Eithne. Their baptism had changed something deep within them.

The next afternoon Patrick announced that he was leaving. He wanted to preach a sermon to the newly baptized.

He once again stood on the rock used now for baptisms not

blood sacrifice, "I've been blessed by your receptivity to me and to Christ Jesus, who I represent."

He turned to Aengus and said, "You will be blessed. I can assure you that you will find God's abundant grace in all your endeavors as you rule this land."

Patrick continued, "But, I must leave you. I must leave able teachers to keep you in the proper faith."

He turned to Boandas, called him to stand on the rock, and put his hand on his shoulder, "I have appointed this man to be your teacher. Christ Jesus has filled him with God's grace. He will continue to study the scripture as diligently as he studied the vile rules of the druid. He will be what we call in the church, your Bishop. He has authority to baptize any who turn toward the way." There was silence.

He pointed down from the rock, "I appoint this man, Giosai, as a teacher. He has learned well and can teach others. Your good queen Eithne has learned well and will be a good teacher of the women and the children."

He looked now at Anaias. "Be with God and turn away from false teachings. Let these who I have appointed guide you."

"All who have been baptized in the true faith shall now share in the Holy Eucharist." He called Boandas to lift the cup of wine and break the bread. Aengus and Eithne came forward as did Ciallach and Giosai. Each received the bread dipped into the cup by Patrick putting the wine soaked bread into their mouth. Anaias and Papallas came forward but Patrick shook his head. He also rejected Luann and Moira.

The bard, Cormonthuc, came out with his harp. He had not been baptized, but he was still permitted to tell the story of the events in song. Then the pipers and drummers started. There was dancing into the night. Anaias and Papallas left early for their home by the river.

Patrick left the next morning with a larger group of followers.

CHAPTER 59 – THE RIVER-SIDE CHAPEL
SOUTHERN EIRE

WISDOM'S GIFT 8 – THERE IS PLENTY OF WORK FOR YOU

Anaias and Papallas had embraced each other through the night. The sun came up over the river. The birds were in chorus. There was a knock at their door.

It was the familiar voice of the bard, "Hello, are you there?"

Papallas jumped up and pulled on his cloak, as did Anaias. "Of course we're here. Welcome."

Cormonthuc was red faced and looking at his feet. "We're not sure how to say this, but my wife, daughters and I would like to be baptized by you. We liked what your teacher Pelagius had to say about Christ Jesus."

Then he looked at Anaias and shook his head, "And we don't like a God who would not give the cup to you, after you have given the cup to others so many times."

Anaias stammered, "I don't know if I can..."

Papallas smiled, "Of course you can! It is about our creator God, water, and Rabboni Yesua and Miraham of Magda. As we experienced baptism, it is about being welcomed into God's family of love. It is about doing good in the world as God has created us be good."

"Well, yes then, I guess I can," Anaias said smiling.

"Good then," Cormonthuc nodded, "I'll go get the girls and we will make a feast of it afterwards like they did on the hill."

Later that morning it was more than Cormonthuc's family that came. Luann and Moira and all the children they cared for came. There were also several from the village who had held back when Patrick invited them to be baptized.

As they stepped into the river each person kneeled letting the water cover their heads, Anaias and Papallas lifted them saying, "May you be baptized and cleansed in the name of the Creator, in the name of the Rabboni Yesua, our teacher, and in name of the Holy Loving Fire within us."

There was laughter in the trees over the river and lights flickered around them. Cormonthuc pulled up his harp and sang about the beauty of the God of creation and the creatures in their midst. He sang of knowing he was cleansed by the pure water and pure light.

Anaias pulled out the honey-wine and honeycakes. Moira had a flask of the wine given to her by Pelagius. All in a circle they shared from the two cups, one as a symbol of the joy of creation; the other as a symbol of the compassion of Christ Jesus. They shared the one loaf remembering the bread of life that comes to us in the name of the sweet God of creation in Christ Jesus.

The next day, when they returned to Shreedrum, they were met by Boandas.

"You will follow my instructions now," he said.

He looked at Papallas and back at her, "I know what you're doing by the river. You will stop!"

Anaias responded, "You do not know what we're doing. You have not been there."

Boandas hissed, "You've brought your people to the brink of disaster too many times!"

Papallas changed the subject, "Will you now support the king?"

Boandas responded, "Bishop Patrick has taught me that Christ is my King. I will support only Him." He returned to his previous subject of insults, "But apparently you have trouble following Christ Jesus."

Papallas and Anaias brushed by him and found Aengus.

They embraced him and Eithne.

"We have great news!" Aengus laughed as he spoke the words. "The day after the waters of baptism washed her head Eithne told me she is to have a child! The power of this God of Christ Jesus is great!"

"Oh Eithne! How wonderful!" Anaias said as she embraced her. She was grateful. This would make Aengus' place on the throne strong.

Bishop Boandas, wearing the same robe he had worn as a druid priest, but now with a cross given to him by Bishop Patrick, walked up to Aengus, between Anaias and Papallas.

He said in a teaching tone to Aengus, "May I remind you, that these two do not know the true faith. You must not listen to any advice they give."

Aengus flared, "I will decide whose counsel I should keep."

"Not if you want to keep in good standing with the church of Bishop Patrick," Boandas continued. "Your whole realm is in danger, not just of eternal punishment, if you let these two counsel you."

Aengus nearly shouted, "And you are the one I should trust!? You have been plotting against me, with my cousin, since our time in Cymru." He looked around. "So who can I trust?"

Boandas knew it was time to back off, "Yes, I have felt Ciallach was more suited to this task. God, though, has made you king. We will all trust in God."

He turned as if to leave but then thought of a last word, "In the garden it was a woman who tempted Adam. Do not trust yourself to a woman." He walked out of the room.

The months went by quickly. There was a lot to get ready. Eithne began to show and feel the symptoms of a pregnant woman. M'alda was hovering around her. The queen grandmother Danathie, showed interest but was weakening with age.

Giosai wandered to the village below the hill, spending time with Luann and Moira.

Giosai was silent most of the time but on this day, he approached Luann.

He took her arm and looked into her eyes, "You were once a daughter of Ana, but now you are baptized in Christ Jesus. Would you consider being my wife?"

Luann stared at Giosai. She had enjoyed his help and was friendly with him, but had never seen him as a lover.

She responded carefully, "As a daughter of Ana and as a follower of Christ Jesus I have chosen not to marry. It gives me time to do work of love. I'm flattered by your proposal."

He looked at his feet and his lower lip trembled. He stuttered, "I know I haven't said this to you before, but I've loved you since my sister first came to Cymru with you. Now that we're both baptized in Christ Jesus, I've felt we were meant by God to be together."

Luann began to feel hot with embarrassment. "Thank you for your words, I can't marry any man."

Giosai suddenly turned and ran away.

Later that day Luann told Anaias what had happened. Anaias promised to talk to Giosai.

Anaias found him out in the field below Shreedrum with the grazing sheep. She stood silently with him until he was ready to talk.

Giosai finally said, "I guess I embarrassed myself with Luann."

Anaias responded, "It was a beautiful thing you said to her. She had never known you had such strong feelings for her."

Giosai cried, "How could she not have known? I've been there at their hut every day doing chores. I've cared for the children that are there. I was even baptized because I thought she would like that."

"We thought you did those things because you chose to do them, not to impress Luann."

Giosai responded somberly. "I hoped she would love me enough to give up her decision not to marry."

"She made that decision a long time ago. It would take time for her to change it," Anaias responded.

Giosai said defiantly, "It is time for her to change."

"Give it time. She never knew of your feelings," Anaias said as she went over to her brother to hug him. This was a side of him that she had never seen. He pulled away.

A few weeks later the festival of the harvest came. There was a celebration in the village below Shreedrum. People from all over Munster came with a part of their harvest. The ritual was a combination of celebrating the God of Christ Jesus and the goddess Eire.

Everyone seemed to agree that the crops came in fuller and healthier now that Aengus was king.

There were a few reports of fighting on the northern border of the Osraige and EiCeinnselaigh land. Conal Err Breg was reportedly fighting with his brothers to the north; trying to carve out territory in more fertile lands.

Anaias continued to see darkness in the southwest. Aengus was not able to summon the loyalty of those on the western peninsula or those to the far south. It was decided that they would not be forced into submission as the brother of EiNeill had tried to do. There were several tribes called the Corco Duibne who made alliances with no one.

Kings in the ancient days created alliances by taking hostages from the tribes. Through the hostages, they would force the tribes into compliance. That was not the way Aengus wanted to rule.

Ciallach continued to criticize him for failing to fight battles and for negotiating rather than engaging and conquering.

Everything seemed calm, except for the darkness that Anaias saw in her visions. The sticky cloud was growing.

Beechna appeared by the river hut. She whispered to Anaias, "The Tywa are concerned about you living in this spot. The evil cloud is growing. You need to be in the safety of Shreedrum."

Anaias, busy with her gardening, responded, "I can't go to the holy hill. Boandas thinks he's the religious leader there. That's where the danger is."

Anaias and Papallas gathered people from the village together at the river hut. Luann, Moira, and Giosai always came with the children. Cormonthuc came with his wife and daughters. They often talked about Rabboni Yesua and about how they were struggling to love one another and help one another as he taught them to. Giosai sat next to Luann, always hopeful.

Anaias often told them stories that Pelagius had told her about Rabboni Yesua. She remembered stories about Miraham of Magda that Susanna had told her. There was the story about the neighbor, who was actually the enemy, but showed love. There was the story of the son who went away and returned and his father had a feast in celebration. Each story told something about both God and people.

Rabboni Yesua said of Miraham, "She is the happy one, beautiful in her speaking, pure spiritual Miraham, the inheritor of light." They talked about how Jesus told them they were the light of the world. What did that mean? Anaias silently thought of the sticky dark cloud that was growing. Could her light be strong enough to defend against it's power?

"Isn't that what we all want," Anaias asked, "to be full of the divine light?"

During the evening gatherings, Cormonthuc came with his harp. He had composed several songs to the glory of creation and Christ. He was especially amazed by the story of Mary who gave birth to the child Jesus. She was, for Cormonthuc, a symbol of the beauty of nature.

Aengus and Eithne joined them. They prayed together and shared the cups of wine and honey and the loaf of bread. Then they sang and laughed until it was time for everyone to go to their homes.

It was a balmy 'full sun season' night and Aengus and Eithne were walking home. They were surrounded by a crowd from the village. They had been part of a night of singing with Anaias and Papallas. Laughter was still in their hearts.

Suddenly a small boy came running into the crowd.

"He's got a knife!" someone yelled.

The boy plunged the knife into Aengus side. As people ran to Aengus side, the boy escaped in the crowd.

Eithne screamed. Aengus slumped to the ground.

Someone wrapped the wound tightly and several men carried him up to the castle on Shreedrum.

Boandas was called to assess the wound. Several others called for Papallas and Anaias to come. They ran to king's hill with Luann and Giosai. When they entered the royal rooms, they saw Boandas bent over Aengus. Papallas pushed him aside to check the wounds.

As it turned out, there was a lot of blood but the wound did not hit any vital organs. As Aengus awoke the next morning Boandas and Anaias were there by his side.

Boandas said softly as Aengus' eyes opened, "There is punishment for being with those who worship demons!"

Papallas sleeping nearby was awakened by Boandas' words. He replied harshly, "There's punishment for attempting to kill the king."

Boandas glared at Papallas but didn't speak.

Several of his Muscraige advisers suggested to Aengus that this could have been some loyal followers of the brothers of the EiNeill. It might have been someone from the Corco tribes to the south or west.

Ciallach appeared, "You've allowed the Corco Duibne tribes to thrive without your leadership. They would easily defeat you and take over the kingdom of Munster."

Ailill, the Muscraige advisor, laughed, "I don't think any of those tribes have such ambitions, but they might have fared better under the EiNeill."

"But the EiNeill took hostages!" objected Aengus through his pain.

Ailill commented, "Ah, but the EiNeill were harder on the Ciarraige and Ei Fidgenti who are now your allies."

Ciallach hissed, "You need an army to go and teach them a lesson!" Caillach looked around him to see if anyone else was listening. He said to himself, "Maybe I should put together my own army if he doesn't have the courage."

CHAPTER 60 – POWER AROUND SHREEDRUM, EIRE

Boandas was sitting quietly in Ciallach's hut below Shreedrum.

Ciallach came in the door and momentarily looked surprised to see him.

Boandas spoke first, "If God was with you, my son, your plans would succeed."

Ciallach looked into Boandas' eyes, "Maybe I don't understand the workings of this God of Christ Jesus. Even the tribes to the west seem to be tired of fighting."

Ciallach shook his head, "And where is the wealth that the Eogan family is supposed to have? I have nothing to offer to pay them for their loyalty."

Boandas said softly, "It will come in due time. First you need to get rid of your cousin."

Boandas continued sitting. "You have almost waited too long. If Eithne has a son, you will lose any chance of ruling. It might be good if she had an accident."

Ciallach responded, "Maybe I've lost anyway. I won't harm a woman about to bear a child. It would be insane to threaten the daughter of the EiCeinnselaigh."

Boandas took on his teaching tone, "You do what God calls you to do. God's ways are beyond us. The wealth, and allies that you hope for will come because of our baptism."

He continued, "Because Patrick has blessed me with this position, I can wield great power. Aengus has been listening to your sister who is considered by the Church to be worse than a non-believer because she follows the beliefs of that Pelagius."

He leaned toward Ciallach saying, "If you are afraid of hurting a pregnant woman, you would do the Church a favor by ridding it of your sister. The Church would understand. The Holy man Patrick himself told me that in the eyes of the church your sister has no rights. She is worse than a pagan. Her continued teaching by the river is putting a stain on the Eogan clan."

Ciallach stood up, and looked shocked, "I couldn't harm my sister!!"

"She hasn't acted like a sister. She's harmed you." Boandas responded.

"How could you...?" Ciallach started to stand. Boandas grabbed his arm and pulled him back down.

"How can you not? You should be king! You know that. That's more important than your sister's health. You must save the souls of your future realm," Boandas said quietly. "They'll be grateful to you."

"I cannot!" Ciallach stood. "I cannot sink so low. Who is this God you worship?" Ciallach turned and ran out of the hut.

The next morning Anaias put on her green cloak. It was time to settle the situation with her brother.

Beechna stood by the door of her hut. "I don't know if you can change him. It's that cloud that is growing in the west. It makes weak people do terrible things"

Anaias looked at Beechna, "I believe that hearts can always be changed. Or maybe you might say people can discover who they were truly created to be. Pelagius taught me that. Rabboni Yesua was always changing people by helping them discover the sacred in them. The daughters of Ana teach that we are all a part of Her mind."

Beechna waved her arms, "There are so many Torca who just don't have anything inside of them. You really think it's just hiding, waiting?" Beechna looked serious. "I've known real deer and robins that have more of a spirit than some people."

Anaias retorted, "I think that there is the fire of creation in everyone. The daughters of Ana called it the green fire, the fire we were created to have. There is fire in the sun, in the earth, in the plants, in the birds and in Tywa and in Torca."

"And in Ciallach and Boandas?" Beechna got a sour look on her face.

"I think so..." Anaias said thoughtfully. "I hope so...whoever attacked Aengus was very foolish. We need to all work together. There can't be prosperity in our land unless we do."

Ciallach was sitting in his hut at the base of Shreedrum, shaken by the thoughts Boandas had shared with him.

Anaias and Papallas arrived at his round hut and got out of the wagon.

Ciallach came out to greet them, "I see you've come checking on me."

"May we come into your home, brother?"

He moved aside for them, "I can't refuse you, sister. I seem to have no choice with the Roman. I have no tea to give you though."

"We can talk without tea," Anaias said.

Anaias sat on a bench covered with dirt. She looked around the house. It smelled of spoiled food and mice.

Papallas said directly, "We want to know if you're still plotting to be king."

Ciallach said in a happy sounding mocking voice, "Why would I do that!? He is such a good king. The people love him so much."

Anaias responded, "I do hope and pray that you accept Aengus as king. Your life can be dedicated to the good of the realm of Munster."

He declared, "I do accept it, just as I have accepted the true baptism." He added, "I'm connected now to the church of Bishop Patrick, with all of that power."

"Good. So you accept Christ Jesus as the teacher of love and forgiveness," Anaias said.

Ciallach responded with a laugh, "You can't be one to teach me about Christ Jesus. You tried to teach us false words."

Anaias sighed, "I'm sorry you feel that way. My teachings about Christ Jesus are the true teachings. Living through love can give you life. There is so much potential in life. Living through hate and plotting only gives you death."

Ciallach turned away from her.

They left him. Anaias felt discouraged, but said silent prayer for him.

There were no more attacks on Aengus for many moon cycles. Many people had opinions about who had planned it. Some thought it was just one of the children left behind by the years of battle and famine, even though many were being cared for in houses like those set up by Luann and Moira.

Papallas and Anaias were sitting quietly before the fire.

Luann came bursting in the room. "I've found him!" Her eyes were glowing.

"He's the son of Laigis. I was summoned by several in a village to the north to investigate some children who were ill. Donaugh worked with me and the children."

She grabbed Anaias hands, "He's the companion I've been waiting for!"

"And will I meet him?" Anaias laughed in her surprise. She had never seen Luann so excited.

"Oh yes, you'll meet him in a few minutes," Luann bubbled. "He has the deep wisdom of the ancient ones." She was obviously in love.

Just then a tall ruddy faced, blond haired man entered the room.

He walked up to Anaias and taking her hand in both of his, he said, "And you must be the Holy Woman Luann has been telling me about." He looked to Papallas, and added, "You are the holy couple I have been looking for." He stepped back, "I am here to learn from you."

Anaias laughed, "I've never seen Luann so excited."

Papallas took Donaugh's hand, "After meeting you, Luann is full of the fire of the earth. I may need to learn from you."

"Yes, I feel the fire from her. We've both felt as though we've been searching for each other all our lives." Donaugh put his arm around Luann and kissed the top of her head.

Seeing that Luann had come home, Giosai burst into the hut.

"Luann ...," He started to say something and then stopped and looked at Donaugh

Donaugh didn't notice Giosai, but continued, "The gods and goddesses have chosen that we be together." He then caught Luann's eyes and stopped. "But she's been teaching me that there is just one God."

He took Luann's hand, "I wish to be baptized into her faith, the faith of Rabboni Yesua." He looked pleadingly at Anaias, "If you agree to teach me."

Anaias smiled gently, "Of course I will."

Donaugh put his arm around Luann. Giosai's eyes grew big.

Donaugh said softly, "We'll be married on the next harvest night. It is many months from now, but my family needs to know you all and assent to the alliance."

Silently Giosai rushed out of the hut and across the fields towards his brother's hut.

For the next several months, Donaugh traveled between his home in the northeast and the village below Shreedrum. When he was there, he would visit the home of Anaias and hear her stories of Christ Jesus.

He brought several members of his family to be baptized, with him, by Anaias, in the river. Luann stood with him and held his hand as he accepted Christ Jesus and his teachings.

CHAPTER 61 – JEALOUSY
SHREEDRUM, EIRE

WISDOM'S GIFT 9 – THE IMPORTANT WORK IS NOT EASY WORK

On the night of the second full moon after the shortest day of the year, a day when the goddess Bride was said to be emerging from the earth, Eithne felt birth pains. She asked Anaias and Moira to come and stay with her. M'alda sat by her side.

Eithne's mother and sister also arrived on Kings Hill from their home in the north.

"This is an excellent time to have a child," Moira declared. "The life within the earth is just awakening. The earth is just beginning its celebration."

Anaias and Papallas were spending the nights on Shreedrum again awaiting the birth.

Aengus shouted in the middle of the night. All the women came running to Eithne. Aengus went with Papallas, a few rooms away.

Eithne let the women guide her as she endured the contractions. Moira had seen many births in the village and the refuge. Eithne's mother, though, at first wanted to be in charge. She backed off as the contractions became stronger and her daughter's cries became more difficult to take.

Two old women from the village came up with herbs and prayers for the coming royal birth.

It was not until early morning that the cry of a newborn baby was heard. Aengus and Papallas burst into the room. Boandas sat at a distance obviously in prayer.

Anaias greeted him, "You have a beautiful daughter! Congratulations!" Anaias hugged Aengus.

Aengus ran to Eithne's side as Moira and Eithne's mother were busy preparing the baby. They placed the infant in her waiting arms.

Boandas came over to the new mother, "We must baptize this infant at dawn." He stiffly intoned, "She must be cleansed from the curse of her birth."

Eithne, looking at this new life in her arms, barely heard Boandas' words. With tears in her eyes, she said softly to Aengus, "We'll call her Bridey for the power of the earth at the moment of her birth." She and Aengus huddled together as a new family in love.

Anaias felt a pang of sorrow that she would never share the joy of birth with Papallas. She felt Papallas' arm around her, comforting her.

Ciallach walked up behind Anaias and Papallas and whispered, "An unfortunate birth, don't you think? A girl can't be king."

He continued, "If Aengus died now, I'd be king."

Anaias whispered. "I thought you had left that dream behind, brother."

Ciallach responded, "I'm only looking for the good of Eire. They need a male Christian king."

Papallas answered, "And are you worthy to be one?"

Ciallach whispered, "We may see."

They silently watched the mother and baby together. Bridey found her mother's breast and began to nurse.

Boandas approached Anaias, "You might consider taking instruction from me and recanting your wrong thinking." He put his hand on her shoulder.

Anaias brushed his hand away without words.

He glared at her, saying, "The heretic who leads others astray has no rights. God's vengeance can be sudden and bloody." He shook his head, "Be careful, my daughter."

It was a month before Eithne and Bridey were ready for the baptism that was urged by Boandas. This would be the first baptism for Boandas as a Christian Bishop. Aengus and Eithne stood on the sacrificial rock in the meadow on top of Shreedrum holding the tiny newborn, Bridey. The valley was bathed in sunshine. Giosai held a silver bowl of water from the river.

Bishop Boandas tried to take Bridey into his arms as he had seen Bishop Patrick do, but Bridey shrieked. Aengus held her during the ritual.

As the water touched Bridey's head, Anaias saw a special light come down and touch her. There were crows around who seemed to be singing a softer song then crows usually sing. Bridey began to cry. The crows matched her noise.

Anaias knew that Beechna and her friends were among them. She wondered if the ancient ones were here. She wondered if goddess Bridey herself were here. She knew that Christ Jesus and Miraham were present.

Anaias returned to the house by the river by herself, Papallas stayed behind to gather men for a trip south.

Giosai was there waiting for her, "Sister, what can we do about Luann?"

Anaias was startled, "What's wrong with Luann?"

He continued, "Since she has promised never to be married, she can't marry Donaugh."

Anaias responded, "She can change her promise. God often changes what's required of us."

Giosai was almost whimpering, "Boandas says that when a Christian woman makes a vow of chastity she can never change it." He softened, "But I loved her before she met Donaugh. She refused me. If she changes her mind, I should be the one she marries."

Anaias said softly, "I'm sorry brother, but God didn't choose you to be with Luann."

Giosai was shouting now, obviously more deeply hurt than Anaias knew, "I'm not so sure that she and Donaugh aren't sinning! Boandas says that if they are they will pay with everlasting fire."

"Giosai! Stop that, I've never heard you talk that way before."

Giosai shouted back, "Boandas said you all are condemned by the God of Christ Jesus! Luann and you and ...all of you." Giosai ran out of the hut.

He had only cleared the door when Eithne and Aengus came though with the tiny Bridey. Papallas was behind them.

When they were alone, Papallas and Anaias embraced.

He whispered, "I will go south again. What gift would you like me to buy for you in my trading?"

She responded, "Just bring yourself and your crew home safely."

Their eyes met.

For some reason her thoughts went to her near drowning when she was a child. She remembered that Papallas' father had drowned at sea. She had not worried before. Suddenly she was frightened.

Papallas laughed, "Although I'm a son of Pallas, I now even have Christ Jesus protecting me."

He kissed her gently. They made love and held each other tightly.

He and the crew left a few days later.

The season of fire came again. The oak trees were in full leaf. The honeybees were dancing through the flower-strewn meadows. Boandas celebrated it as the season of his conversion. He called the people in the village to come to the Kings Hill to be baptized. Some came just to see the king and queen and new baby. They accepted the ritual of baptism from Boandas as a courtesy.

During the next months, Anaias didn't see Giosai. She also didn't see Boandas. It seemed odd, but she didn't have time to worry about it. The rumors were that Boandas was expanding his Bishopric to include the Corco Baiscind to the west. Boandas had taken Giosai with him as an apprentice in the faith. Anaias was concerned that these people were actively hostile to the Eogan family.

Ciallach seemed to have heard her words. He had actually visited Shreedrum and held the baby Bridey

Luann and Donough were preparing for their wedding in the harvest season. It would be several months before the wedding.

Donough's family often visited Shreedrum, hoping to bring an alliance between the Eogan clan and the Laigin clan. For years, the Laigin clan had been on the borderlands between the EiNeill and kingdom of Munster. They had suffered each time the EiNeill clan expand its territory.

Aengus was delighted by this new alliance.

Beechna appeared in Anaias' window. "The cloud is growing! The Tuatha de Danaan don't even seem to have the power to control it. They asked me to warn you that there may be violence."

CHAPTER 62 – A CELEBRATION
SHREEDRUM, EIRE

It was harvest season. The oak trees were golden and there was a chill in the air. Preparations for the wedding were in full speed. Aengus would perform the ceremony. Anaias would serve the two cups of wine and of honey to the couple as they made their sacred promise to each other.

Anaias was filled with a deep and gnawing fear. Papallas and the others had not returned yet. She hadn't heard any reports of an accident at sea. But would she? She would like to think that the spirit of Papallas would reach out to her if there had been trouble.

The day came when Luann and Donough would be married.

After they recited their vows before Aengus and he blessed them, a procession of instruments and dancers brought Luann and Donough to the river. There Anaias gave them the blessing.

The banquet and celebration began. Everyone laughed and danced at the joyful moment. Cormunthuc sang of the wedding and of the future of this partnership between Donough, son of Laigin, and Luann, a woman of Cymru who was a healer and a gardener.

Anaias wandered up the hill, away from the crowd, to sense more clearly the mood of the land. Her anxiety was growing.

As she sat in silence, she felt the cloud of sticky evil come over the place she sat. She asked for the help of the partnership of Rabboni Yesua and Miraham of Madga.

Suddenly the dog that was with her started barking furiously. Beechna, with a cloud of Tywa, flew by her, down the hill.

"They are here!" Beechna shrieked and she flew past Anaias.

Suddenly there were screams from the clearing below. Anaias jumped up and ran down the hill following the Tywa.

CHAPTER 63 – WHY?

IN HER OWN WORDS
IN THE FOREST CLEARING IN THE AHERLOW VALLEY

I heard screams as I pulled myself out of my meditation. It was as if I were pushing my way through a dark spider web, the kind of web that has grown old and is covered with soot. I tripped down the hill.

I could hear screams and the sound of swords against sword and shouts of men and women. As I came to the clearing, I saw several men dressed in robes to cover their faces. One came at me with a sword high. I screamed the deafening scream of Ana as I picked up my staff and caught his sword mid air knocking it out of his hand. I swung again and could hear the bones breaking in his side. He screamed in pain and fell to the ground. His voice sounded familiar. I didn't have time to stay with him.

I ran across the field to Luann who was lying on the ground with blood gushing from her side and a deep gash in her head. Donaugh was fighting her attacker with knife against sword.

Before I knelt to see to Luann, I saw a man on top of Moira. He had her robe up and was slamming her head with his one fist, while he was preparing to rape her. I came up behind with my knife and pulling him by the hair was able to slam the blade into his neck. Blood spurted onto Moira as she lay semi-conscious but sobbing. The man fell to the side and in his dying moment struck me on the head with a rock he found on the ground. I reeled from the blow but stood up to find Luann,

The robed men ran into the woods taking their swords with them.

All was silent. Donaugh and I ran to Luann's side.

As I held her, we were surrounded by a rainbow of color and I screamed, "Why!!!"

The sound reverberated in my head and around me. I screamed for anyone who had ever lost a friend or child or mother in senseless violence. I screamed from the depth of every time and place I had lived or would live in body."

Donough and I sunk together to embrace Luann's lifeless body. It seemed like an eternity. But then I knew I needed to move to the injured, to see if there was anyone I could heal.

I gave Luann to Donough and slowly stood, though my head was throbbing and my legs could barely carry me.

On the ground I saw Cormunthuc, with his wife and daughters. He was lying still in a pool of blood. His wife saw me approach, "He defended us. I didn't know he could fight like that, I thought he could only sing." She touched his still face. "We're safe, but he is leaving us."

I knelt down to Cormunthuc and put my head near his mouth to feel any breath. I was startled to hear a faint voice. "Sister of Ana, take the harp. Tell the story."

I whispered back, "You will live to tell this story, to tell why!" I said fervently.

All he said was, "No, I am going." He stopped breathing and was still.

Then it was darkness. Anyone who was there simply saw my body crumple on the ground. But I saw the caves of the Tuatha de Danaan.

The swirling rainbow surrounded me as I saw tall redheaded men and women lift me up and fly me to the edge of the Galtees. They carried me into a cave and cared for my head wound.

A tall woman with long blond hair came to me and sat down.

"You can not leave your people now. You cannot leave us now. You have work to do."

I could barely talk, but thought she might know, "Who did this? Where is my love, Papallas?"

She looked at me with her deep blue eyes, "It was not people, it was a power of darkness that comes in the form of passion, lust for power, greed, and anger." She took my hand.

"As for Papallas, you will see him again, but we can't say when."

I fell asleep.

I woke up in the meeting room in Shreedrum surrounded by Aengus and Eithne.

I heard a voice say, in the distance, "She's waking up!" It was my mother M'alda.

I heard a baby crying and I knew it was Bridey.

Then I was startled to hear the booming voice of Boandas. "Give her more tea. She'll recover well."

I fell back to sleep.

CHAPTER 64 – CHANGES
SHREEDRUM, EIRE

As she came to consciousness she saw Aengus and Eithne sitting next to her mat. Occasionally she would hear the cry of little Bridey.

She was reassured by their presence. As she slept she relived the horror of Luann's death. She saw the blood all around. She was once again holding Cormunthuc's dying body, hearing the cries of his daughters. In some of the dreams she actually saved them all with her herbs and prayers.

She awoke and tried to search the faces for Luann and Cormunthuc. She saw Moira and the pain on her face. She knew the massacre had really happened.

"Anaias, are you awake now?" She heard Aengus' voice.

"I'm trying to be," she said. She realized a sob came from her as she spoke those words.

"Is Papa home yet?" she asked.

There was silence.

Her grief sent her back into a deep sleep. But the dreams were there and there was no soothing rest.

Eventually she awoke. Knowing she had to face life, she forced herself to sit up. Cormunthuc's harp was by her mat. She was alone. She picked up the harp and sitting it in her lap, tried to make the same sort of music that he had made. Her sounds were harsh. She sighed.

She continued to strum the strings. The music became softer. The story of what happened started to flow through her mind.

She felt the soothing presence of Rabboni Yesua and Miraham, of Ana. She saw Beechna sleeping in a corner.

She strummed the strings of the harp for the rest of the afternoon.

The sun was setting when Aengus came into the room. Behind him were Boandas and Ciallach. She put down the harp.

"Cousin," Aengus was sounding so formal, "we need to talk."

She looked from Aengus' face to Boandas. Boandas was smiling. Ciallach was standing behind him looking triumphant.

"How are you sister?" Ciallach came over to her and touched the wound on her head. Dread shot through her like lightening.

"She will be fine, after some rest," Boandas said softly. She looked at Aengus, trying to read his eyes.

"Ani," Aengus sat next to her and took her hand. "The attack on you and your women proves that we can no longer be a people of peace."

"But the teachings," she said as firmly as she could.

"Are false ones." Boandas cut her off.

Aengus spoke, "I've decided that I need to listen more closely to Bishop Boandas, God may be speaking through him now." His eyes were harder than she had ever seen them.

"No, you can't," she tried to speak with strength, but she knew her words sounded weak. Her body was weak.

"It's over, daughter," Boandas said softly. He leaned over to her and put his lips next to her ear and whispered, so no one else could hear, "You have lost."

Aengus held her hand, "Sleep well, Ani, your mother and Eithne will be checking on you."

As they left the room Beechna was sitting up. Her eyes were huge. "Let's go see the wise ones. We can't let him win."

Anaias stared at the place they had been standing. What could she do?

As events unfolded, Ciallach was declared commander of an army. Preparations were made to invade the Corco tribes. Some of the dead men were from that region. Suspicions were that they had been responsible for the attack on Aengus and the wedding massacre.

Many of the people of the village had been outraged about the attack. Boandas told them that God wanted them to avenge the killings. The young men of the local tribes were anxious to show their courage.

It took Anaias a lot time to return to health. She had terrible headaches. Her body was wracked with pain without a source. She kept getting reports of victories in battle that came at a high cost of many deaths. She stayed on Shreedrum while she recovered.

She spent a lot of time with her mother and grandmother. Danathie told her stories of battles she had known, trying to convince her that it was the only way to respond to the violence that had caused her wounds. M'alda could see the pain in Anaias' heart, but could not say anything to relieve it. She often talked about the gloriful days as a child living in Shreedrum.

Occasionally Eithne and Bridey would come into her room. The baby made Anaias laugh and forget the sorrow and loss.

She found her way to laughter through many small ways.

CHAPTER 65 – IT SPITE OF IT ALL.
BY THE SUIR RIVER

WISDOM'S GIFT 10 – DESPITE APPEARANCES, ALL CREATION GIVES ITS POWER TO THE GOOD AND LIFE AFFIRMING.

Eventually Anaias was able to return to her home by the river. Friends came by with food and others gifts. The good news that everyone kept telling her was that crops were quickening in the fields. The rains were coming in this season of the new sun. The trees were showing new leaf.

They knew she didn't like the wars and the killing. They all wanted her to know that they considered the quickening of life and gentle rains to be good blessings of her God.

A pain continued in her heart as she realized that Papallas would not be returning from his voyage. She found herself talking to his spirit.

She talked to Rabboni Yesua and Miraham of Magda. She was comforted with the sense that Miraham knew about the loss of one she loved, and about loss through violence. They seemed to respond to her with words of comfort, but no advice on how she could change Aengus' heart.

Beechna stayed with her, occasionally bringing a crowd of Tywa friends. They seemed to have accepted the new order of things. Beechna's Tywa friends were cautious of Anaias at first. They disappeared when anyone else visited.

She continued to keep bees and heal by the river. People came by for her various types of honey. She collected herbs and sorted them, ready for any ailment.

As the years went by Eithne and Bridey would come to visit, and laughter would fill the hut. She especially liked it when Bridey, who was just learning to talk, would call Boandas 'Bishie sourface.' She would then pucker as though she had eaten an un-leached acorn.

Anaias and Eithne would laugh until their sides hurt.

Donaugh married Moira and they had five boys.

Giosai disappeared. The rumors were that he went north to find Bishop Patrick. Some thought he might have gone south to study to be a priest of Christ Jesus.

Her grandmother and then mother died on Shreedrum, happy to

be home.

Aengus never came to see her. Ciallach and Boandas had his full attention.

She kept trying to learn to play the harp, but she could not sing the story of what happened to her and to her world. The words would not come.

CHAPTER 66 – SEARCHING

IN HER OWN WORDS
SOUTHERN IRELAND AT THE MOUTH OF THE SUIR RIVER AND INTO THE SPACE BETWEEN DIMENSIONS

    Life can be startling in its inconsistencies, but we need, sometimes to accept the strange twists and turns. Never, in this life, did I learn who murdered Luann and the bard. Was it the Corco, who Aengus, with Boandas help, blamed?
    Was it an alliance Boandas had made with the Corco so that he could gain power? Then had he turned against them?
    Was it Giosai and his jealousy?
    Was it someone from the tribe of EiNeill getting revenge?
    Was it the sticky, dark cloud, made up of unspoken sorrow and anger, that smothered the good in people's hearts?

    In a dream, I heard Susanna calling for me to return to the refuge.
    I took the harp of Cormunthuc to the shore where several curraghs were moored.
    I prepared one of the boats and balanced it with food for the few days of crossing back to Cymru, if I made it that far. The oars would guide me back to the community on the cliff. My sisters would be there, and Elihf with her family. Susanna, David, their daughter, Mary, Jacob, Tinai, Jeremiah and their son, Morgan, would be there.
    If I didn't make it across the sea in this small boat, maybe I would find my way to that shimmering island I had seen so long ago, and maybe to Papallas.
    I got into the boat. I pulled on my cape, the red one that I had received so long ago, that had been given for me by my aunt: the eagle, the light. The wind whipped up along the shore.
    I prayed, "Guide me Ana. Guide me Rabboni Yesua. Guide me Miraham." Stars filled the sky. Suddenly three lights shot across the darkness of the night.
    I heard a splashing in the water and a rustling. It was Beechna and Rodnic and dozens of Tywa, Beechna said with a giggle, "You're not going anywhere without us." She settled down in the boat with her friends.

I began to hear distant drumming and chanting. It was voices of people praying. The voices did not come from the shore; they seemed to come from the sea, from the sky, from the stars.

I picked up the oars, and with all my strength, I pulled the boat away from the Irish shore. The Tywa didn't touch the oars. They did, though, seem to help me row.

I didn't look back, only forward.

CHAPTER 67
EPILOGUE

Legend reports that King Aengus ruled into his 90's. He was overthrown by a grand-nephew. He was tauntingly called the 'king of 30 defeats'. That is until he took on a druid adviser and began to win battles. The Kings of Munster ruled over southern Ireland for many centuries, fighting the Vikings under Brian Boru and to the invasion of the Normans.

The Christians, in the region around the holy hill, were always a bit different, stressing loving action over words; peacemaking over violence.

POSTLUDE – THE LATEST TRIP TO IRELAND – 2002

The journey of writing this story has taken me on many trips around Celtic County. I took one year long, unpaid sabbatical, but the savings ran out before I could finish it. This story was not yet completed.

I put the manuscript into a drawer as I took an appointment, in 1997, to Marysville and met some extraordinarily creative people. I met my life partner, Earl and married him in 1999. He had a beautiful rustic home in Oro Fino and the Bishop got romantic and appointed me to the two small churches in the valley, in the towns of Etna and Fort Jones.

I kept hearing, in my dreams, sleeping and during walks, "Tell my story!" So I asked Earl if he would go with me. He had never been out of the country before. He courageously said, "Yes!"

April 06, 2002 – Here we are in Dublin! My husband, Earl, and I made the trip. We were married just two years before, this was the first long trip we had taken together.

We had an awful night on the plane, but it was a non-stop out of Los Angeles. In a sleepy stupor, we got our luggage and took a taxi to a b&b I had rented on the internet. It was in downtown Dublin. The room was small and the shower didn't work well. We fell into a deep sleep. Around 3 p.m., we woke up hungry and wandered the streets for food. We found a place on O'Connell that sold pizza by the slice. Now, Bridey, guide us!

At 2 a.m., we woke up hungry again. I had saved a couple of rolls, cheese and juice from the food service on the plane. That kept us fed until it was time for breakfast.

I've always been amazed at the amount of food they feed a person in an Irish bed and breakfast. There was cold cereal, fruit, ham or bangers (sausages), eggs and juice with toast. Most importantly to me on this morning was that there was good rich (probably instant) coffee. We were very sleepy and slow.

It was, though, Sunday and Earl and I wanted to try out a church. We chose the Presbyterian Church on O'Connell. A huge imposing exterior revealed a small friendly congregation. Most of the people there were visitors. The sermon was pleasant.

We napped after church and then walked across the Liffey to try to find a nice restaurant. After about a half mile of walking, we found a wonderful seafood place. I had chowder with mussels, salmon and shrimp. Earl chose Fish and Chips.

When I was back in the room and Earl was sleeping, I pulled out the manuscript for Greenfire (yes, I packed all 300+ pages). Here was the story that had unfolded over the last decades. I wanted to finish it.

Suddenly I thought of Beechna. Was she still here? Did the Tywa live forever or just a very long time? Would I know her? Would she know me? I began to meditate on the fairy world. Were there fairies in my home in California? How would I know?

The next morning we rented a car (automatic) and headed out without reservations.

I had the route planned. We were going to go around Dublin and head south. As it turned out, we didn't go around Dublin at all. We accidentally took the wrong exit and went north. We pulled off on N1 at Balbriggan, got a snack and checked the map. We were heading right for the mysterious ancient site of Newgrange.

Well, okay, so much for plans. This was, after all, a good idea. Newgrange is one of the most sacred sites in Ireland. We bravely took N2. By this time it was 3:30 p.m. and too late for a tour. The tourist office made us a reservation at a bed and breakfast in Drogheda.

On the way, we stopped to see Moasterboice Abbey build in 510 CE. The crosses were like books, with stories of the bible and the gospel of Jesus. There was a round tower but it was in disrepair.

The next day we traveled back to Newgrange. I had bought some books on the site the night before. I was well versed on its mysterious history. For centuries, they appeared as round, grass covered hills. No one knew that the mounds were man-made and hollow inside. The Kings of Tara had used the site for coronations. They knew it was sacred somehow, as it sat at a curve of the River Boyne. The tour took us into the excavated New Grange. Deep inside the mound was a room. It was found that at the moment of winter solstice the room would be illuminated with the light of the new sun.

Archeological evidence pointed to the construction being over 10,000 years ago. Stone had been brought from the Wicklow hills miles to the south. How did these people know so much about the stars and seasons? Why did they go to so much trouble? It did not seem to be a burial site. There were no bodies. It seemed to be ceremonial only. It is one of the many deep, sacred mysteries of Ireland.

I was anxious to get back to Kildare. I had remembered my magical visit years ago. What would I find? I found a new, wealthier, Ireland. We decided to drive down back county roads. Earl and I noticed that the drivers did not care that the roads were narrow with hedgerows, and with no pull-offs. They would come up behind us at high speed and pass on blind curves. Where was the sleepy Ireland of 17 years ago? Now everyone seemed prosperous and drove SUVs.

In Kildare, I wanted to show Earl what I had found at Bridget's Cathedral. It was changed. There was no more sign of the ancient fire.

The grounds had been cleaned up. We walked down the street to the well. There were newly built subdivisions. There was a sign pointing to the well, but we walked and walked and couldn't find it.

Disappointed, we drove as fast as we could on the crowded highways to Cashel.

Somehow, the approach to Cashel wasn't the same. I remembered the trip on the bus, the shock at seeing the rock, the rainbow, the voice. All I saw was a traffic jam on the way into town. However, there was Shreedrum.

The bed and breakfast was reserved for a full week. It was a beautiful clean room. What a relief. I had found it on the internet, where it looked nice, but you never know. The room had a window seat with a view of Shreedrum, now known as Saint Patrick's rock. I could sit and write while gazing at the holy hill.

None of the Cathedrals or round tower or crosses on the rock dated back to the 5th century. We were, however, able to crawl all around the rock from the outside and inside. What did it look like when Aengus and Anaias were here? Were the buildings round, or square? Did they have more than one story?

All the museums had information about Ireland from Saint Patrick, then skipping to the Normans. The library had a book on the kings of Munster, with a chapter on Aengus. It was here that I learned about his marriage to Eithne. I also learned here that he died in his 90's. The librarian told me I should return and stay for a year to really learn what I needed to know.

The next morning I was out at sunrise, before all the traffic. Earl slept as I walked around the town. I walked to the rock, climbed up the side, and meditated. Crows flew overhead.

Earl and I drove to the valley of Aherlow. We had a picnic lunch of Irish bread and cheese.

We drove to Rosslare and took a ferry to Pembroke on the Welsh coast, the former Cymru, to again see the land of the Eogan exile. Earl enjoyed the engine room of the ferry, but the crossing was rough. I saw the Dale Peninsula and the islands of Owain and Torrida from a distance.

We drove back to Dublin swinging through the Wicklow Hills. I wanted to wander around Glendalough and see the home of Saint Kevin. As we approached Glendalough, the beautiful days in Ireland gave way to drenching rain. The rain came down hard as we forced ourselves to walk slowly around Kevin's community and up to the second lake. There was a labyrinth. We walked it in the rain.

We found a bed and breakfast in Laragh with good heaters to dry our clothes and a breakfast of scrambled eggs and salmon.

As this trip ended, I was proud that I returned the car to the rental company, this time, with Earl's help, without a scratch on it. We made it to the airport with time to spare to get through customs.

The flight home was long. The dog, who spent time in the kennel, and two cats, who stayed home and got 'fed' by strangers, were a little distressed, but happy to see us.

The next Sunday I returned to my ministry. I had many warm greetings.

I walked my dog, Popcorn, through the hills of Oro Fino and thought, "Now this is where I want to live. And we do, actually live here!!

I came home to my congregations in Etna and Fort Jones. The churches became, for me, a dance of the artist in us all, it was a joy to be the spiritual leader of these people.

I began work on a Doctor of Ministry at the University of Creation Spirituality. This story became the dissertation.

My ministry has brought me so close to people in their lives, their joys and sorrows, the questions and struggles. It has also allowed me to just care for people and be a friend. I thank all the people who have touched my life, and whose lives I've touched for their openness to God's grace with us. I was caught up in my ministry of celebration of life.

"Tell my story!!" I heard in my dreams, sleeping and waking.
So in 2006 I took a second unpaid sabbatical.

I needed to make sure I wrote the story that Anaias wanted to tell. I can't play the harp as Cormonthuc might have. But, then, Anaias couldn't play it well either. As you read, make your own music.

CONCLUSIONS – BUT NOT THE END

The story of Anaias, including her scream of horror because of the massacre, may seem unremarkable in human history. Massacres happen every day. People scream in horror and cry in sorrow every day. Forgetfulness is part of most of the events of our life no matter how traumatic they have been. They will be forgotten, unless we do the work of remembering. Yet, it is a story that is vitally important to humankind. That to me is the importance of studying history.

What events were so terrible that we have turned away from them and tried to deny they ever happened? What traumatic events happened in the midst of chaos or victory and the sufferers merely had to 'get over it' and move on? What events were joy filled and glorious but were interpreted as mundane and trivial?

The writing of history, though, often simply recounts the dates and events of those in power. It is through 'storytelling' history that we can actually attempt to know the heart of what happened to the individuals living in the time of our story. That is the gift of 'intuitive history'. We carefully and thoughtfully listen for the story.

By telling the story, we can remember wisdom learned, but we can also find wounds that have not healed. There are some wounds from historical calamities that are still affecting peoples and countries today. By intentionally remembering with compassion, I sense that we can heal the past and through that healing, heal the present. Can you think of any places in the world that have a dark sticky cloud of sorrow and anger?

One conclusion I have drawn from this experience with Anaias, is that I need to continue to write history from the intuitive, storytelling mode. I will continue to research and tell the story of periods of history that need healing.

Another conclusion I have drawn from this experience with Anaias, is that she has a lot of wisdom to give us today.

There are many ancestors who have wisdom that we need to hear. I include the journey of her Christian teacher, Pelagius, who needs to be heard by our age, and whose memory needs to be healed. With her, I include the teachings of Miraham of Magda, who was considered a prize student by Rabboni Yesua. We are beginning to recognize her in this present age.

Could it be that our ancestors are inviting us now to be mindful of all that has happened in the ancient past? Maybe our mindfulness can cause healing. Maybe our mindfulness can lead us away from the repeating the mistakes, even glorifying the mistakes, of those who have lived before us.

I believe that by writing, researching, and reporting the story of Anaias, I have provided some healing. Hopefully Anaias and I have opened some hearts to compassion and possibility.

BIBLIOGRAPHY

Bede, Venerable. *Ecclesiastical History of the English People. 731 a.d.*. Translated by Leo Sherley-Price Edited by D. H. Farmer, Penguin Classics, 1990

Carr, David. *Time, Narrative and History*. Indiana University Press, 1986

Carr-Gomm, Philip. *The Elements of the Druid Tradition*. Element Books Limited, 1991

Julius Caesar, *De Bello Gallico VI*

Christie-Murray, David. *A History of Heresy*. Oxford Press, 1976

Delaney, Frank. *Legends of the Celts*. Sterling Publishing Co., 1989

Delaney, Mary Murray, *Of Irish Ways*, Harper and Row, 1973

Bill Devall, George Sessions, *Deep Ecology, Living as Though Nature Mattered*, Peregrine Smith Books, 1985

Discovery Magazine, June 2003 Volume 24, Number 6

Dugdales, *Monasticon Anglicanum*

Evans, R. F. *Pelagius, Inquiries and Reappraisals*. London Press, 1968

Evans-Wentz, W. Y. *The Fairy-Faith in Celtic Countries*. New Page Books, 2004 (1911)

Ferguson, J. *Pelagius: a Historical and Theological Study*. Cambridge, 1978 and 1956

Fox, Matthew, ed. *Western Spirituality, Historical Roots, Ecumenical Routes*, Bear & Company 1980

Fox, Matthew. *Creation Spirituality, Liberating Gifts for the Peoples of the Earth*. Harper, 1991

Fox, Matthew, Rupert Sheldrake, *The Physics of Angels, Exploring the Realm Where Science and Spirit Meet,* Harper, 1996

Freeman, Mara. *Kindling the Celtic Spirit,* Harper, 2000

Goodenough, Ursula, *The Sacred Depths of Nature* .

Greene, Brian. *The Elegant Universe, Superstrings, Hidden Dimensions, and the Quest for the Ultimate Theory*, W.W. Norton. 2003

Greene, Brian. *The Fabric of the Cosmos, Space, Time and the Texture of Reality,* Knopf. 2004

Haskins, Susan. *Mary Magdalene: Myth and Metaphor*, Riverhead Books, 1995

Hurley, Jack. *Legends of Exmoor,* The Exmoor Press, 1993

Jones, Kathy. *Spinning The Wheel of Ana, A Spiritual Quest to Find the British Primal Ancestors.* Ariande Publications, Glastonbury, England, 1994

Jones, Kathy. *The Ancient British Goddess, Her Myths, Legends and Sacred Sites,* Ariadne Publications, 1991

Jung, C. G. *Memories, Dreams, Reflections*, Vintage, 1965

Logan, Patrick. *The Holy Wells of Ireland.* Colin Smythe, Ltd England. 1995

Mac Niocaill, Gearoid. *Ireland Before the Vikings*, Gill and Macmillan, 1972

McGiffert, Arthur Cushman. *A History of Christian Thought, Volume II, The West From Tertullian to Erasmus.* Charles Scribner's Sons, 1947

Markale, Jean,. *Women of the Celts.* Inner Traditions International, Ltd, 1986

Mead, G. R. S., *Pistis Sophia, The Gnostic Tradition of Mary Madgalene, Jesus, and his Disciples*, Dover Publications, Inc, New York, 2005 (original 1921)

Moss, H. St. L. B. *The Birth of the Middle Ages 395-814*, Oxford University Press, 1964

O'Driscoll, Robert, ed. *The Celtic Consciousness*, George Braziller, New York, 1981

Otto, Rudolf. *The Idea of the Holy,* Oxford, 1923

Pagels, Elaine. *The Gnostic Gospels,* Vintage Press, 1979

Powell, T. G. E. *The Celts.* London: Thames and Hudson, 1980

Piggott, Stuart. *The Druids*, London: Thames and Hudson, 1975

Progoff, Ira. *Jung, Synchronicity, and Human Destiny,* Dell, 1973

Rees, B. R. *Pelagius, A Reluctant Heretic*, The Boydell Press, Woodbridge, England, 1991

Rees, B. R. *The Letters of Pelagius and His Followers,* Oxford, 1995

Renfrew, Jane. *Food, and Cooking in Prehistoric Britain History and Recipes,* English Heritage, 1985

Robinson, James M. *The Nag Hammadi Library in English*, Harper/San Francisco, 1990

Roberts, Tony. *Guide to the Pembrokeshire Coast Path*, Abercastle Publications, 1992

Ross, Anne, Don Robins, *The Life and Death of a Druid Prince,* Touchstone, New York, 1991

Ruether, Rosemary Radford. *Gaia and God, An Ecofeminist Theology of Earth Healing,* Harper Collins, 1992

Seymour, John. *About Pembrokeshire* , Local Press, 1982

Sheldrake, Rupert. *The Rebirth of Nature, the Greening of Science and God*, Bantam Books, 1991

Skeat, W.W. editor. *Broughton in his Ecclesiastical Historie of Great Britaine, 1633 (Joseph of Aramathia, pg xxvii)*

Talbot, Michael. *Mysticism and the New Physics, Beyond Space-Time, Beyond God, to the Ultimate Cosmic Consciousness*. Bantum, 1981

Thomas, Patrick. *Candle in the Darkness, Celtic Spirituality in Wales*. Llandysul, Dyfed, Wales: Gomer Press, 1993

Van de Weyer, Robert. *The Letters of Pelagius, Celtic Soul Friend,* Worcestershire, England: Arthur James, Ltd, 1995

Thurstan, Violetta *The Use of Vegetable Dyes*, London: Dryad Press, 1978

Wallace-Hadrill, J. M. *The Barbarian West, A. D. 400-1000,* Harper Torchbooks, 1962

White, Hayden. *Metahistory.* Johns Hopkins, 1973

Yourgrau, Palle. *A World Without Time*, Basic Books, 2005

ENDNOTES

[1] Carl Jung, *Memories, Dreams and Reflections*, Vintage Books, 1965, pg. 100

[2] Rupert Sheldrake, *The Rebirth of Nature, the Greening of Science and God,*, Bantum Books, 1991, pg. 165

[3] Sheldrake, pg. 175

[4] Sheldrake, pg. 176

[5] Palle Yourgrau, *A World Without Time, The Forgotten Legacy of Godel and Einstein*, Perseus Books, 2005, pg. 7

[6] Yourgrau, pg. 8

[7] Brian Greene, *The Fabric of the Cosmos*, Knopf, 2004, pg.178-80

[8] Greene, pg. 452

[9] Greene, pg. 456

[10] Ira Progroff, *Jung, Synchronicity and Human Destiny*, Dell Publishing Co., 1973, pg. 3

[11] Greene. pg 458

[12] Progoff, pg. 128

[13] Progoff, pg. 132

[14] Ursula Goodenough; *The Sacred Depths of Nature* pg. 170

[15] Bill Devall, George Sessions, *Deep Ecology, Living as Though Nature Mattered*, Peregrine Smith Books, 1985 pg. 67

[16] Gearoid Mac Niocaill, *Ireland Before the Vikings, pg. 3,*

[17] Kathy Jones, *Spinning The Wheel of Ana*, Ariadne Publications, Glastonbury, Pg. 43

[18] ibid

[19] W. Y. Evans-Wentz, *The Fairy Faith in Celtic Countries*, pg. 29

[20] Evans-Wentz, pg. 52

[21] Rupert Sheldrake and Matthew Fox, *The Physics of Angels*, pg. 27

[22] ibid

[23] Michael Talbot, *Mysticism and the New Physics*, pg. 127

[24] Talbot, pg. 129

[25] Rosemary Radford Ruether, *Gaia & God*, pg 136

[26] Jones, pg. 43

[27] Mara Freeman, *Kindling the Celtic Spirit*, Pg. 137

[28] Mary Aileen Schmiel, pg. 168

[29] Jones, pg. 42

[30] Robert Evans *Pelagius, Inquiries and Reappraisals*, pg. ix

[31] Anne Ross and Don Robbins, *The Life and Death of a Druid Prince*, Pg. 84

[32] Jones, pg. 6

[33] Philip Carr-Gomm, *Elements of the Druid Tradition*, Element Books, pg. xii

[34] ibid. pg. 43

[35] Carr-Gomm, pg. 44

[36] ibid, pg. 50

[37] ibid, pg. 57

[38] ibid pg. 60

[39] Ibid

[40] Carr-Gomm, pg. 62

[41] *Discovery Magazine*, June 2003 Volume 24, Number 6, pg. 30

[42] Rees, pg. xiii

[43] J. Ferguson wrote, *Pelagius, a Historical and Theological Study*, 1956, pg. 40

[44] Ferguson, pg. 41

[45] Ferguson, pg. 46

[46] Venerable Bede, *Ecclesiastical History of the English People*(673 – 735) – Penguin Classics, pg. 56

[47] Bede, pg. 64

[48] David Christie-Murray, *A History of Heresy* Oxford Press, 1989. pg. 91

[49] Matthew Fox, *Creativity, Where the Divine and Human Meet*, Tarcher, Putnam, 2002, pg. 91

[50] Matthew Fox, *Creation Spirituality, Liberating Gifts for the Peoples of the Earth,* Harper/San Francisco, 1991, pg. 1

[51] Van de Weyer, *The Letters of Pelagius, Celtic Soul Friend,* Arthur James, Ltd. Worcestershire, England, pg. 49

[52] .ibid

[53] Ruether, pg. 136

[54] Ibid

[55] Mary Aileen Schmiel, "*Exploring Celtic Spiritual Legacies*" within *Western Spirituality, Historical Roots, Ecumenical Routes*, ed Matthew Fox, p176

[56] B. R. Rees, *Pelagius, A Reluctant Heretic* in 1991 pg. ix

[57] Rees, pg. x

[58] Julius Caesar, *De Bello Gallico* VI, 14

[59] Broughton in his Ecclesiastical Historie of Great Britaine, 1633 (Joseph of Aramathia Edited by W.W. Skeat, pg xxvii)

[60] *The Holy Bible, Revised Standard Version,* World Bible Publishers, 1972

[61] Dugdales Monasticon Anglicanum pg. xxiv

[62] Jack Hurley, *Legends of Exmoor,* The Exmoor Press, pg. 46

[63] Mead, GRS, *Pistis Sophia,* Dover, 2005 (1921) pg. 20

[64] ibid, pg. 47

[65] ibid, pg. 102

[66] Holy Bible, RSV, Luke 24:8-11

[67] *Thunder Perfect Mind,* Trans by Gordon W. MacRae, *The Nag Hammadi Library,* pg. 271, passim

[68] *Psalm 148* passim

[69] *Holy Bible,* John 20:16

[70] George W. MacRae, Translator, Douglas Parrott, Editor, *"The Gospel of Mary"* James M. Robinson, Editor, *The Nag Hammadi Library,* pg 471-4, passim

[71] G. R. S. Mead, *Pistis Sophia, The Gnostic Tradition of Mary Madgalene, Jesus, and his Disciples*, Dover Publications, Inc, New York, 2005 (original 1921), pg. 103

[72] Mead, pg. 47

[73] Wesley W. Isenberg, Translator, "The Gospel of Philip", James M. Robinson, Editor, *The Nag Hammadi Library,* pg. 138

[74] J. M. Wallace-Hadrill, *The Barbarian West* , Harper, 1962. Pg. 21

[75] H. St. L. B. Moss, *The Birth of the Middle Ages,* Oxford Press, 1964 pg. 9

[76] Moss, pg. 13

[77] Patrick Thomas, *Candle in the Darkness, Celtic Spirituality from Wales,* Gomer Press. Pg. 23

[78] ibid

[79] Gearoid Mac Niocaill, page 6